Mass Torts: Cases and Reflections

Tort and Insurance Law

Edited by the
European Centre of Tort
and Insurance Law

together with the
Institute for the European Tort Law

Volume 34

Mass Torts in Europe: Cases and Reflections

Willem H. van Boom
Gerhard Wagner

With Contributions by
Jenny Boldon • Willem H. van Boom • Moritz Brinkmann • Filippo Andrea Chiaves • Nadia Coggiola • Melissa R. Ferrari • Michele Graziadei • Christopher J.S. Hodges • Bernhard A. Koch • Harald Koch • Otto Ernst Krasney • Hermes Marangos • Claudio Perrella • Francesca Rolla • Thomas A. Roth • Astrid Stadler • Philip Tansley • Andreas W. Tilp • Gerhard Wagner

DE GRUYTER

European Centre of Tort and Insurance Law
Reichsratstraße 17/2
A-1010 Vienna
Tel.: +43 1 4277 29650
Fax: +43 1 4277 29670
E-Mail: ectil@ectil.org

Institute for European Tort Law
Reichsratstraße 17/2
A-1010 Vienna
Tel.: +43 1 4277 29651
Fax: +43 1 4277 29670
E-Mail: etl@oeaw.ac.at

ISBN 978-3-11-034945-0
e-ISBN 978-3-11-034946-7
ISSN 1616-8623

Bibliographic information published by the Deutsche Nationalbibliothek
The Deutsche Nationalbibliothek lists this publication in the Deutsche Nationalbibliografie; detailed bibliographic data are available in the Internet at http://dnb.d-nb.de.

Datenkonvertierung und Satz: jürgen ullrich typosatz, 86720 Nördlingen
Druck und Bindung: CPI books GmbH, Leck
♾ Gedruckt auf säurefreiem Papier
Printed in Germany

www.degruyter.com

Preface

In recent years, the issue of mass tort litigation and the fair and efficient settlement and adjudication of mass torts have drawn increasing attention in academic discourse, legal practice and policy debates.

Undoubtedly, the quantity and quality of the extant literature on mass litigation and class actions is overwhelming. Within the European legal debate, however, the emphasis seems to be mostly on 'massification' in competition, consumer and securities law. This book adds to the existing literature by collecting a number of case studies mostly on tort cases and, by combining these with thematic chapters in which the challenges concerning mass torts are mapped, explores and analyses them from a European perspective. By implication, this book thus combines substantive law and procedural law aspects on the one hand, and issues concerning the practical operation of law and related mechanisms of behaviour modification and dispute settlement on the other. It does not follow the standard approach of analyses within the area of collective redress, namely the design of institutions that allow for aggregate litigation before the civil courts. Rather, it adopts a broader perspective that includes other, and perhaps unexpected, modes of settling mass disputes, namely mechanisms of Alternative Dispute Resolution, bankruptcy reorganisations, and even criminal trials. As a result of the studies in this volume, a broad range of options emerges from which the parties may choose their most-preferred dispute resolution mechanism. This raises the question whether the resultant competition between jurisdictions, and sometimes even between various branches within the same jurisdiction, is a good or a bad thing.

The setup of the book is briefly as follows. The introductory chapter sketches the contours of the issues of mass torts and related problems of substantive and procedural law. Then, the book follows two main threads. In the first section, case reports written by expert practitioners give an insight into the practical operation of the law in various cases of mass tort. These chapters cut through jurisdictions and vary from mass breast implant scandals to large-scale financial fraud. In the second section, we have brought together academic reflections on wider issues of mass torts. The two sections paint a varied picture of the many challenges posed by mass torts. A final chapter draws together the key insights from the case studies and the academic papers. In doing so, it tries to answer the question whether we can hope for a race to the top in the strive for efficient and adequate institutions of collective redress or whether we are witness to a race to the bottom.

As always, assembling an edited volume is a joint effort. Therefore, we owe thanks to the authors for their proficient contributions, to ECTIL staff members

Marlene Steininger and Reinhard Pesek for their much appreciated management of the editorial process, to Munich Reinsurance Company, in particular Ina Ebert, for supporting and promoting the project, and to professors Oliphant and Koziol for endorsing and hosting the project.

Willem van Boom & Gerhard Wagner

Table of Contents

Willem H van Boom

1 Mass Torts: Debates and Pathways

I. Setting the Scene

In recent years, the issue of mass tort litigation and the fair and efficient settlement and adjudication of mass torts has drawn increasing attention in academic discourse, legal practice and policy debates. Indeed, academics, practitioners, courts, legislatures and policymakers throughout Europe have been struggling with the 'massification' of private law relationships, both in and outside of tort law.[1] The subject is, however, not easy to demarcate. It moves between the law of civil procedure, substantive tort law, access to justice debates and regulatory frameworks for mass consumer disputes. I understand the definition of the subject matter of this volume to include the broad concept of monetary compensation for wrongs committed vis-à-vis individuals. The adjective 'mass' in 'mass torts' denotes different cases. One variation is a one-time accident which directly and simultaneously causes widespread damage (eg, a train derailment disaster; a chemical plant explosion). Another variation of a mass tort may involve a long-latency disease incurred by many and caused by the defective product of one manufacturer or several manufacturers of an identical or similar product (eg, defective breast implants, asbestos). Each of these variations has its own peculiarities as far as standards of conduct, standard of proof of causation, prescription periods, damages and fair distribution of compensation, and rules of civil procedure are concerned. 1/1

This book aims at bringing together viewpoints from both legal practice and academic debate on the above-mentioned issues of mass tort. Thus, it meanders between substantive law and procedural law on the one hand, and the practical operation of law and related mechanisms of behaviour modification and dispute settlement on the other. As a result, this book does not only involve reference to 'the law in the books' but extends well into the domain of 'the law in action'. 1/2

From a practical point of view, I set out to collect insights from legal practice on the practical business of mass tort procedures: how are such cases set up 1/3

1 On the concept of 'massification', see *J Steele/WH van Boom*, Mass Justice and its Challenges, in: J Steele/WH van Boom (eds), Mass Justice – Challenges of Representation and Distribution (2011) 1 ff. On the notion of 'mass' see also *A Guégan-Lécuyer*, Dommages de masse et responsabilité civile (2006) 53 ff. See also *H Koch/A Willingmann* (eds), Großschäden – Complex Damages (1998); *H Koch*, Haftung für Massenschäden – Recht, Abwicklungspraxis, rechtspolitischer Handlungsbedarf, 53 Juristenzeitung (JZ) 1998, 801 ff.

by claimants, how do respondents react? What strategic considerations are involved, what practical obstacles and pitfalls exist? How do courts deal with the fundamental change that 'massification' seems to have set into motion?

1/4 Admittedly, the literature on mass litigation, class actions, group and representative action is abundant.[2] Yet, most of the existing European literature focuses on competition law and consumer law rather than on tort law. Moreover, recent academic projects on mass tort law are invariably influenced by the well-known class action vehicles in the USA, Canada and Australia. Against this backdrop, this book adds to the existing literature by collecting a number of case studies mostly on tort cases and, by combining these with thematic chapters in which the challenges concerning mass torts are mapped, explored and analysed from a European perspective.

1/5 In this introductory chapter, I set out to introduce the subject matter of this volume, the two sections of this volume and its component chapters. First, I briefly introduce the relevant concepts, terminology and the basic legal framework to facilitate the understanding of the entirety of the book (no 1/6 ff below). Secondly, I sketch debates and pathways in the domain of mass torts. Here, I give a brief overview of the discourse at EU-level on mass litigation (no 1/21 ff below). Then inventory is made of the various pathways of litigating, adjudication and resolving mass disputes (no 1/23 ff below). There, I outline some of the issues that merit consideration both in academic and policy debate when considering steps towards modification of the legal framework for resolving mass torts. Fourthly, I give an overview of the contents of this volume and its subdivision into two main sections. Here, I introduce the practitioners' case studies and the thematic academic contributions (no 1/25 ff below). I conclude with some final considerations (no 1/44 ff below).

II. Concepts and Basic Legal Issues

1/6 In Europe, private law systems traditionally consider the basis for monetary compensation for wrongs committed vis-à-vis individuals to lie in the law of tort or contract. In turn, tort and contract law are traditionally conceptualised as

---

2 Of the recent literature, I merely mention: *PG Karlsgodt* (ed), World Class Actions – A Guide to Group and Representative Actions around the Globe (2012); *JG Backhaus/A Cassone/GB Ramello* (eds), The Law and Economics of Class Actions in Europe – Lessons from America (2012); *C Hodges/A Stadler* (eds), Resolving Mass Disputes – ADR and Settlement of Mass Claims (2013). For an overview of the various forms of class action in common law jurisdictions, see eg *R Mulheron*, The Class Action in Common Law Legal Systems (2004).

systems offering individual remedies to individual creditors and victims, which are to be exercised by individuals in their individually lodged proceedings. In short, the individual and his individual assets and debts are central to the philosophy of private law.

As a result, the concept of *class action*, the construction of aggregation of claims into one consolidated legal action, well known to the legal systems of the United States of America, Canada and Australia, is different in many ways from this traditional look on the aims and functions of private law.[3] The basic notion of class action is that one representative of a class of individuals (numerosity) with comparable individual causes of action sharing a 'commonality of issues' files a claim and petitions the court to appoint him as 'lead plaintiff' for the entire class. This procedure for class certification may or may not end in actual certification. If it does, the lead plaintiff is the sole legal representative in the proceedings. The class action institute relies heavily on monitoring activities by courts of the lead plaintiff and his entrepreneurial attorney. 1/7

By contrast and notwithstanding the potential inefficiencies of this principled approach, the European concept of private law adheres to individual entitlement and responsibility as the foundation of private law relationships. Hence, individual claimants have individual *causes of action* and an individual *right of audience*: the right to be heard in a court of law when in pursuit of a cause of action for monetary compensation for wrongs committed against them individually. Usually, the cause of action accrues to the harmed individual who has actually suffered the infringement and/or the economic consequences thereof. 1/8

The principle of *res judicata* denotes the situation in which there has been a final judgment which is no longer subject to appeal. It is also used to refer to the doctrine which bars or precludes re-litigation of such cases between the same parties (*preclusive effect*). In this latter usage, the term *res judicata* is synonymous with 'preclusion'.[4] So, claim preclusion and/or issue preclusion (also known as 'collateral estoppel' or 'issue estoppel') is the principle which posits that a determination of an issue as a necessary element of a judgment should 1/9

3 On the functions of private law generally and tort law specifically in a European context, see eg, *G Wagner*, Prävention und Verhaltenssteuerung durch Privatrecht – Anmaßung oder legitime Aufgabe?, 206 Archiv für die civilistische Praxis (AcP) 2006, 352ff; *WH van Boom*, Efficacious Enforcement in Contract and Tort (inaugural lecture Erasmus University Rotterdam 2006). Cf *G Wagner*, Collective Redress – Categories of Loss and Legislative Options (2011) 127 Law Quarterly Review 55ff.

4 Definition derived from *Ministry of Justice*, The Government's Response to the Civil Justice Council's Report: 'Improving Access to Justice through Collective Actions' (2009) 20.

generally not be re-examined in a subsequent dispute in which the same issue is presented.[5]

1/10 In principle, *res judicata* does not extend to third parties who were not formally implied in the litigation of the case. Thus, where a court establishes certain facts in a tort case between a tortfeasor and one victim, these facts can easily be re-litigated in proceedings with other victims of the same or similar wrongdoing. Moreover, the starting point for many legal systems is that points of law decided in one case do not have any official status in other proceedings. In practice, however, the concept of *precedence* – either in an official, rigid *stare decisis* sense or in a more flexible version of informal *authority* – may somehow remedy this inefficiency.

1/11 Others than the individual may have an economic stake in the claim for compensation. For instance, an agent for the harmed individual may lodge proceedings by issuing a writ on the basis of a proxy, a power of attorney or even assignment. *Assignment* of the claim, that is the actual transfer of ownership in the claim – be it for the purpose of legitimate transfer or for the purpose of collecting the proceeds of the claim – may or may not be possible. Here, the various legal systems have different approaches to assignment of claims. Some legal systems are quite comfortable with others (assignee) than the original claimant (assignor) pursuing claims in court as long as the original claimant has expressed his consent with such assignment. Others simply deny the possibility of 'commodification' of some or all types of claims. As a result, the latter jurisdictions may also experience difficulties with *third-party funding* arrangements where the pursuit of the claim is somehow delegated to the third party with or without assignment.[6]

---

5 ALI/Unidroit Principles of Transnational Civil Procedure (2004) 48 (comment on principle 28). On the *res judicata* effect in the international mass tort context, see eg, *A Pinna*, Recognition and Res Judicata of US Class Action Judgments in European Legal Systems, 1 Erasmus Law Review 2008, 31 ff.

6 On the legal restrictions imposed on third party funding, the literature abounds. I merely refer to the definitions and further references at *WH van Boom*, Financing Civil Litigation by the European Insurance Industry, in: M Tuil/L Visscher (eds), New Trends in Financing Civil Litigation in Europe – A Legal, Empirical, and Economic Analysis (2010) 92 ff; *WH van Boom*, Third-Party Financing in International Investment Arbitration, SSRN eLibrary 2011, 1 ff. Cf *S Madaus*, Keine Effektivität einer europäischen class action ohne "amerikanische Verhältnisse" bei deren Finanzierung, Zeitschrift für Europäisches Privatrecht (ZEuP) 2012, 99 ff. On practical experience with funding mechanisms in the Dutch context, see, *IN Tzankova*, Funding of Mass Disputes: Lessons from the Netherlands, 8 Journal of Law, Economics & Policy 2012, 549 ff.

Ultimately, the goal of a civil procedure for monetary compensation is to obtain a court order to pay compensation. Such a verdict for compensation may be dissected into various elements: it usually contains statements of facts, applicable legal principles and qualification of facts as fitting the operative parts of a particular legal construct or doctrine. The court *orders* the payment of an amount in *damages*, to be calculated according to principles of the *law of damages*. Usually, the private law of damages centres on the principle of full compensation (*restitutio in integrum*). 1/12

However, proceedings may also be confined to a petition for *declaratory judgment*. For instance, where a multiplicity of victims chooses to wait with issuance of a writ until one of them obtains a favourable ruling on a point of law in a *test case* proceeding. In the test case, the court is petitioned to render a declaration specifying the legal relationship between claimant and respondent rather than order the payment of compensation. The basic idea is that the outcome of the test case – eg, on whether a particular product design was flawed, whether an auditor neglected a duty of care vis-à-vis investors when approving an annual report, etc – effectively decides the fate of all the other dormant, stayed or pending court cases on that particular point of law. Some legal systems do not have specific procedural rules for test case procedures; there, the authority of the verdict is informal, not official. Others have a specific procedure for test case proceedings (*Musterprozess, lead action*) which extend *res judicata* effect to third parties implicated in the wider conflict. 1/13

Alternatively, *injunction* may be part of the tool-box of the claimants as well. If in a particular case monetary compensation is not deemed part of the law of damages but rather the law of restitution or unjust enrichment, the cause of action may be one for restitution of an amount paid without legal justification. The appropriate procedural tool may be a mandatory injunction ordering the restitution. Such actions may be either loss-oriented or gain-oriented and may, depending on the legal system, form part and parcel of substantive causes of action or constitute a discretionary power of the court.[7] 1/14

The person held liable for monetary compensation for the wrong committed vis-à-vis the victim is individually responsible. When summoned to enter civil proceedings, however, the respondent may have a right to compel a third party to join the proceedings (*interpleader; indemnity claim proceedings*). This may be especially relevant where the respondent is not exclusively liable but one of multiple jointly and severally liable wrongdoers. 1/15

---

7 Further on this topic *WH van Boom*, Comparative Notes on Injunction and Wrongful Risk-Taking, 17 Maastricht Journal of European and Comparative Law 2010, 10 ff.

1/16 *Joint and several liability* is the legal doctrine where each of two or more persons can be held individually liable in full for the payment of the monetary compensation due to the victim.[8] Such joint and several debtorship may arise in case of joint torts (eg, where two companies deliberately collude to contravene competition law restrictions), concurrent torts (eg, where the acts of two or more tortfeasors concurrently and incidentally contribute towards the genesis of one undivided damage), vicarious liability (where one is held liable ancillary to the primary tortfeasor) and several other situations.[9]

1/17 On the side of the claimant, most European legal systems allow a basic form of *aggregation* of individual claims on the basis of *voluntary joinder* or *consolidation* of claims. This essentially means that claimants join forces and jointly issue a writ against the tortfeasor to have their case heard in one and the same procedure. Where allowed, a joinder may actually take the form of an *opt-in* collective action procedure, where several claimants authorise one of them – or an agent – to lodge proceedings in their name and on their joint behalves. As a rule, joinder does not alter the status of the individual claims that underlie the proceedings (so, one plus one does not equal three). Sometimes, courts have the discretionary power to join related and concurrently pending court cases as well in order to efficiently deal with these in one procedure. However, not much use is to be expected from these powers in those legal systems where existing civil procedure rules are predominantly moulded to the 'one-versus-one model' of civil procedure. Bringing multiple claims or tortfeasors together may in fact render the judicial management task even more complex than it already is with single claimant/respondent proceedings.

1/18 Other forms of collective action go under various names: *collective action*, group action, representative action, etc. There is no fixed terminology in use, so it is relevant to distinguish on the basis of the characteristics of the procedure instead of the heading under which such actions are brought. Usually, legal systems provide for some sort of *legal standing* for *representative organisations* (ie, associations and/or foundations, that is: incorporated not for profit legal persons with capacity to perform legal acts, obtain assets and incur debts) to have some cases for injunction heard. In the enforcement of European con-

---

8 *BA Koch*, Multiple Tortfeasors in Mass Tort Cases, in this volume no 12/18 prefers the use of the expression 'solidary liability'. Both expressions pertain to the situation where each of a number of tortfeasors is individually liable for the whole of the damage suffered by the victim.

9 On joint and several liability and its scope, eg, *I Gilead/MD Green/BA Koch* (eds), Proportional Liability: Analytical and Comparative Perspectives (2013); *K Oliphant* (ed), Aggregation and Divisibility of Damage (2009); *WVH Rogers* (ed), Unification of Tort Law: Multiple Tortfeasors (2004).

sumer law, such collective actions are widely acknowledged.[10] In some countries, designated associations have special statutory powers to claim restitutionary damages (for the benefit of the public purse) on behalf of a represented class of detrimented consumers. In others, such associations and/or foundations have a special role in obtaining amicable settlements for the benefit of individual victims, subject to court approval.[11] It is unusual in Europe, however, for associations and/or foundations – let alone individuals – to be authorised to initiate damages proceedings on behalf of individual victims without their explicit consent. That would in fact amount to a class action model, where one claimant is the exclusive representative of an entire class. The closest any European legal system has come to the USA-style class action, is the collective action procedure with an *opt-out* damages award (eg, the WCAM procedure in the Netherlands). It seems that this model is currently slowly but surely gaining momentum in Europe.

Once a collective procedure for the payment of the monetary compensation due to the collective of victims is successful, there is a *follow-up phase* where the proceeds need to be administrated, distributed and/or invested for the benefit of the collective of the victims. Since most European legal systems do not have a fully-fledged collective action procedure as such, it comes as no surprise that such a follow-up phase does not exist either. Unless a specific statutory arrangement for the creation, administration, governance and distribution of a fund exists, perhaps general principles can be applied. In common law traditions, the *trust* may be useful. In other jurisdictions, the incorporation of a dedicated 'special purpose vehicle' may be useful. Accepting the notion of a collec- 1/19

---

10 Directive 98/27/EC of the European Parliament and of the Council of 19 May 1998 on injunctions for the protection of consumers' interests, Official Journal (OJ) L 166, 11.6.1998, 51–55; Regulation (EC) No 2006/2004 of the European Parliament and of the Council of 27 October 2004 on cooperation between national authorities responsible for the enforcement of consumer protection laws (the Regulation on consumer protection cooperation), OJ L 364, 9.12.2004, 1–11. Further on collective enforcement from a consumer law perspective, eg, *W van Boom/M Loos* (eds), Collective Enforcement of Consumer Law – Securing Compliance in Europe through Private Group Action and Public Authority Intervention (2007); *C Hodges*, The Reform of Class and Representative Actions in European Legal Systems – A New Framework for Collective Redress in Europe (2008); *F Cafaggi/H-W Micklitz* (eds), New Frontiers of Consumer Protection – The Interplay between Private and Public Enforcement (2009).

11 This is essentially the Dutch system of the WCAM, on which *A Stadler*, Mass Damages in Europe – Allocation of Jurisdiction – Cross-Border Multidistrict Litigation, in this volume no 13/29 ff. Cf *F Weber/WH van Boom*, Dutch Treat: The Dutch Collective Settlement of Mass Damage Act (WCAM 2005), Contratto e impresa/Europa 2011, 69 ff; *T Arons/WH van Boom*, Beyond Tulips and Cheese: Exporting Mass Securities Claim Settlements from the Netherlands, European Business Law Review (EBLR) 2010, 857 ff.

tive damages action in mass tort cases inevitably raises issues of damages calculation (quantum) and distribution. Moreover, in the process the function of the *law of damages* may also have to be scrutinized. Rather than paying lip service to the doctrine of full compensation, forms of damage-scheduling, restitutionary damages (skimming off of illegal gains[12]) and cy-près solutions[13] would need to be explored.

1/20 A related issue in the follow-up phase is insolvency. *Insolvency* is a complication under any circumstances – so it will not come as a surprise that insolvency of the liable party adds to the already complex distributional issues involved with mass torts. To some extent, the multiplicity of liable parties may render the problem less complicated for the victim. In that case, joint and several liability may offer solace to victims. Obviously, this contrasts with the plight of the solvent parties thus held liable. In other respects, the follow-up phase of administration and distribution much resembles insolvency proceedings, where a trustee in bankruptcy is assigned the task of taking stock of the bankrupt estate and fairly distributing proceeds.

III. Debates and Pathways

A. The Debate in Europe

1/21 During the past decade or so, the European Commission has been struggling with the subject of mass litigation without reaching definite conclusions or policies. Diverging pathways seemed to emerge from the two Directorates responsible for competition policy and consumer policy.[14] Then, in 2011, 'a coherent ap-

---

12 See further on skimming-off procedures according to German law, eg, *G Wagner*, Neue Perspektiven im Schadensersatzrecht – Kommerzialisierung, Strafschadensersatz, Kollektivschaden (Gutachten zum 66. Deutschen Juristentag Stuttgart 2006) (2006) 111 ff; *J Neuberger*, Der wettbewerbsrechtliche Gewinnabschöpfungsanspruch im europäischen Rechtsvergleich (2006); *M Leicht*, Gewinnabschöpfung bei Verstoß gegen die lauterkeitsrechtliche Generalklausel (2009) 213 ff; *S Sieme*, Der Gewinnabschöpfungsanspruch nach § 10 UWG und die Vorteilsabschöpfung gem. §§ 34, 34a GWB (2009). Cf *Wagner*, 206 AcP 2006, 352 ff.

13 On *cy-près* distribution in a European context, see eg, *G Howells*, Cy-près for Consumers: Ensuring Class Action Reforms Deal with 'Scattered Damages', in: Steele/van Boom (fn 1) 58 f; generally on cy-près in litigation *R Mulheron*, The Modern Cy-près Doctrine: Applications & Implications (2006) 213 ff.

14 Cf Green Paper, Damages Actions for Breach of the EC Antitrust Rules (COM(2005) 672 final); White Paper, Damages Actions for Breach of the EC Antitrust Rules (COM(2008) 165 final); Green Paper, Consumer Collective Redress (COM (2008) 794 final).

proach to collective redress' seemed to herald convergence of the competition and consumer policy areas.[15] In 2013, the Commission unfolded two pillars of its new comprehensive policy. Firstly, it unveiled a proposal for a Directive on competition law damages actions.[16] Secondly, it published a communication titled 'Towards a European Horizontal Framework for Collective Redress',[17] which was accompanied by a Recommendation 'on common principles for injunctive and compensatory collective redress mechanisms in the member states concerning violations of rights granted under Union Law'.[18] The Recommendation suggests that Member States should ensure that representative organisations have legal standing to bring representative actions, that opt-in damages actions are to be sustained and that courts are to take on an active managerial role in dealing with such cases. However, none of the above documents lays down a binding instrument for the Member States to enact particular collective redress remedies.[19] Instead, Member States are invited to introduce adequate procedures for collective action procedures concerning injunction and redress for damages in the coming two years. After this period, the Commission will revisit the subject and assess whether further action at EU-level is opportune. It seems that, for the time being, the Commission accepts that the developments in this area at Member State level are still in their infancy and that the time for harmonisation has not yet come (if it ever will).

Indeed, as far as developments at Member State level are concerned, new initiatives and innovative developments are rife. In countries such as Denmark, the Netherlands and Portugal, some form of opt-out damages procedures was introduced some time ago.[20] The serendipitous success of the Dutch WCAM in attracting cross-border settlements in mass financial and investment disputes is noteworthy.[21] If anything, the WCAM has fuelled debate within Europe on whether 1/22

---

15 Commission Staff Working Document Public Consultation: Towards a Coherent European Approach to Collective Redress (SEC (2011) 173).

16 Proposal for a Directive of the European Parliament and of the Council on certain rules governing actions for damages under national law for infringements of the competition law provisions of the Member States and of the European Union (COM (2013) 404 final).

17 COM (2013) 401/2.

18 C (2013) 3539/3.

19 Cf *A Stadler*, Die Vorschläge der Europäischen Kommission zum kollektiven Rechtsschutz in Europa – der Abschied von einem kohärenten europäischen Lösungsansatz?, Zeitschrift für das Privatrecht der Europäischen Union (GPR) 2013, 279 ff.

20 See the brief overview of countries at *WH van Boom*, De Minimis Curat Praetor – Redress for Dispersed Trifle Losses, 4 Journal of Comparative Law (J Comp L) 2009, 171 ff.

21 On the WCAM, see *Weber/van Boom*, Contratto e impresa/Europa 2011, 69 ff; *Arons/van Boom*, EBLR 2010, 857 ff; *WH van Boom*, Collective Settlement of Mass Claims in the Netherlands, in: M Casper et al (eds), Auf dem Weg zu einer europäischen Sammelklage? (2009) 171 ff;

mass damages procedures should be cobbled together on *opt-in* or *opt-out* bases.[22] Recently, further momentum for the introduction of so-called opt-out collective actions seems to be building. For instance, in the United Kingdom concrete suggestions for the introduction of such procedures have been made in the area of competition law and consumer law.[23] In Poland, the 2009 Act on Pursuing Claims in Group Proceedings was introduced.[24] In France, a legislative draft on a limited opt-out collective action in consumer law is currently pending before Parliament.[25] Meanwhile, in Belgium a Parliamentary Bill on collective redress was recently introduced.[26] One can easily conclude that it appears that there is a competition going on between Member States in designing the most attractive alternative for the USA class action while retaining the national legal cultural texture.

B. Pathways

1/23 When considering the various pathways to damages adjudication, settlement and compensation, one cannot but investigate tort law in conjunction with other systems of deterrence, compensation and vindication.[27] The same is even more true

---

A Mom, Kollektiver Rechtsschutz in den Niederlanden (2011) 311ff. Cf *Van Boom/Loos* (fn 10); *H van Lith*, The Dutch Collective Settlements Act and Private International Law (2011) 13ff. Cf *WA Kaal/RW Painter*, Forum Competition and Choice of Law Competition in Securities Law after Morrison v. National Australia Bank, 97 Minnesota Law Review 2012, 132ff.

22 Cf on the dichotomy opt-in/opt-out, *R Mulheron*, The Case for an Opt-out Class Action for European Member States: A Legal and Empirical Analysis, 15 Columbia Journal of European Law 2008, 409ff.

23 *Department for Business Innovation & Skills (BIS)*, Private Actions in Competition Law: A Consultation on Options for Reform (2013); *BIS*, Civil Enforcement Remedies: Consultation on Extending the Range of Remedies Available to Public Enforcers of Consumer Law (2012).

24 *JM Szewczyk*, Selected Issues Concerning Pursuing Claims in the Polish Group Proceeding, 1 Journal of Education, Psychology and Social Sciences 2013, 60ff.

25 Projet de loi relatif à la consommation, introduced in Parliament on 2 May 2013. On French developments generally, see eg, *S Brunengo-Basso*, L'émergence de l'action de groupe, processus de fertilisation croisée (thèse 2009 Universite Paul Cezanne – Aix-Marseille III) (2011) 235ff; *Guégan-Lécuyer* (fn 1) 403ff.

26 Parliamentary Bill on Causes of Action for Collective Redress, 17 January 2014, Doc 53, 3300/001. Cf on Belgian law *S Voet*, Een Belgische vertegenwoordigende collectieve rechtsvordering (2012); *B Allemeersch et al*, Vers une 'class action' en droit belge? (2008).

27 This point was raised and addressed in some of my earlier writing. See eg, *WH van Boom/MG Faure*, Introducing 'Shifts in Compensation Between Private and Public Systems', in: WH van Boom/MG Faure (eds), Shifts in Compensation between Private and Public Systems (2007) 1ff; *WH van Boom*, Compensating and Preventing Damage: Is there any Future left for Tort Law?, in: H Tiberg/M Clarke (eds), Festskrift till Bill W. Dufwa – Essays on Tort, Insurance

for mass damages, where the limits of fair, balanced and expedient court adjudication come in sight even quicker than in 'single victim/single tortfeasor' cases. As *Figure 1* illustrates, there are competing pathways that may fulfil comparable roles as tort law. These alternatives may not render exactly the same results in the strict legal sense but they may well suffice from a societal point of view. Indeed, they may turn out to be superior in other respects such as speed and accessibility of procedure. For instance, it has been suggested that in regulated markets (eg, financial services, telecommunications) there should be a discretionary power for the relevant market authority to coerce a regulatee who contravenes statutory standards to provide redress according to some predefined compensation standard. This could indeed be a viable alternative to the arduous route of private litigation.[28] Also, the promise of ADR bodies has been highlighted in this respect.[29]

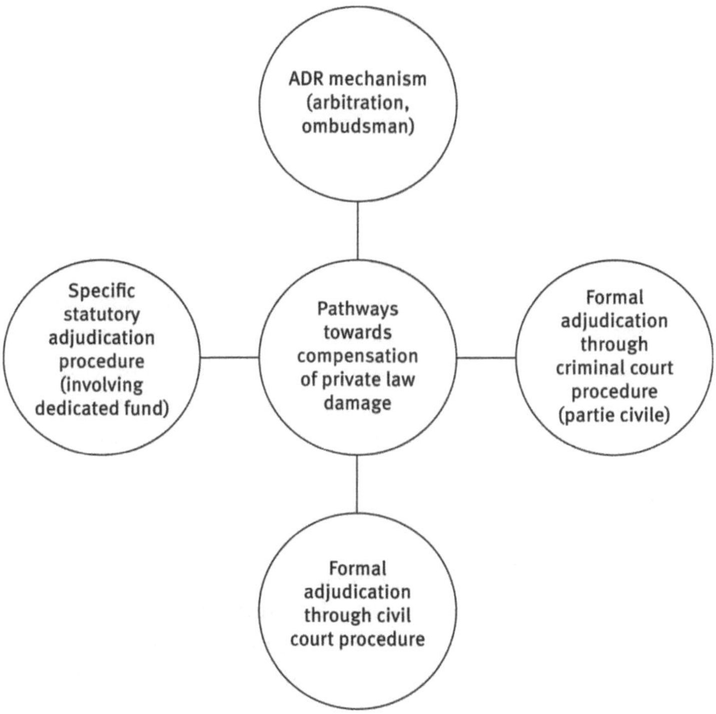

Figure 1: Pathways towards compensation

Law and Society in Honour of Bill W. Dufwa, vol I (2006) 287 ff. Cf also the literature referred to in *Van Boom* (fn 3).

28 See eg *Hodges* (fn 10) 207 ff.

29 Cf *S Roberts/M Palmer*, Dispute Processes – ADR and the Primary Forms of Decision-Making (2005).

1/24 Furthermore, in some countries it is not uncommon for mass tort cases to become part of criminal proceedings, where the law allows victims of a crime to submit their claim (follow-on 'partie civile'). There are some advantages for victims involved: it is the State prosecution service that provides the expert witnesses, investigates the facts and causation issues and covers the legal expenses for the prosecution. Furthermore, it can make use of investigative powers which ordinary victims lack. Criminal conviction may also open up access to a national Criminal Injuries Compensation Authority. The obvious drawback of the *partie civile* pathway is that the victims are not in full control of the proceedings. The route towards redress hinges on the actual prosecution and successful conviction of the tortfeasor. Moreover, others who are jointly and severally responsible but are not prosecuted are not affected. This merely shows that each pathway has its inherent limitations and that one should be suspicious of the suggestion that 'one size fits all torts' exists.

IV. The Contributions to this Book

A. Cases and Reflections

1/25 The book consists of two main sections: 1) case reports from legal practice and 2) academic reflections on wider issues of mass torts. Thus, the first section brings together concrete examples of how mass tort litigation, settlement and administration work out in practice. The chapters in this section were written by expert practitioners in their field and thus give an insight into the practical operation of the law in the cases at hand. In the case reports, a sketch of the case and its facts is presented, the legal and factual issues involved as well as an impression of the stakeholders involved (eg, primary and secondary victims, liable parties, lawyers, interested associations and pressure groups, insurance companies, regulatory authorities, media and political involvement). As concerns the legal issues, questions arise such as which jurisdictions were involved (and why)? What substantive rules were relevant (tort, contract, administrative law, etc)? Were there attempts at settling out of court? And if so, which stakeholders were involved? How did these attempts work out? If court intervention was involved, how did they manage the case? As to the dynamics of the case, issues are covered such as what were the decisive elements of the case that tipped the balance one way or the other (eg, pressure exerted by a regulatory authority? Media attention may cause a business to settle rather than go to court over a case, etc). Finally, it may be considered whether in hindsight the case could have been dealt with differently (more efficiently, effectively)? And if so, what would be the conditions under which this alternative scenario could have worked?

Here, some words on the scope of the book are in order. Mass torts come in different shapes and sizes and the word 'tort' seems malleable when combined with 'mass'. Furthermore, mass claims need not be based on tort law exclusively; they may also arise under contract law, as in cases involving the transport sector (cancellation of trains or flights, late departure) and in cases involving the sale of securities by banks, investment funds or brokers. In fact, the concept of tort heavily depends on the delineation between contract and tort in the various jurisdictions. Thus, a case of misleading information to potential investors may be considered a true tort case in one jurisdiction and a case of (quasi-)contract in the other, just as much as a case of personal injury may be framed as either the result of negligence to perform a common law duty of safety in tort law or the contractual non-performance of contractual obligations to provide safety. 1/26

Therefore, some of the issues raised in this volume may well fall within the scope of both tort and contract law. Nevertheless, the book as a whole focuses on what can be understood to be mass torts. Set in other terms, the book may even have been divided not only in two main sections but also into a number of distinct categories. As can be gleaned from what follows, at least three main areas of interest are involved: personal injury claims (airplane crashes, ship wrecking, defective products), investment claims and consumer cases (eg, boarding denial and late departure cases, mis-selling of endowment policies). Note, however, that these three areas of interest do not necessarily have a traditional 'tort' focus and their relative relevance for policymakers (at least at a European level) is not identical. Therefore, we decided not to over-emphasise these categories but instead we categorised the contributions to the book along the two sectional lines as referred to earlier. 1/27

B. Case Studies

Although other orders would have been perfectly tenable, we have decided to arrange the case studies in the following order.[30] First, under the heading of 'several events with common causes', there are two case studies on defective products and business processes which endangered life and health: asbestos and silicone breast implants. Secondly, under the heading 'one event with mul- 1/28

30 Cf on the typology of mass tort cases *S Lange*, Das begrenzte Gruppenverfahren (2011) 3ff.

tiple victims' we deal with two salient disasters that caused widespread death and injury: the grounding, tilting and capsizing of the Costa Concordia (2012, Italy) and the derailment and collision of a high-speed train in Eschede (1998, Germany). Thirdly, the theme of 'multinationals and multi-district actions' deals with the accountability in tort of multinational corporations for mass damage caused elsewhere, illustrated by the litigation of African silicosis claims against mining companies and environmental claims against Shell before UK courts. The fourth and final category of case studies involves financial markets and mass damage. One case study involves the allegedly misleading annual report of the German Telekom, a second one the Italian bank (over)charge class action and a final third one the claw-back actions by the trustee in the Madoff bankrupt estate.

1. Several events with a common cause

1/29 In the chapter titled 'The Italian 'Eternit Trial': Litigating Massive Asbestos Damage in a Criminal Court', Coggiola and Graziadei report on the criminal prosecution in Torino, Italy of former managers and related group companies of the international asbestos manufacturing company Eternit who were held accountable for the historical actions and omissions of Italian Eternit factories. The criminal indictment was based on the lack of safety measures at the factories, which had exposed numerous employees, relatives and inhabitants living in the vicinity to the risks of asbestos related diseases. The criminal trial involved numerous individuals, organisations and public authorities who joined as *parti civili*. Coggiola and Graziadei show how the Italian legal system grapples with both the prosecution of a complex string of corporate actions and omissions – which is rather more complicated than the prosecution a one-off act with a single victim – and the involvement of multiple victims claiming compensation for hugely disparate damage in the context of one and the same criminal proceeding. The authors identify a number of pertinent questions that the Italian Eternit trial raises, such as whether the criminal trial is the most efficient way of dealing with such complicated mass damages cases. One obvious advantage the criminal trial has over tort trials is that the huge investment in the investigation of facts and causation is borne by the State judicial authorities rather than by private claimants. The downside obviously is that victims have less say in how the criminal prosecution is conducted.

1/30 Ferrari discusses the rise of mass litigation concerning silicone breast implants. After an in-depth comparative analysis of the US-origins of litigation in this area, Ferrari turns her attention to the recent PIP scandal and the implications it has had for European medical devices safety policies. She furthermore shows that the EU product liability framework[31] may at first sight offer adequate protection against defective implants but since defectiveness and causation need to be shown by the claimant, cases involving ruptured implants are by no means clear-cut. Moreover, since manufacturers of implants and recipients may well reside in different countries (including the USA), there are inevitably issues of jurisdiction and applicable law involved. Moreover, Ferrari demonstrates that the fact that the manufacturer may enter into bankruptcy further adds to the complication of obtaining compensation. She concludes that some form of aggregation of claims – be it through class action or otherwise – is key to resolving the obstacles for individual victims and can offer judicial economy as concerns both fact-finding, leverage for settlement negotiations and 'closure' for defendants.

2. One event with multiple victims

The capsizing of the Costa Concordia cruise ship off the coast of Il Giglio, Italy, 1/31
on 13 January 2012 is discussed by Perrella. Perrella's contribution offers insight into the different aspects involved in this mass damage event. Apart from the deplorable loss of lives and the great number of injured, there are substantial insurance claims, wreck removal costs and environmental claims involved. One of the issues here is to ascertain which legal regime applies to the claims, whether maritime limitation (treaty) regimes apply[32] and what courts have competence to hear the various claims. Indeed, a class action was filed in the USA. Perrella also shows that the way in which offers for settlements are phrased and framed in the immediate aftermath of a mass damage event can be decisive for its pick-up rate and therefore its success.

Krasney reports on his experience as the Ombudsman for the victims of the 1/32
1998 rail disaster in Eschede, Germany. In Eschede, a high speed train derailed and collided with a concrete bridge after material fatigue caused a wheel to disintegrate. The disaster left 101 persons dead and some 88 injured. The German railway company DB accepted responsibility and appointed Krasney as Om-

31 Council Directive 85/374/EEC of 25 July 1985 on the approximation of the laws, regulations and administrative provisions of the Member States concerning liability for defective products, OJ L 210, 7.8.1985, 29–33.

32 Here, one of the conflicting issues may well be that the *lex sitae* of the ship's flag is decisive for the applicable regime to limitation while the contract of carriage may well be subject to a different law.

budsman for the victims involved. The assistance supplied by DB was aimed to be comprehensive and to include both financial compensation and other support such as psychological help. As Krasney shows, the appointment of an Ombudsman by the responsible corporation itself to distribute compensation does require careful balancing in order to avoid any perceived conflict of interest or appearance of partiality and to bolster trustworthiness of the official involved. As Krasney demonstrates, it seems that the Ombudsman successfully acted as an intermediary between the disaster victims and the liable company.

3. Multinationals and multi-district actions

1/33 In his contribution titled 'International environmental mass litigation in the UK', Marangos firstly deals with claims against Shell Petroleum for environmental damage sustained by communities in the Niger Delta following accidental oil spillage. The claims are pursued before the London High Court, which raises all sorts of conflict of laws issues, such as whether damages should be assessed in accordance with the Nigerian or English law of damages. Marangos then turns to comparable foreign cases litigated in the UK such as the BP oil spill in Colombia, the *Cape* asbestos proceedings. He asks what will be the future consequences of such cases reaching UK courts, especially in light of differences in the levels of compensation awarded in domestic courts.

1/34 Tansley discusses the pending 'South-African silicosis litigation in London'. Here, the UK courts were called upon to consider damage relating to wrongs allegedly committed in South Africa. As far as jurisdiction was concerned, the issue is whether the defendant company had its place of domicile in London – which necessitates an interpretation of the Brussels 1 Regulation (Council Regulation (EC) No 44/2001) on what constitutes 'central administration' and 'principal place of business'. Moreover, the main substantive questions turn to the duty of care of a mining company vis-à-vis workers contracting silicosis, whether there was a breach of that duty and if so, what the appropriate level of compensation is.

4. Financial markets and mass damage

1/35 Rolla reports on the use of the Italian class action procedure for recouping consumer overcharges by banks. The Italian class action statute entered into force in 2010. It allows an opt-in consolidation of homogenous claims on initiative of the original claimant. The bank charges case offers an interesting example of how the new statutory regime can be used by consumer organisations in building a mass damages case. Meanwhile, it also shows the inherent restrictions of the opt-in consolidation process. Before engaging in such a process, the original claimant(s) needs to assess the chances of others opting in and how the costs incurred can ideally be distributed (and financed).

Tilp and Roth report on the 'The German Capital Market Model Proceedings **1/36**
Act as Illustrated by the Example of the Frankfurt Deutsche Telekom Claims'. The Telekom case involves private investors in Deutsche Telekom claiming compensation for allegedly false, incomplete and misleading prospectuses. The facts date from the late 1990s, the first individual cases were brought to court in 2001, the *Kapitalanleger-Musterverfahrensgesetz* (Act on Exemplary Proceedings in Capital Market Disputes, KapMuG) was enacted in 2005 and only in 2012 were the first so-called 'model decisions' (verdicts in the KapMuG test case) handed down. And the end is not yet in sight, as Tilp and Roth demonstrate. Perhaps, what this test case procedure shows is that meticulous mass adjudication is not necessarily expeditious. Indeed, it seems that the experience with the German KapMuG shows that efficiency, expedience and pace are not easily reconciled without abandoning the foundations of procedural autonomy and the opt-in principle in mass litigation.[33]

The contribution by Boldon discusses various tort aspects in the aftermath **1/37**
of the collapse of Bernie Madoff's global Ponzi scheme. The trustee in bankruptcy of Bernoff's business and estate initiated legal actions to obtain restitution of payments made to hedge funds and investors who had profited from payments before the fraudulent nature of the scheme was uncovered and who could not argue that they had received these payments in good faith; some banks were also held responsible for not preventing some of these transactions. The scale of the trustee's recovery operation is immense: more than 1,000 legal actions worldwide were started for a total amount of over USD 17 billion. Settlements were reached with various defendants, enabling the trustee to claw back more than USD 9 billion and to distribute the proceeds to the fraud victims. Boldon shows that because of the international nature and the vast scale of the investments involved, both the recoup efforts and the distribution of proceeds involve numerous issues of jurisdiction, applicable law and cross-border recognition and execution. Meanwhile, the trustee's fees and legal costs are coming close to USD 1 billion.

---

33 Recent amendment of the KapMuG has not changed the basic design of the Act. Cf *A Stadler*, Developments in Collective Redress: What's New in the 'New German KapMuG'?, EBLR 2013, 723ff.

C. Academic Reflections

1/38 The second section of the book concerns the academic reflections on some of the themes that surfaced in the first section. The section covers a broad range of underlying legal and policy concerns. The chapters were written by outstanding scholars, experts in their fields, with a broad and comparative vision on the issues involved. Here, the volume focuses at a more general level on many of the problematic issues that were raised at case level in the case studies. How do fundamental principles of substantive tort and insurance law (such as joint and several liability, standards of proof of causation), as well as principles of civil procedure (such as rules of evidence, burden of proof and the right to be heard) stand up in face of the challenges posed by 'massification'? Can civil procedure effectively deal with aggregation of claims, collective damage actions, model cases and test case proceedings? What alternatives to litigation have developed in terms of dealing with mass dispute adjudication in tort law and related areas? Have alternative pathways to compensation been successful in addressing all stakeholders' interests in a fair and balanced way? What is the role of conflict of laws in the market for dispute adjudication services within Europe? And finally, what is the relevance of insolvency proceedings in examining responsibility and fairly distributing compensation?

1/39 The contribution by Harald Koch, entitled 'Mass Damage in Europe: Aggregation of Claims, Effective Enforcement and Adequate Representation', provides an extensive overview of the wider issues involved in designing adequate responses to mass tort phenomena in private law systems. If courts are to distribute 'effective enforcement' in mass damages cases, the question is what the goals of the underlying substantive rules are and whether the emphasis should be laid on deterrence values, fair and swift compensation or something else. Koch thus points out that both the foundations of substantive law and the suitability of the concomitant procedures need to be addressed. He then touches upon alternative pathways towards mass dispute resolution such as ADR, arbitration and settlement, the limited value of test case procedures, methods of aggregation, issues of accountability in representative actions and the framework for funding mass litigation. In conclusion, he draws attention to the logistics of mass torts and the need for risk management by the companies involved.

1/40 Bernhard A Koch's contribution entitled 'Multiple Tortfeasors in Mass Tort Cases' deals with the issue of attributing liability in mass tort cases where more than one tortfeasor is involved and it is uncertain who caused the damage. Obviously, the first hurdle is the standard of proof. Koch shows that legal systems have adopted different approaches to this problem and that, besides the dichotomous approach of either fully attributing responsibility or fully denying it, there are such alternatives as proportionate liability, the loss of a chance doctrine and various variations of joint and several liability. Koch then moves on to model the different case scenarios in which multiple tortfeasors are involved and may or may not have contributed to the damage, and in which the injured party is or is not attributed contributory fault. Koch argues that both economic efficiency and equity should be considered in finding the most equitable framework for attributing responsibility. Moreover, he lists several factors such as the type of harm involved, the nature of the relationship between the parties and the basis of liability as relevant for the limits to imputation of legal causation. In essence, Koch poses the question whether the traditional bipartite model of litigating torts is fitted to suit mass damages cases.

In her contribution entitled 'Mass Damages in Europe – Allocation of Jurisdiction – Cross-Border Multidistrict Litigation', Astrid Stadler analyses the existing framework for litigating and settling mass tort claims with an international dimension and then discusses the need to reflect on private international law to ensure adequate responses to such issues as parallel court cases and contradictory court rulings across Europe and beyond, national differences in the civil litigation playing-field and the ensuing chances of a genuine *forum shopping* of claimants for the most favourable jurisdiction to push their claims. One of the conclusions that can be drawn from Stadler's analysis is that the EU rules on competence, applicable law, recognition and execution do not fit the legislative innovations at Member State level concerning mass tort damages procedures. Stadler concludes that the recent initiatives at EU level fail to address the private international law dimensions of mass tort litigation in Europe and that therefore the challenges posed by forum shopping within Europe will be further exacerbated. One of the possible ways to overcome these challenges is by adopting a rule of concentration of proceedings in one Member State, or so Stadler suggests. 1/41

Hodges' contribution on 'Delivering Redress through Alternative Dispute Resolution and Regulation' seeks to analyse the gradual movement from classical litigation models – or even their replacement – to alternative and online dispute resolution mechanisms (ODR and ADR). After an overview of the various methods of compensating victims outside tort law, the alternatives for resolving contract disputes (such as commercial arbitration), he turns to consumer ADR as the prototype of contemporary alternatives to litigation, the *partie civile* method of piggy-backing on criminal proceedings and the growing involvement of regulatory authorities in particular markets (such as Ombudsmen, Financial Services Authorities, etc) to ensure swift and adequate redress to (mostly) wronged consumers. Hodges foresees that the use of instruments such 1/42 as ADR and ODR will further spread and will indeed change the role of litigation and legal services generally.

1/43 Brinkmann's contribution entitled 'Mass Tort Related Insolvency Proceedings: Choice of Jurisdiction, Treatment and Discharge of Tort Claims' deals with the insolvency aspects of mass litigation. Three main issues are analysed, namely which court is competent to deal with mass tort claims where the tortfeasor has been declared bankrupt (the gravitational force of insolvency), whether tort victims enjoy priority or other preferred treatment in the *pari passu* distribution of assets and how discharge of the bankrupt's debts affects tort victims present and future. The insolvency aspect of mass torts is rather important conceptually as well.[34] Insolvency procedures are mainly a method of distribution scarce resources according to transparent rules. As such, the concept of insolvency, the method of asset restructuring and the role of the trustee in distributing the funds can inform policymakers and legislatures when considering new ways of dealing with the 'scarcity problem' that may be associated with mass damages.[35] Moreover, as Brinkmann aptly demonstrates, we may experience a development towards *forum shopping* of corporate tortfeasors in view of the threat of insolvency to find the most attractive 'centre of main interest' within Europe.

V. Final Considerations

1/44 As can be concluded from the previous paragraphs, this volume covers the breadth and depth of mass tort litigation, negotiation, settlement, adjudication and compensation. In doing so, it offers further guidance in a highly complicated area of the law which involves concepts and principles derived from both substantive and procedural law. This volume does not offer rough and ready answers to the challenges posed by mass torts. Underlying the cases and reflections, however, is at least one issue that may merit further discussion: are we ready yet for a common pan-European approach to mass tort litigation? Is the legislature willing to step away from the traditional doctrine which holds that individuals have individual claims which are to be heard individually? Here, a balance between the fundamental right of individual audience and efficiency in

34 On the conceptual similarities and differences between insolvency and mass tort actions, see cf *RA Nagareda*, Mass Torts in a World of Settlement (2007) 161 ff.

35 Another procedure that may offer fresh insights into how to distribute among mass tort victims is the maritime procedure for general average procedure (dispatch).

judicial dispute resolution is to be sought.[36] This search for balance is decided by several factors. One of the factors that influences legal change is *legal culture*. Where the culture within a particular legal system tends to be such that emphasis is put on principles of due process, fair hearing and precise adjudication, it will have difficulty in delivering on speed, flexibility and equal treatment of single cases. There, constitutional restrictions arguments may well be used to justify the legal status quo.[37] In other legal cultures, members of the bar are considered entrepreneurs first and 'servants of the law' second, courts are deemed to provide a legal service rather than constitute a state institution, and market solutions are preferred over state-administered and corporatist solutions. Perhaps, in such cultures certain legal solutions for the challenges posed by mass tort litigation would be considered more appropriate than others.

If European legal systems are to tackle the issue of mass tort litigation and **1/45**
the fair, efficient and expedient settlement and adjudication of mass torts, they need to rebalance both substantive and procedural law and principles. So, if procedural rules need to be adjusted in light of mass tort cases, perhaps so does substantive law. For instance, in dealing with mass trifle loss cases (ie, those cases where a large number of persons are affected but each suffers a minor financial loss), both the procedural right of individuals to a fair hearing and the substantive law of damages (skimming-off, restitutionary damages, cy-près solutions) may need rethinking.[38] If we acknowledge that mass torts are 'different' and that they deserve different rules, why would that only apply to rules of civil procedure? In turn, this raises the question whether victims of mass torts deserve 'special treatment'. Bernhard A Koch raises the interesting point that it seems that, in mass tort cases, victims have higher chances of receiving (higher) compensation than single victims in singular tort scenarios do.[39] Does the fact that there is a multitude of victims indeed lead to higher success rates, eg, through the increased legal pressures on the tortfeasor(s) and the leverage that crowds have, the involvement of media and politics and other such factors? If so, this might also explain the pressures on the legal system to amend procedural rules and even substantive rules (eg, on burden of proof concerning causation) to deal with mass tort cases more effectively, swiftly and efficiently.

---

36 *Van Boom*, 4 J Comp L 2009, 177.

37 Further on constitutional limitations according to German law, eg, *L Fiedler*, Class Actions zur Durchsetzung des europäischen Kartellrechts (2010) 237 ff.

38 For an interesting sociological approach of the various interests that collective (damages) actions could ideally take into account, see *L von Moltke*, Kollektiver Rechtsschutz der Verbraucherinteressen (2003) 101 ff.

39 *Koch* (fn 8) in this volume 12/62 (fn 52).

1/46 The way forward for the European Union is unclear. Given the differences in national legal culture, and the simmering hotchpotch of legislative innovations at Member State level, perhaps the recent decision to keep to recommendations is the wisest possible for now. Yet, the contributions by Stadler and Brinkmann as well as the some of the case studies show that, in the near future, the least that the European Union could do is to design unambiguous rules on court competence, applicable law, stay and priority of proceedings, recognition and execution and insolvency aspects in mass tort litigation.

Nadia Coggiola and Michele Graziadei*

2 The Italian 'Eternit Trial': Litigating Massive Asbestos Damage in a Criminal Court

I. Introduction

The so-called 'Eternit trial' is the largest criminal case ever prosecuted in Europe for asbestos-related deaths, injuries and damage.[1] News on the trial was published in most major European newspapers, as well as on Italian television for months. The gravity of the facts, the stakes involved in the litigation (including the recovery of damages by the very high number of victims and other civil claimants appearing before a criminal court), the communication campaigns of the victims' associations, supported by several non-profit associations, including the unions, explain its resonance. 2/1

The first instance proceedings of the Eternit trial ended on 13 February 2012, with the conviction of the defendants, the two top managers accused of the crimes, the Belgian Jean Luis de Cartier de Marchienne and the Swiss Stephan Schmidheiny, by the *Tribunale di Torino* (the first instance court of Torino), in Italy, to sixteen years of imprisonment and an award of damages for millions of Euros. Compensation was to be paid jointly and severally by them and by some defendant companies that were held civilly liable for the damage suffered by a very large number of claimants who participated in the proceedings in the quality of *parti civili* (see below no 2/15). 2/2

The second stage of the proceedings ended on 3 June 2013, when the *Corte d'Appello* (Court of Appeal) of Torino sentenced Stephan Schmidheiny to eighteen years of imprisonment, and an award of damages in favour of about half of the claimants who were successful before the first instance court. During these proceedings, the other defendant, Jean-Louis de Cartier de Marchienne, died at the age of 92. The *Corte d'Appello* has released only its ruling and the full judgment of the appellate court will be published later this year. Therefore, given that the appeal decision confirmed at least in part the rulings of the first in- 2/3

* This chapter is the result of a collaboration: Michele Graziadei authored marginal numbers (nos 2/1–23); Nadia Coggiola authored nos 2/24–48.

1 The full text of the first instance decision is available on the following web site: <http://www.diario-prevenzione.it/docbiblio/sentenza_eternit.pdf> (last consulted on 25 July 2013).

stance judgment, this chapter will concentrate on this. A few points of the first instance decision which were overturned or modified by the appellate court will be mentioned briefly, which explains why the number of successful claimants on appeal was not as high as before the first instance court.

2/4 A further appeal before the *Corte di Cassazione* (Court of Cassation) is pending, hence the criminal case is not yet closed. Furthermore, many civil claimants will still have to turn to civil courts to collect their money, or to pursue full compensation, because both the first instance and the appellate court ordered interim payments of damages to the victims or their successors, and left the determination of the precise quantum of their damages to the civil courts.

2/5 The Eternit trial is surely not the first case in Italy on this matter, although it is unprecedented as regards the extent of the damage that the court had to consider. Eternit was not the only company in Italy which, by working with asbestos, involved its managers in committing criminal offences related to the violation of rules on safety at work. In the last two decades or so, many criminal courts in our country have pronounced judgment on the criminal and civil liability of Italian entrepreneurs and managers who have caused deaths or illnesses related to the production or the use of asbestos products in Italy.[2] More

---

2 See eg Corte di Cassazione (Italian Supreme Court, Cass) 22 March 2012 no 24997; Cass 17 September 2010, no 43786, Cassazione penale (Criminal Court, Cass Pen) 2011, 5, 1679, annotated by *R Bartoli*; Rivista italiana di medicina legale 2011, 2, 489 annotated by *M Barni*; Cass 1 April 2010, no 20047; Tribunale (Trib) Milano, 4 June 2007, Corriere del merito 2007, 11, 1289; Cass 9 May 2003, Foro italiano (Foro it) 2004, II, 69, annotated by *R Guariniello*, Tumori professionali da legno e amianto; Cass 11 July 2002, Foro it 2003, II, 324, annotated by *R Guariniello*, Tumori professionali da amianto e responsabilità penale; Cass 30 March 2000, Foro it 2001, II, 278, annotated by *R Guariniello*, Dai tumori professionali ai tumori extraprofessionali da amianto, Diritto e pratica del lavoro (Dir e prat lav) 2001, 1151, Rivista critica di diritto del lavoro (Riv crit dir lav) 2001, 519; Corte di Appello (App) Venezia, 15 January 2001, Rassegna di giurisprudenza del lavoro nel Veneto (Rass giur lav Veneto) 2001, fasc 1, 68, annotated by *D Parolin*, Nesso di causalità nelle malattie professionali causate da esposizione all'amianto, Rivista trimestrale di diritto penale dell'economia (Riv trim dir pen econ) 2001, 439; App Milano, 29 June 2001, Riv crit dir lav 2001, 781; Trib Milano, 20 December1999, Foro it 2001, II, 53; Cass 2 July 1999, Foro it 2000, II, 260, annotated by *R Guariniello*, Malattie professionali, tumori da amianto, asbesto, Dir e prat lav 2000, 706; Cass 5 October 1999, Foro it 2000, II, 259, annotated by *R Guariniello*; Malattie professionali, tumori da amianto, asbestosi; Riv trim dir pen econ 2000, 1096; Rassegna giuridica della sanità (Ragiusan) 2000, fasc 198, 108; Giur it 2001, 1709; Pretura (Pret) Milano, 20 December 1999, Riv crit dir lav 2000, 483, annotated by *A Culotta*, *S Cantoni*, *P Ricci*; Cass 11 May 1998, Foro it 1999, II, 236, annotated by *R Guariniello*, I tumori professionali nella giurisprudenza, Dir e prat lav 1998, 2509; Pret Torino, 2 June 1998, Riv crit dir lav 1998, 1066; Pret Bergamo, 3 April 1997, Foro it 1998, II, 484, annotated by *L Tramontano*, Ancora in tema di morte per intossicazione da amianto: brevi rilievi problematici sulla "ri-descrizione dell'evento" nella verifica del nesso causale; Cass 28 January 1997, Riv crit dir lav 1997, 657;

recently, civil courts have also decided claims concerning the civil liability of defendants for similar facts.[3] Readers who are not so familiar with the Italian legal system should bear in mind that Italian criminal courts are empowered to decide whether compensation should be awarded to victims under art 185 *Codice Penale* (Penal Code). This article provides: 'Ogni reato obbliga alle restituzioni, a norma delle leggi civili. Ogni reato, che abbia cagionato un danno patrimoniale o non patrimoniale, obbliga al risarcimento il colpevole e le persone che, a norma delle leggi civili, debbono rispondere per il fatto di lui.' ('Every crime requires restoration according to the civil law. Every crime which has caused patrimonial or non-patrimonial damage obliges the perpetrators and the persons who, according to the civil law, are responsible for his or her actions to pay compensation'). This power of the court is exercised on the initiative of the *parte civile*, who may be present in the proceedings as mentioned no 2/15 below.

II. Facts of the Case

A. The Accusations

Following a long investigation, a pool of prosecutors of the *Tribunale di Torino*, led by Raffaele Guariniello, accused a Belgian and a Swiss citizen, Jean Luis de Cartier de Marchienne and Stephan Schmidheiny respectively, of the violation of art 437 of the Italian Penal Code, which punishes those who intentionally 2/6

App Torino, 15 October 1996, Rivista italiana di diritto e procedura penale (Riv it dir e proc pen) 1997, 1448, annotated by *C Piergallini*, Attività produttive e imputazioni per colpa: prove tecniche di "diritto penale del rischio"; App Torino, 24 October 1996, Giurisprudenza Piemontese 1997, 131, annotated by *G Carosso*, Orientamenti della giurisprudenza del lavoro (Orient giur lav) 1997, I, 261; Pret Torino, 9 February 1995, Foro it 1996, II, 107, annotated by *L Termini*, Riv crit dir lav 1995, 1059, annotated by *M Mariani*; Pret Crema, 12 February 1996, Nuovo diritto 1996, 529; Trib Bologna, 11 May 1994, Rivista penale (Riv pen) 1994, 1025, annotated by *L Palladino*, Malattia professionale ed omicidio colposo: brevi note in margine ad una interessante pronuncia; Trib Casale Monferrato, 30 October 1993, Riv crit dir lav 1994, 697; Pret Pordenone, 7 July 1992, Foro it 1992, II, 720; Pret Milano, 16 July 1984, Rivista giuridica del lavoro 1984, IV, 486. For commentary, see the literature cited in fn 10.

3 The first decision of a civil court awarding damages for death caused by mesothelioma of a worker exposed to asbestos is: Cassazione sezione lavoro (Cass sez lav) 9 May 1998, no 4721, Orient giur lav 1998, I, 651, Giustizia civile 1999, I, 593. There are also a very high number of cases concerning social insurance issues related to asbestos, which will not be considered here.

omit to install systems, devices or signals that must be installed to prevent disasters or work accidents, and of having caused a disaster, in violation of art 434 of the same Code in the four Italian factories owned by Eternit in Italy (see below nos 2/18–22). These violations caused the deaths of 2,191 individuals and 665 cases of personal injuries. The factories in question were located in the cities of Casale Monferrato, Cavagnolo, Rubiera, and Napoli Bagnoli.

2/7 The alleged crimes mainly referred to acts and omissions that took place long before the indictment of the defendants, although the consequences of those acts and omissions have lasting effects, or produce effects which will provoke more injuries and deaths in the future. The peak of deaths related to the production of asbestos products in Italy will occur in 2020. All the Eternit companies based in Italy were declared insolvent by the *Tribunale di Genova* between December 1985 and June 1986.

B. The Stakeholders

2/8 While there were only two defendants, there were a large number of claimants seeking compensation.

2/9 First of all, there were those suffering from asbestos-related diseases, who had been exposed to asbestos dust in the Italian factories, either because they were employed by Eternit, or because they worked in Eternit plants, although actually employed by other companies. Secondly, there were those who had been exposed to asbestos dust, but who had not worked in those factories, such as those living with the workers exposed to asbestos, or near the Eternit factories, and all those exposed by other means to asbestos dust produced by Eternit. A third group was comprised of the relatives of the victims of the asbestos, who either claimed compensation for harm suffered as a consequence of their relatives' death or personal injuries, or as successors to the victims' rights to compensation.

2/10 A final class of claimants consisted of a variety of legal entities. These included local governments, such as the Regione Piemonte and Emilia Romagna, the Provincia di Torino and Alessandria, and the municipalities where the factories were located (or those that were close to them). Their claims aimed at obtaining compensation for the environmental pollution and the reclamation of land as well as for non-material damage. Other entities such as INAIL (the public insurer for work injuries and illnesses) and INPS (the national social insurance system for retirement and disability pensions) introduced claims to recover sums paid as pensions to the workers suffering diseases caused by exposure to asbestos. The *Azienda Sanitaria Locale* (ASL) of Alessandria (the local Nation

Health Service Unit) claimed an amount equivalent to the extra costs incurred as a result of the asbestos-related diseases. Lastly, some Unions, environmental associations, and associations of victims' families also claimed compensation for their losses.

The number of lawyers involved in the trial was quite large: 3 general pro- 2/11
secutors, 82 lawyers for the *parti civili*, 6 for the defence, and 3 for the companies which were held to be jointly liable with the criminal defendants for the civil wrongs ascribed to them appeared before the court. Equally noteworthy was the number of medical and scientific experts consulted. Such a huge investment in a criminal investigation can be explained by taking into account certain features of criminal and civil proceedings in Italy, which shall be clarified in the following.

C. Public Resonance

The case received much attention and considerable media coverage, although, 2/12
as mentioned above, it was not the first case in which managers of a company were convicted for deaths and illnesses caused by asbestos. The issue of compensation for asbestos-related damage has also been at the centre of public debate for a long time in Italy. The large number of victims who were exposed to asbestos due to the activities of the Eternit factories in Italy and the names of the defendants certainly contributed to the attention this case received. The high reputation of chief prosecutor, Raffaele Guariniello, who is well-known in Italy as a champion of workers' and consumers' health protection, also explains why the case attracted so much attention.

The activism of the associations of the families of the victims of asbestos 2/13
exposure contributed to the attention the case was given in the general public. They participated in every hearing of the case. These associations managed to highlight the case in the media and to establish contacts with foreign associations representing victims of asbestos in their fight for justice, thus enhancing the international resonance of the case. Their participation in the Eternit trial and some stories about the experiences of the victims and their relatives were documented in: 'Polvere. Il grande processo dell'amianto' (Dust. The great asbestos trial), a documentary directed by Niccolò Bruna and Andrea Prandstraller which was released in 2011. In addition, several news reports of the case and the story behind it went on air before, during, and after the trial – a normal occurrence in Italy when issues of major public concern are at stake. Furthermore, the proceedings were followed by a number of victims' associations from several European countries and there was extensive coverage by the foreign press.

D. Jurisdictions Involved

2/14 In Italy, the criminal prosecution of managers and employers for the death or serious personal injury caused by unsafe working conditions is common. The Italian Constitution (art 112 Cost) and the Italian Code of Criminal Procedure (art 50 CPC) obliges public prosecutors to bring a criminal action against the defendants in cases of homicide, or serious personal injury, as well as for most other criminal offences. Minor personal injuries are prosecuted only following a complaint by the injured parties, in accordance with the provisions of art 582 *Codice penale* (Penal Code, CP). The criminal charges for which the defendants were indicted are subject to compulsory prosecution under Italian law.

2/15 In principle, all those who are harmed by a crime can claim compensation and restitution by appearing as *parte civile* before a criminal court, in accordance with art 74 of the Italian Code of Criminal Procedure.[4] The *parte civile* is an institution which features in all codes that are influenced by the French Code of Criminal Procedure.[5] Readers who are not familiar with the role played by the *parte civile* in criminal proceedings should therefore turn to general works on comparative criminal and civil procedure to get acquainted with it. The essential point is that, under the Italian Code of Criminal Procedure, those who have suffered damage as a consequence of a crime, may decide to be a party to the criminal court proceedings as *parte civile*, to claim compensation, possibly on an interim basis, or restitution in kind, from the defendant (and\or the parties who are jointly liable with the defendant). As an alternative, they may decide not to play any role in the criminal proceedings, but to rely on the findings and the records of the criminal court, whose judgment shall be *res judicata* in this respect in subsequent civil proceedings to recover damages. Furthermore, any claimant who does not pursue either course may start parallel and independent civil proceedings (see arts 75, 651, 652 Code of Criminal Procedure). In the latter case the criminal and civil court proceedings and their outcomes shall be completely independent from one another, and may eventually lead to different and conflicting outcomes.

---

4 Legittimazione all'azione civile. 1. L'azione civile per le restituzioni e per il risarcimento del danno di cui all'articolo 185 del codice penale può essere esercitata nel processo penale dal soggetto al quale il reato ha recato danno ovvero dai suoi successori universali, nei confronti dell'imputato e del responsabile civile.

5 *M Chiavario*, Private Parties: The Right of the Defendant and the Victim, in: M Delmas-Marty/JR Spencer (eds), European Criminal Procedures (2005) 541ff; *C Howard*, Compensation in French Criminal Procedure (1958) 21 Modern Law Review 386.

The *parte civile* has the autonomous power to bring evidence to the criminal court, to assist the prosecutor in proving the guilt of the defendant. It therefore can, for example, inspect documents and cross-examine witnesses at the trial, and present its own conclusions to the court. Quite often, the reason for the claimant being present in the criminal proceedings as *parte civile*, rather than initiating parallel civil proceedings, is to take advantage of the fact that the court provides the often needed, but expensive, scientific and medical expert opinions, paid by the court (*consulenti tecnici d'ufficio*), although the *parte civile* can also appoint experts. Furthermore, if a claimant appears before the court in the capacity of *parte civile*, the evidence heard by the court is formed with the material contribution of the *parte civile*, who has the power, for example, to cross examine witnesses, which may be important to reach a single decision on the issue of criminal and civil liability. As mentioned above, the claimant may also forego the right to present his case to the court as *parte civile*, and decide to bring a separate civil action for damages before a civil court. In this case, however, the burden of proof concerning the facts of the case is entirely on him. In the light of the extensive nature of the factual enquiries required in the Eternit case, which did not concern a single action or event, but numerous actions and events over a considerable period of time, it is not surprising to learn that most of the Eternit claimants presented their case to the court as *parti civili* in the above mentioned criminal proceedings. The possibility of taking an active part in the criminal proceedings by cross-examining witnesses and bringing evidence to the court in such a complex case was vital given the difficulty of replicating such a penetrating and wide ranging enquiry before a civil judge once the criminal case was closed, or while the criminal proceedings were pending. From a more general point of view, it should also be considered that a criminal trial offers to civil claimants a unique opportunity to present to the public opinion the case for the victims' claims. While the hearings of a criminal court case are public, civil proceedings in Italy are mostly written, and do not really offer to those claimants 'a day in court'. The criminal court is entitled to deliver compensation under the provision of art 185 of the Italian Penal Code, which states: 'Every crime requires restoration according to the civil law. Every crime which has caused patrimonial or non-patrimonial damage obliges the perpetrators and the persons who, according to the civil law, are responsible for his or her actions to pay compensation'.[6] 2/16

6 Art 185 Codice Penale (CP): 'Ogni reato obbliga alle restituzioni, a norma delle leggi civili. Ogni reato, che abbia cagionato un danno patrimoniale o non patrimoniale, obbliga al risarcimento il colpevole e le persone che, a norma delle leggi civili, debbono rispondere per il fatto di lui.'

2/17 For both the criminal charges and the related claims for full or interim compensation, the *Tribunale di Torino*, a first degree criminal court staffed by three professional judges, had jurisdiction to hear the case.

E. The Main Legal Questions

2/18 The defendants were accused of two crimes.

2/19 Firstly, they were accused of violating art 437 of the Italian Penal Code,[7] which punishes those who intentionally omit to install systems, devices or signals that must be installed to prevent disasters or working accidents (or removes or damages them). Such conduct is a crime regardless of whether or not an incident or a disaster occurs but, if an incident or a disaster does in fact occur, the punishment is between three and ten years' imprisonment. The prosecutors accused the defendants – who had control over the management of the production process and who were involved in decisions concerning the safety of the Italian Eternit plants – of omitting to take the preventive and safety measures which should have been taken according to the law under the circumstances.

2/20 Secondly, the defendants were indicted for the violation of art 434 of the Italian Penal Code,[8] which prohibits any intentional conduct aimed at causing the ruin of a building, or of a part of it, or another disaster.[9] The creation of dangerous conditions by violating this provision is enough to trigger punishment. If a building or part of it is ruined or a disaster occurs, the punishment is between three and twelve years' imprisonment. The defendants were accused of causing a disaster, by omitting to adopt the technical, hygienic and organisational

---

7 Art 437 CP: 'Rimozione od omissione dolosa di cautele contro infortuni sul lavoro. Chiunque omette di collocare impianti, apparecchi o segnali destinati a prevenire disastri o infortuni sul lavoro, ovvero li rimuove o li danneggia, è punito con la reclusione da sei mesi a cinque anni. Se dal fatto deriva un disastro o un infortunio, la pena è della reclusione da tre a dieci anni.'

8 Art 434 CP: 'Crollo di costruzioni o altri disastri dolosi. Chiunque, fuori dei casi preveduti dagli articoli precedenti, commette un fatto diretto a cagionare il crollo di una costruzione o di una parte di essa ovvero un altro disastro è punito, se dal fatto deriva pericolo per la pubblica incolumità, con la reclusione da uno a cinque anni. La pena è della reclusione da tre a dodici anni se il crollo o il disastro avviene.'

9 The Corte Costituzionale (Constitutional Court) 1 August 2008, no 327, Giurisprudenza costituzionale (Giur cost) 2008, 3529, rejected the question of constitutionality raised with respect to this article, which was based on the vagueness of the concept of 'disaster', holding that the proper interpretation of this article, in the light of the system of the Code, makes it applicable to a form of prejudice which is extensive, complex and very serious.

measures which should have been put into place to protect the workers' health. In particular, they had either omitted to carry out or had carried out insufficient tests on the workers' health conditions, and had not informed them about the risks related to asbestos. Furthermore, the defendants had supplied asbestos products and waste to private and public administrations (for paving the streets, courtyards, and for the thermal isolation of attics) without providing warnings of the associated risks. They had also exposed the workers' relatives and co-habitants to asbestos dust, inter alia, by failing to clean the workers' working clothes on the plants. In addition, they had polluted the environment surrounding their factories, which led to the population of several towns being exposed to asbestos. This situation continued at least until 1976, when some remedial action was taken, although their effect was not sufficient, and did not effectively eliminate the production and the spreading of asbestos dust either at the work or in the environment, nor did it prevent the hazards to human health.

The accusations were noteworthy because the prosecutors assumed that the **2/21** defendants had acted (or had failed to act) with the intention to cause damage. In cases of death and personal injuries resulting from poor working conditions, the employer is often accused of crimes that imply a lack of due care, such as *omicidio colposo* (manslaughter, art 589 CP), and *lesioni personali colpose* (negligent personal injuries, art 590 CP), namely those which do not require proof of such an intent. But in this case, the prosecution opted for a different approach. This choice was related to the unusual facts of the case, involving a large number of victims and claimants. The charges based on arts 434 and 437 CP are easier to substantiate in cases involving large numbers of victims, compared to those based on individual injuries or deaths (such as *omicidio colposo* or *lesioni colpose*), which would be more demanding in terms of evidence pertaining to each victim and possibly more difficult to prosecute due to the limitation periods established for these crimes.[10] To establish the relevant intent, the prosecutors provided testimonial and documentary evidence as proof to the court that the directors of the plants and the accused knew of the evolving scientific knowledge concerning the dangers posed by asbestos to human health in the 1960s. To mention one example, the internal correspondence from the director

---

10 For further commentary on asbestos related injuries and consequent judicial proceedings in Italy, see: *A Di Amato*, La responsabilità penale da amianto (2003); *L Montuschi/G Insolera* (eds), Il rischio da amianto. Questioni sulla responsabilità civile e penale (2006); *N Coggiola*, Alla ricerca delle cause. Uno studio sulla responsabilità per i danni da amianto (2011). In English: *N Coggiola*, Causation in Mesothelioma Cases in the Italian Courts (2013) 21-1 European Review of Private Law (ERPL) 331 and *N Coggiola*, Asbestos Cases in the Italian Courts: Duelling with Uncertainty (2009) 3 InDret, Barcelona 1–34, in <http://www.indret.com/pdf/678_en.pdf>.

of the marketing department of the plant located in Casale Monferrato to the other directors of the Italian company contained a copy of a New York Times Magazine article published on 13 January 1973 mentioning the research by Dr Irving Selikoff which, in a symposium held at the New York Academy of Sciences in 1964, had documented the relationship between asbestos dust and mesothelioma, the dangers created by even brief exposure to asbestos dust, as well as the worsening effects caused by prolonged exposure to asbestos dusts. In that Symposium, Dr Enrico Vigliani and others presented data documenting 172 asbestos-related deaths from Piedmont and Lombardy.[11] Stephan Schmidheiny himself, in an internal seminar on the dangers of asbestos held in Neuss in June 1976 for the managers and the staff of the Eternit companies, acknowledged that scientific evidence concerning asbestos, which had been available since the 1960s (with a specific reference to the work of Dr Selikoff), was examined carefully by the company, although until 1976 no investment in safety had been considered necessary. Vigliani announced that from then on the company intended to launch a programme of remedial action, but also that the problems for the industry, which were highlighted by the scientific evidence, were problems to live with. The expert witnesses for the defendant gave evidence about the fact that in the 1960s and in the early part of the 1970s scientific evidence concerning the dangers of asbestos was not yet 'consolidated' as it is now, in part because scientific measurements of the level of exposure to asbestos and systematic observations of the effects of exposure had not been developed at that time. On this point the court held that, although it can be conceded that such knowledge was not yet 'consolidated', it was abundantly clear in the light of the evidence presented at trial that major industrial groups such as those represented by the defendants knew, from the second half of the 1960s onwards, that asbestos could cause pleural cancer (and that crocidolite in particular could be lethal), affecting not only workers in the industry, but also those who came into contact with it in other ways.

2/22 Given the long time which had elapsed between the alleged actions or omissions of the accused and when they were charged with the crimes, the prosecutors faced the possibility that the charges could not be upheld by the court, because the crimes could be time-barred. The prosecutors avoided this obstacle by relying on the classification of the two crimes of which the defendants were accused as continuing crimes (*reati permanenti*), in which all the actions and omissions, as well as the continuing state of affairs caused by them, are considered as relevant. With respect to the crime punishable according to art 437 CP,

11 *EC Vigliani/G Mottura/P Maranzana*, Association of Pulmonary Tumors with Asbestosis in Piemont and Lombardy, Annals of the New York Academy of Sciences (1965) vol 132, 558.

the prosecutors maintained that the limitation period begins to run from the moment when the last injury was suffered by a victim, while in the case of a crime stipulated in art 434 CP, the limitation period had not yet started to run, because the danger in question was considered to be ongoing in light of the conditions in the area which had been polluted by the asbestos dust produced by Eternit. The court of first instance accepted their argumentation but, on appeal, the decision was reversed with respect to one of the charges, and it was thus held that the limitation period for the crime punishable under art 437 had lapsed. As the full judgment of the appeal court is not yet available, it is too early to comment upon the decision rendered on appeal on this point.

F. Out-of-Court Procedure

Pending the first instance trial, the Becon company, in the name of Stephan 2/23
Schmidheiny, offered the *Comune di Casale* (Municipality of Casale) € 18.3 million to withdraw its *parte civile* in the Eternit case, and to renounce all future claims for compensation. Initially, the town council was willing to accept the settlement, but the fierce opposition of the citizens of the town eventually led the council to turn it down. Other smaller towns also refused similar offers, while a few accepted them. On appeal the Municipality of Casale was awarded € 30,934,446. Whether and when the Municipality shall be able to collect this money is open to question, however. The death of one of the defendants during the appeal resulted in the exclusion from the proceedings of the ETEX Group SA. This is a Belgian holding company with substantial assets, which would otherwise have answered jointly for the compensation of the damage attributable to Louis de Cartier de Marchienne and to Eternit, according to the ruling of the first instance court on the claims of the *parti civili*.

G. Court Procedure: The Proceeding of the Trial

The trial before the *Tribunale* was quite long, lasting from 6 April 2009 to 2/24
13 February 2012, with 66 hearings. It was also burdensome to manage because of the large number of victims and *parti civili* claiming compensation, and the complexity of the factual and legal issues at stake. The number of documents examined by the court and the experts was huge, for example.

At the beginning of the trial there were more than 6,000 *parti civili*, not only 2/25
the victims themselves, if still alive, and/or their relatives or successors, but also local authorities, unions and various associations. The large number of

parti civili reflected the high number of alleged victims and the staggering economic and ecological damage that the asbestos manufacturing process caused to people and places over the previous thirty years in several areas of the country. Under the Code of Criminal Procedure, the court had to decide on the compensation claims of the *parti civili* to make its task easier. To carry out its duty, namely setting the criminal punishment first, the court granted standardised interim payments in the range of € 60,000, € 35,000, and € 30,000 to the victims (or their successors), depending on the respective situation, thus leaving to the civil courts the task of assessing the precise amount of damages for each claimant. On the other hand, as mentioned below, the court awarded full compensation of the damage which was claimed by legal persons and other entities, such as municipalities and other public authorities, trade unions and environmental associations, which could be assessed more easily.

2/26 The accused denied wrongdoing and never appeared in court. They were never interrogated during the investigations leading to the trial and they never addressed written statements to the court.

H. Court Procedure: The First Instance Court Findings of Fact

2/27 The judgment of the *Tribunale di Torino* is 713 pages long. The list of the victims alone covers 180 pages. The first part of the judgment sets out the historical development of the asbestos industry and the creation of an international cartel among the firms involved in the production of asbestos products. This part tells the cross-border history of Eternit and demonstrates the real power and influence held by the defendants over the management of the Italian factories at the relevant moments in time. Then, the judges move on to illustrate the law on the protection of workers against illnesses caused by asbestos exposure, which was in force in the relevant period. Those laws considered a criminal offence the exposure of workers to dust in general and imposed specific preventive measures to abate them and to avoid their diffusion in the working environment (and imposed annual medical check-ups for workers exposed to asbestos dust).[12] In the interpretation of the Italian courts, which were at first slow to sanction these violations, the Italian legislation obliged employers to provide every possible means to protect workers from health dangers at work, having regard to the sci-

12 Decreto del Presidente della Repubblica (Dpr) 19 March 1956, no 303, Norme generali per l'igiene del lavoro (SOGU 30 April 1956, no 155), arts 4, 21, 58 ff. For commentary see, among others, *G De Santis*, Gli effetti del tempo nel reato. Uno studio tra casistica e dogmatica (2006) 53 ff, 77 ff.

entific and empirical knowledge available.[13] But from the evidence given to the court, in the Eternit factories located in Italy, the violations of these norms was related to Eternit's failure to implement minimal precautions.

The judgment goes on to describe the production processes in the four Eternit factories. With the help of many witnesses, the court thoroughly assessed the working conditions in the factories. The presence of high levels of asbestos dust in the factories and the poor working conditions of the workers were related to the nearly total lack of aspirator fans, filters and similar devices that could have at least reduced the level of dust in the working places up until 1976, and to the insufficient safety measures which were put in place afterwards. Furthermore, the workers were neither provided with adequate means of protection against the dust, nor obliged to use or wear them when provided. They were not informed about the dangers of the asbestos dust and of the need to protect themselves against such dangers. The workers washed their own overalls at home. The medical inspections in the plants were rare or non-existent, and the workers suffering from asbestosis were not always assigned to safer jobs. The levels of asbestos dust in the working areas were regularly above the limits established by law. The improvements to the working conditions undertaken by the employers always took a significant amount of time. They only followed after repeated inspections and warnings by the public authorities. In two of the factories the so-called 'blue asbestos', that is to say the crocidolite asbestos, the most carcinogenic kind of asbestos, was used until the closing of the plants, and therefore also in the period of time under investigation. **2/28**

Regarding the pollution of the places outside the factories, the evidence established that asbestos was transported using jute sacks. These were often ripped, and thus asbestos dust was dispersed for years in the Casale railway station and in the train wagons. The sacks were also often transported on open trucks, passing through the towns where the plants where located, with a further dispersion of the dust. The holes in the sacks were mended by Eternit workers in their homes. The areas surrounding the factories were covered by the dust from the production process, because the existing aspirator fans had no filters, and the waste products were generally crushed in the open air. In addition, no precautions were taken in the transportation and dumping of the waste. The workers' overalls, covered in dust, were washed at home and worn to go back home, contributing to the dispersion of asbestos fibres outside the factories. In Casale and Cavagnolo the liquid waste was directly dispersed into the **2/29**

---

13 This is standing case law. For commentary see eg *A Di Amato*, Codice di diritto penale delle imprese e delle società. Annotato con la giurisprudenza (2011) (the author was a member of the defence team).

Po River, where the asbestos dust created artificial beaches where people went in their free time. The factories in the two towns and in Bagnoli were not cleaned up when they were eventually closed down. Workers and others could buy or receive the powder waste (so-called *polverino*) and other by-products of the production such as felt and used sacks free of charge. In the towns of Casale and Cavagnolo the *polverino*, or the waste products, were used to pave roads and yards. In Casale the *polverino* was used for the thermal insulation of attics. Both towns are therefore still exposed to dangers linked to the presence of these materials. They therefore need large investments to return to normal the places where the factories were located and the buildings and places where the asbestos products were used. Presently, the air pollution levels of the towns where the Eternit factories were located are, however, below the prescribed thresholds.

2/30 The judgment addresses in depth the issue of what knowledge was available regarding the dangerousness of asbestos fibres for human health and the policy of major industrial groups regarding it. The evidence established that, by the end of the 19th century, the manufacture of asbestos was, for the first time, considered an activity dangerous for human health. By the beginning of the 20th century, the relationship between asbestos exposure and asbestosis was ascertained, and as mentioned above, in 1964 an international conference presented solid evidence on the relationship between asbestos and lung cancer.[14] The industry was then alerted to this association and the implications of these scientific discoveries for it were not ignored by its managers. They tried to minimise any alarming information and to avoid the implementation of restrictive legislative measures that could have reduced the profitability of their business in some countries. The various companies connected to the asbestos industry acted as a lobby to achieve these aims, as evidenced from the judgment.

2/31 Many pages of the judgment are devoted to the various scientific issues related to the illnesses caused by asbestos. With the support of expert knowledge and scientific literature on the effects of asbestos exposure, the court held that such exposure is the cause of various illnesses. The first is asbestosis, caused by the accumulation of asbestos dust in the lungs. Asbestosis is a cumulative illness. There is a direct relationship between the amount of dust inhaled and the seriousness of the illness. Another frequent illness is the lung carcinomas that can be caused by different factors. The scientific consensus is that these can also be initiated by the asbestos alone, however, and that their occurrence is directly related to the amount of asbestos exposure, generally to high or at least

---

14 Expert witnesses Mara, Thieme, Carnevale and *BI Castleman* – who is the author of Asbestos: Medical and Legal Aspects (4th edn 2005) – were consulted on this point in the proceedings.

medium amounts of asbestos dust. The latency of this illness is around 10 years, but can be higher or lower in some types of cancers.

Lastly, a very frequent illness in those exposed to asbestos dust is mesothelioma. This is a cancer that is exclusively caused by asbestos, which is characterised by a very long latency, at least 10 years. It can be caused by a very small amount of asbestos dust, but it is still debated whether it is dose-dependant or not. In the former case, any exposure to asbestos dust can be considered a causative factor of mesothelioma, because it at least shortened the latency of the mesothelioma, or aggravated the same illness. In the latter case, the defendant can try to establish previous exposure to argue the lack of causation with respect to successive exposure, as previous exposure in which he is not implicated may be the cause of the illness. In Italy, the *Corte di Cassazione* held that the three diseases are all dose-dependant. The single exception to these rulings is the *Corte di Cassazione* judgment *Cozzini*,[15] in which the court held that it must be ascertained if the theory of the accelerating effect of the subsequent exposure on the initiated mesothelioma is shared by the scientific community; whether it is a statistically universal or probabilistic law, and, in the latter case, if that accelerating effect actually occurred in the concrete case; and, lastly, if the previous exposure caused the mesothelioma with certainty. This last point is not a minor one, in the light of the margins of uncertainty surrounding the scientific knowledge available with respect to the precise etiology of mesothelioma. The *Tribunale di Torino* held that the preponderant opinion in the scientific community is that mesothelioma is a dose-dependent illness, considering that the alternative model of causation, involving the hypothesis of a trigger dose, which would be the sole causal factor, is not supported by the available data and scientific opinions. Therefore, it considered that every exposure has a causal impact until the development of the mesothelioma, and that an increase in exposure cannot be ruled out as irrelevant to the development of the pathology. 2/32

I. Court Procedure: The Trial and Appellate Court Decisions

The *Tribunale di Torino* then examined the judicial precedents concerning the provisions of arts 437 and 434 CP, and their applicability to the facts of the case. The following paragraph covers only those issues that are more relevant to a foreign reader. 2/33

15 Cass 17 September 2010, no 43786 – *Cozzini e altri*.

2/34 Undisputedly, a long period of time intervened between the first deaths and injuries related to the activity of Eternit and the prosecution of the above mentioned crimes by the prosecutors of the *Tribunale di Torino*. On this basis, the defendants objected that the crimes of which they were accused were time-barred due to the lapse of the limitation period fixed by the Penal Code. The *Tribunale di Torino* held, however, that the defendants were accused of a continuing crime (*reato permanente*), and the acts and omissions constituting a violation of art 437 CP, taken together with their consequences, constituted a single crime. According to this approach, the limitation period runs from the date of the last diagnosis of the illness (formulated on 13 August 1999) for all the cohort of victims for which the criminal charges were brought. Regarding the second crime, punishable according to art 434 CP, the court held that, in the towns of Casale and Cavagnolo, the dangers created by the presence of asbestos were still real. Hence, the limitation period for the crime in question had not yet ended. The crimes committed in the towns of Napoli Bagnoli and Rubiera were, on the contrary, time-barred because the dangerous situation created by the violation of that article no longer existed.

2/35 The *Corte d'Appello* overturned this last decision, holding that the crimes committed in Napoli Bagnoli and Rubiera were not statute-barred. The accused was held liable under art 434 CP. However, as mentioned above (no 2/21) the *Corte d'Appello* also held that the crime punishable under art 437 CP was statute-barred. At the moment, the full judgment of the appeal court is not yet available and therefore the basis for this holding is not fully clear. As a consequence of this ruling, the number of claimants for whom damages were awarded was less that half compared to the claimants compensated by the first instance court.

2/36 The court then examined the relationship between the managerial positions held by the two defendants and the occurrence of the facts of which they were accused. The defence lawyers tried to establish that the two defendants never had any control over the operations carried out in the Italian factories.[16] The *Tribunale di Torino* rejected this defence. According to the documents and witnesses examined in the course of the hearings, the accused were aware of the conditions in the factories, and omitted to take or impose precautions and

16 Italian law did not contain provisions on the criminal liability of firms up to the reform introduced with *Decreto legislativo* (d lgt) 8 June 2001, no 231, Disciplina della responsabilità amministrativa delle persone giuridiche, delle società e delle associazioni anche prive di personalità giuridica, a norma dell'articolo 11 della legge 29 settembre 2000, n. 300 (Gazzetta Ufficiale (GU) 19 June 2001, no 140). Even before that date, however, claims for the civil liability of firms for wrongful acts or omissions of their managers were allowed on the basis of the *respondeat superior* rule, as explained below no 2/39.

safety measures in violation of the law. Therefore, considering that the pathologies and deaths caused by asbestos exposure are dose-dependant, the court held that the accused had committed a crime according to art 437 CP. As already mentioned, the appeal judgment reversed this holding, maintaining instead that the limitation period for this crime had lapsed. The first instance court held that the accused had also committed a crime according to art 434 CP, because they had not taken measures to prevent what was happening in the Eternit factories in Italy and in the surrounding area (the cession or selling of the *polverino* and other production waste and its use by the population, for example). Given the gravity of the violations and of their consequences, they were sentenced to sixteen years' imprisonment by the first instance court. As already mentioned, this ruling was modified on appeal because of the death of one of the two defendants, and it was considered that the limitation period for these crimes had not expired for the factories in Napoli Bagnoli and Rubiola. This explains why the prison sentence imposed on the only surviving defendant – namely Stephan Schmidheiny – was increased to 20 years.

Civil liability for the wrongs committed by the defendants raised the question of the applicable limitation periods. The court applied art 2947/IIII of the Italian Civil Code (CC), which provides that, if a civil wrong is also a crime, the limitation period applicable to it is that of the crime if more favourable to the aggrieved party, as is usual in similar criminal cases. Therefore the limitation period applicable to the compensation claims for damage caused by the violation of art 434 CP had expired for the wrongs committed in Rubiera and Napoli Bagnoli. The same was true for the consequences of the violation of art 437 CP with respect to deaths following illnesses that had been diagnosed before 13 August 1999. All the other compensation claims could still be pursued because the limitation period had not yet lapsed for these. 2/37

The appellate court reversed the first instance judgment on the point of the lapse of the limitation period for the crimes committed in Rubiera and Napoli Bagnoli, and consequently affirmed the liability of the only surviving defendant. 2/38

The two accused and the companies to whom civil liability for their wrongs could be ascribed were held jointly and severally liable by the *Tribunale di Torino* for the compensation of all the damage that was the consequence of the violation of arts 434 and 437 CP, during the respective periods of management. These companies were held jointly liable with the two defendants because they were held vicariously liable under arts 2049 and 2395 CC for the civil wrongs committed by their managers. The first provision holds employers liable for wrongful acts and omissions of their employees on a *respondeat superior* basis, without the need to prove negligence in their hiring or supervision. The second 2/39 provision extends the same regime to company managers with regard to the companies employing them. With respect to most claims brought by the victims or their successors, the court awarded interim payments of damages. The precise determination of the quantum of damages owed to each claimant was thus left to the civil courts, being too complicated to be determined in the criminal proceedings. Before the civil courts, the *res judicata* effects of the criminal judgment will most likely preclude further inquiry into the acts and omissions of the defendants and their relevance in terms of causation of damage with respect to the victims who were represented in the proceedings (see also below).

2/40 Following the death of one of the two accused while the appeal proceedings were still open, the *Corte d'Appello* convicted Stephan Schmidheiny of the crime sanctioned by art 434 CP and held him responsible for the compensation to be paid to the injured parties, jointly with the companies which are civilly liable for the corresponding wrongs committed by him. However, with respect to the other defendant, the proceedings were closed due to his death. As a consequence, the appeal court also revoked the ruling of the first instance court concerning the civil liability of the companies which had been held liable for wrongs committed by the deceased, such as the ETEX Group SA.

2/41 Both INAIL, the national insurance system for workers' injuries and illnesses and INPS, the national social insurance system for retirement and disability pensions, received interim compensation for the indemnities and pensions paid because of the illnesses that were the consequence of the criminal facts (respectively € 15,000,000 and a sum to be quantified by the civil court) in the first instance, but on appeal their claims were rejected, probably because the relevant limitation periods had lapsed.

2/42 Regione Piemonte, Provincia di Alessandria, Provincia di Torino, Comuni of Casale Monferrato, Mirabello Monferrato, Morano sul Po, Coniolo, Villanova Monferrato, Pontestura, Balzola, Ozzano Monferrato, Cavagnolo, Motta de' Conti, Caresana, Stroppiana, Candia Lomellina and *ASL di Alessandria* obtained compensation for both economic and non-economic losses.[17] In particular, they were compensated for the prejudice to their historical, cultural, political and economic identity, and for the environmental damage to the specific area. The *Regione Piemonte* obtained an interim award of € 20,000,000 covering the expenses incurred for land reclamation, for the maintenance of the Mesothelioma Register, for the Regional Asbestos Centre, and for the treatment of asbestos-

---

17 Non-economic losses are now recognised as a matter of course in Italian law to legal persons and associations as well: see *N Coggiola/B Gardella Tedeschi/M Graziadei* in: B Winiger/H Koziol/BA Koch/R Zimmermann (eds), Digest of European Tort Law, vol 2: Essential Cases on Damage (2011) 1016.

related pathologies by the Regional Health Service. The *Comune di Casale Monferrato* was compensated with an interim award of € 25,000,000 for the costs of land and buildings reclamation. The *ASL di Alessandria* was awarded € 5,000,000 for its loss of prestige and the frustration of its tasks, and for the loss caused by the general increase of the medical expenses caused by the exposure of workers and citizens to asbestos dust. *Regione Emilia Romagna, Provincia di Reggio Emilia* and *Comune di Rubiera* received compensation for the prejudice to their historical, cultural, political and economic identity, and for the expenses incurred by their health services to provide care for the people affected by diseases caused by asbestos.

The workers' unions, which also claimed damages, were compensated for 2/43 the economic and non-economic losses related to the loss of confidence in them provoked by the systematic violation of the regulations that should have protected the workers' health and ensured a safe working environment (€ 100,000, or another sum to be awarded in a civil suit). Compensation for non-economic losses was also awarded to five associations, namely the *Associazione italiana esposti amianto* (€ 100,000), *Associazione famigliari vittime amianto* (€ 100,000). *Legambiente* (€ 100,000), *WWF Italia* (€ 70,000), and *Medicina democratica* (€ 70,000). They obtained compensation for the prejudice caused to their interests and aims, either because of the moral prejudice they were assumed to have suffered, or because the resources and the efforts devoted to preserve the environment or the health of the victims of asbestos were frustrated by the actions and omissions of the defendants.

The workers and/or their relatives were compensated for the harm caused 2/44 by the exposure to asbestos. On the issue of causation, the court held that the causal link between the intentional exposure of the victims to asbestos and those pathologies and deaths was proved by the expert evidence made available to the court. The evidence presented to the court in this respect involved an analysis of the level of exposure to asbestos dust linked to the personal life of each individual, as attested by the available data collected for each individual over the years, the diagnosis of the pathology formulated while the worker was alive or post mortem, and an epidemiological study of the cohort in question. The workers were also compensated for the documented cases of pleural plaques. To hold the defendants liable for this type of harm, the court maintained that it sufficed to ascertain the exposure of the workers to the asbestos dust, which was known to cause prejudicial consequences. To understand this part of the judgment it is necessary to bear in mind that the crimes for which the defendants were charged also allowed compensation for moral damage under art 185 CP. The compensation awards covered once more only deaths or injuries caused by illnesses diagnosed (or which had become manifest) after 13 August

1999, because the relevant limitation period for civil claims had expired for damage that had materialised prior to that date. Given the long period of latency of mesothelioma, this explains why victims exposed to asbestos dust decades ago or their successors were to be awarded compensation. The defendants were, however, also held liable if workers initially suffering from asbestosis were subsequently diagnosed with lung cancer. Harm which could not be ascribed to the actions or omissions of the defendants was left uncompensated. In other words, the court took into account the specific periods in which each of the defendants carried out managerial tasks for each plant when deciding on the question of their liability.

2/45 The defendants were also held liable for the harm suffered by the citizens of Casale Monferrato, Cavagnolo and Brusasco who developed a pleural mesothelioma and other illnesses related to asbestos (such as pleural plaques and lung cancer), on the same causal basis which supported the compensation awards in favour of the workers and their relatives. Moreover, the defendants were also held liable for all non-pecuniary damage suffered by the citizens of Casale Monferrato, Cavagnolo and Brusasco and their successors, for the so-called *danno da esposizione*, that is to say the fear of contracting an illness caused by the exposure to the dust. Almost 3,000 claimants obtained an award of interim damages which recognised the civil liability of the defendant and companies that were jointly liable.

2/46 Although this case was covered by a large number of articles in the press and received considerable attention by the media, the judgment of the *Tribunale of Torino* on the Eternit case has not yet been extensively commented upon in Italian law journals and reviews.[18] More comments will probably be available after the publication of the judgment by the Court of Appeal and the Court of Cassation.

2/47 Pending an appeal to the Court of Cassation on such complex litigation, it would be unwise to provide here more than an outline of the issues which may be discussed following the Eternit trial. First of all, it is hardly surprising to learn that substantial resources went into the investigation of conduct and facts that caused a huge loss of lives, an epidemic of very serious or fatal diseases, and large scale environmental pollution. True, recourse to a criminal trial to do justice in such a case may surprise readers who know little about Italian law.

---

18 The comments available so far are: *A Palma*, In primo piano, Studium iuris 2012,1181–1191; *V Musacchio*, Eternit, diritto penale e morti da amianto: una breve opinione sull'argomento, Riv pen 2012, 472ff; *M Formica*, Omissione dolosa di cautele destinate a prevenire patologie da amianto e disastro doloso, Danno e responsabilità 2012, fasc 8-9, 908; *S Zirulia*, Caso Eternit: luci ed ombre nella sentenza di condanna in primo grado, Riv it dir e proc pen 2013, 471ff.

This is why this case was selected for the foreign reader: it is surely an instructive litigation. It is worth recalling that, from the point of view of Italian law, the case is an outlier only in so far as it dealt with the largest industrial disaster caused by the asbestos industry in Italy. The criminal prosecution and the conviction of defendants accused of violation of rules on safety at work is not rare under the law in Italy. Of course, it is impossible in this context to provide a full account of the law in action in Italy in this respect. With regard to asbestos litigation, it is nonetheless worth recalling that Italian criminal courts have released defendants from liability for lack of a causal link when their causal contribution to the production of damage was not beyond doubt.[19] In the Eternit plants, however, disregard for basic preventive and safety measures was the rule for decades, and investments in safety were consistently null or insufficient. The trial court in Torino examined the scientific evidence available at the relevant periods of time in depth. This examination was carried out with the help of experienced prosecutors and leading defence lawyers, with an impressive team of experts at work. The risk of imputing knowledge with the benefit of hindsight was avoided. This evaluation can be supported by abundant elements of fact that this litigation documented in detail. The industry was alert to the dangers that asbestos posed to human health and deeply troubling scientific evidence was available years before any remedial action to save lives or spare the environment was taken.[20] On the other hand, it is still too early to know whether the claimants will be able to collect their compensation. Some doubts are justified in this respect after the death of one of the defendants resulted in the revocation by the *Corte d'Appello* of the order to pay damages which would otherwise have been shouldered by Etex group SA as well. Nevertheless money was not all that was at stake for many parties in this trial. The uproar caused by the offer of € 18.3 million in settlement to the Municipality of Casale was caused by public outrage at the idea that the town would not have been represented in the criminal proceedings if the settlement had gone through. Although it was clear to all that that recovery of damages under the circumstances was uncertain and costly, the decision was still not to forego an opportunity to ask the court to do justice and to put on the judicial record the tragedy of an entire community.

---

19 Cass Pen, sez IV, 12 July 2013, no 30206.

20 In other words, this is not the case of parents smoking in the presence of their children when smoke was not considered by the population to be a toxic habit. It is rather the case of the tobacco industry selling its products knowing that they are toxic, without releasing warnings about them.

2/48 An assessment of the case in broader perspective would require a separate contribution, given the numerous questions that litigation like this raises. What are the pros and cons of the 'mass claims procedure' through the criminal courts: is this an efficient and fair alternative to civil court adjudication? Are there drawbacks? Advantages? In addition, is it appropriate to shift industrial injuries into the sphere of the criminal law? Civil litigation relating to a complex set of facts involving a very large number of people, over such a long time span, would also have been extremely difficult to manage before an Italian civil court. Italy does not have a comprehensive and efficient regime for group litigation or class actions in civil cases. The reform of group litigation first introduced in 2005, to deal with mass litigation in consumer cases (*azione di classe*: art 140bis *Codice del consumo*) even in its latest version would not have covered this type of litigation. Furthermore, the lack of efficient discovery of evidence and the burdens relating to the acquisition of complex scientific evidence in a civil trial in Italy would have put the claimants at a serious disadvantage anyhow. Surely, relief to the victims from workers' compensation systems, the social security system and the national health service alleviated at least some of the suffering of the victims of asbestos and their families and this is not to be forgotten, because litigation and the judicial process is a very expensive means to compensate those who have suffered damage. From a more general point of view, there is no doubt that the prosecution of industrial accidents in criminal courts is an inefficient way to enforce safety regulations at work.[21] A good question would be, therefore, why prevention and inspection services did not do more to stop what was going on in Casale Monferrato and in the other Eternit plants in Italy. Not all kept silent, or did nothing. Among the scientific teams that first documented at the world level the dangers of asbestos and its lethal nature in 1964 there was a team of Italian scientists who dealt with cases that must have come from Casale as well. The trade unions of the plant of Casale in 1974–1975 raised the question of the pollution of the workplace, and of the seriousness of the dangers for human health associated with asbestos. The latter initiative may lie at the origins of the decision of the owners of the plant to begin to address the issue of safety at work. But prevention of health risks at work which do not end up in isolated incidents runs into glaring conflicts of interests, set by the corporate search for profits, the push to maintain workers' occupational levels, and the demands of protection of public health. In France it has been noted, for example, that medical doctors employed by the industry to check the health of the

21 As a matter of fact, when the Torino prosecutors took up the case, they were not acting to enforce safety measures in active industrial plants. Criminal law often arrives too late to provide specific prevention.

workers exposed to asbestos did not react promptly to the threats posed by asbestos, and that inspection services in the factories where asbestos entered the production process were not equipped for the task assigned to them.[22] In the Eternit case, this was true as well. At the end of the day, if nothing else works, it should be borne in mind that willful violations of preventive and safety measures at the workplace may be considered serious offences under the criminal law applicable in the country, and that convictions for these offences may open the way to awards of damages. Such violations of the law are punished under the criminal law in several countries, and certainly not only in Italy.[23] Tort law scholars may still object that a criminal courtroom is not the ideal place to discuss compensation for personal injuries and deaths. The wisdom of this observation is reflected in the fact that in this case the criminal ruling and the interim orders for payments handed down by the court are just a peg for a more precise determination of the damage to be compensated by the civil courts if no settlement is offered. Nonetheless, this wise remark should not make us blind to the range of solutions that are available in Europe on this point,[24] unsatisfactory as they may otherwise be: the Eternit case has something to teach in this respect too.

---

22 Le drame de l'amiante en France: comprendre, mieux réparer, en tirer des leçons pour l'avenir (rapport au Senat Français), Rapport d'information no 37 (2005–2006) de MM *Gérard Dériot* et *J-P Godefroy*, fait au nom de la mission commune d'information, déposé le 26 octobre 2005 ("Le silence de la médecine du travail et de l'inspection du travail").

23 Nonetheless some legal systems may hinder actual recourse to criminal law in a variety of ways, to the dismay of those who have suffered serious consequences for those offences. See further on this point the report to the French Senate cited in the previous footnote.

24 For more on this in comparative perspective, see eg *M Dyson*, Connecting Tort and Crime: Comparative Legal History in England and Spain since 1850, (2009) 11 Cambridge Yearbook of European Legal Studies 247.

Melissa R Ferrari

3 Silicone Breast Implants: Mass Tort and Massive Damage in Europe

I. Introduction

Silicone breast implant litigation 'is one of the world's largest mass tort litigations'.[1] Initiated about 35 years ago, the litigation is not over yet. Most of the activity related to the lawsuits has taken place in the United States, although the claimants, breast implant recipients, hail from all over the world. 3/1

Mass tort litigation, lawsuits involving a large group of similarly situated plaintiffs, also known as 'group actions',[2] 'multi-party actions',[3] or 'collective redress'[4] in the European Union (EU), is sometimes referenced in the US as 'aggregate litigation'.[5] Mass tort litigation has been utilised in the US for the adjudication of large personal injury actions including silicone breast implants, asbestos, Agent Orange and Vioxx (rofecoxib), to name just a few. 3/2

The complex and prolonged US silicone breast implant litigation took on several different 'mass tort' forms as it evolved over the years and, as a result, the litigation provides a few practical examples of successful resolution of groups of factually similar claims using differing procedures. In addition to settlement and jury trials of numerous individual cases in both state and federal courts throughout the US, silicone breast implant litigation has included the settlement of a multi-district litigation (MDL) class action involving the compa- 3/3

---

1 *In re: Dow Corning Corporation* Opinion Relating to Appeals from and Motions Regarding the Bankruptcy Court's November 30, 1999 Confirmation Order (Eastern District of Michigan (ED Mich), 13 November 2000) at 43.

2 *Lovells*, Product Liability in the European Union, a Report for the European Commission (February 2003) MARKT/2001/11/D at 37 (last visited 13 December 2013) <http://www.ec.europa.eu/enterprise/policies/single-market-goods/files/goods/docs/liability/studies/lovells-study_en.pdf >.

3 *M Napier*, Journal of Personal Injury Litigation 1994, 173–177.

4 See *V Reding*, Vice-President of the European Commission, EU Justice Commissioner, Collective Redress: Examining the way forward, Hearing of the JURI Committee: A Horizontal Instrument for Collective Redress in Europe? (12 July 2011) (last visited 13 December 2013) <http://www.europa.eu/rapid/press-release_SPEECH-11-517_en.htm?locale=en>.

5 See *S Issacharoff/C Kuhl/F McGovern/S Middleton/Moderator: J Beisner*, The American Law Institute's New Principles of Aggregate Litigation, 6th Annual Judicial Symposium on Civil Justice Issues, George Mason Judicial Education Program (2011) 8 Journal of Law, Economics and Policy (JLEP) 183.

nies Bristol, Baxter, and 3M,[6] 'limited fund' class action settlements regarding the companies Inamed and Mentor requiring findings by the court that, at that time, the total assets of the manufacturers were insufficient to pay each claimant in full,[7] and a bankruptcy reorganisation proceeding pursuant to Chapter 11 of the US Code[8] regarding the manufacturer Dow Corning Corporation (Dow Corning).[9]

3/4 Silicone breast implant litigation has also utilised several aggregate claim litigation 'tools' available to the US courts for managing mass tort litigation including the appointment of special masters,[10] the appointment of a mediator,[11]

---

6 The 'Settling Defendants' included Bristol-Meyers Squibb Co, Medical Engineering Corp, Baxter Healthcare Corp, Baxter International Inc, and Minnesota Mining and Manufacturing Co (3M), Exhibit B1 to Bristol, Baxter, 3M, McGhan & Union Carbide Revised Settlement Program, Order No 27 (Approval of Revised Settlement Program and Injunctions), *In re: Silicone Gel Breast Implant Products Liability Litigation (MDL 926) Heidi Lindsey et al v Dow Corning Corp et al* (Northern District of Alabama, 22 December 1995).

7 *In re: Silicone Gel Breast Implant Products Liability Litigation (MDL 926) v Inamed Corporation et al*, Order and Final Judgment Certifying Inamed Settlement Class, Approving Class Settlement, and Dismissing Claims Against Inamed and Released Parties, Order 47A (1 February 1999); *In re: Silicone Gel Breast Implant Products Liability Litigation (MDL 926) v Inamed Corporation et al*, Order Determining Inamed Distribution Plan, Order 47B (7 July 1999). The Court approved a pro rata distribution of approximately $ 32 million to a mandatory, non-opt out class, noting that '... there cannot be any serious dispute about this being a "limited" fund case, indeed an extremely "limited" fund case to the extent of providing what most claimants would view as only *"de minimis"* distributions.' Ibid, fn 6: Each claimant received US$ 725. See also *In re: Silicone Gel Breast Implant Products Liability Litigation (MDL-926), Butler et al v Mentor Corp et al*, Order 14 Approving Mentor Settlement and Certifying Mentor Settlement Class; Final Judgment as to Claims against Mentor (10 September 1993).

8 11 United States Code (USC) §§ 1101 ff.

9 *In re: Dow Corning Corp*, 211 Bankruptcy Reporter (BR) 545 (Bankr ED Mich 1997).

10 Judge Robert Jones in Oregon appointed Dr Richard Jones, MD, PhD as Special Master to help him identify scientists to serve as technical advisors in the Hall v Baxter Healthcare Corp group of cases. *Hall v Baxter Healthcare Cor*, 947 Federal Supplement (F Supp) 1387, 1392–93 (District of Oregon 1996). In 1996, Judge Jack B Weinstein appointed three Special Masters to serve on a panel to select scientific experts for breast implant litigation; Judge Weinstein's panel selection process was adopted by Judge Sam C Pointer in the MDL litigation.

11 The US Bankruptcy Court and District Court appointed Prof Francis McGovern as a Mediator to work as an intermediary amongst all parties, chiefly the Tort Claimants Committee, the Debtor's Representatives and the Court. See Order Appointed Mediator, Case No 97-CV-00001-DT (ED Mich, 11 November 1997). Later, Prof McGovern was appointed Special Master with regard to functions related to the Litigation Facility and was appointed member of the Finance Committee by the District Court. *In re: Dow Corning Corp*, Order Appointing Francis E McGovern as Special Master, Case No 00-CV-00001-CT (Litigation Facility Matters) (ED. Mich, 2001).

the referral of a scientific issue to an expert science panel,[12] the appointment of experts as 'technical advisors' to the Court,[13] and the appointment of class counsel.[14]

A. A Brief History of Implants and the US Litigation

Although exact figures are not available, the US health regulatory authority, 3/5
the Food and Drug Administration (FDA), estimated in 2011 that between 5 and 10 million women worldwide had been implanted with silicone breast implants.[15] How did breast implant surgery get started though?

Years ago, attempts to enlarge the female breast led to adventurous proce- 3/6
dures including transplantation of the body's own fat tissue, the implantation of paraffin or sponges, or even the injection of non-medical grade silicone directly into the breast tissue. These procedures often caused disastrous cosmetic results, and of course pain, as reported in the medical literature.[16] In response to the need for a better surgical option, in the early 1960s, plastic surgeons Dr Thomas Cronin and Dr Frank Gerow developed a medical device designed for surgical implantation in the breast essentially consisting of a sealed packet surrounding a viscous silicone core.[17] In conjunction with Dow Corning, they de-

---

12 The '706 Panel' set up by Judge Sam C Pointer in the multi-district litigation proceeding pursuant to Federal Rule of Evidence 706 was charged with developing video-taped testimony for presentation at trial of about 27,000 individual cases regarding the issue of general causation, in other words, the issue 'do silicone breast implants cause systemic disease?' *In re: Silicone Gel Breast Implants Products Liability Litigation*, 793 F Supp 1098 (Judicial Panel on Multidistrict Litigation (JPML) 1992). See also *Laura L Hooper/Joe S Cecil/Thomas E Willging*, Assessing Causation in Breast Implant Litigation: The Role of Science Panels, 64 Law and Contemporary Problems (Law & Contemp Probs) 139 (2001).

13 *Hall v Baxter Healthcare Corp*, 947 F Supp 1387, 1392 no 7 (District of Oregon 1996). See also *Hooper/Cecil/Willging*, 64 Law & Contemp Probs 139 (2001).

14 Federal Rules of Civil Procedure (Fed R Civ P) 23(g).

15 *FDA Update on the Safety of Silicone Gel-Filled Breast Implants*, (June 2011) Center for Devices and Radiological Health US Food and Drug Administration, p 3 (last visited 13 December 2013) <http://fda.gov/downloads/MedicalDevices/ProductsandMedicalProcedures/Implantsand Prosthetics/BreastImplants/UCM260090.pdf>.

16 *K Boo-Chai*, The Complications of Augmentation Mammaplasty by Silicone Injection (1969) British Journal of Plastic Surgery (Brit J Plast Surg) 22(3-4) 281–285; *N Ohtake/Y Koganei/M Itoh/N Shioya*, Postoperative Sequelae of Augmentation Mammaplasty by Injection Method in Japan (1989) Aesthetic Plastic Surgery 13(2) 67–74.

17 *In re: Dow Corning Corp*, 211 BR 545, 550 (Bankr ED Mich 1997).

veloped a product that has become known as a silicone gel breast implant, a product introduced to the market in 1964.[18]

3/7 Silicone breast implants were marketed for reconstructive surgery as well as for elective breast augmentation surgery.[19] Indeed, soon after having been developed, several US manufacturers sold and shipped breast implants worldwide, partly of a substandard quality for shipment abroad.[20]

3/8 In 1976, the US Congress amended the Federal Food, Drug and Cosmetic Act giving the FDA the authority to review and approve the safety and effectiveness of medical devices; at that time silicone breast implants had already been on the market for over ten years and were considered Class II devices, those with a moderate risk. Consequently, breast implants already on the market were 'grandfathered in' whereas new implants were reviewed through the pre-market notification or 510(k) process.[21] The 510(k) process requires the applicant to demonstrate that the product for which FDA approval is sought is 'substantially similar' to, and therefore as safe and effective as, a medical device already legally on the market,[22] thereby effectively short-cutting the regulatory process.

---

18 Ibid.

19 *FDA Update on the Safety of Silicone Gel-Filled Breast Implants*, (June 2011) Center for Devices and Radiological Health US Food and Drug Administration, p 3 (last visited 13 December 2013) <http://fda.gov/downloads/medicaldevices/productsandmedicalprocedures/implantsand prosthetics/breastimplants/ucm260090.pdf>.

20 It has been reported that documents obtained during pre-trial discovery reveal that some breast implants of a quality substandard for the US market were authorised for shipment abroad. 'According to the Foreign Plaintiffs' Subcommittee, a 1979 Bristol-Meyer memorandum indicated that the company had 140 gel-filled mammaries which had "incomplete adhesion of the gel to the shell" including handwritten notes stating "these units can be packaged for shipment to any country *other* than USA, Western Europe, Australia & New Zealand. They are excellent for South America, Near East, *Eastern* Europe, Africa and the Far East', *S Alexander, Heidi Lindsey, et al, v Dow Corning Corp, et al*: The Exclusion of Claimants from Australia, Ontario and Quebec, 4 Pacific Rim Law & Policy Journal (Pac Rim L & Pol J) 419, 420 f (1995), citing Memorandum of Law of Foreign Plaintiffs' Sub-Committee of Plaintiffs' Steering Committee in Opposition to Proposed Settlement. The Foreign Plaintiffs' Subcommittee also claimed that another manufacturer, McGhan, in a company document dated 22 October 1977 signed by the Quality Assurance Manager stated: '[p]roduct deviates from specifications due to visible flaws. Request approval to release product for shipment to Mexico.' Ibid, at 13 (quoting from Shainwald Affidavit, para 16). See also *K Carter-Stein*, In Search of Justice: Foreign Victims of Silicone Breast Implants and the Doctrine of Forum Non Conveniens, 18 Suffolk Transnational Law Review (Suffolk Transnat'l L Rev) 167, 180 (1995).

21 Ibid. See also Regulatory History of Breast Implants in the US, US Food and Drug Administration, (last visited 13 December 2013) <http://www.fda.gov/MedicalDevices/Productsand MedicalProcedures/ImplantsandProsthetics/BreastImplants/ucm064461.htm>.

22 21 Code of Federal Regulations (CFR) 807.92.

The safety of the implants started to be questioned in the late 1970s when 3/9
women began to allege that the implants caused untoward health effects. The door to years of litigation was opened in 1977 when a woman with a ruptured[23] implant won a jury trial in Texas against her implant's manufacturer.[24] In 1980, the Public Citizen's Health Research Group, a consumer advocacy organisation affiliated with Ralph Nader, warned that silicone implants might cause cancer.[25]

During the 1980s, more and more lawsuits were filed by implant recipients 3/10
who argued over the manufacturers' vehement objections that the implants caused systemic injuries such as auto-immune diseases. Cases progressed to trial, with some juries deciding in favour of the plaintiffs.[26]

In 1988, the FDA reclassified silicone breast implants as Class III devices re- 3/11
quiring, from then on, their pre-market approval[27] and requiring that the manufacturers of implants already on the market document by mid-1991 that the implants were safe and effective. The breast implant controversy quickly became a matter of public debate throughout the US, particularly following a national television broadcast 'Face to Face with Connie Chung' outlining the alleged dangers of silicone breast implants in 1990.[28]

---

23 The FDA published an October 2000 report confirming, in the population of 344 women with silicone breast implants studied, that 77% of the women had at least one breast implant that was ruptured or suspicious for rupture, that silicone gel could be seen outside the body's fibrous capsule surrounding the implant in 21.2% of the women, and the median implant age at the time of rupture was 10.8 years. *S Brown/M Middleton/W Berg/M Scott Soo/G Pennello*, Prevalence of Rupture of Silicone Gel Breast Implants Revealed on MR Imaging in a Population of Women in Birmingham, Alabama, American Journal of Roentgenology (AJR) 175 (October 2000); (last visited 13 December 2013) <http://www.fda.gov/downloads/ScienceResearch/SpecialTopics/WomensHealthResearch/UCM247715.pdf>.

24 *M Higgins*, Mass Tort Makeover? 84 American Bar Association Journal (ABAJ) 53, 55 (1998).

25 *M Kalfus*, 50 Years of Fake Breasts, The Orange County Register (15 May 2012). More than 30 years later, on 26 January 2011, the US Food and Drug Administration (FDA) did announce reports of some cases of a specific type of breast cancer, anaplastic large cell lymphoma, in women with breast implants: *FDA Medical Device Safety Communication: Reports of Anaplastic Large Cell Lymphoma (ALCL) in Women with Breast Implants*, 26 January 2011, (last visited 13 December 2013) <http://www.fda.gov/MedicalDevices/Safety/AlertsandNotices/ucm240000.htm>.

26 For example: In 1984, a jury in San Francisco awarded breast implant recipient Maria Stern $ 211,000 in compensatory damages and $ 1.5 million in punitive damages. *Stern v Dow Corning Corp*, No C83-2348 MHP (ND California, 15 November 1984).

27 Regulatory History of Breast Implants in the US, US Food and Drug Administration (last visited 13 December 2013) <http://www.fda.gov/MedicalDevices/ProductsandMedicalProcedures/ImplantsandProsthetics/BreastImplants/ucm064461.htm>.

28 Face to Face with Connie Chung (CBS television broadcast 10 December 1990).

3/12 In 1992, the FDA concluded that none of the silicone breast implant manufacturers' pre-market approval applications contained enough data to support general admission to the market, restricting the use of silicone breast implants to reconstructive surgery patients and for the replacement of silicone implants. The FDA pointed out that implantation even for those purposes should be considered investigational requiring the women who received the implants to be followed in adjunct clinical studies. In short, since the data submitted by the manufacturers did not conclusively prove the safety of silicone breast implants, beginning in 1992 silicone breast implants were no longer available in the US for elective breast augmentation.[29]

3/13 Between 1992 and 1994, more than 16,000 lawsuits were filed.[30] Around that time, individual lawsuits against implant manufacturers proceeded to trial, and, despite the lack of conclusive medical evidence[31] establishing that silicone implants actually cause systemic disease, some led to substantial plaintiff verdicts.[32]

---

29 In the year 2006, following re-evaluation of the data, in reversal of its moratorium in 1992, the FDA permitted the implantation of silicone breast implants for augmentation. Regulatory History of Breast Implants in the US, US Food and Drug Administration, (last visited 13 December 2013) <http://www.fda.gov/MedicalDevices/ProductsandMedicalProcedures/ImplantsandProsthetics/BreastImplants/ucm064461.htm>.

30 *K Stine*, Silicone, Science and Settlements: Breast Implants and a Search for Truth, 53 Defense Counsel Journal (Def Couns J) 491 (1996).

31 Some examples of medical studies that have concluded that silicone breast implants do not pose a statistically significant risk of causing connective tissue disease include: *J Sanchez-Guerrero/GA Colditz/EW Karlson/DJ Hunter/FE Speizer/MH Liang*, Silicone Breast Implants and the Risk of Connective-Tissue Disease and Symptoms, (1995) New England Journal of Medicine (NEJM) 332 (25) 1666–1670 (an analysis of 14 years of data from the Nurses' Health Study cohort at the Department of Rheumatology, Harvard Medical School). *SM Edworthy/L Martin/SG Barrr/DC Birdsell/RF Brant/MJ Frizler*, A Clinical Study of the Relationship between Silicone Breast Implants and Connective Tissue Disease (1998) Journal of Rheumatology, 25 (2) 254–260. *Institute of Medicine of the National Academies*, Safety of Silicone Breast Implants, 1 June 1999 (last visited 13 December 2013), <http://www.iom.edu/reports/1999/safety-of-silicone-breast-implants.aspx>. *EC Janowsky/LL Kupper/BS Hulka*, Meta-Analysis of the Relation Between Silicone Breast Implants and the Risk of Connective-Tissue Disease (2000) NEJM 342 (11) 781–790.

32 In December 1991, Marianne Hopkins was awarded $ 7.34 million by a federal jury in San Francisco who determined that her mixed connective tissue disease had been caused by her ruptured silicone breast implants based upon claims of breach of warranty and fraud. *Hopkins v Dow Corning Corp*, No 92-16132, 1992 WL 176560 (ND Cal 27 May 1992), *aff'd* 33 Federal Reporter, Third Series (F 3d) 1116 (9th Circuit Court (Cir) 1994). In December 1992, in *Johnson v Bristol-Meyers Squibb*, $ 25 million ($ 5 million actual damages plus $ 20 million punitive damages) was awarded for mixed connective tissue disease and autoimmune disease caused by ruptured implants. In March 1994 in *Doss v 3M Corp*, a Houston, Texas jury awarded three

The fact that a breast implant plaintiff could be awarded significant damages based upon a doctor's 'expert testimony' at trial confirming that implants were the cause of the patient's medical problems, despite several studies concluding that there was no definitive link between silicone implants and systemic disease, led to cries of 'junk science'.[33] The controversial issue prompted Marcia Angell, executive editor of the well-respected medical journal New England Journal of Medicine, to author a book entitled 'Science on Trial: The Clash of Medical Evidence and the Law in the Breast Implant Case'[34] where she outlined the scientific evidence and the legal claims and concluded that there was no basis for either the FDA moratorium or the plaintiffs' verdicts. 3/14

This was just the beginning of what turned out to be decades of litigation and appeals in multiple jurisdictions encompassing numerous sub-issues. To describe the US silicone breast implant mass litigation as contentious is somewhat of an understatement; each single issue was vigorously prosecuted by claimants and defended tooth and nail by implant manufacturers. 3/15

B. Meanwhile in Europe ...

The actual number of silicone breast implant recipients in Europe is not precisely known due to, at least in part, the absence of databases[35] tracking the implantation of medical devices and the lack of applied standards for comprehensive medical documentation. 3/16

---

women a total of $ 27.9 million ($ 12 million compensatory damages plus $ 15 million punitive damages), *B Feder*, 3 are Awarded $ 27.9 Million in Implant Trial, New York Times, 4 March 1994, (last visited 13 December 2013) <http:www.nytimes.com/1994/03/04/us/3-are-awarded-27.9-million-in-implant-trial.html>. As reported by Judge Pointer in 'Breast-implant cases tried' from 1992 to 1999, the *Doss v 3M Corp* case settled after judgment for an undisclosed amount, (last visited 13 December 2013) <http://www.fjc.gov/BREIMLIT/trials.htm>. The New York Times reported on 5 August 1994 that one lawsuit involving 18 women was settled by the parties during *voir dire* or jury selection for a confidential amount totalling millions of dollars (last visited 13 December 2013) <http://www.nytimes.com/1994/08/05/us/further-us-ban-of-breast-implants-is-urged.html>.

33 See, for example *D Bandow*, The Decade of 'Junk Science' (10 May 1999), (last visited 13 December 2013) <http:www.cato.org/publications/commentary/decade-junk-science>.

34 *M Angell*, Science on Trial: The Clash of Medical Evidence and the Law in the Breast Implant Case (1996).

35 The European Parliament, in a resolution regarding breast implants in the year 2003 noted at No 24 '[c]onsiders that national breast-implant registers are an essential means of enabling both producers and patients to be traced (in the event of defective implants being identified they will, in particular, be essential in tracing the patients concerned after the operation) ...'

3/17 US silicone breast implants first reached the European markets in the late 1960s; since then, silicone breast implants have been continuously marketed, sold, and implanted in European patients. Prior to 1992, US manufacturers including Dow Corning, Bristol, Baxter, 3M, Cox-Uphoff, McGhan, Mentor and Bioplasty supplied the European markets from their US production facilities, often via European distributors. Detailed records tracking the importation of breast implants in Europe are not available, however, the largest US manufacturer, Dow Corning, acknowledged having received $ 68 million attributable to the sale of 579,000 breast implants outside the US;[36] this represented nearly half of its total sales.[37]

3/18 Following the FDA's 1992 partial ban of silicone breast implants from the US market as discussed above, some manufacturers, including Dow Corning, terminated their implant production entirely whereas at least one company simply transplanted its manufacturing facility from the US to Europe. The massive supply gap left behind by Dow Corning was quickly filled by other producers, amongst them the Japanese manufacturer Koken and European manufacturers[38] which entered the lucrative market with their implants in the 1980s.

3/19 Since having been introduced to the market in the late 1960s in Europe, silicone breast implants have been continuously available in all European countries with one exception: France. The French national health agency, at that time the Medicines Agency,[39] restricted the use of silicone implants in 1992 and

---

European Parliament Resolution on the Communication from the Commission on Community and National Measures in Relation to Breast Implants, COM(2001)666 – C5-0327/2002 – 2002/2171(COS); (last visited 13 December 2013) <http://new.eur-lex.europa.eu/legal-content/EN/TXT/PDF/?uri=CELEX:52003IP0063&rid=1>.

36 *Alexander*, 4 Pac Rim L & Pol J 419, at 426 (1995).

37 *Carter-Stein*, 18 Suffolk Transnat'l L Rev 167, at 183 (1995), citing Supplement to the 13 March 1993 Response of Dow Corning Corporation to Plaintiffs' Second Set of Interrogatories, *In re: Silicone Gel Breast Implant Products Liability Litigation*, MDL No 926, Case No CV 92-P-10000-S (1993).

38 European silicone breast implant manufacturers include/included Polytech-Silimed in Germany; Eurosilicone SAS, Lab Sebbin, Medically Applied Plastics (MAP), Simaplast and Poly Implant Prosthese (PIP) in France; Nagor Ltd in the Isle of Man; BioSil Ltd in Scotland; Rofil Medical Nederland BV in the Netherlands; and Inamed (formerly McGhan) in Ireland.

39 The AFSSAPS, the French health and safety authority set up in 1999 and predecessor of the current French National Agency of Medicine and Health Products Safety established in 2012, ANSM, was the successor to the Medicines Agency. AFSSAPS 2008 Annual Report (last visited 14 December 2013) <http://docsfiles.com/pdf_afssaps_annual_report.html> file name: f041acf df73129ac6b0487e7bb21a020.pdf.

three years later barred all breast implants except saline filled.[40] In 2001, the Medicines Agency's successor, *Agence française de sécurité sanitaire des produits de santé* (Afssaps), permitted silicone breast implants back on the market in France.[41]

The FDA has only ever permitted breast implants filled with saline, silicone, 3/20
or a combination of silicone and saline, so called bi-lumen implants, to be sold in the US, but in Europe breast implants filled with materials other than silicone gel or saline were marketed too. Questions regarding the safety of those products, however, in the end led to their being removed from the EU market.

For example, Trilucent™ breast implants consisting of a silicone elastomer 3/21
shell filled with soy bean oil were generally available throughout the EU between 1995 and March 1999. It is estimated that 11,000 women in Europe were implanted with Trilucent™ breast implants.[42] Due to reports of inflammation associated with rupture and concerns about long-term health risks associated with the breakdown of the lipid filler, women who had been implanted with soy oil filled implants were advised to have them removed.[43] Implants filled with hydrogel, a polymeric material with the ability to swell in water without dissolving, were generally available in the EU until 2000 when concerns about the safety of the fill material, including an increased risk of rupture, were voiced. Hydrogel filled implants manufactured by Poly Implant Prothèse (PIP) as well as NovaMed's NovaGold were voluntarily removed from the market.[44] TiBREEZE implants manufactured by GfE Medizintechnik GmbH in Germany consisting of a titanium coated silicone elastomer shell filled with a silicone gel material manufactured by PIP were also withdrawn from the EU market in 2004.[45]

---

40 *R Watson*, EU Parliament Calls for Tougher Rules on Breast Implants (2003) 326 British Medical Journal (BMJ) 414 no 6.

41 *F Petit*, Breast Implants in France. New Regulations, and Qualitative and Quantitative Study of Breast Implants Sold between 1995 and 2004, Annales de Chirurgie Plastique Esthétique 50 (2005) 685–693.

42 *X Bosch*, Spanish Women to Sue over Breast Implants (2000) 321 BMJ 403.

43 See the UK's Medical and Healthcare Products Regulatory Agency's report 'Types of Breast Implants' (last visited 13 December 2013) <http://www.mhra.gov.uk/PrintPreview/DefaultSplashPP/CON019576?ResultCount=10&DynamicListQuery=&DynamicListSortBy=xCreationDate&DynamicListSortOrder=Desc&DynamicListTitle=&PageNumber=1&Title=Breast%20implants>.

44 *J Hadwicke/NR Gaze/JK Laitung*, A Retrospective Audit of Novagold 'Hydrogel' Breast Implants (2007) Journal of Plastic, Reconstructive & Aesthetic Surgery 60 (12) 1313–1316.

45 Report of the *Bundesinstitut für Arzneimittel und Medizinprodukte*, (German Federal Institute for Drugs and Medical Devices) '*Brustimplantate TiBREEZE der früheren GfE Medizintechnik GmbH ebenfalls betroffen*' or, translated into English 'TiBREEZE Breast Implants from the former GfE Medizintechnik GmbH are also affected', 26.01.2012. In 2012, the Institute also recom-

3/22 The most recent breast implant controversy surrounds PIP silicone implants, generally available in Europe until March 2010[46] when the French medical device regulatory authority, Afssaps, suspended the marketing, distribution, export and use of PIP silicone gel breast implants. Following an inspection of the PIP plant, Afssaps discovered that breast implants manufactured since 2001 had actually been filled with silicone gel with a composition that differed from that previously approved.[47] Non-medical grade or industrial grade silicone was apparently used to fill the implants already implanted in thousands of women throughout Europe. This led to the initiation of criminal proceedings in France against PIP owner Jean-Claude Mas, criminal investigations in other European countries, and personal injury litigation in France,[48] Germany,[49] and England. With the assets of PIP being scarce or non-existent, and insurance coverage limited and contested, additional defendants have been named including doctors and hospitals, an insurance carrier, the German company that had delivered the industrial silicone to PIP, the Afssaps and TÜV Rheinland, the entity that had

mended that women with these implants have them removed; (last visited 13 December 2013) <http://www.bfarm.de/DE/Medizinprodukte/risikoerfassung/empfehlungen/Silikon_Brustimplantate_PIP.html>.

46 According to the European Commission, around 400,000 PIP silicone breast implants were sold worldwide. They were available in nearly all EU countries and extensively implanted in women in the UK (around 40,000), France (about 30,000), Spain (approx 10,000) and Germany (about 7,500). European Commission – Press Release 'Medical devices: European Commission asks for further scientific study and draws first lessons from the recent fraud on breast implants', IP/12/96 (2 February 2012) (last visited 13 December 2013) <http://www.europa.eu/rapid/press-release_IP-12-96_en.htm?local=en>.

47 Both the French and UK device regulatory authorities carried out additional testing of the PIP implants, generally concluding that there is no increased risk of cancer or chemical toxicity, although there is a significantly greater risk of rupture described as two to six times higher than for other silicone implants with ruptures occurring within 5 years, leakage of silicone, local reaction and lymph node enlargement: *Agence française de sécurité sanitaire des produits de santé* (AFSSAPS), 'Résultats des tests complémentaires sur les Implants mammaires à base de gel de silicone de la société Poly Implant Prosthèse' (14 April 2011); *Medicines and Healthcare Products Regulatory Agency* (MHRA), Summary report on tests performed on extracts of silicone gel filler material from PIP silicone breast implants. Commissioned by the MHRA in July 2010 (January 2012). See also Department of Health, NHS Medical Directorate, 'Poly Implant Prothese (Pip) Breast Implants: Final report of the Expert Group', Sir Bruce Keogh, NHS Medical Director (18 June 2012).

48 As reported in *'PIP-Opfer klagen deutschen TÜV und Silikon-Lieferanten an'*, WAZ, 5 January 2012, more than 2,000 women have filed suit in France.

49 *'Gericht zweifelt Anspruch auf Schadenersatz wegen minderwertiger Brustimplantate an'*, Süddeutsche.de, (13 November 2012) (last visited 13 December 2013) <http://www.sueddeutsche.de/panorama/skandal-um-minderwertige-pip-brustimplantate-gericht-bewertet-schadenersatzklage-kritisch-1.1521801>.

granted European CE certification[50] to the product following evaluation of its safety. Litigation is ongoing.

In an editorial published in the British Medical Journal, Mr Heneghan summed it up nicely: 'Complete and utter confusion now reigns over Poly Implant Prosthèse breast implants and what to do, particularly with regard to the evidence needed for their regulation, effectiveness, and, more importantly, safety.'[51] 3/23

It was the PIP scandal that finally launched a discussion in Europe amongst the various Member States as well as at the EU level in Brussels and Strasbourg regarding the safety of medical devices.[52] Triggered by the PIP fiasco, the European Parliament (Parliament) adopted a Resolution on 14 June 2012 calling on the European Commission (Commission) to develop an adequate legal framework to guarantee the safety of medical technology.[53] On 26 September 2012, the Commission adopted a package on innovation in health consisting of proposals for stricter regulation of medical devices[54] and *in vitro* medical devices[55] and issued a communication regarding medical devices.[56] The Commission's proposals include clearer and wider scope of the EU legislation; tightening the requirements for clinical evidence to ensure patient safety; more powers and obligations for the assessment or 'notified bodies'; thorough supervision of the assessment bodies by national authorities; an extended database regarding medical devices; and better ability to trace medical devices permitting more rapid response to safety concerns.[57] The Commission's proposals will be dis- 3/24

---

50 Following an evaluation by an assessment body or 'notified body', products rated as safe for use in the EU, EFTA countries and Turkey are granted a 'CE rating' certifying safety; currently there are approximately 80 notified bodies.

51 *C Heneghan*, The Saga of Poly Implant Prosthèse Breast Implants (2012) 344 BMJ e306.

52 *R Watson*, Europe Launches Investigation into Health Risks of Faulty Breast Implants (2012) 344 BMJ e939.

53 European Parliament resolution of 14 June 2012 on defective silicone gel breast implants made by French company PIP (2012/2621(RSP)); P7_TA-PROV(2012)0262, (last visited 14 December 2013) <http://www.europarl.europa.eu/sides/getDoc.do?type=TA&reference=P7-TA-2012-0262&format=XML&language=EN>.

54 European Commission 'Proposal for a Regulation of the European Parliament and of the Council on medical devices, and amending Directive 2001/83/EC, Regulation (EC) No 178/2002 and Regulation (EC) No 1223/2009'.

55 European Commission 'Communication from the Commission to the European Parliament, The Council, The European Economic and Social Committee and the Committee of the Regions', COM(2012) 540 final 26 September 2012.

56 Ibid.

57 Ibid.

cussed in the Parliament and in the Council with a view to being adopted in 2014 and are expected to gradually become effective between 2015 and 2019.[58]

3/25 Between 1998 and 2003, the EU debated the issue of breast implants and their safety. The discussion was initiated at that time by breast implant self-help groups filing petitions with the Parliament seeking to ban silicone breast implants.[59] The Parliament's Committee on Petitions requested a study of the issues surrounding silicone implants, particularly breast implants, within the framework of the Parliament's Scientific and Technological Options Assessment Series (STOA). An independent group contracted by STOA carried out a comprehensive assessment, the results of which were completed in May 2000[60]. In response, the Parliament passed a resolution in June 2001 focusing on product safety, also recommending better pre-operative and post-operative support for patients.[61] The Commission published a communication in November 2001 proposing tighter controls on the safety of breast implants, new provisions for information and labelling, better informed consent for patients, documentation of all breast implants in national registries as well as post-operative clinical evaluation, and reconsideration of safety requirements regarding medical devices.[62] In February 2003, the Commission issued a directive making breast implants a Class III device, effectively tightening the requirements for CE certification.[63]

3/26 Before the recent wave of PIP claims, silicone breast implant related litigation in Europe had been comparatively limited. A few reported[64] as well as an

---

58 <http://europa.eu/rapid/press-release_MEMO-12-710_en.htm?locale=en> (last visited 13 December 2013).

59 *L Gorgojo/J González-Enríques/W Wisbaum/J Martín-Moreno*, Update Report 'Health Risks Posed by Silicone Implants in General, with a Special Attention to Breast Implants', European Parliament's Scientific and Technological Options Assessment Series, STOA 116 EN, 06-2003.

60 *JM Martín-Moreno/L Gorgojo/J González-Enríques/M Wisbaum*, Health Risks Posed by Silicone Implants in General, with Special Attention to Breast Implants, PE 168.396/Fin.St/rew 2000.

61 'European Parliament Resolution on the Communication from the Commission on Community and National Measures in Relation to Breast Implants' COM(2001)666 – C5-0327/2002 – 2002/2171(COS); (last visited 16 December 2013) <http://www.europarl.europa.eu/sides/getDoc.do?pubRef=-//EP//NONSGML+TA+P5-TA-2003-0063+0+DOC+PDF+V0//EN>.

62 *Gorgojo/González-Enríques/Wisbaum/Martín-Moreno*, European Parliament's Scientific and Technological Options Assessment Series, STOA 116 EN, 06-2003.

63 Commission Directive 2003/12/EC of 3 February 2003 on the reclassification of breast implants in the framework of Directive 93/42/EEC concerning medical devices, Official Journal (OJ) L 28, 4.2.2003, 43–44; (last visited 16 December 2013) <http://new.eur-lex.europa.eu/legal-content/EN/TXT/PDF/?uri=CELEX:32003L0012&rid=2>.

64 For example, in *O'Keefe v Harvey-Kemble* (1998) 45 Butterworths Medico-Legal Reports (BMLR) 74 (Court of Appeal Civil Division) 24 April 1998, the claimant was granted GBP 13,500 in general damages and GBP 11,650 in special damages for informed consent and negligence

unknown number of unreported cases involved individual patient's lawsuits against their surgeons asserting, for example, lack of informed consent[65] and/or professional negligence.

Product liability lawsuits were also filed against implant manufacturers pursuant to EU Council Directive 85/374/EEC[66] concerning liability for defective products. For example, in *Hems v Poly Implants Prosthesis*, the claimant's implant ruptured causing silicone to migrate to her lymph nodes, requiring removal and later replacement of the implants. The Court ruled that, pursuant to EU and English law, the defendant was required to pay for the cost of the private surgery to replace the implants but not for the claimant's insurance policy.[67] In *Foster v Biosil*,[68] a case involving rupture of an implant within seven months of implantation plus leakage of the implant on the opposing side, the Court held that, pursuant to the English Consumer Protection Act 1987 and Council Directive 85/374/EEC, the claimant had to prove not only that the implants failed in an unsafe manner contrary to her expectations, but also that the implants were defective.[69] The Court ruled in favour of the defendant manufacturer reasoning that the claimant, who had the burden of proof, had not established that the implants were defective and, notably, the cause of the defect. 3/27

European recipients of silicone breast implants manufactured by US companies were included in the multiple manufacturers' global multi-district litigation settlement as well as the bankruptcy proceeding involving Dow Corning. Both proceedings included foreign claimants who timely registered with the MDL-926 Claims Office[70] and in the Dow Corning bankruptcy proceed- 3/28

---

claims stemming from her post-operative hematoma requiring surgical evacuation, loss of sensitivity, and breast asymmetry requiring five additional surgeries.

65 In *Williamson v East London and City HA*, 1997 Westlaw 1104570 (Chancery Division, Ch D), (1998) 41 BMLR 85, [1998] Lloyd's Law Reports Medical (Lloyd's Rep Med) 6 (Ch D), 24 October 1997 (Eng), the claimant was awarded GBP 20,000 for the surgeon's failure to obtain her informed consent to the performance of a subcutaneous mastectomy associated with the dispersion of silicone in her breast tissue and axilla following silicone breast implantation.

66 Council Directive 85/374/EEC of 25 July 1985 on the approximation of the laws, regulations and administrative provisions of the Member States concerning liability for defective products, OJ L 210, 7.8.1985, 29–33.

67 *Hems v Poly Implants Prosthesis* (2006) Current Law Yearbook (CLY) 1063 (Nottingham County Court) 30 August 2006.

68 *Foster v Biosil* (2000) 59 BMLR 178 (County Court Central London), 19 April 2000.

69 See also *P Shears*, The EU Product Liability Directive – Twenty Years On (2007) Journal of Business Law (J Bus L) 884–908.

70 The deadline for foreign claimants to register with the MDL-926 Claims Office was 5 March 1995 to qualify as an 'Other Registrant'; in order to qualify for the status 'Current Claimant' medical records documenting disease had to be filed by October 1994.

ing.[71] In the MDL proceeding, claimants, including foreign claimants, were able to 'opt-out' of the settlement and, instead, pursue individual litigation against the manufacturers.[72] Similarly, a claimant in the Dow Corning bankruptcy who decided not to settle her claim could elect to litigate.

II. Legal Issues, Negotiations, and Resolutions

A. The Multi-District Litigation Settlement

3/29 After the FDA had removed silicone breast implants from the market in the US in 1992, more than 400,000 cases were filed in various federal and state courts[73] alleging damage from implants that had ruptured or leaked.[74] Plaintiffs' claims were based on several different causes of action including negligence, fraud, misrepresentation, breach of express or implied warranties, strict liability and violation of consumer protection laws. The alleged injuries were initially local such as capsular contracture or hardening around the implant, rupture, the need for replacement or removal of the implants, migration or shifting of the implant, temporary or permanent disfigurement, granulomae or siliconomae, infection and pain. Later, systemic injuries such as immune system dysfunction or connective tissue diseases were alleged. Medical research regarding the alleged systemic problems was ongoing at that time.

---

71 The 'bar date' for foreign claimants to register with the Dow Corning proceeding was 14 February 1997 (15 January 1997 for US claimants). *In re: Dow Corning Corp*, Amended Joint Plan of Reorganization, (Bankr ED Mich, 4 February 1999).

72 It has been argued that, as a practical matter, foreign claimants had no choice to opt-out due to insufficient, ineffective or non-existent redress in the foreign forum coupled with the potential legal obstacles imposed by the legal issues *forum non conveniens* and choice of law. *Carter-Stein*, 18 Suffolk Transnat'l L Rev 167, 180 (1995).

73 'In recent mass torts, the cases have been filed almost simultaneously in the federal and state courts. The state cases are often congregated within the state, either by operation of statutes, court administration powers, or voluntary agreements. The same plaintiffs' lawyers almost always represent the plaintiffs in the federal and state case, especially because diversity jurisdiction problems may lead the same law firm to file in various courts. And, of course, the defense firm is usually the same in state and federal litigation.' *P Rheingold*, Comments on Judicial Federalism: A Proposal to Amend the Multidistrict Litigation Statute, 73 Texas Law Review (Tex L Rev) 1581, 1581 f (1994-1995).

74 *Hooper/Cecil/Willging*, 64 Law & Contemp Probs 139, 142 (2001).

In 1992, the Judicial Panel on Multi-District Litigation consolidated all the breast implant cases filed in federal courts for pre-trial proceedings[75] pursuant to USC § 1407.[76] Amongst the 27,000 cases transferred was a class action lawsuit brought on behalf of foreign plaintiffs.[77] The Multi-District Litigation (MDL-926) was assigned to Chief Judge Sam C Pointer of the US District Court for the Northern District of Alabama. As cases became ready for trial, they were transferred back to the district courts from whence they came; it was anticipated that the early trials would set the benchmark for possible settlement. 'While consolidation simplifies discovery, it won't necessarily avoid costly trials. The leading theory in mass torts holds that parties won't settle claims until they have tried enough to know roughly what the claims are worth.'[78] 3/30

The major issue presented in the silicone breast implant products liability cases, hotly disputed by the parties and still debated to this day, is whether silicone implants actually cause symptoms and disease. Claimants are convinced that the implants cause not only localized problems due to implant rupture, leakage, or by the body's formation of capsular tissue around the implant, but also systemic diseases such as rheumatoid arthritis, scleroderma, systemic lupus erythymatosis, Sjroegren's syndrome and other connective tissue diseases, as well as a litany of symptoms including joint pain, muscle pain, chronic fa- 3/31

75 'Hundreds of depositions of plaintiffs, corporate representatives and experts have been taken in the MDL and related state court proceedings. In addition, millions of documents are available for inspection through the MDL Depository in Cincinnati, Ohio.' *In re: Dow Corning Litigation*, ED Mich, Civil Action No 00-CV-00001, Case Management Order No 1 at 9. As noted by Rheingold, P, '... when MDL discovery is getting underway, courts and the parties almost universally agree to utilize the federal work product, allowing state discovery only on local, nonrepetitive issues. The best example of federal-state coordination, and the one that promises to be a model for future mass torts, is that in the breast implant cases. Here, an experienced federal judge, appointed to manage the MDL, moved rapidly to involve state court judges in the discovery. Judge Sam Pointer appointed a master as state court liaison and held meetings periodically with the state court judges to keep them informed of developments and to encourage them to avoid repetitive discovery. The great majority of the state courts then agreed to utilize the federal work product and not to order or permit depositions or document discovery on their own.' *Rheingold*, 73 Tex L Rev 1581, 1582 (1994–1995).

76 *In re: Silicone Gel Breast Implants Prod Liab Litig*, 793 F Supp 1098 (JPML 1992). 28 USC § 1407(a) states in part '[w]hen civil actions involving one or more common questions of fact are pending in different districts, such actions may be transferred to any district for coordinated or consolidated pretrial proceedings.'

77 *Ashley v Dow Corning Corporation*, 92 CV 10221-BC (ED Mich 1992). The defense *forum non conveniens* was raised by Dow Corning in opposing certification of the class. Motion to Dismiss, *Ashley v Dow Corning Corporation*, ibid.

78 *Higgins*, 84 ABAJ 53, 56 (1998).

tigue, dryness of the eyes and hair loss. The defendant manufacturers deny the systemic problems while often admitting that rupture and silicone 'bleeding', the gradual leeching of silicone through the silicone membrane covering the silicone gel core, does occur in some instances, particularly with older implants containing a less 'cohesive' gel core.

3/32 In other words, the primary legal issue presented in the silicone breast implant litigation was one of proximate causation. Pursuant to the applicable US tort law, the burden of proving causation is on the plaintiff. The legal issues and standards regarding the presentation of evidence to support causation, generally via expert testimony, are complex and were evolving as cases were being tried. The comparatively lenient standard applicable at that time for determining the admissibility of scientific evidence and expert testimony undoubtedly led to some plaintiff verdicts. In 1993, the US Supreme Court in the landmark decision *Daubert v Merrell Dow Pharmaceuticals, Inc* made the qualifications for giving scientific testimony in a federal trial stricter, essentially making the trial court the 'gatekeeper' for all expert testimony.[79] At the same time as the cases were being tried, medical research results addressing silicone implants, utilising differing research methodologies, were also being published, making the 'cases among the most difficult ever presented in federal courts'.[80]

3/33 The increased scrutiny of the FDA coupled with news of plaintiffs' verdicts and women's reports of ill health following implantation prompted the filing of even more cases. The sheer magnitude of the litigation was a matter of concern for the defendant companies faced with escalating defense costs.[81]

3/34 In response to the rising flood of litigation, in September 1993, Dow Corning proposed a global settlement of the controversy. In April 1994, Judge Pointer provisionally certified *In Re: Silicone Gel Breast Implant Products Liability Litigation, Heidi Lindsey, et al v Dow Corning Corp et al* as a class action for settlement purposes under Rule 23(b)(3) of the Federal Rules of Civil Procedure.[82]

---

79 *Daubert v Merrell Dow Pharmaceuticals, Inc*, 509 United States Supreme Court Reports (US) 579 (1993).

80 *Hooper/Cecil/Willging*, 64 Law & Contemp Probs 139, 142 (2001).

81 In the year 1994 alone, Dow Corning Corporation claimed to have spent more than $ 200 million in litigation costs. *In re: Dow Corning Corp*, 211 BR (Bankr ED Mich 1997) 545 at 552.

82 Rule 23 of the Federal Rules of Civil Procedure addresses class action suits. The rule provides that one or more members of a class may sue as a representative of all members of a class only if the class is so numerous that joinder of all members is impracticable, there are questions of law or fact common to the class, the claims or defenses of the representative parties are typical of the claims or defenses of the class, and the representative parties will fairly and adequately protect the interests of the class. A court's finding pursuant to Rule 23(b)(3) means that the court found that 'questions of law or fact common to class members predominate over any

Cases pending in various state courts were also progressing. For example, a complaint was filed in 1994 against Dow Corning in a Texas state court on behalf of 27 breast implant recipients. 'Dow Corning found itself "under significant pressure" to settle these twenty-seven cases, especially since any findings of fact made in these cases (the "Texas cases") could have significant adverse effects upon Dow Corning's position in a related multi-district case and related global settlement discussions then pending in federal court in Alabama. Dow Corning was also motivated to settle because of its view that Texas was a "plaintiff-friendly" forum. Dow Corning thus hired Ken Feinberg, a noted expert in settlement practice, to engage in settlement negotiations with the Plaintiffs.'[83] The case was settled in 1994 for a total of $ 17 million to be paid in yearly installments over seven years.[84] 3/35

After a year of negotiation,[85] the parties agreed to a global settlement of the federal MDL and on 1 September 1994, the District Court approved a $ 4.25 billion global settlement of the silicone breast implant class action[86] representing at that time the largest products liability class action settlement in US history.[87] The settlement addressed women in the US as well as claimants from sixty-five other countries.[88] 3/36

The settlement plan generally provided compensation for certain defined illnesses or symptoms, documented implant rupture, and separate payment for explantation or removal of an implant not replaced by another silicone implant. 3/37

---

questions affecting only individual members, and that a class action is superior to other available methods for fairly and efficiently adjudicating the controversy', Fed R Civ P 23(b)(3).

83 *In re: Dow Corning Corp, Bear Stearns Government Securities, Inc v Dow Corning Corp*, No 04-1916, (6th Circuit, 22 August 2005), at 2.

84 The settlement terms included Dow Corning's agreement to payment of $ 100 per day to each claimant in the event payments were late. The plaintiffs later sold their rights to Bear Stearns. Dow Corning ceased payment following the filing of the Chapter 11 bankruptcy petition in 1995. Bear Sterns attempted to enforce the $ 100 liquidated damages clause via a bankruptcy claim. The District Court granted Dow Corning's motion for summary judgment on the grounds that the $ 100 per day clause was a penalty unenforceable under Texas law, the applicable law as agreed by the parties. On appeal, the 6th Circuit Court of Appeals affirmed the decision of the District Court – (ibid).

85 In the US legal system, it is common for the attorneys representing the parties, outside the courtroom and either independently from the court or at the prompting of the court, to negotiate the terms of a settlement as well as the settlement agreement, usually also drafting the court's orders implementing the settlement for the review and approval of the court.

86 *In re: Silicone Gel Breast Implant Products Liability Litigation (MDL 926), Heidi Lindsey, et al v Dow Corning Corp, et al*, No CV 94-P-11558-S. 1994 US Dist Lexis 12521 (Northern District of Alabama, 1 September 1994) [hereinafter: *Lindsey Opinion*].

87 Ibid, at 1.

88 Ibid, at 6.

Pursuant to the plan, each claimant had to meet certain filing deadlines and prove her eligibility for each element of every claim: proof of manufacturer, disease, rupture and/or explantation.

3/38 For purposes of the MDL settlement, the hotly disputed proximate causation issue did not have to be proven. Stated differently, pursuant to the settlement plan, a claimant did not have to prove that, more likely than not, her disease or symptoms were caused by one or more silicone breast implants; she had to prove only the presence and severity of her disease or symptoms. The elements of proof were the same for both foreign and domestic claimants.

3/39 The amounts to be paid to foreign claimants were reduced, however, compared to domestic claimants. According to the terms of the settlement agreement, there was a three (3) percent cap on the Disease Compensation Program funds that could be paid to foreign claimants while the remainder was dedicated to domestic claimants.[89] Domestic claimants generally favoured the plan while foreign claimants, particularly those living in Canada and Australia, were against the plan primarily due to its unequal treatment of foreign claimants.[90] Additionally, foreign women objected to the reduced notification program for foreign claimants compared to US claimants[91] and maintained that they were inadequately represented in the proceeding. None of the seven named plaintiffs, the plaintiffs whose names were listed on the complaint filed to initiate the proceeding, resided outside the US.[92] Even more significantly, none of the attorneys on the Plaintiffs' Negotiating Committee represented foreign claimants.[93]

3/40 After Dow Corning filed for bankruptcy protection in 1995, the MDL-926 global settlement collapsed but, following further negotiations, a separate settlement for foreign claimants was approved, the Foreign Settlement Program (FSP).[94] Pursuant to the FSP, foreign claimants who had timely registered with the MDL-926 Claims Office were compensated for disease and explantation; rup-

89 *Lindsey Opinion* (fn 86) at 16, 18.

90 Due to objections to the proposed settlement, Australian, Quebec and Ontario claimants were excluded from the settlement.

91 Plaintiffs' Class Counsel reported that 5,894 notification packages were sent to non-US residents although Dow Corning acknowledged that it had overseas sales of at least 579,000 breast implants and had earned $ 68 million in overseas sales.

92 *Lindsey Opinion* (fn 86) at 15.

93 The Court was aware of this but did not find it necessarily fatal to the certification of the class and approval of the settlement, even though treatment was not equal to all under the terms of the settlement. *Lindsey Opinion* (fn 86) at 15.

94 *In re: Silicone Gel Breast Implant Product Liability Litigation (MDL 926)*, Order No 45 Approving Notice of Foreign Settlement Program and Providing Parallel Settlement Option for Domestic 'Other Registrants', Master File CV 92-P-10000-S (26 June 1998).

ture benefits were not paid to foreign claimants. The amount of compensation paid to a foreign claimant was less than the amount paid to a similarly situated domestic claimant under an otherwise comparable Revised Settlement Program (RSP).

Although the litigation and negotiation of innumerable common issues had been concluded by the time the MDL-926 Claims Office began to evaluate individual claims, for each claimant the pursuance of her own claims was akin to new multiple mini-proceedings with limited appellate rights. For example, as in all products liability cases, the first step for each claimant was proving that she had been implanted with a product manufactured by one of the settling defendants. Only certain types of proof, generally contemporaneously written medical records proving the fact of implantation and the manufacturer of the implant, were deemed sufficient according to the settlement plan. Often years had passed between the time of implantation and the filing of the claim and the required records were not available; these women were denied compensation. 3/41

Following years of evaluating and paying compensation pursuant to the RSP and FSP, the MDL-926 Claims Office accepted its last medical record for evaluation on 15 December 2010, closing a long chapter in the history of silicone breast implant litigation. 3/42

B. The Dow Corning Corporation Bankruptcy Proceeding

In the US, bankruptcy does not always imply a complete inability to pay one's debts or obligations; there are various types of bankruptcy, all governed by federal law. One variety, a bankruptcy reorganisation proceeding pursuant to Chapter 11 of the US Code[95] permits a debtor, under certain circumstances, to be relieved of its debts and thereafter continue business as a reorganised debtor. The Chapter 11 reorganisation procedure ensures finality to the defendant while, at the same time, providing at least limited compensation to creditors such as silicone breast implant recipients who assert claims against a debtor company. '... [T]he bankruptcy court, as a forum for resolving large and complex mass litigations, has substantial power to reorder creditor-debtor relations needed to achieve a successful reorganisation.'[96] 3/43

Dow Corning Corporation utilised the Chapter 11 procedure to resolve all of its then existing and future liabilities related to its manufacture of silicone 3/44

95 11 USC §§ 101 ff.

96 *In re: Dow Corning Corporation*, 2002 FED App 0043P, p 12 (6th Cir 29 January 2002).

products.[97] The massive number of lawsuits that had been filed against the company had made the proposed MDL-926 settlement of $ 4.2 billion appear to be under-funded and therefore less appealing to claimants who, notably, had the option to opt-out[98] and pursue litigation. Consequently, from the company's perspective, there was continued exposure to litigation[99] offering less 'finality' than desired. The company faced 90 different state court trials in the year 1995, some with overlapping dates, causing the company to conclude that defense was logistically and financially impossible. In response, on 15 May 1995, Dow Corning filed a voluntary petition for bankruptcy protection under Chapter 11 of the Bankruptcy Code. 'Unlike most debtors in bankruptcy, Dow Corning was fully solvent at the time it filed its bankruptcy case; it has remained so throughout the proceedings and has never disputed its ability to pay all its creditors. Rather, the purpose of the bankruptcy petition was to enable prompt and uniform settlement of the numerous breast-implant-related lawsuits pending against Dow Corning at the time of the petition.'[100]

3/45 The bankruptcy filing effectively removed the manufacturer from the MDL-926 settlement and started a whole new round of litigation with entirely separate, although sometimes related, legal issues. One of the vigorously litigated issues involved the potential liability and disputed insurance coverage of Dow Corning's two equal shareholders, Dow Holdings Inc. (a wholly owned subsidiary of Dow Chemical) and Corning Inc.[101]

---

97 In addition to silicone breast implants numbering in the thousands, Dow Corning also sold silicone gel to other breast implant manufacturers and manufactured other medical devices made of silicone including, for example, chin implants, and penile implants.

98 The New York Times reported on 5 August 1994, that 15,000 women opted out of the federal MDL-926 settlement (last visited 14 December 2013) <http://www.nytimes.com/1994/08/05/us/further-us-ban-of-breast-implants-is-urged.html>.

99 'Dow Corning abandoned a $ 4.2 billion global class action settlement when the number of women who stepped forward to collect under the agreement far exceeded the company's expectations.' *Higgins*, 84 ABAJ 53, 57 (1998).

100 *In re: Dow Corning Corporation, Official Committee of Unsecured Creditors, et al v Dow Corning Corporation, Dow Chemical Corporation and Corning Incorporated*, Nos 04-1608/1643/1720/1721/1722, p 2 (6th Cir 26 July 2006).

101 In an Opinion dated 8 May 1997, the 6th Circuit Court of Appeals issued a Writ of Mandamus ordering the District Court 'to transfer the claims against Dow Chemical and Corning Incorporated to the Eastern District of Michigan,' *In re: Dow Corning Corp*, 113 F 3d 565, 572 (6th Cir 1997). Approximately 14,000 cases were transferred pursuant to the Writ of Mandamus. *In re: Dow Corning Litigation*, Order Dismissing Cases Against Dow Chemical Co and Corning Incorporated, (ED Mich 2005). See also *E Caplan*, Milking the Dow, 29 Rutgers Law Journal 121 (1997).

The Dow Corning bankruptcy project was mammoth and a resolution was years in the making. In fact, some issues are still unresolved, including, for example, if and when the 'premium payments' envisioned by the Plan will be paid. After years of litigation, it has only recently been decided that a Dow Corning tissue expander[102] does qualify as a breast implant pursuant to the definition of 'breast implant' in the reorganisation plan.[103] The expander issue is a good example of the protracted nature of the litigation. After the District Court ruled in 2009 that tissue expanders are breast implants,[104] Dow Corning appealed the decision to the 6th Circuit Court of Appeals.[105] The Court of Appeals remanded the issue to the District Court for consideration of what it called 'a formidable dump' of extrinsic evidence in order to determine the intention of the parties when the Plan was drafted.[106] After examining the evidence, the District Court in 2013 concluded that the parties had intended tissue expanders to be included under the definition of 'breast implants'.[107] Thereafter, Dow Corning once again appealed to the 6th Circuit Court of Appeals. 3/46

Even more complex than the MDL-926 proceedings, the Dow Corning bankruptcy also included resolution of non-implant claims including, for example, those of physicians and health care providers who claimed that Dow Corning advertised that breast implants were safe but, instead, delivered unsafe products, as well as the US government, who claimed to have lost money through health care and pension payments to breast implant victims. The largest and 3/47

---

102 A tissue expander, generally saline filled, is implanted provisionally and is usually gradually enlarged in order to expand the breast tissue for a later more permanent implant.

103 Memorandum Opinion and Order Regarding Breast Tissue Expander Issue on Remand, *In re: Settlement Facility Dow Corning Trust*, Case No 00-00005, Docket No 924 (8 October 2013).

104 In its Memorandum Opinion and Order Regarding Tissue Expander Issue dated 10 June 2009, the District Court decided that tissue expanders fit the Plan's definition of 'breast implant'. *In re: Settlement Facility Dow Corning Trust*, Case No 00-00005, Docket No 673, 10 June 2009.

105 *In re: Settlement Facility Dow Corning Trust, Dow Corning Corporation v Claimants' Advisory Committee*, 628 F 3d 769 (Court 6th Cir, 17 December 2010).

106 In its Opinion dated 17 December 2010, the 6th Circuit Court of Appeals stated: 'Here, each party amassed a formidable dump of such evidence; and each side argues, in great detail, that its evidence shows that the other's interpretation would confound everyone's expectations as to what the Plan was supposed to mean ... The district court in this case ... is far-better equipped, not least in terms of background knowledge, to sort through that evidence and determine what is important.' (ibid, at 5). The 6th Circuit held that the term 'breast implant' as written was ambiguous, requiring the District Court to review the parties' extrinsic evidence, remanding the case to the District Court for this purpose (ibid, at 6). A petition for rehearing en banc to the 6th Circuit Court of Appeals was denied per Order dated 24 January 2011.

107 Memorandum Opinion and Order Regarding Breast Tissue Expander Issue on Remand, *In re: Settlement Facility Dow Corning Trust*, Case No 00-00005, Docket No 924 (8 October 2013).

most vociferous group of claimants was the silicone breast implant recipients, numbering 170,000.

3/48 Within the framework of the bankruptcy proceeding, Dow Corning made two settlement proposals, neither of which merited nor received the enthusiastic acceptance of the claimants. On 8 November 1998, after intense negotiation with the active intervention of court appointed Mediator Prof Francis McGovern,[108] a 'Joint Plan of Reorganisation' was proposed by the debtor Dow Corning together with the Official Committee of Tort Claimants,[109] which negotiated[110] on behalf of all personal injury claimants.

3/49 After some changes had been made, an Amended Joint Plan of Reorganisation (the Plan) establishing a $ 2.35 billion fund was filed with the Bankruptcy Court on 4 February 1999.[111] The Plan established 33 different classes,[112] only a few dealing with breast implants: Class 5 for domestic or US claimants, Class 6.1 for claimants in Europe, Class 6.2 for claimants in Asia, Africa or South America, and Class 7 'gel' or 'raw material' claimants, women who were implanted with silicone breast implants manufactured by a company other than Dow Corning but filled with silicone gel supplied by Dow Corning.[113]

3/50 Pursuant to the Plan, compensation is paid for rupture, explantation and disease. A Class 6.1 European claimant receives only 60% of the amount payable to a US claimant.[114] Amounts paid to Class 6.2 claimants are even more sharply limited at 35% of the domestic payment.[115]

3/51 In accordance with bankruptcy law, the plan was put to a vote class by class and more than the required number of classes, including Class 6.1 foreign

---

108 *In re: Dow Corning Corp*, Opinion Relating to Appeals From and Motions Regarding The Bankruptcy Court's November 30, 1999 Confirmation Order (hereinafter: Opinion Relating to Appeals From ... Confirmation Order) (ED Mich, 13 November 2000) at 9. See also Order Appointing Mediator, Case No 97-CV-00001-DT (ED Mich, 11 November 1997).

109 The Official Committee of Tort Claimants was appointed by the US Trustee pursuant to its authority per 11 USC §§ 1102 and 1103 to appoint various committees, *In re: Dow Corning Corp*, Opinion Relating to Appeals From ... Confirmation Order (fn 108) 8, 52.

110 The Bankruptcy Code at sec 1103(c) grants official creditors' committees broad authority in formulating a plan and performing 'such other services as are in the best interest of those represented'. 11 USC § 1103(c).

111 *In re: Dow Corning Corp*, Amended Joint Plan of Reorganization, (Bankr ED Mich, 4 February 1999).

112 *In re: Dow Corning Corp*, Opinion Relating to Appeals ... Confirmation Order (fn 108) at 69.

113 *In re: Dow Corning Corp*, Amended Joint Plan of Reorganization, (Bankr ED Mich, 4 February 1999) at 26.

114 Schedule III to Dow Corning Settlement Program and Claims Resolution Procedures, Annex A To Settlement Facility and Fund Distribution Agreement, Annex A-108.

115 Ibid.

claimants, voted in favour of the plan.[116] Hearings were held in Bankruptcy Court in 1999 addressing the fairness of the plan and the objections filed against the plan, including the objections of foreign claimants who generally contested their inequitable treatment compared to US claimants. Experts testified and the parties presented arguments; thereafter, the Bankruptcy Court confirmed the Plan on 30 November 1999.[117] In a separate opinion, the Court held that there was a legitimate reason for classifying breast implant claimants in three separate classes.[118]

Consistent with breast implant litigation's protracted history, the bankruptcy plan's confirmation was appealed to the US District Court. Numerous legal issues[119] were addressed on appeal including several appeals filed on behalf of foreign claimants. Following hearings in April 2000, District Court Judge Denise Page Hood affirmed the bankruptcy plan in a 168-page opinion on 13 November 2000.[120] 3/52

With reference to foreign claimants, Judge Hood held that the Bankruptcy Court's approval of the Plan's separate classification and disparate treatment of foreign claimants as compared to domestic claimants was not clearly erroneous for several reasons.[121] The Court acknowledged that both Class 6.1 and Class 6.2 3/53

---

116 *In re: Dow Corning Corp*, Opinion Relating to Appeals From ... Confirmation Order (fn 108) at 107.

117 *In re: Dow Corning Corp*, Confirmation Order (fn 108).

118 *In re: Dow Corning Corp*, Classification and Treatment Opinion, 244 BR 634, 658 (Bankr ED Mich 1999).

119 One of the major issues addressed by the appeal was the Bankruptcy Court's 21 December 1999's issuance of an opinion regarding the Joint Plan's release and injunction provision holding that the release and injunction provisions in the Amended Joint Plan apply only to claimants who had voted in favour of confirmation of the plan. *In re: Dow Corning Corp*, Opinion Relating to Appeals From ... Confirmation Order (fn 108) at 19. The Released Parties, according to §§ 8.3 and 8.4 of the Plan include the Settling Physicians, the Settling Health Care Providers, the Debtor-Affiliated Parties, the Shareholder-Affiliated Parties and Settling Insurers (ibid, at 33). Having earlier addressed this issue, the Sixth Circuit had ruled that the Court's § 1334(b) 'related to' jurisdiction did exist over the actions pending against the Shareholders, Dow Chemical and Corning Inc and the joint insurance policies between the Debtor and the Shareholders. *In re: Dow Corning Corp (Lindsey I)*, 86 F 3d 482, 494, 495 (6th Cir 1996). In November 2000, there were approximately 14,975 cases filed with the District Court against Dow Corning's Shareholders. *In re: Dow Corning Corp*, Opinion Relating to Appeals From ... Confirmation Order (fn 108) at 43. The District Court ruled that the Plan's release and injunction provisions are proper in this case, reversing the Bankruptcy Court's release and injunction provisions in its 21 December 1999 Opinion (ibid, at 45, 46, 69).

120 *In re: Dow Corning Corp*, Opinion Relating to Appeals From...Confirmation Order (fn 108).

121 Ibid, 107.

voted to accept[122] the Plan and noted that the Plan Proponents' experts credibly testified in the Bankruptcy Court to differences in the foreign legal systems that justify the different treatment of foreign claimants. '...[T]he Proponents have shown that verdict amounts, economic, cultural and legal differences between the countries support separate classifications of the foreign claimants in this case.'[123]

3/54 After appeals to the 6th Circuit Court of Appeals,[124] the reorganisation plan became 'Effective' on 1 June 2004,[125] ten years after the MDL-926 settlement plan had been approved by Judge Pointer.

3/55 The plan of reorganisation provided for the establishment of a settlement facility[126] (the Settlement Facility – Dow Corning Trust or SF-DCT), an entity charged with reviewing and paying claims pursuant to the plan. The reorganisation plan also provided for the establishment of a litigation facility.[127] Claimants who did not agree to the terms of the settlement could elect to proceed via litigation, provided the election was made within six months of the Effective Date.[128] Litigating claimants had to prove causation and medical research has not confirmed a causal link between silicone implants and systemic disease. Not surprisingly therefore, comparatively few claimants elected to litigate. A foreign claimant also had to consider the possibility that her claim would be referred to her home jurisdiction for trial pursuant to *forum non conveniens* principles.[129]

3/56 From a European claimant's perspective, the process of pursuing an individual claim is arduous and, even if successful, the compensation paid by the SF-DCT pursuant to the Plan is often 'too little, too late'.[130] As in the MDL-926

---

122 At least 66.7% of a class is needed to constitute an accepting class. 11 USC § 1126(c). 78.9% of Class 6.1 claimants voted to accept the Plan; Class 6.2 eventually also became an accepting class (ibid, at 107).

123 Ibid, at 120.

124 *In re: Dow Corning Corp*, 2002 FED App 0043P, p 12 (6th Cir 29 January 2002).

125 *In re: Dow Corning Corp*, Notice of (A) Confirmation and Effective Date of Amended Joint Plan of Reorganization, as Modified, (B) Discharge of Dow Corning and (C) Release and Injunction of Claims Against Certain Third Parties, Case No 94-20512 (Bankr ED Mich, 1 June 2004).

126 *In re: Dow Corning Corp*, Amended Joint Plan of Reorganization, (Bankr ED Mich 1999) at 28.

127 Ibid, 15.

128 Ibid, 38.

129 Ibid, 46 f.

130 The Plan provides for three possible avenues leading to compensation for a Class 6.1 Dow Corning silicone implant recipient. A base payment is made for proven rupture of a Dow Corning implant in the amount of $ 12,000.00. Additionally, there is a possible 'premium payment' that may be paid up to $ 3000.00. For removal of a Dow Corning silicone implant without replacement with another silicone implant, a separate and independent Explant payment of

proceeding, no compensation is paid until the proof of manufacturer is deemed acceptable according to the strict proof rules prescribed by the plan.[131] Strict deadlines for the submission of records to prove disease, explant and rupture are established by the SF-DCT pursuant to the Plan; many times it is impossible for claimants to obtain the records they need within the time limitations set by the SF-DCT. Some claimants only receive compensation after numerous submissions, arguments, and appeals to Error Correction, the Claims Administrator and sometimes even the appeals judge.[132]

The SF-DCT will accept claims from previously registered claimants until 3/57
3 June 2019. Thereafter, the facility will close but, if the past is any indication of the future, implantation of silicone breast implants will continue as will litigation addressing silicone breast implants.

Perhaps future litigation will address the safety of the relatively new nano- 3/58
technology[133] and the usage of nanomaterials in breast implants?[134]

III. Conclusion

Although imperfect, resolution of complicated litigation addressing numerous 3/59
intertwining clusters of complex issues involving a large number of claimants is, it seems, best reached via class action or another form of aggregate litigation. Individual trials of each silicone breast implant case would have rapidly de-

$ 3000.00 is made. For the presence of a proven disease or a group of symptoms as defined by the Plan, a separate payment is made to Class 6.1 claimants between $ 6000.00 and $ 180,000.00 depending upon the disease and the disability or severity level. Alternatively, in lieu of documenting the presence of disease or symptoms, Class 6.1 claimants may elect an expedited payment in the amount of $ 1200.00. See generally, Schedule III to Dow Corning Settlement Program and Claims Resolution Procedures, Annex A To Settlement Facility and Fund Distribution Agreement.

131 Schedule III to Dow Corning Settlement Program and Claims Resolution Procedures, Annex A To Settlement Facility and Fund Distribution Agreement, Annex A-7.

132 Ibid, Annex A-53, 54.

133 *T Fleischer/J Jahnel/S Seitz*, NanoSafety – Risk Governance of Manufactured Nanoparticles, European Parliament's Scientific and Technological Options Assessment Series (STOA 2012) (last visited 16 December 2013) <http://www.europarl.europa.eu/stoa/webdav/site/cms/shared/4_publications/Options%20Brief/STOA%20Options%20Brief%202012-06%20-%20Nanosafety.pdf >. See also *L Laska*, What Every Personal Injury Lawyer Should Know about Nanotechnology, Science & Law, September 2012, vol 48, no 9.

134 *Judit E Puskas/Matthew T Luebbers*, Breast Implants: the Good, the Bad and the Ugly. Can Nanotechnology Improve Implants? (2012) 4 WIREs Nanomedicine and Nanobiotechnology (Wiley Online Library) 153–168.

pleted the assets of the defendant companies due to the expense of discovery and trial, risking involuntary bankruptcies potentially leaving no assets with which to compensate the claimants. As exemplified by the silicone breast implant litigation, the aggregate litigation approach to resolution of mass tort claims promotes judicial economy by fusing discovery as well as settlement negotiations into one proceeding.

3/60 Looking at all the relevant factors, mass tort or aggregate litigation provides a legal framework for developing an algorithm or a tool for rapid processing and resolution of numerous similar claims vis-à-vis a single defendant or a group of defendants, providing all litigants with the possibility of moving on after resolution, leaving the burdensome litigation behind within a foreseeable time frame. At the same time, it frees the legal system from a panoply of individual trials.

3/61 Class action or any other form of aggregate litigation does provide the claimant with a rather uncomplicated access to justice and comparatively expeditious compensation of the claim at an affordable cost. On the other hand, it also enables the defendant to draw a perimeter or borderline around all the potential single cases he would otherwise be confronted with allowing definition of the extent of the problem and resulting potential exposure, permitting resolution of the controversy at one time thereby ensuring 'finality'.

Claudio Perrella

4 The 'Costa Concordia' Case

I. Foreword

The 'Costa Concordia' capsized on 13 January 2012, while carrying about 3,200 passengers and 1,000 crew members. The disaster is one of the worst in the cruise industry's recent history, and the largest marine insurance loss on record. The ship sailed too close to the coastline of the Il Giglio Island, and struck a rocky reef, known to locals as 'Le Scole', a few hundred yards out. Islanders said they had never seen the ship try to pass so close before. Ships usually pass by up to five miles away. 4/1

A 40-metre long gash was torn in the £ 370 million ship's hull, causing it to take on large quantities of water in minutes and list violently. The 4,200 passengers and crew were told to abandon ship. The Concordia capsized after the captain tried to turn around and head into the island's port in an apparent attempt to facilitate the evacuation. 4/2

In September 2013 the ship was rolled and pulled upright. The efforts of 430 professionals have successfully completed what has been called the most challenging salvage operation ever performed; rescue teams managed to stabilise the ship, which was anchored to underwater granite with four submarine anchor blocks and wires, each able to withstand a thousand-ton force. Twenty-five welders worked to reinforce the hull of the Concordia on the sea side, where the wires and hull projections used for stability and to pull up the vessel, were attached. 4/3

Once sea-ready, the ship will be pulled to a large and deep harbour located a convenient distance from the shipwreck site. This strategy has been used on a smaller scale but not with a ship of this size.[1] The 'one piece' approach – rather than slicing the ship up and barging it off bit by bit – aims to minimise environmental impact and to maximise safety. After the ship is removed, the sea bottom will be cleaned and marine flora replanted. 4/4

The loss sustained by the insurance industry is currently estimated at around € 1 billion. In addition to the total loss of the vessel's hull, for which US$ 500 million has already been paid as the sum insured, the P&I Club[2] and 4/5

---

1 Concordia is 950 feet long and weighs 44,612 metric tons.

2 P&I stands for Protection and Indemnity. P&I is insurance in respect of third party liability and expenses arising from owning ships or operating ships as principals. An insurance mutual, a Club, provides collective self insurance to its Members. The membership is comprised of a

the reinsurers are facing the impact of immense salvage costs. Originally estimated at US$ 230 million by the salvage firms, these costs have already more than doubled to over € 500 million at present.

II. The Wreck Removal Operations

4/6 The legal framework to which wrecks are subject is a combination of the coastal state's national legal framework and international maritime law, and there is often a lack of uniformity which can create confusion due to differences between jurisdictions and uncertainty over the geographical extent of responsibility. Under the 1976 Convention on Limitation of Liability for Marine Claims (LLMC) – which gives shipowners the right to limit their liability – states which ratified the Convention were given the option to opt out of the liability limitation regime in the case of wreck removals, and most ratifying states did so.

4/7 Statutory authorities in coastal states exercise great power in wreck removal, and political considerations usually have a significant impact on operations. Public concern for the protection of the environment appears to be greater than in the recent past, and in many parts of the world there is a zero tolerance approach towards ship-sourced pollution.

4/8 The International Maritime Organisation (IMO) recognised international legal inconsistencies in respect of wrecks, and encouraged the creation of a more uniform international legal framework through the 2007 IMO Convention on the Removal of Wrecks, adopted at a conference held in Nairobi, Kenya. The process of ratification is still underway. Over the last year, two further states have signed the Nairobi Wreck Removal Convention, bringing the number of signatories to eight, two fewer than the ten required for the Convention to enter into force.

4/9 The goal of the IMO Convention is to harmonise the approach of the various states to wrecks and the decision-making about whether wrecks should be removed.[3] It also intends to create a liability and compensation regime for the removal of wrecks, which is to be paid for by shipowners and their insurers. The Convention applies to a state's Exclusive Economic Zone which extends to 200 nautical miles from shore. States may choose to apply the Convention within their 12 nautical mile territorial waters, but may also apply their own domestic

---

common interest group who wish to pool their risks together in order to obtain insurance cover 'at cost'.

3 Article 2 of the Convention requires state response to be proportionate to the hazard and not to go beyond what is reasonably necessary.

law to those inshore waters. This may lead to inconsistency of approach as most wrecks that represent a hazard are likely to be within the 12 mile limit.

As regards the contractual background, wreck removal operations are chiefly conducted under commercial contracts that usually fall into the category of a lump sum or fixed price agreement – sometimes with staged payments according to progress – or a daily hire rate for the personnel, craft and equipment required to complete the job. The most widely used contracts have a standard form as produced by the shipping association, the Baltic and International Maritime Council (BIMCO). These are the daily hire contract, Wreckhire, and the lump sum contract, Wreckfixed, and its staged payment version, Wreckstage. **4/10**

Traditionally, daily hire contracts were considered potentially unfavorable to the insurer because of the risk of limited cost control associated with the open-ended nature of the arrangement. At the same time, fixed price contracts were considered risky for the contractor, since wreck removals are notoriously subject to uncertainties (namely bad weather which could extend the time of the job with no additional compensation for the contractor).[4] **4/11**

III. The Impact on the Local Industry and the Legal Issues at Stake

The carriage of passengers by sea is a sizable industry in Italy, which includes both ferry services between the mainland and the islands and pleasure cruises. In 2009, Italy overtook Greece, becoming the largest European industry with 92 million passengers. In the same year, Italy, Greece and Denmark accounted for more than 50% of passenger flux in the EU (22.9% Italy; 21.9% Greece and 10.8% Denmark). The Italian ports of Messina and Reggio di Calabria are among the ten busiest European ports, with more than 10 million passengers each.[5] **4/12**

Equally sizable is the pleasure cruise industry: according to reliable forecasts, in 2012 the number of passengers was in the region of 10,740,000, with 4,891 vessels calling on Italian ports.[6] **4/13**

---

4 The latest, 2010, edition of the BIMCO Wreckhire contract attempts to deal with these concerns by introducing a bonus incentive scheme, encouraging the contractor to complete the operation within agreed time limits.

5 Trasporto marittimo – Anni 2005–2009, Tavole di dati, 27 aprile 2011, Istat, Annuario statistico italiano, 2011 <www.istat.it/it/archivio/trasporti>.

6 Source: Seatrade Cruise Shipping Miami.

4/14 It is no surprise therefore that the accident was a real shock for the local industry, raising serious concerns about its short and long term impact. The legal issues at stake are numerous and complex: the liability regime applicable to the claims filed by passengers and third parties;[7] the possibility for the shipowners to invoke limitation of liability (and the regime applying to such limitation); the consequences arising from the possible spill of bunker and fuel oil on board, and the proliferation of civil actions against the cruise line company in court rooms around the world (and the validity of the forum selection clauses contained in passenger ticket contracts).

4/15 The implications and lessons to be learned from this accident are indeed far reaching and involve issues far beyond this case: international regulations applicable to the cruise industry, including for instance the ISM Code; the role of classification societies in approving cruise vessels for safety; cruise ship safety, including how they handle passenger training for emergency response. The position must necessarily be considered from the viewpoint of Italian law, because (this has been too easily and frequently forgotten or neglected in the aftermath of the accident) actions and claims are – and will be – first and principally brought against the owners of the ship, Costa Crociere Spa, a company based in Italy and established under Italian law.

IV. Liability Regime Applying to the Actions Brought by the Passengers

4/16 It has proven rather difficult and controversial to identify the liability regime applying to the actions which will be brought by the passengers and the relatives of the deceased. There are indeed three different theories:

4/17 The claims brought by passengers should be subject to the provisions of the International Convention on Travel Contracts (CCV) adopted in Brussels in 1970, ratified by Italy, and the Council Directive 90/314/EEC of 13 June 1990 on package travel, package holidays and package tours (equally enacted by Italy), since the incident occurred during a cruise included in a package offered by Costa. Costa Crociere in fact submitted to the passengers a package incorporating Costa's general terms and conditions, which in the 2012 edition refers to the provisions of the CCV 'unless there is a national or international regulation

7 Apart from the tragic toll of deaths and injuries, it is clear that the accident had several consequences on the economy of Giglio Island.

compulsorily applying to the stage or service during which the damage took place' (in other words, the CCV is referred to as a 'residual' regulation in case there is no mandatory domestic or international law applicable to the claim). The application of the CCV and the EU law and Italian legislation on package tours and travel contracts would be justified by the fact that although the accident took place during the sea transit, this was part of a cruise offering a vast array of activities (likely ranging – as is now normal on board mega cruise ships – from rock climbing to ice skating, and of course several excursions ashore), exposing passengers to risks which are only faintly related to the carriage by sea. If the claims were brought under the CCV, limitation of liability under art 13 would apply, namely 50,000 Germinal golden francs for cases of personal injury, equal today to around € 600,000, whilst limitation for loss or damage to baggage would be slightly less than € 24,000 per passenger.

In the aftermath of the event some commentators have considered the matter governed by the provisions of the Athens Convention[8] which established a comprehensive integrated system to govern the liability of cruise ship operators for personal injuries and property damage sustained by its passengers and contains standards for establishing liability and permissible defenses as well as its own statute of limitations and venue provisions. As part of this comprehensive system, the Athens Convention allows the carrier to limit its liability for passenger personal injury or death, but the carrier loses its right to limit liability where it is proven that the damage resulted from an act or omission committed with intent to cause damage or recklessly and with the knowledge that such damage would probably result. However, Italy was not a signatory of the Athens Convention 1974 and the following Protocol of 2002 at the time of the accident. 4/18

The applicability of the liability and limitation regime of the 2002 Protocol has been argued in light of the following. The essential provisions contained in the Athens Convention as amended by the 2002 Protocol have been transposed in EU Regulation (EC) No 392/2009, which was adopted in order to overcome the delay by several Member States in ratifying the Athens Convention and which introduced an effective system in respect of the liability of carriers of passengers by sea in the event of accidents. Pursuant to its art 12, the Regulation 'shall ap- 4/19

8 Athens Convention relating to the Carriage of Passengers and their Luggage by Sea (PAL) adopted on 13 December 1974, entered into force on 28 April 1987; the 2002 Protocol was adopted on 1 November 2002 and will enter into force on 23 April 2014. The Convention was designed to consolidate and harmonise two earlier Brussels conventions dealing with passengers and luggage (adopted in 1961 and 1967 respectively) and was primarily motivated by a series of uninsured ferry disasters, but the Convention has so far had limited success and the number of States which have ratified it is limited.

ply from the date of the entry into force of the Athens Convention for the Community, and in any case from no later than 31 December 2012'. Following Council Decision dated 12 December 2011, the Union has deposited its instrument of accession to the Athens Protocol on 31 December 2011, and has required Member States to take the necessary steps to deposit the instruments of ratification of, or accession to, the Athens Protocol within reasonable time (if possible by 31 December 2011).

4/20 However, several states, including Italy, have not ratified the Protocol and, lacking such a ratification, it seems very unlikely that the question of liability in the Costa Concordia accident could indeed be regulated by the Athens Protocol. The consequences of the applicability of the 2002 Protocol and/or EU Regulation (EC) No 392\2009 would be significant. EU Regulation 392/2009, under art 3 'Liability and insurance' makes a reference to arts 3 to 16 of the Athens Convention, which follow the 'two-tier system' adopted by the Montreal Convention on international carriage by air. As regards damage to passengers, a carrier is liable unless he can prove that the event was not caused by an act of war, hostility, civil war, civil unrest or natural phenomena of an exceptional, inevitable and irresistible character or was solely caused by the act or willful omission of a third party. If the extent of the damage arising from a maritime loss exceeds 250,000 Special Drawing Rights (to a maximum of 400,000 SDR), the carrier is only liable for negligence. As regards damage to passengers arising from an event other than a 'shipping incident', a carrier's liability is always, whatever the amount of the damage, negligent within the ceiling of 400,000 SDR and the burden of proving the negligence on the part of the carrier rests on the passenger.[9]

4/21 Finally, according to some claimants, Italian law (ie Italian Navigation Code) should apply in consideration of the fact that the accident took place on board a ship flying the Italian flag and inside Italian territorial waters and the fact that the package tour was booked with an Italian-based company. In this case there would be no limitation of liability for death or injuries (because the Code does not contain a provision limiting the amount of damages which can be awarded in favour of a passenger or his/her relatives in case of death or injury), but a very low limitation of liability for loss of baggage (€ 6.20 per kilo of goods lost or damaged).

9 Athens Convention 2002 forbids the signatories from setting limits lower than 400,000 SDR, or from allowing the parties to an agreement setting a lower limit, but admits that the limit can be increased. This can take place either through specific provisions of national law, which could set a higher ceiling or eliminate it altogether (art 7.2) or through a specific written agreement between carrier and passenger (art 10).

Furthermore, it should be considered that the limitations set out by the CCV and/or 2002 Protocol could be disregarded by the Italian courts if the judge considered that the Italian Navigation Code should apply excluding the provisions of the aforesaid Conventions, especially if this would allow an award of higher damages. The position reached by the Italian courts over the last two decades as regards compensation for death or serious injuries is towards a progressive increase of the amount of compensatory damages, and it is not uncommon now that the sums awarded considerably exceed the limits applicable under the CCV or Athens Protocol. 4/22

Finally, it is worth mentioning that clauses excluding or limiting liability are considered potentially unfair by Italian law, and subject to specific and strict conditions of validity: pursuant to art 1341 *Codice Civile* (CC), similar clauses must be referred to in an ad hoc clause at the end of the contract or the general terms and conditions, and must be specifically approved and accepted; moreover, several clauses of this kind are void if contained in contracts with consumers. 4/23

In light of the above, it seems likely that claims which are brought on behalf of passengers injured or killed will argue the applicability of Italian law to the accident, seeking compensation beyond the limitation set out by the Conventions. 4/24

V. Damage Assessment for Bodily Injury in Italian Case Law

Over the last twenty years the amount of damages awarded for bodily injury cases in Italy has been constantly increasing. The courts have added to pecuniary damages a (often rather confusing) array of non-pecuniary damages, and the class of parties entitled to claim non-pecuniary damages in the case of the death of a relative has been substantially expanded. 4/25

The Italian Supreme Court, however, recently handed down a couple of landmark rulings aimed at reorganising the subject matter and ensuring legal certainty and uniformity. It emphasised that, while the courts must take into account the factual circumstances and relevant case law when assessing damages according to equity (in accordance with art 1226 CC), the criteria enshrined in the tables drafted and updated by the court of Milan must also be applied nationwide. 4/26

According to these criteria, following the death of a relative, claimants may seek compensation for non-pecuniary damage which could easily be in excess 4/27 of 400,000 SDR (around € 460,000). Ruling no 26972 of 2008[10] sets the foundations for a new unitary notion of non-pecuniary damage, which, according to the Supreme Court, can only be claimed if the law explicitly states so, which means:

- when the tortious act is also a felony,
- when the law expressly allows compensation for non-pecuniary damage,
- when the tortious act constitutes a serious violation of rights affirmed at constitutional level.

4/28 More recently, in order to reduce uncertainty, the Supreme Court ruled that, when determining damages, the courts must take into account the circumstances in fact and the relevant case law,[11] and may assess the damages according to equity (pursuant to art 1226 CC) but the criteria in the tables drafted and updated by the Court of Milan should be adopted throughout the country.

4/29 According to these criteria, in the case of the death of a relative, claimants are entitled to seek compensation for non-pecuniary damage which could very easily be in excess of 400,000 SDR. When claims are brought by foreign nationals, a classic issue is the proof of reciprocity pursuant to art 16 of the 'General provisions' (so-called *preleggi*) of the Italian Civil Code. Article 16 states that: 'The foreign national enjoys the same civil rights as the citizen upon condition of reciprocity and exception made for provisions contained in specific legislation'.

4/30 Italian case law has long established that the exercise of civil rights by a foreign national is conditional upon the proof of reciprocity (if challenged in Court). However, the Italian Supreme Court has progressively reduced the scope of art 16, especially when dealing with mental and bodily integrity or with inalienable rights, such as the right to health and to equitable compensation. Italian case law now no longer requires proof of reciprocity from EU citizens[12] and foreign nationals legally residing in the territory of the Republic. Recently the *Cassazione*[13] stated that the condition of reciprocity can only be required with regard to non-fundamental rights, since fundamental rights such as life, health

---

10 Corte di Cassazione (Cass) 11 November 2008, no 26972, *Alfonsi v Sartori*, Responsabilità e risarcimento 2008, fasc 11, 14; Nuova giurispurdenza civile (Nuova giur civ) 2009, I, 102; Assicurazioni 2008, II, 2, 439; Diritto e giurisprudenza 2008, 526; Nuova giur civ comm 2009, I, 102; Danno e responsabilità 2009, 19; Corriere giuridico (Corr giur) 2009, 48.

11 Cass 7 June 2011, no 12408, *Pantaleo v Rana*, Foro italiano (Foro it) 2011, I, 2274; Corr giur 2011, 1075; Guida al diritto 2011, fasc 26, 17; Nuova giur civ 2011, I, 1058.

12 Corte di Appello Venezia, 9 June 2004, Foro it 2005, I, 550.

13 Cass 11 January 2011, no 450, *LA v Italiana Assicurazioni*, Foro it 2011, I, 394; Corr giur 2011, 495; Archivio giuridico della circolazione e dei sinistri stradali (Arch circolaz) 2011, 291.

and bodily integrity are enshrined in the Constitution and must be guaranteed regardless of nationality.

Italian case law has furthermore tackled the issues related to the need to take into account the social and economic situation of the victim when determining damages, and to consider the cost of living in the country where the claimants is domiciled if the action is brought by a foreign citizen. The Supreme Court[14] held that: 'the purpose of damages is to indemnify the victim for the suffering arising from the tortious act and if the compensation that can derive from a certain amount of money varies depending on how the money is used, then the amount awarded must vary and not the compensation'. Recently the Court of Turin held that the need to provide equal compensation to all victims cannot be satisfied by awarding the same amount of money to all of them, regardless of the financial situation of the victim, since this would entail an unjust enrichment of victims living in countries where prices are lower or where the economy is less prosperous. 4/31

VI. Costa's Right to Limitation of Liability

Pursuant to art 7 of the Italian Navigation Code, limitation of liability is regulated by the law of the ship's flag. The ship was flying under the Italian flag, the owners (Costa Crociere Spa) are an Italian company, the accident took place inside Italian territorial waters, and there is little doubt therefore that limitation of liability (and Costa Crociere Spa is likely preparing the application) would be regulated by Italian law. Italy has not ratified the 1957 and 1976 Conventions or the 1996 Protocol (the ratification procedure was started some time ago, but has not been completed yet); hence, the Italian Navigation Code will apply. The system (set out by art 275 of the Navigation Code) is peculiar, and there are quite a few significant differences between Italian law and the Conventions. 4/32

First of all, limitation under Italian law is afforded only to the operator (*armatore*, in Italian) whilst the Conventions extend the limitation to other parties involved (eg manager, charterer and Master). Secondly, the Italian Navigation Code provides for an 'all inclusive' system, since it extends the limitation to all acts or events which occur during the voyage (including, for instance, salvage awards, or removal of wreck charges, and liability claims for the injured and dead passengers), whilst the Conventions exclude several sources of liability and the damages arising from limitation. A major difference exists in respect of 4/33

---

14 Cass 14 February 2000, no 1637, *Ranalli v Nuova Maa assicurazione*, Rivista giuridica di circolazione e trasporto 2000, 732.

the calculation of the limitation fund. Under Italian law, the fund is based on the value of the ship, not on her tonnage. In order to limit liability, the operator of the ship must establish a limitation fund by way of actual payment of a sum to the court; the amount is equal to two-fifths of the sound value of the ship (plus the ship's earnings at the end of the voyage), but if the value of the ship at the time when the limitation is applied for is lower than one-fifth of the sound value, then the limitation fund is equal to one-fifth. In other words, in the case of total loss, the fund will coincide with one-fifth of the sound value of the ship, whilst if the ship is rescued and her value is above two-fifths of the sound value, two-fifths of this value will be the limit. Finally, under Italian law, limitation is excluded in case of fraud or gross negligence of the operator.

4/34 It is well known that the Captain (Schettino) has been under house arrest for a long time and faces criminal charges for manslaughter and for abandoning the ship, because there is clear evidence that he left the cruise liner before all the passengers were evacuated ashore; furthermore, the Italian Prosecutor has qualified Captain Schettino's behaviour as 'reckless and inexcusable' in performing a very risky manoeuvre sailing too close to the coast. The recklessness of the Captain in principle does not prevent Costa Crociere from benefiting from the limitation clause but, under Italian law, owners are prohibited from invoking limitation in the case of 'gross negligence' (*colpa grave*), which does not coincide at all with the recklessness required by the LLMC[15], and implies a degree of negligence far less severe. Whilst in fact the LLMC provides for a virtually unbreakable system of limitation of liability, and a party will be unable to limit liability only if 'it is proved that the loss resulted from his personal act or omission, committed with the intent to cause such a loss, or recklessly and with knowledge that such loss would probably result', under Italian law the owners may lose the right to limit liability if there was a clear breach of the duty of control and management on their part. This explains why it has become so important to understand whether the cruise ship intentionally deviated from its original course and whether (in spite of Costa Crociere's allegations) it was common practice for the Costa Concordia to deviate from its original route and to sail dangerously close to Giglio Island, and whether the so-called 'flyby' or 'showboating' was part of Costa's promotional policy.

15 Convention on Limitation of Liability for Maritime Claims (LLMC Convention), done in London, enacted on 19 November 1976 and entered into force in 1986.

VII. Class Actions and Punitive Damages

Costa Cruises, the shipping company which operated the Concordia, initially offered survivors a 30% discount on future cruises as compensation. The proposal was immediately dismissed and unanimously branded 'insulting'. Costa then put forward a new offer. Unharmed passengers were to receive € 11,000 (approx US$ 14,250) in compensation for items lost and psychological damage, as well as a further sum of € 3,000 to reimburse the costs incurred after the disaster. 4/35

An agreement was reached with virtually all the Italian consumer associations. Similar agreements were also reached in other countries, such as the United Kingdom and France, where settlement has proved more complex and time-consuming than expected by Costa. 4/36

Costa had originally set a very tight deadline for acceptance of its offer and passengers were expected to make their decision by February 2012, that is, within one month of the accident. This deadline was extended when the *Fédération Nationale des Victimes d'Attentats & d'Accidents Collectifs* (FENVAC – National Federation of the Victims of Catastrophes), which represented a large number of passengers, claimed that the deadline was too close and unreasonable. 4/37

It is worth noting that the sums Costa agreed to pay exceed the average compensation which have been awarded by Italian courts over the last decade for claims brought by unharmed passengers against travel organisers for breach of travel contract (so-called claims for 'ruined holidays'). On the other hand, the Costa Concordia disaster is an exceptional case, and the shipping company no doubt preferred to settle the vast majority of claims arising from this accident as quickly as possible. The more serious cases have already been brought to court in Italy and other countries, particularly the US. 4/38

Despite the many settlements, numerous claims for compensation are still pending. Most of the pending claims have been filed by passengers who were injured in the accident: many had to jump from the ship and swim ashore in cold water and total darkness. Some suffered physical injuries, while others are claiming psychological injuries, such as post-traumatic stress disorder (PTSD), nightmares or flashbacks. A number of these passengers claim that the evacuation was chaotic, with crew members giving contradictory instructions and the captain delaying the evacuation order for a full hour after the accident. 4/39

Three members of the crew filed a lawsuit seeking to annul their settlement agreement. They allege that they had signed the agreement at a time when they were vulnerable, psychologically impaired and in financial straits. They also claim that Costa implied that crew members would only remain employed if 4/40 they agreed to the settlement. In early 2013, one family received an indemnity of € 22,000 per passenger: double the amount offered by Costa following the disaster. The sum of € 22,000 has been confirmed by Costa. This could well prompt further claims for indemnification and an attempt to invalidate the settlements which have already been accepted.

4/41 A class action has been filed in the US[16] seeking larger compensation amounts and the award of punitive damages. The complaint, alleging negligence and breach of contract, was filed in federal court in Chicago by Gary Lobaton, a member of the Costa Concordia crew who is seeking class-action status to represent all victims of the disaster. The claimant alleges that 'the defendants failed to properly and timely notify all plaintiffs on board of the deadly and dangerous condition of the cruise ship as to avoid injury and death' and that the passengers and crew 'were abandoned by the Captain'.

4/42 To substantiate their claims, other passengers have argued that the ship's design was defective: Carnival Corp and the Costa Concordia's engineers allegedly neglected security reservations when designing the ship in order to accommodate more passengers (and generate higher earnings). This made evacuation following the accident more difficult. These product liability claims not only concern damages for passengers several times higher than the settlement offered by Costa Cruises, but also the award of punitive damages totalling hundreds of millions of US dollars. From the plaintiffs' point of view, the advantage of arguing an allegedly faulty design is that it makes it easier to justify the jurisdiction of US courts.

4/43 It is proving difficult however to elude the enforceability of the forum selection clause in the passenger tickets (providing for the jurisdiction of the Court of Genoa) and the possibility to direct the claim against Carnival bypassing Costa Crociere Spa and Italian jurisdiction, in light of the position already expressed by the US Supreme Court[17] which held that United States federal courts will enforce forum selection clauses so long as the clause is not unreasonably burdensome to the party seeking to escape it, and passes the test for judicial fairness. The lawsuit, which also names Costa Crociere Spa, seeks damages up to $ 100 million in punitive damages.

4/44 It is worth noting in this respect that Italian courts (in the leading case *Parrott v Fimez Spa*) have expressed the view that private lawsuits brought by

---

16 *Lobaton v Carnival Corp*, 12-cv-598, United States District Court, Northern District of Illinois (Chicago).

17 *Carnival Cruise Lines, Inc v Shute*, 499 United States Supreme Court Reports (US) 585, 111 Supreme Court Reporter (S Ct) 1522, 113 US S Ct Lawyers' Edition, Second Series (L Ed 2d) 622 (1991).

injured people must aim at obtaining compensation for a loss, and allowing separate awards intended to punish the defendant is contrary to public policy. The case was decided by the Court of Appeal of Venice, by a judgment confirmed by the Supreme Court,[18] refusing the enforcement and recognition of a judgment of the District Court of Jefferson County, Alabama, rendered in a tort case, where an Italian manufacturer had been ordered to pay $ 1,000,000 in punitive damages having allegedly caused the death of the plaintiff's son who was involved in a road accident, due to a defect in the design of the buckle of the crash helmet that he was wearing. The US Court did not specify the apportionment of compensatory and punitive damages against the Italian defendants, and the Court of Appeal of Venice concluded that the award was punitive in nature, and therefore contrary to domestic public policy. A very recent decision of the Italian *Cassazione*[19] has confirmed that judgments awarding punitive damages are non-enforceable in Italy, because they are contrary to public policy. The Court of Appeal of Turin had granted the enforcement in Italy of a judgment of the Supreme Court of Cambridge, Massachusetts, ordering an Italian company to pay damages up to $ 8 million in favour of an employee who had suffered serious injuries following an accident which had occurred at the defendant's US subsidiary. The Court of Appeal of Turin had considered the reasonability and fairness of the quantum awarded in favour of the plaintiff in consideration of the seriousness of the injuries suffered by the employee, with no consideration though of the criteria traditionally adopted by Italian courts when assessing and awarding compensatory damages, and despite the fact that the US decision did not contain any indication of the criteria for the quantification. The Italian defendants appealed the enforcement order, and the Supreme Court overturned the ruling on the grounds that the US decision awarded punitive damages and the Italian civil liability system is strictly compensatory, not punitive.

Whilst the position on punitive damages now seems rather clear-cut, it is 4/45 worth noting that an approach sometimes adopted by Italian courts is to grant enforcement of compensatory damages, refusing however the enforcement of punitive elements. An interesting decision in this respect is the judgment of the Court of Appeal of Trieste[20] where the Court was requested to grant a conserva-

---

18 Cass 19 January 2007, no 1183 *Parrott v Soc Fimez*, Massimario 2007, 486; Nuova giur civ 2007, I, 981; Rivista di diritto internazionale privato e processuale (Riv dir internaz priv e proc) 2007, 777; Foro it 2007, I, 1460; Appello Venezia, 15 October 2001, Riv dir internaz priv e proc 2002, 1021; Nuova giur civ 2002, I, 765.

19 Cass 8 February 2012, no 1781/2012 *Soc Ruffinatti v Oyola-Rosado*, Foro it 2012, I, 1449.

20 Court of Trieste, 3 December 2009, *DTFT v Ayhan Nakliyat Sanayi Ve Ticaret AS*.

tory arrest aimed at securing the recovery of a claim awarded in a Turkish judgment. The Trieste Court ruled that the decision of the Court of Istanbul was indeed enforceable, save for the part where the judgment had awarded interest which would have been usurious under Italian law. The Court therefore granted the arrest up to the amount equalling the capital sum on the grounds that the plaintiffs would subsequently seek the enforcement of the Turkish judgment for capital alone, leaving interest aside. Hence, any judgment including punitive damages against Costa Crociere Spa would face serious problems during enforcement, and the exequatur would face an uphill battle.

VIII. The Possible Damage to the Environment Arising from the Spill of Bunker Oil

4/46 The risk of damage to the environment arising from the spill of the bunker oil on board caused great concern because Giglio Island is a place of great beauty and a wildlife sanctuary. Most of the bunker oil on board was luckily removed in the aftermath of the accident.

4/47 The fuel represents a substantial pollution hazard – in many cases the greatest pollution threat. A fully-fuelled vessel may carry thousands of tonnes of fuel. Salvors may be engaged on a specific ad hoc contract – often a BIMCO Wreckhire contract suitably amended – to remove the bunkers, with the operation undertaken in parallel with the main wreck removal. The primary concern is that there should be no spillage during the operation, which can be delicate and complicated and may require rigging of temporary pipe work and fuel heating systems. In modern salvage, contractors may use 'hot tapping' (drilling into the fuel tanks from the exterior and inserting probes and hoses to extract the pollutant).[21]

4/48 Pollution caused by the spill of the bunker oil would trigger the applicability of the provisions of the Bunker Oil Convention 2001, ratified by Italy on 2010. The Convention (modelled on the International Convention on Civil Liability for Oil Pollution Damage, 1969) was adopted to ensure that adequate, prompt, and effective compensation is available in the case of damage caused by spills of oil, when carried as fuel in ships' bunkers. The Convention applies to damage caused on the territory, including the territorial sea, and in exclusive economic

21 The cost of bunker fuel removal from a wreck lies with the ship owner's P&I Club and can form a large part of the incurred cost of dealing with a wreck.

zones of States which are parties to the Convention, and requires ships over 1,000 gross tonnage to maintain insurance or other financial security, such as the guarantee of a bank or similar financial institution, to cover the liability of the registered owner for pollution damage. A key provision (art 7.10) is the possibility for direct action, which would allow a claim for compensation for pollution damage to be brought directly against the insurer or other person providing financial security for the registered owner's liability. In such a case the defendant may invoke the defences (other than bankruptcy or winding up of the ship owner) which the ship owner would have been entitled to raise, including limitation pursuant to art 6.

However, there might be a potential problem of inconsistency between the provisions of the Bunker Oil Convention 2011 and the limitation of liability as set out under Italian law because, pursuant to art 6 of the Bunker Oil Convention: 'Nothing in this Convention shall affect the right of the ship owner and the person or persons providing insurance or other financial security to limit liability under any applicable national or international regime, such as the Convention on Limitation of Liability for Maritime Claims, 1976, as amended'. Hence, there is an explicit reference to the LLMC system of limitation, while – as illustrated above – the Italian system differs considerably from the Convention, and its limitation based on the ship's value could have the effect that limitation under Italian law is substantially lower than the limitation under the LLMC. 4/49

Overall, the quality of the water around the half-submerged ship has not been significantly polluted, according to Tuscany's Regional Agency for Environmental Protection, which is in charge of monitoring the site. 4/50

Otto Ernst Krasney*

5 Ombudsman for the Victims of the Rail Accident at Eschede on 3 June 1998

I. Appointment of the Ombudsman

The idea of appointing an ombudsman for the victims of large-scale accidents was not new, but, as far as we can see, it had previously not actually been done in Germany. There was therefore a lack of usable experience to draw on following the rail accident at Eschede. 5/1

The Deutsche Bahn AG (DB) decided to appoint an ombudsman immediately after the Eschede accident.[1] It was not possible for an ombudsman to be appointed other than by DB (the tortfeasor and the party liable to pay any compensation), for example by the injured and bereaved, both because of the need to move quickly and for practical reasons – at the time, the names of all of the victims, and notably their addresses, were not known. Even later, they would not have been able to find a common candidate in the short time available. 5/2

However, consideration needs to be given to finding a way of allaying victims' fears that an ombudsman appointed by the company from which compensation would be sought following an accident might be a 'company man', for example by having the ombudsman formally appointed by an impartial person (eg the prime minister of the state, a bishop or the president of a court). 5/3

II. Responsibilities of the Ombudsman

In the initial meetings with the then Chairman of DB, Johannes Ludewig, on the responsibilities of the ombudsman and the resources to be placed at his disposal, it was agreed that the ombudsman should be a point of contact for victims (both the injured and the bereaved) on any issues of concern to them. In particular, the ombudsman's area of responsibility was not to be confined merely to the role of adjudicator on the amount and extent of any financial compensation in individual disputes. Instead, he was also responsible for making proposals for support, 5/4

* The translation of this contribution from German into English was not carried out by the author.

1 For further information on the Eschede ombudsman see: *M Reiter*, Eschede und danach. Erfahrungen aus der Arbeit des Ombudsmannes der Deutschen Bahn (2005).

and offering and providing it after consulting the company. It was agreed that the ombudsman would attach particular importance to the provision of psycho-social treatment and psychological and psycho-social after-care for victims. An initial sum of DM 5 million was placed at his disposal to provide support and all-round psycho-social treatment and care for victims.

5/5 If an ombudsman has already been appointed independently of any large-scale accident having occurred, one of his first responsibilities should be to assist with one of the most important tasks, namely care for the injured and the bereaved at the scene of the accident – this also helps to build up a relationship of trust with them.

5/6 The next DB Chairman, Hartmut Mehdorn, gave his full support to the ombudsman.

III. Position of the Ombudsman

5/7 The DB Board agreed that the ombudsman would naturally not be subject to any general or specific instructions from DB. However, outside his own organisational structure, the ombudsman likewise was not empowered to take decisions on compensation or give instructions relating to it to DB staff. The ombudsman was not to have any general authority to issue instructions or take decisions that could draw him from the outset into the often inevitable difficulties surrounding the determination of compensation in individual cases, as this could have quickly impaired the victims' trust in his role. The ombudsman was to discuss fundamental issues with DB's Board, who would then communicate its decisions within DB. He discussed any problems with individual cases first with the staff responsible at DB. If the matter could not be resolved, which was seldom the case in view of the Board's general instructions to their staff to be as supportive as possible, it was referred to the Board after discussion with the Head of the Legal Department, Margret Suckale, or the Chairman, Johannes Ludewig and later his successor, Hartmut Mehdorn.

5/8 The ombudsman himself took the necessary decisions relating to the important task of arranging for and providing psychological treatment and psycho-social after-care for the victims and the bereaved. He was provided with the organisational and (substantial) financial means required to do so. He received assistance from a number of specialists at DB, notably psychologists in the company's management, though the psychological examinations, treatment and after-care were performed exclusively by independent practising psychologists. A suitably qualified university faculty was contracted to assist with this work. It was not only the large number of victims and the consequent public interest and loss of confidence in DB's high technology that led to the company appointing an ombudsman.

It was also the personal experiences of the Board members at the scene of 5/9
the accident on the day it occurred that led them to want to do everything within their power to at least mitigate the suffering of those affected.

IV. The Work of the Ombudsman

A. Extensive Personal Assistance

As point of contact for all of the injured and bereaved, the ombudsman was 5/10
called upon to provide help in a wide variety of areas. Not only was initial financial support needed, but also help with many practical and personal problems such as organising travel to visit close relatives who had been injured, especially for disabled or old people, help with looking after young children whilst their mother was visiting their father, and moving patients to hospitals nearby or even to where they lived. An important aspect of the help provided proved to be the intense personal contact starting with the initial discussions, which made the injured and the bereaved feel that they had not been left alone in their suffering.

B. Offer of Legal Aid and Community of Interests

In view of the fact that the Ombudsman had been appointed by DB, to create a 5/11
relationship of trust it was decided to offer victims the possibility of obtaining legal advice at DB's expense. The aim was to avoid any impression that their right to legal advice had been limited in any way and that only advice from the ombudsman was free of charge. The lawyers instructed by the victims generally provided invaluable help in assessing their claims.

At the memorial service for the victims, a relative of a victim who had died 5/12
had distributed a list for victims, their relatives or the bereaved to enter their names if they wished to become members of a community of interests for the victims of the accident. The ombudsman was then asked to provide the community of interests with the names and addresses of all of the injured and the bereaved. The ombudsman was unable to comply with the request for reasons of data protection, but advised all of the injured and the bereaved of the existence of the community of interests in two letters.

C. Psychological Help and Treatment

5/13 Initially – not just for data protection reasons – psychological care could only be offered to the victims by the ombudsman in writing. Questionnaires, produced by specialists not employed by DB with the help of the university, were attached and the responses, which were sent exclusively to the ombudsman, were used to establish the medical and psychological findings. Only when the written consent of those concerned had been obtained did the psychologists offer treatment. There were problems due not only to the reluctance of many to accept that they needed treatment, but also to not infrequent resistance on the part of relatives and regrettably of not a few doctors. However, the victims who were not prepared to agree to any treatment and/or care were assured that they could request it at any time if they changed their minds. The early examination of victims and their subsequent treatment proved invaluable in helping them to deal with the traumatic burden they had to bear.

5/14 The psycho-social after-care was provided in local groups in the presence of psychologists. The care did not constitute actual treatment, but support for the injured and bereaved in dealing with their trauma. It proved necessary to have separate groups for the injured and the bereaved as far as possible. The psycho-social aftercare was from the outset not intended to be provided indefinitely, though no specific time limit was set. Most of the groups were in existence for around two years.

5/15 The psycho-social after-care also encompassed work trial periods including support when starting a new job and help with all the formalities people had to go through.

5/16 Another issue was the need for psychological support, especially when the luggage held by the police was handed over to the bereaved relatives. In most cases, the severe damage caused to the luggage by the violence of the accident and the objects it contained painfully brought back memories of the lost loved ones.

5/17 Finally, the building of a memorial has helped the bereaved in coming to terms with their grief. The artistic design of the memorial took account both of the personal feelings of the people affected, most of whom live in southern Germany, and its location in northern Germany.

D. Help for the Helpers

5/18 Psychological treatment and psycho-social care was also given to the many local people from Eschede and members of the fire service and other rescue workers who provided help following the accident. A special office was set up for this purpose in cooperation with the Lower Saxony authorities.

E. Compensation for People Affected

The victims were not referred to DB's liability insurers for financial compensa- 5/19
tion. DB's own liability group assessed each case on its merits and determined the amount. There was close consultation with the ombudsman on principles and the detail of decisions. Meetings were held daily in the first few weeks to enable provisional payments to be made quickly. Differences of opinion with victims on compensation were regularly resolved not through lengthy written correspondence, but through personal discussions with the people concerned at their place of residence. Standard compensation for damaged luggage and possessions was paid with no need to provide proof. This procedure enabled the financial compensation paid to the injured and the bereaved (which was never the subject of legal action relating either to the amount or the way it was determined, with the exception of the test case mentioned below brought by relatives on the amount of damages for pain and suffering) to play a not inconsiderable role in helping people to come to terms with the accident.

This decidedly does not happen in cases where liability is disputed for a 5/20
long time after an accident. To eliminate this problem as far as possible, it was agreed with DB at a very early stage that victims would receive compensation as if DB were liable for the accident without DB acknowledging such liability. The main effect of this was that damages for pain and suffering could be paid which, according to the law at the time, victims could only have claimed in cases of culpable liability.

Damages for pain and suffering for the injured were based on the severity of 5/21
the consequences of their injuries. The rates that had been generally used in past cases – usually the upper limit – were applied. We cannot be totally certain of the overall amount of damages for pain and suffering paid to the injured. Only the total amount of compensation was specified in many cases where there were differences between the injured and DB on individual components of the compensation, but agreement on the total amount.

According to legal practice, damages for pain and suffering are only 5/22
awarded to bereaved relatives if the loss of a close relative has caused them to suffer psychological damage themselves. To avoid the need for lengthy assessments by experts and the possible subsequent disputes, it was agreed with DB that, for close relatives within a family unit, it would generally be accepted that such psychological damage had been incurred, with no examination by a spe-

cialist being required. However, one difficulty was the question of whether standard damages for pain and suffering should be payable to all of the bereaved or whether they should be based on the degree of impact, notably on the actual role the deceased had played in their lives. In the end, standard damages for pain and suffering of DM 30,000 were assumed for all concerned. At that time, in cases where courts had awarded damages for pain and suffering to bereaved people at all, amounts of between DM 5,000 and DM 10,000 had been considered appropriate. A test case brought by the community of interests with the aim of achieving higher damages for pain and suffering was unsuccessful.

5/23 By the end of 2004, DB had paid out a total of € 30 million in compensation and damages for pain and suffering.

V. Conclusion

5/24 Experience has shown that appointing an ombudsman for the victims of an accident (the injured and the bereaved) can be of considerable help not only to the victims, but also to the liable company. It therefore seems advisable not just to use an adjudicator to decide on disputes over the amount of financial compensation, but to appoint an ombudsman, whose role extends far beyond that.

5/25 The ombudsman's responsibilities should include the organisation and provision of psychological treatment and psycho-social care and aftercare, and personal support in the wide range of situations that arise. Undertakings in which accidents at some time in the future appear inevitable would be well advised to make general use of an ombudsman to look after accident victims rather than waiting until a large-scale accident occurs. The pain and suffering of the victims and their need for help and care are there, irrespective of how many victims there are in a particular case. Indeed, a single victim feels more alone and lost than victims in a community with others. In addition, only an ombudsman already in place can care for victims at the scene of the accident. DB has therefore appointed a permanent ombudsman.

Hermes Marangos

6 International Environmental Mass Litigation in the UK

I. Introduction

Oil major Shell is facing a suit in its home base in England based on particulars of a claim filed by the Bodo Community based in the Niger Delta alleging that its operations resulted in two large oil spills in 2008 and caused environmental damage to the claimants' lands and fishing waters and have had a profoundly detrimental impact on the life of the community. The suit focuses on the consequences arising from Shell's oil exploration activities specifically in Ogoniland in the Niger Delta. 6/1

According to the Particulars of Claim, filed in March 2012, oil spills have resulted in soil and water that could not be used for agriculture or fishing. Nigeria's oil regulator has asked Shell to pay $5 billion (£3.2 billion) for the oil spill.[1] 6/2

Shell almost immediately acknowledged responsibility for both spills in response to the claimants' letter of claim dated 1 July 2011 but have argued that three-quarters of the oil that escaped, during 2007–2011, from the Shell Petroleum Development Company (SPDC) facilities is due to criminal activities including sabotage, oil theft and illegal refining and that these activities are causing huge environmental damage in the Niger Delta. Further, Shell maintained the position that it has always accepted that it should compensate, in accordance with Nigerian law, those affected by the oil spills. 6/3

Negotiations recently took place between Shell and Leigh Day & Co (Leigh Day), the law firm acting for the Bodo community in the Niger Delta. No agreement was reached which Shell state failed in a formal mediation process because the compensation/remedial measures sought were disproportionate to Nigerian standards to allow a mediated process to work. The legal action continues. 6/4

1 <http://www.bbc.co.uk/news/world-africa-18875731>.

II. Facts of the Case

6/5 It is accepted by the claimants and Shell that on or about 28 August 2008 and 7 December 2008 respectively, oil spills occurred allegedly as a result of equipment failure causing an extensive spill of crude oil into the Bodo creek.

6/6 It is estimated that 500,000 barrels of crude oil were spilled in the Niger Delta. Shell was provided with notice of the spills but the claimants allege that no or no adequate steps were taken to reduce the oil spills or contain them.

6/7 The loss essentially comprises of environmental damage consisting of – (a) a reduction of marine life throughout the Bodo Creek; (b) a dramatic reduction in the mangrove population of the Bodo Creek; (c) contamination of the farmland along the coastal areas affecting farm productivity as a consequence of soil toxicity levels; and (d) high levels of hydrocarbons in the water in breach of Nigerian legal standards and international standards.

III. Legal Liability

6/8 In August 2011 the Shell oil group admitted liability for two spills in Nigeria, which they said had been caused by operational failures. Following a legal claim brought in the UK, Shell agreed to concede to the English jurisdiction and court system.

6/9 The claimants state that the applicable law governing the determination of the claim however is the law of Nigeria pursuant to sec 11, alternatively sec 12 of the Private International Law (Miscellaneous Provisions) Act 1995. Section 11 of the Oil Pipelines Act 1990 provides that Shell is strictly liable to compensate – *'any person suffering damage (other than on account of his own default or on account of the malicious act of a third person) as a consequence of any breakage of or leakage from the pipeline or an ancillary installation, for any such damage not otherwise made good. If the amount of such compensation is not agreed between any such person and the holder, it shall be fixed by a court in accordance with Part IV of this Act.'*

6/10 Further, the Petroleum Drilling and Production Regulations of 1969. Regulation 25 requires companies to:

> *'... adopt all practicable precautions including the provision of up-to- date equipment approved by the Director of Petroleum Resources to prevent the pollution of inland waters, rivers, watercourses, the territorial waters of Nigeria or the high seas by oil, mud or other fluids or substances which might contaminate the water, banks or shoreline or which might cause*

> *harm or destruction to fresh water or marine life, and where any such pollution occurs or has occurred, shall take prompt steps to control and, if possible, end it.'*

Further, the operators of oil pipelines are also required by Regulation 37: 6/11

> *'to maintain all apparatus and appliances in use in his operations ... in good repair and condition, and shall carry out his operations in a proper and workmanlike manner in accordance with these and other relevant regulations and ... take all necessary steps practicable –*
> *a) to control the flow and prevent the escape or avoidable waste of petroleum discovered in or obtained from the relevant area; ...*
> *b) to prevent the escape of any petroleum into any water, well, spring, stream, river lake, reservoir, estuary or harbour; and*
> *c) to cause as little damage as possible to the surface of the relevant area and to the trees, crops, buildings, structures, and other property thereon.'*

Nigerian statutory law further requires operators of oil pipelines to comply with 6/12 'good oil field practice' and explicitly adopts international standards of best practice. The Mineral Oils (Safety) Regulations 1962 provide by Regulation 7:

> *'Where no specific provision is made by these Regulations in respect thereof, all drilling, production, and other operations necessary for the production and subsequent handling of crude oil and natural gas shall conform with good oil field practice which for the purpose of these Regulations shall be construed to be adequately covered by the appropriate current Institute of Petroleum Safety Codes, the American Petroleum Institute Codes or the American Society of Mechanical Engineers Codes.'*

It is alleged that Shell was further required to comply with the Environmental 6/13 Guidelines and Standards for the Petroleum Industry (2002) ('the Guidelines') with regard to the clean up operation following an oil spill. The Guidelines require the operator of an oil pipeline to promptly clean up an oil spill irrespective of its cause. Section VIII B.4.1 states:

> *'An operator shall be responsible for the containment and recovery of any spill discovered within his operational area, whether or not its source is known. The operator shall take prompt and adequate steps to contain, remove and dispose of the spill.'*

Pursuant to Sec VIII B.2.6.3 of the Guidelines, the clean up must commence 6/14 within 24 hours of the occurrence of the oil spill. The Guidelines further require the operator to keep a daily log of all spills until the clean up is complete. Within 24 hours of a spill the operator must submit an 'oil spill notification report' to the director of the Department of Petroleum Resources of Nigeria. A follow up report should be submitted 14 days after the spill and a clean up report should be submitted four weeks after the spill.

6/15 Pursuant to Sec VIII B.2.11.1 of the Guidelines, it is the responsibility of the operator to restore the environment in so far as it is possible to do so to its original state. Section VIII B.2.11.3 of the Guidelines stipulates that: i) For all waters there shall be no visible sheen after the first 30 days of the occurrence of the spill no matter the extent of the spill; ii) For swamp areas, there shall not be any sign of oil within the first 60 days of occurrence of the incident.

6/16 The Guidelines further provide that oil contamination of soil, sediment and surface water may not exceed specified levels that are consistent with internationally recognised standards for maximum levels of oil pollution. Section VIII B.2.11.3 of the Guidelines stipulates that: iii) For land/sediment, the quality levels ultimately aimed for (target value) is 50mg/kg of oil content.

6/17 Once the clean-up report is submitted, the operator is required to conduct an Environmental Evaluation (Post Impact) Study of the adversely impacted environment pursuant to Sec VIII B.7.1 and art 2 of the Environmental Impact Assessment Process Guidelines.

6/18 The claimants also rely on the Nigerian law of tort by claiming that Shell is strictly liable for the damage caused under the rule in *Rylands v Fletcher*[2] in that Shell transported crude oil in the pipelines – that product was hazardous and an unnatural use of the land and likely to cause harm to property in the surrounding area in the event of escape of oil.

IV. Damages Rules

6/19 A court hearing is due to take place to determine the timetable for the case and for Shell's response to the legal arguments presented by Leigh Day. However, a point of dispute is whether the measure of damages should be determined by English rules or Nigerian. While the liability of a company registered in Nigeria should be determined by Nigerian law, as this was the law of the place where the oil spills occurred and damage was caused – but as Nigerian law is largely based on English law – the bringing of proceedings in the English courts largely reflects the reputation of the English courts procedure in the fair and expert administration of justice. Further, it follows what appears to be a pattern for multinationals to be held accountable in their home jurisdiction for damage which has been caused by, or is related to the operations of one of their foreign

2 (1868) Law Reports (LR) 3 House of Lords (HL) 330.

subsidiaries abroad – often referred to as so-called 'foreign direct liability'. Shell argues that they are prepared to compensate in accordance with Nigerian law and standards. Such difference in compensation levels was believed to be the principal reason for the failure of the formal mediation process between the parties.

V. Similar Cases

A. BP Oil Spill Colombia

In 2011, a group of 73 Colombian farmers lodged documents at the High Court in London accusing BP of negligence and breaching a duty of care over the building of a new oil pipeline which led to poisoned water, caused crops to fail and livestock to die. **6/20**

The farmers have accused BP of failing to abide by the proper environmental procedures when constructing the Ocensa pipeline in Colombia. **6/21**

Lawyers acting for the farmers commissioned a scientific investigation and claim that BP's negligence caused water to be poisoned, livestock to perish and crops to fail, as well as damage and erosion to groundwater and soil. The lawsuit claims that BP could have done more to prevent this by taking proper soil erosion control measures on land owned by the farmers. The farmers say that BP engaged in 'risky or dangerous activity' and add that an environmental impact study submitted by BP to the Colombian Ministry of the Environment in 1994 was 'inadequate and defective'. **6/22**

The lawyers acting for the farmers[3] have said that emerging evidence in this case has brought to light BP's central role in the construction of the Ocensa pipeline, and its failure to adequately appreciate risk and implement basic measures to protect the local environment and the livelihoods of impoverished local communities: **6/23**

'Rather than accepting responsibility for its actions, BP has, in the same way as it has done in the Deepwater Horizon spill, sought to distance itself as far as possible from the environmental destruction that has taken place.' **6/24**

The farmers are claiming damages against BP for breach of contract and negligence. BP denies that it acted negligently and that construction of the pipeline has caused long-term damage to the farmers' property. It argues that the main cause of soil erosion and sedimentation is the removal of forests by farm- **6/25**

3 Paul Dowling of Leigh Day & Co.

ers for cattle grazing. The farmers dispute this. BP has not yet lodged a response to the new evidence.

B. Lubbe and Others v Cape Plc[4]

6/26 In this case over 3,000 plaintiffs made a claim for damages for personal injuries (and in some cases death), against Cape Plc ('Cape'), allegedly suffered as the result of exposure to asbestos and related products in South Africa. In some cases the exposure is said to have occurred in the course of the claimant's employment, in others as a result of living in a contaminated area. When the proceedings were issued by the Lubbe claimants in 1997, the defendant had no presence in South Africa.

6/27 The House of Lords overruled an earlier Court of Appeal decision (*Lubbe*[5], Court of Appeal on 24 August 1999). The House of Lords gave the claimants permission to bring an action in England against Cape as the parent company of the South African operating subsidiaries. An important consideration was that to stay proceedings in England, where legal representation and legal aid are available, in favour of the South African forum where they are not would deny the plaintiffs any realistic prospect of pursuing their claims to trial.

6/28 Prior to 1948, Cape operated mines and mills in South Africa. In 1948 the company set up a wholly owned subsidiary in South Africa CASAP, which in turn established subsidiary companies to operate the mines and mills. The Lubbe case commenced in 1997 when five South African residents issued proceedings against Cape plc, in England where is it domiciled.

6/29 *Forum non conveniens* is a common law doctrine which allows a court discretion to refuse to hear a case if the claimants' choice of forum is inappropriate or inconvenient for the defendant. An application to stay a case cannot be made where both parties are domiciled in countries bound by the Brussels Convention 1968 ('the Convention'), now replaced by the Brussels Regulation which applies to most European countries. The Convention was incorporated into English law by the Civil Jurisdiction and Judgment Act 1982. Article 2 of the Convention provides for a defendant to be sued in its place of domicile.

6/30 Where the Convention does not apply or only one party is bound, the principles for determining a dispute on jurisdiction were set down by the Court of Appeal in *Spiliada Maritime Corporation v Cansulex Limited*[6]. Where proceedings

4 (2000) 4 All England Law Reports (ALL ER) 268.

5 *Lubbe v Cape Plc* [1999] England and Wales Court of Appeal, Civil division (EWCA Civ) 2107.

6 (1987) 1 Appeal Cases (AC) 460.

are brought as of right against an English multinational, the courts have recognised that England may not automatically be the most appropriate forum for the trial.

This is a discretionary decision for the court. In applying its discretion in a forum application, the court will consider whether there is some other available forum with jurisdiction, which is the more appropriate forum for the trail. The court must consider the 'connecting factors' including the location of the witnesses and documents as well as the law governing the claim. If the court is satisfied that there is another available forum which appears to be the appropriate forum for the trial, the burden will shift to the claimant to show that there are special circumstances requiring that the trial should take place in England. 6/31

In *Lubbe* the High Court initially accepted that the case should be stayed on the grounds that South Africa was the appropriate forum for the trial. The witnesses, documents and experts were all located there and South Africa was the place where the alleged damage occurred. In 1998 the Court of Appeal lifted the stay on a technical point: South Africa was not 'available' to the claimants as Cape had no presence there when the proceedings were issued. The South African courts had no jurisdiction until Cape had given an undertaking to submit to their jurisdiction. This had occurred after the proceedings were issued in England. 6/32

C. Afrika and Others v Cape plc

Within a few days of service of the defence, another Writ was served which named a further 1,539 South African residents, the *Afrika* case. They had also been granted legal aid by the Legal Services Commission and the allegations were identical to those in the Lubbe case. Cape then applied to stay the Afrika proceedings and to re-impose the stay in Lubbe. The defendant's position was that the claimants had misled the courts by failing to reveal the extent of the group litigation behind the original five *Lubbe* claimants. 6/33

In July 1999 the High Court stayed both the Lubbe and Afrika actions stating that South Africa was clearly the more appropriate forum. The Court of Appeal upheld this judgment, citing the 'public interest factor' referred to in the Bhopal litigation in the USA. In Bhopal, India, a lethal gas was accidently released from a chemical plant operated by Union Carbide India Limited. More than 2,000 Indian citizens died and 200,000 were injured. Union Carbide, a multinational corporation, had its headquarters in Connecticut, although the Bhopal plant was operated by a subsidiary, Union Carbide India Limited. 6/34

6/35 The parent company in the USA submitted to the jurisdiction of the Indian courts. The New York court stayed the claim in the USA on the basis that it should be heard in India and that 'the Indian interest far outweighs the interests of the citizens of the United States in this litigation.'

6/36 In the *Afrika* case the Court of Appeal judgment was appealed by the claimants. They were supported in the appeal by the South African government, who instructed London lawyers to make formal submissions on their behalf. In 2000 the House of Lords held that the South African claims could proceed in England. Although based on the specific facts of the case, their reasoning is a clear indicator to other companies who many find themselves in litigation of this type: the court's sympathy is with the claimants.

6/37 The principal argument was that the claimants could not bring their case in South Africa because of lack of funding and civil procedures. This is despite South Africa having an established and independent judiciary and a form of contingency fee funding. The absence of group action procedures in South Africa was cited to support the claimants' arguments on funding and procedure. In fact, the *Lubbe/Afrika* case has led to a claim in the South African courts against South African mining companies, including Glencor Limited. The South African claimants were supported by the National Union of Mineworkers and represented by English and South African lawyers. The claims related to asbestos exposure and the allegations are similar to those made in *Lubbe/Afrika*.

6/38 Despite the House of Lords finding that South Africa was the most appropriate forum for the trial on the grounds that 'the personal injury issues tipped the balance very clearly', they still refused the defendant's application to stay the claim, and thus allowed the action to proceed in England.

6/39 Lord Bingham gave the leading judgment and found that the claimants could not get 'substantial justice' in South Africa, in accordance with the precedent in the *Spiliada* case.

6/40 There was a settlement out of court without a hearing. On 12 March 2003, Cape plc and Gencor Ltd, which took over many of Cape's asbestos operations in 1979, signed settlement agreements totaling £10.7 million (approx $16.5 million).

6/41 If the allegation made by the claimants in the *Lubbe/Afrika* case was upheld by the English courts, this could overturn legal precedent and the principle of corporate separateness in this jurisdiction.

6/42 English law has, for over a century, acknowledged that a company has a separate legal identity which operates independently of its shareholders. Limited liability companies are liable for their acts or omissions in law only to the extent of their assets.

A shareholder, even a majority shareholder, is not currently responsible for the acts of a company in which he has a shareholding. 6/43

There are some circumstances in which a third party can be liable for the acts of a company, these include: where a company employs an agent – the company, as principle, can be liable for the acts of the agent; a company can be vicariously liable for the acts of its employees and shareholders can be liable in certain circumstances for example if there is evidence of fraud or the company is a sham. 6/44

The *Lubbe/Afrika* claimants were attempting to make new law either by piercing the corporate veil; circumventing it or holding the parent company liable for the acts of its subsidiaries. 6/45

D. Adam v Cape Industries Plc[7]

In this case, Cape's corporate structure was scrutinised by the Court of Appeal. 6/46
Until 1979 Cape was the parent of a group of subsidiary companies which included a South African mining company, EGNEP and a US company, NAAC, based in Illinois. An asbestos factory in Texas bought asbestos from EGNEP and in the 1970s personal injury claims were brought by individuals who worked in the factory and lived near it. The defendants included individuals who worked in the factory or lived near it. The defendants included Cape, EGNEP and other Cape companies. Cape had no assets or legal presence in the USA. Default judgments were obtained which the plaintiffs then tried to enforce against Cape in the High Court in London. The Court of Appeal dismissed their claim in 1998, rejecting the plaintiffs' argument that the Illinois company, NAAC, was the 'alter ego' of the parent company, Cape. The court also rejected the 'single economic unit' argument, finding that the managing director of the subsidiary (NAAC) controlled that business.

VI. Conclusion

If this issue is ever successfully litigated against a corporation in the UK, it 6/47
could open the floodgates for further claims. These would not necessarily be restricted to personal injury claims or pollution claims in the event of an environmental disaster but could extend to employment or financial services industry related claims. *Lubbe* raised important legal and public policy issues for

7 (1991) 1 ALL ER 929.

companies and their insurers who may have provided cover in the past for little or no premium for what appeared to be an unlikely or unforeseen risk.

6/48 Despite the claims and settlements, there is no example of where a case has fought to trial and liability for a transnational tort has been established against a multinational company. It remains to be seen how the English courts will in future interpret the types of allegation made in the *Afrika* case.

6/49 There are very important issues to be decided if further cases reach trial, which include, the extent to which the parent company was involved in the business of its subsidiary which could give rise to a challenge to the corporate veil; whether the defendant owed a duty of care to the claimants in the absence of the usual degree of proximity; whether English law or local law applies to the claim; the governing law including limitation and whether the court has discretion to allow time barred claims and the damages which will apply if the claimants succeed, either English levels or local levels which may be far lower than the English damages.

Philip Tansley

7 South African Silicosis Litigation in London. A Case Study

Recently several large collective actions were launched against mining companies in London and Johannesburg. More are likely to follow. The claimants are black South African miners who have contracted silicosis as a result of their work in South African gold mines, allegedly as a result of the negligence of the mine operators. The actions raise interesting questions regarding the ability of impoverished workers in the developing world to seek redress against multinational companies, the nature of corporate liability and jurisdiction. 7/1

Epidemiological studies in the mid-1990s revealed very high and hitherto unknown levels of silicosis amongst ex-gold miners in South Africa and neighbouring countries which provided the mines with workers. This, coupled with inadequate levels of compensation available through statutory compensation schemes, has sparked a number of collective actions in South Africa and London by former mineworkers seeking compensation. Although probably overstated, the potential liability of the mines has been put at as much as $ 100 billion and may well run into the hundreds of millions of dollars. 7/2

This case study examines the silicosis litigation in general and, in particular, the collective actions brought in London against one of the most well-known South African mining houses: Anglo America South Africa (AASA). 7/3

I. What is Silicosis?

Silicosis is one of the oldest latent industrial diseases. It is an incurable, progressive lung disease caused by exposure to dust containing high levels of crystalline silica over a number of years. Onset is typically at least 15–25 years from first exposure. The slow progression of the condition means that at onset symptoms are generally quite mild. However, once the disease has progressed, it can cause serious loss of lung function. In addition silicosis significantly increases the sufferer's susceptibility to other lung diseases such as TB. According to the World Health Organisation, South Africa has the highest rate of TB in the world and the rates of TB in miners, who often live in crowded hostels at the mines, is particularly high. Silico-tuberculosis (silicosis in conjunction with TB) is a very serious, and often life threatening, condition. 7/4

II. Silicosis in South Africa

7/5 There is a long-standing history of silicosis in South African gold mining as the ore bearing rock in the region has particularly high silica content. Since the early twentieth century, the South African mining industry has attempted to control dust in mines through a variety of methods such as ventilations and 'wetting down' (ie using water to suppress dust). Until the mid-1990s it was generally thought that these measures had reduced the level of dust in mines to acceptable levels. However, two studies in Botswana (Steen 1997) and the Eastern Cape (Trapidio 1998) revealed rates of silicosis in former mineworkers of between 22% and 36%. Subsequent research appears to have confirmed that there are very high levels of silicosis in former black mine workers. Estimates of the extent of the problem vary; although most studies converge on estimates of 300,000 to 500,000 affected mineworkers. Many mineworkers are completely uncompensated and the others have received very low levels of compensation under the South African statutory scheme (see no 7/8 below).

7/6 It appears that a so-called 'hidden epidemic' of silicosis went undiscovered due to a combination of factors. Although from at least the 1960s the mines regularly screened working miners for conditions such as silicosis and TB, it appears that there was no surveillance for retired miners. In addition, the labour patterns of miners made such monitoring difficult as miners were often migrants who worked short contracts at a number of mines before returning to their homes in remote areas which provided workers to the mines. Worker advocate groups also assert that the mines deliberately turned a blind eye to the problem.

7/7 Ex-miners with silicosis have a range of symptoms ranging from the mild to the very serious. Typical cases involve loss of income, costs of future care and significant pain and suffering.

7/8 Statutory compensation is available in South Africa under the Occupational Diseases in Mines and Works Act 1973 (ODIMWA). However, the ODIMWA compensation is generally recognised as inadequate. In particular, ODIMWA provides a single lump sum payment which is significantly below the levels of compensation available under South Africa's general manual workers' compensation regime (the Compensation for Occupational Injuries and Diseases Act 1993, COIDA) or which would be available if the miners were able to sue their employers for breach of their duty of care in delict. Historically it was thought that both COIDA and ODIMWA provided 'no fault' regimes which removed eligible individuals' right to a direct action against their employers.

7/9 The issue of silicosis amongst former mineworkers is politically charged. Worker advocate groups claim that the conditions experienced by mine workers over the relevant periods were the result of the deliberate exploitation of black mineworkers as a result of apartheid era attitudes. The mines counter that they provided the safest working environment that they could consistent with the scientific knowledge available at the time and that allowing the claims to succeed (rather than for example providing for enhanced ODIMWA compensation) could cause serious damage to one of South Africa's most important industries.

III. The Litigation

A. The Stakeholders

The silicosis issue has led to a complex web of litigation in London and South Africa. Although this case study focusses on the litigation which is on-going in London, it is important to understand the position in South Africa in order to put the English proceedings into context. 7/10

In August 2004 test cases were commenced against Anglo America South Africa (AASA) by a group of claimants, represented by the Legal Resource Centre in South Africa and English public interest law firm Leigh Day & Co, in Johannesburg. AASA was the head company of a group consisting of a large number of South African mines until 1998. The claimants, who are all former miners at those mines, allege that AASA owed them a direct duty of care to ensure that the mines provided safe working conditions. They say that they have contracted silicosis as a result of AASA's breach of that duty of care. The duty of care was alleged to arise either because AASA had control of the mines or because AASA assumed a direct duty of care as a result of technical services it provided to the mines under various contracts. The rationale for claiming against AASA, rather than the mines, was apparently to circumnavigate the ODIMWA bar on claims against employers. The original arbitrations settled in late 2013 on undisclosed terms. 7/11

In 2006 a further test case was commenced against Anglogold Ashanti. The Anglogold litigation was brought by Richard Spoor, a lawyer who had previously been involved in the *Cape* asbestos litigation – actions brought in England and South Africa on behalf of employees at South African asbestos mines belonging to the English Cape group of companies. The test case was a direct attack on the ODIMWA regime and argued that the statute bar on claims against employers (which was explicit in COIDA but also thought to apply to ODIMWA claims) did not apply. That claim failed at first instance and on appeal. However, in March 2011 the South African Constitutional Court held that the COIDA 7/12 statute bar did not apply to claims by miners. Sadly the test claimant, Mr Mankayi died the day before judgment was delivered. As a result of the ruling that the compensation limit was unconstitutional, opening the way for claims directly against employer mines.

7/13 In September 2011 Leigh Day & Co commenced a collective action in London on behalf of a group of named miners and a further group comprising all miners with silicosis who are, or were, employed by AASA. AASA did not accept the jurisdiction of the English courts and at present the English courts are determining the question of jurisdiction (see no 7/26 below). If the miners are successful on the jurisdictional issues, the Court will still have to decide whether the groups, as defined, are procedurally permissible before those actions can proceed.

7/14 In August 2012 proceedings were commenced on behalf of a group of some 3,000 claimants represented by Hausfeld LLP, a Washington based law firm specialising in class action litigation, and South African firm Abrahams Kiewitz. Those actions consist of an English collective action against AASA and Anglo American plc, which closely follows the Leigh Day & Co claim, and three class actions in South Africa against the three largest mining companies Anglogold, Harmony and Goldfields in which the miners bring employers' liability claims taking advantage of the *Mankayi* judgment. In December 2012 Richard Spoor, in conjunction with US class action firm Motley Rice, commenced a further class action against 30 mining companies, including AASA, on behalf of a group of said to total 17,000 former mineworkers. The application for class certification indicates that, if the classes are certified, the Spoor and Hausfeld class actions will be consolidated.

7/15 None of the applications for class certification have yet been heard and the final form of any class action(s) eventually approved is difficult to predict as the right to bring class actions in South Africa was itself only definitively established by the Supreme Court decision in *Children Resource Centre v Pioneer Foods*[1] in November 2012.

7/16 The claims are supported by a number of trade unionists, including the South African National Union of Miners and other worker-advocate groups. However, the South African government's response to the claims has been relatively muted (see no 7/29 below). The mining industry as a whole has yet to develop a unified response to the claims. In particular, although the mines have individually denied the allegations against them, they have given no indication of whether there will be an industry wide response to the problem.

1 [2012] South Africa Supreme Court of Appeal (ZASCA) 182.

B. Collective Actions in England and Wales

Before discussing the London proceedings in detail, it is convenient to briefly set out the forms of collective action which can be brought in England and Wales. These are: 7/17

- *Multiple Party Claims:* This procedural route allows any number of separate claims to be brought at the same time and case-managed together where they can be '*conveniently disposed of in the same proceedings*'. This form of collective action is most appropriate for small actions where all the claimants are ascertainable or for bringing test cases involving a small number of claimants. It has the advantage that the court has a broad discretion to allow cases to be brought together in this way where it is in the interests of justice. The main restriction is that the claimants need to be represented by the same lawyers and present similar factual and legal issues.
- *Group Litigation Orders:* This procedure allows a single claim to be brought, with court approval, on behalf of all members of a defined class where the case gives rise to '*common interests of law or fact*'. In particular, a group litigation order will bind all potential claimants within the definition of the group, whether they are aware of and consent to the proceedings or not. Group member must inform the Court if they wish to be removed from the group. In practice, the procedure is used relatively seldom. Since the procedure's introduction in 2000, only 82 group litigation orders have been issued. The limited take up is often attributed to the difficulties in agreeing funding and the courts' reluctance to agree orders unless they are narrowly defined.
- *Same Interest Representative Claims:* This procedure allows a single claimant to bring a claim as the representative of a group of individuals who all have the same legal interest. This form of collective action is of limited application because the requirement of the same legal interest tends to limit the procedure to groups such as beneficiaries of an estate or a trust. For example, in *Emerald Supplies v British Airways*,[2] it was held that victims of an alleged cartel did not have sufficiently similar interests for a same interest claim to be brought.

2 [2010] Law Reports, Chancery Division (3rd Series) Ch 48.

C. The Allegations

7/18 All of the proceedings against AASA contain common allegations. The main issues are:

- *Establishing a duty of care:* AASA did not own or operate the mines at the relevant times. In essence, AASA's business was to identify mining opportunities and then develop mines with the assistance of outside investment, listing them on the Johannesburg stock exchange. AASA did however provide services to the mines pursuant to service agreements and, it is alleged, have considerable *de facto* control over the mines as a result of its influence over the South African mining industry. It is also alleged that the relationship between AASA and the mines in general and/or the specific duties undertaken under the service agreements, gave rise to a duty of care between AASA and the miners. As well as evidential issues regarding the degree of AASA's influence over the mines, a key issue is likely to be whether, as a matter of law, this sort of relationship was capable of giving rise to a duty of care. In particular, these allegations raise interesting issues regarding the extent to which companies which have no direct legal relationship with the claimants can owe them a duty of care.
- *Establishing breach:* The claimants' case on breach of duty is essentially that the dangers of dust in the gold mining industry have been well known for many years but, notwithstanding that, South African mines took a reckless approach to the health of workers by, for example, failing to provide adequate safety equipment, permitting levels of dust in the mines which they knew to be dangerous and allowing unsafe working practices. In response it is likely that AASA will argue that they did everything possible to provide a safe workplace consistent with the industry knowledge at the time regarding the dangers of silicosis and best practice in the mining industry.

D. The London Proceedings

7/19 The London proceedings are split into two claims:

- A same interest representative claim seeking damages on behalf of several thousand named claimants with silicosis and a further class of all other South African miners who have worked for AASA and have been certified as having silicosis.
- Separate multi-party claims in which the claimants allege that AASA breached a duty of care to provide them with a safe workplace.

Tactically it is probable that separate claims have been commenced so the multi-party claim can proceed as a test case if the court determines that one or both of the groups defined in the representative action are too wide. 7/20

The Hausfeld claim is a representative action brought on behalf of approximately 1,000 miners. It substantially mirrors the claims against AASA. It is likely that the Hausfeld claim will not proceed until there is a decision in the Leigh Day & Co group claim on jurisdiction and the composition of the collective claims. 7/21

E. Why London?

Given that the London proceedings relate to wrongs allegedly committed in South Africa, it is not at first sight apparent why the claimants would bring their claims in London. However, there are several tactical reasons why the claims might have been brought in London: 7/22

- *Procedural convenience and efficiency*: English law has established procedure for collective actions which adds certainty to the process. By contrast, although South African law provides in principle for collective actions, there is no established procedure and the certification and form of class actions rests largely on the court's discretion. The English courts also have the resources and case management powers which allow them to handle large and complex cases of this sort. As noted above, eight years after they were commenced, substantive hearing has yet to take place in the South African proceedings. By contrast, although they give rise to complex preliminary issues with the potential for the process being slowed down by appeals, the English proceedings are likely to proceed relatively quickly.
- *Quantum*: Damages which are recoverable will be calculated on an English basis[3] meaning that they will be higher than those which would be awarded in South Africa. This may arguably extend to allowing the recovery of losses which are not recoverable in South Africa, such as compensation for the provision of gratuitous care and additional compensation for the families of those claimants who die before a verdict can be obtained.
- *Funding*: From a claimant perspective, England provides a relatively benign funding environment. Firstly, legal costs are recoverable from the losing

---

3 If the English court accepts jurisdiction, it will apply South African law, the *lex loci*, as the substantive law of the dispute (under the Private Law (Miscellaneous Provisions) Act 1975). However, the *calculation* of damages (as opposed to the available heads of loss) is treated as a procedural question governed by the *lex fori*, rather than the *lex loci*.

party. This is an incentive for claimant lawyers who, prior to the 'Jackson' civil procedure reforms in April 2013, were able to take claims under a conditional fee agreement (CFA), and recover an uplift of up to 100% on their fees from the losing party. Claimants can also protect themselves against the cost consequences of losing a claim by purchasing 'After the Event' (ATE) legal expenses insurance (the premium for which was, prior to the Jackson reforms, recoverable from the defendant if the claim succeeded). The availability of CFAs was a significant incentive to lawyers seeking to fund class actions in London or third party funders. The cost consequences of these forms of funding structure can be substantial. In another collective action against Trafigura relating to the dumping of waste off the Ivory Coast, Trafigura was presented with a bill of costs of £ 140 million, including an ATE insurance premium of £ 9 million, for litigation lasting four years (although it was later reduced to approximately £ 40 million on taxation). This compares to a £ 30 million liability payment to the claimants, raising obvious questions regarding the overall efficiency of pursuing claims of this sort through the litigation route. Examples such as this created pressure for the reforms of the English system which were implemented in April 2013. At the time of writing it is uncertain how claimant firms will respond to these changes. Both the London claims are based on funding mechanisms utilising CFA's and ATE insurance. The pre-April 2013 system was intended to provide access to justice and incentivise parties to early settlement. However, as cases like *Trafigura* illustrate, the sometime draconian consequences of the funding system were felt to unfairly tip the balance in favour of claimant firms in cases of this kind.

- *Legal advantages*: Developments in English and EU law over recent years have made it increasingly easy to bring claims on behalf of groups of individuals in countries with emerging economies who allege that they have suffered harm as a result of the activities of large multinationals with a substantial presence in England. In particular, it has become easier to obtain English jurisdiction (see below) and the courts have shown a willingness to impose liability on parent companies for the actions of their subsidiaries (which was not previously the case in England and for which there is no precedent in South Africa). In particular, the decision in *Chandler v Cape*[4] held that, in certain cases, the parent company of a multinational might owe a direct duty of care to the employees of a subsidiary. There are particular parallels between the *Chandler* and Anglo American cases.

4 [2012] England and Wales Court of Appeal, Civil Division (EWCA Civ) 525.

Chandler was the employee of a subsidiary of the Cape group who had contracted asbestosis. The subsidiary was insolvent and there was no insurance coverage in place. The court found that the parent company had breached a direct duty of care towards the employee and that such a duty of care would arise where the parent and subsidiary had similar businesses, the parent company had superior knowledge of issues relevant to health and safety, the parent company knew or ought to have known about unsafe practices at the subsidiary and it was foreseeable that the subsidiary would rely on the parent company's greater knowledge of the risks.

- *Publicity*: It appears probable that the claimants consider that they will be able to place Anglo American under greater pressure to settle by bringing high profile claims in England as opposed to South Africa. Although the silicosis litigation has a high profile in South Africa and the ANC government generally aligns itself with the causes which favour and/or and have the objective of remedying the perceived wrongs of the past, the claimants appear likely to have limited traction. This is perhaps unsurprising, given the critically important position of the mining industry to the South African economy (which in 2011 accounted for, depending on sources, as much as 18% of South Africa's GDP and 50% of its foreign currency earnings) and the traditionally strong lobby of the mining industry. By contrast Anglo American plc, together with many of its investors, is headquartered in London and the publicity associated with the litigation may put Anglo American's senior management under much greater pressure to settle.

IV. Jurisdictional Issues

Jurisdiction in the London proceedings is based on art 2 of the Brussels 1 Regulation (Council Regulation (EC) No 44/2001). Article 2 states that a claimant may commence proceedings against a defendant domiciled in the EU in its country of domicile. Further, the rule in *Owusu v Jackson*[5] states that, if proceedings are commenced first in the country of domicile, a court cannot decline those proceedings on the basis that another jurisdiction is more favourable (subject to the specific provisions of the Regulation in relation to EU states and the possible 'reflexive' application of those provisions in the case of non EU states – see *Ferrexpo v Gilson Investment*[6]). 7/23

5 European Court of Justice (ECJ) C-281/02, *Owusu* [2005] European Court Reports (ECR) I-1383.

6 [2012] England and Wales High Court (EWHC) 721 (Comm).

7/24 However, questions arise regarding AASA's place of domicile. Article 60 of the Regulation states that a company has its domicile in the place of its statutory seat, central administration or principal place of business (with the effect that a company can, in principle, be simultaneously domiciled in more than one country). It is the claimants' case that AASA has its central administration was in London. In particular, they argued that AASA was dormant by the time the proceedings were issued, was administered by its parent company Anglo American Plc, most of its officers were Anglo American Plc officials, routine administration took place in London and AASA's board only met infrequently in South Africa.

7/25 In July 2013, at first instance, the High Court found that AASA's central administration was in South Africa, not London because (1) for intermediate holding companies, of the sort which AASA had become, the assumption was that the central administration was in the place where the underlying business was conducted and (2) although day to day management occurred in London, the 'entrepreneurial' decisions of the company were taken by the board which met in South Africa. An appeal against the first instance jurisdiction decision is to be heard shortly.

7/26 It should also be noted that, in addition, by accepting jurisdiction under art 2 of the Brussels Regulation the English courts will also accept jurisdiction in limited cases where the claimant can demonstrate that a refusal to accept jurisdiction would amount to a denial of justice. Examples of where this might occur include; where the claimants can demonstrate that they would not receive a fair hearing in the natural jurisdiction (*AK Investments CJSC v Kyrgyz Mobil Tel Ltd*[7]) or where the claimants cannot obtain the remedy sought due to a lack of procedure to deal with collections actions or lack of funding for impoverished claimants (*Lubbe v Cape Plc*[8]).

V. What Next?

7/27 The outcome of the appeal on jurisdiction will not be known until summer 2014. In addition, the issues in the case are such that there is the potential for an appeal to the European Court of Justice and/or the English Supreme Court.

7/28 Despite the claimants' presumed reasons for commencing proceedings in London, it appears that much will also hang on the outcome of the collective

7 [2011] United Kingdom Privy Council (UKPC) 7.

8 [2000] United Kingdom House of Lords (UKHL) 41.

actions in South Africa. All of the claimant groups and the South African Mining Minister have advocated the benefits of some form of negotiated settlement but, even if the mines agree to such as solution, it is not clear what form such a solution might take. Possible outcomes might be a reformed and enhanced ODIMWA compensation scheme or a separate settlement fund similar to the asbestos fund agreed in the *Cape* litigation.

There are many obstacles in the way of an industry solution. The *Mankayi* decision has opened up the possibility of claims against all current and former mine operators in South Africa, rather than Anglo American and Anglogold alone. This dynamic will add considerable complexity to the agreement of a fund as the mines have diverse interests and exposures which will need to be reconciled if there is to be an overall solution to the problem. For example, the mines may not be able to reach a consensus on the level or contributions or structure. Some may also fight the cases, either as a matter of principle, because they think they will win or to place tactical pressure on the claimants. The position can often change quickly. For example the claims brought against Cape plc arising from its South African asbestos business were settled rapidly after English jurisdiction was obtained. 7/29

VI. Lessons for the Future

The Anglo American litigation illustrates a number of trends which are important from an insurance and risk management perspective: 7/30

- *Expansion of the jurisdiction of the English courts:* The claims demonstrate a trend towards the development of England as a forum for claimants who have suffered harm as a result of the actions of multinationals domiciled or having a significant commercial presence in England. Other recent examples of this sort of claim include the *Trafigura* litigation (see no 7/22 above), pollution claims brought by residents of the Niger delta against Royal Dutch Shell and claims brought by Columbian farmers in respect of the environmental impact of an oil pipeline (a rare example of a group litigation order in this context). This may significantly increase the legal exposure of companies in jurisdictions where limited access to justice and/or low levels of available compensation may previously have permitted more relaxed attitudes to corporate responsibility than those found in Europe and North America. The willingness of the English courts to accept extra-territorial jurisdiction in such cases may be particularly significant given the more restrictive approach adopted by the US Supreme Court to its extra-territorial jurisdiction under the Alien Tort Act as a result of the appeal in *Kiobel v Royal Dutch Petroleum Co*[9].

- *New medical research/surveillance in previously unfashionable or developing areas:* No-one had realised that there was a significant problem in the labour sending populations in South Africa for over 70 years due to labour trends and lack of epidemiological interest in the labour sending communities. It seems quite possible that similar trends could emerge in worker populations in, for example, South and Central America, the Indian subcontinent and many countries in Eastern Asia.
- *Claimant lawyers:* The case illustrates the activities of claimant law firms in England and the US who are increasingly prepared to put together 'called to account' cases of this sort. Typically such firms identify potential claimant groups, involve local public interest lawyers and worker advocate groups to assist in preparing local litigation and/or assembling claimant groups, fund the initial stages of the litigation and negotiate complex funding arrangements in order to pursue the substantive proceedings. Whilst this development allows groups to obtain access to compensation in cases where they would not otherwise be able to do so, the fees recovered in the *Trafigura* litigation (see no 7/22 above) illustrate that it can often be the lawyers who are the main beneficiaries of such actions.
- *Changes in the political climate:* Regardless of the merits of the parties' cases, it is clear that litigation of this sort would have been unlikely in South Africa before the 1990s. The litigation also demonstrates how unforeseen changes in the political environment and the realignment of key institutions can significantly increase the legal risk companies are exposed to. Although the political changes like those which have occurred in South Africa over the last 20 years are not commonplace, more subtle changes, such as improvements in access to justice and the rule of law and the advent of sympathetic governments, can also rapidly change the potential exposure of corporates operating in those countries.

9 *Kiobel v Royal Dutch Petroleum Co*, 13 Supreme Court Reporter (S Ct) 1659 (2013).

Francesca Rolla and Filippo Chiaves

8 Bank Charges

I. General Introduction

A. The New Class Action Law

Class action law in Italy was introduced by Act no 99/2009, effective from 1 January 2010 following much debate and previous drafts. The law finally resolves the long-standing issue on means of collective redress, apparently overcoming the scant sense of scepticism that had led business representatives, stakeholders and main market players to prefer individual lawsuits.[1] The new provisions are included in the Consumers Code (Legislative Decree no 206/2005) under sec 140 *bis*, entitled Class Actions ('*Azioni di classe*'). 8/1

The introduction of class actions in the Italian legal system has been welcomed by the most important Italian consumer associations and was primarily introduced with the aim of strengthening the protection of consumers. Class actions were initially regarded as a potentially modern, flexible and successful means of defence, capable of offering solid protection in instances that traditionally could only be protected by means of individual remedies. 8/2

1 New legislation to govern consumers' class actions in Italy was initially enacted in December 2007, and was originally intended to come into force in June 2008. However, in January 2009 the date of introduction was postponed in order to address some of the concerns raised and to examine the proposals for amendments to the original version expressed by leading Italian industry associations and following strong criticism by Italian scholars. Indeed, the first version of the law gave certain associations capacity to sue collectively for claims based on standard term contracts, tortious liability, unfair trade practices, and anti-competitive behaviour (including antitrust violations) on behalf of consumers and users, provided that a 'collective interest' was at stake.

The draft was based on an opt-in mechanism and provided for a two-step procedure, the first dedicated to assessing the admissibility of the collective action and the right to compensation, and the second devoted to quantifying the damage on an individual basis with no court involvement. A reform draft was proposed on 23 December 2008 to address the concerns expressed in connection with the 2007 version aiming, among others, at abolishing the two-step procedure, providing clearer criteria to identify the features of the 'class rights' and setting a stricter time limit for the opting-in of class members and to avoid the risk of identical or similar class actions. Parliament finally adopted the bill as part of a larger piece of legislation on 23 July 2009 and the Law entered into force on 1 January 2010.

8/3 *Scope of application* – Section 140 *bis*, which has now been amended by a recent reform,[2] provides that 'individual homogeneous rights of consumers and users', as well as 'collective interests', may (also) be enforced through class action, in relation to (i) contractual rights of a group of consumers/users in homogenous circumstances vis-à-vis the same company (such as in the case of standard term agreements), (ii) homogeneous rights of end consumers and final users of a product vis-à-vis the manufacturer (irrespective of a direct contractual relationship between them[3]), and (iii) homogeneous rights of consumers in respect of unfair business practices or anti-competitive behaviour . It is worth noting that Act no 99/2009 also provides that sec 140 *bis* applies only to acts committed after 15 August 2009. Also, following the recent reform, besides seeking redress claimants can also ask the court to simply assess and declare the defendant's liability without necessarily awarding damages.

B. Italian Class Action Proceedings

8/4 The Italian law on class actions sets forth a special procedure for bringing claims, which is significantly different from the proceedings for individual claims. First, class action provisions provide that standing to sue only lies with the class members. Nonetheless, a primary role in the class action suit is bestowed upon the consumer associations as – pursuant to sec 140 *bis*, para 1 – they can be mandated by consumers to file class action claims before the competent court.

8/5 *The admissibility phase* – The claim must be brought before the ordinary court of the regional capital of the district where the defendant company is based, and has to be served upon the Public Prosecutor.

8/6 Following the first hearing, the court decides on the admissibility of the class action. The action is declared non-admissible when any of the following occur:

- the claim is manifestly groundless; or
- there is a conflict of interests; or
- the individual rights claimed are not homogenous; or
- the claimant does not appear to be able to adequately pursue the interest of the class.

2 Legislative Decree no 1/2012: so-called 'Liberalisation Decree', now Act no 27/2012.

3 Thus this category may also deal with product liability claims.

The court order on the admissibility or inadmissibility of the class action is appealable within thirty days from notice or service of the relevant decision (depending on which occurred earlier). In the event of an admissibility decision, the court shall also: 8/7

- define the terms and conditions for publicly circulating the class action claim, in order to allow other potential class members to exercise their opt-in right. Indeed, as opposed to US opt-out class action law, the Italian provisions prescribe that class action members may decide to join the class action once it has been declared admissible;
- determine the criteria according to which any individual may be included in the class;
- set a peremptory deadline within which the opt-in documents shall be filed with the court.

The merits phase – The order of admissibility entails the opening of the second phase of the proceedings aimed at assessing the claims on the merits. As prescribed by the law, the court ensures that the relevant proceedings (including the taking of evidence) are carried out swiftly and without formalities. If the claim is deemed grounded by the court, an order is issued awarding damages to those who joined the class action suit. Alternatively, the court may simply establish the criterion for liquidation of damages; in such a case, the plaintiffs and the defendant will have a three-month period to reach an agreement on the specific amount of damages. If no agreement is reached, any party may require the court to liquidate the damages in favour of each of the class action members. 8/8

The impact of the new law – Despite the enthusiasm surrounding the introduction of sec 140 *bis*, class actions have not proven as appealing as expected and thus have not ultimately had a significant impact on the overall litigation scenario in Italy, especially in the areas of product liability and unfair practices. Indeed, despite initial expectations, very few class actions have been filed so far and, among these, only four have been declared admissible by courts.[4] 8/9

A multiplicity of reasons may explain why the law on class actions has not been very successful in the Italian context. Firstly, it may be worth noting that under sec 140 *bis*, litigation funding is to be entirely sought by the initial plaintiffs. Secondly, the lead plaintiff(s) can be ordered to pay attorneys' fees and further costs if the class claim is found non-admissible in the preliminary phase, and to bear the costs of publication of the non-admissibility decision. As such 8/10

4 It is worth recalling that in the United States this collective means of protection is widely used: 239 class actions were brought in 2010 and 260 in 2011.

costs are borne by the original plaintiff(s),[5] cost distribution among class members is purely theoretical, as other class members can opt-in only after the claim is declared admissible.

8/11 Another reason why the law on class actions has not proven successful is related to the limited criteria under which a class may be declared admissible. Indeed, class actions may only be employed by consumers seeking protection of claims belonging to the areas specifically identified by the law (namely: contractual rights, product liability and unfair trade practices, as detailed in sec 140 *bis*). Furthermore, and more importantly, it is often very difficult to meet the 'homogeneity of rights' test, which is one of the main requisites for the class to be admitted.

C. Class Actions for Bank Charges

8/12 Although class actions have not been particularly successful in connection with product liability matters and in instances of unfair trade practices, the new provisions have been used in defending consumers' rights in disputes against banking institutions.

8/13 Indeed, a number of class actions have been filed by customers claiming the undue imposition of overdraft fees by banks.

8/14 In 2009, for example, one of Italy's main consumers' associations, CODACONS (*Coordinamento delle associazioni per la difesa dell'ambiente e dei diritti degli utenti e dei consumatori*), filed two different class actions against UniCredit Banca di Roma SpA (now Unicredit SpA) before the Court of Rome, alleging that, in order to compensate for the legal ban on maximum overdraft commissions, the bank would have purportedly introduced new, heavier commissions for customers. However, both class actions were eventually dismissed by the Court on grounds that the allegedly illicit conduct occurred before 15 August 2009.[6]

8/15 A similar class action was brought against Intesa SanPaolo, the largest Italian bank. The claim was submitted by a consumer association named Altroconsumo and was declared admissible by the Turin Court of Appeals.

8/16 This class action will form the object of the present case study.

---

5 Although in principle the named plaintiffs could be funded by the consumer organisation sponsoring the class action, such funding would likely be limited to the attorneys' fees to prepare the initial pleadings in the class action.

6 As already mentioned, the new class action law applies only to acts committed after the date of its entry into force, that is 15 August 2009 (see no 8/3 above).

II. Overview of the Case

A. The Plaintiffs

Altroconsumo is one of the largest Italian group consumer associations with more than 345,000 members. The main goal of the association is to promote and protect consumers' interests and fundamental rights. To this end, Altroconsumo has filed three class actions so far: the first one was brought against RAI – *Radiotelevisione Italiana*, the Italian state-owned public radio and television broadcaster, for damage arising from having arbitrarily interrupted public information TV programmes; the second lawsuit was served against four shipping companies for having agreed to significantly increase their prices for ferries crossing to Sardinia. The present case study focuses on the last class action filed by Altroconsumo together with three bank customers against Intesa SanPaolo, which was the only one to be declared admissible. **8/17**

B. The Defendant

Intesa SanPaolo was formed by the merger of two major Italian banks, Banca Intesa and San Paolo IMI, which occurred in 2006 and which has been legally effective as of 1 January 2007. Today it is the leading banking group in Italy, with nearly 11 million customers and 5,600 branches distributed all over the country. Also, Intesa SanPaolo is amongst the top banking groups in the Eurozone, with a market capitalisation of € 16.8 billion and over 1,500 branches in 12 countries. **8/18**

C. The Class Action Suit

The case was initiated by Altroconsumo and was filed against Intesa SanPaolo on 17 November 2010.[7] The consumer association was acting on behalf of three **8/19**

---

7 A similar class action had already been filed against Intesa SanPaolo. On 5 January 2010, CODACONS, on behalf of an account holder (who also happened to be chairman of CODACONS), summoned the bank under sec 140 *bis*. The plaintiffs questioned the lawfulness of the new fee system introduced by Intesa SanPaolo to replace the overdraft charges demanding € 1,250 as compensation for the damage suffered by the claimant and by all other customers belonging to the same class who would choose to opt in. The class action was deemed inadmis-

account holders. Basically, the court was requested to declare the nullity of the bank's contractual clauses which specified the overdraft charges to be paid by clients, and to sanction the new fee imposed by the bank upon customers who had overdrawn accounts without any prior agreement with the account provider to do so. Also, the plaintiffs alleged that the 'threshold rate' set out in the Italian law on usury (Act no 108/1996) had been exceeded and sought reimbursement of any amounts collected by the bank in excess of that threshold.

8/20 By extensively using its official website, Altroconsumo heavily publicised its intention to promote the class action in the preliminary stage of proceedings, and sought to reach as many consumers as possible subsequent to the order admitting the class action. In other words, even if sec 140 *bis* provides that associations may only act as representatives of individual consumers, Altroconsumo played a primary role in promoting the claim. In simple terms, Altroconsumo may be considered the actual driving force behind the class action brought against Intesa SanPaolo.

8/21 Altroconsumo's lawsuit was not immediately deemed admissible. Indeed, by an order issued on 28 April 2010, the first instance court of Turin rejected the class action. The plaintiffs appealed the decision before the Turin Court of Appeals which overturned the previous decision on 16 September 2011, declaring the suit admissible insofar as it was related to overdraft fees effective from 16 August 2009. The case was sent back to the first instance court to be assessed on the merits, whilst the appeal decision was challenged before the Italian Supreme Court of Cassation.

8/22 The decision of the Turin Court of Appeals has been considered extremely important by scholars and consumer associations, as it is the first Italian class action brought against a bank to be admitted by a court, and potentially opens the way to a number of actions in the future.[8]

---

sible by the Court of Turin both in first instance and on appeal. CODACONS challenged the appeal decision before the Italian Supreme Court of Cassation, which confirmed the previous decisions. The courts held that the allegedly illicit conduct at issue had been performed before 15 August 2009 and, thus, the claim could not be admitted.

8 In an order dated 16 November 2011, for instance, the court of Naples declared the admissibility of a class action launched by the consumer association Assoconsumo Onlus against Banca della Campania S.p.A. As with the class action filed by Altroconsumo against Intesa SanPaolo, the consumer association alleged that two bank customers had been unduly charged overdraft fees.

III. Dynamics of the Case and Legal Issues Involved – The First Instance Proceedings

A. Plaintiffs' Claims

Voidness of overdraft fees – In 2009 a law was enacted prohibiting banks from charging overdraft fees either to bank account holders with a negative balance for less than thirty days, or to overdrawn account holders who had not entered into an agreement with the account provider to do so (Act no 2/2009). On 17 November 2010, three holders of overdrawn accounts who had not entered into an agreement with the account provider, and the consumer association Altroconsumo, served a writ of summons upon Intesa SanPaolo for a class action suit, seeking as follows: 8/23
- as to the period prior to 16 August 2009[9], the court was asked to declare the voidness of the contract clauses which set out the overdraft fees (prohibited by Act no 2/2009) and the penalties in case of a negative account balance;
- as to the period following 16 August 2009, the court was asked to declare the voidness of the new fee for overdrawing accounts imposed by the bank which, according to the plaintiffs, *de facto* supersedes the ban set forth by Act no 2/2009.

Further, the plaintiffs alleged that the above-mentioned charges and penalties infringed the Italian law on usury (Act no 108/1996) and resulted in an unfair trade practice. 8/24

In light of the above, the plaintiffs asked for the restitution of the charges that, in their view, had been unduly imposed on them, as well as compensation for damage. A total compensation amount of € 456 for each account holder was claimed. 8/25

Constitutionality issues – The plaintiffs raised several constitutionality issues. One concerned sec 140 *bis*, para 9, of the Consumer Code insofar as it provides that the publication of the order on the admissibility of the class action claim is a procedural condition to pursue the claim. In the plaintiffs' view, the provision at issue would violate, inter alia, the following fundamental principles: 8/26
- Article 3 of the Italian Constitution, which promotes the substantial equality of all citizens before the law, and art 24, which grants every citizen the right to take legal action in court to protect his/her rights and interests;

---

9 As explained in no 8/3 above, Law no 99/2009 makes the class action remedy available only if the unlawful conduct has been put in place after 15 August 2009.

- Article 169 (titled 'Consumer Protection'[10]) of the Treaty on the Functioning of the European Union;
- Articles 38 (titled 'Consumer Protection'[11]) and 47 (titled 'Right to an Effective Remedy and to a Fair Trial'[12]) of the Charter of Fundamental Rights of the European Union.

8/27 According to the plaintiffs, sec 140 *bis* significantly infringes upon a consumer's right of defence as huge expenses may have to be borne by the latter to comply with the order to publicly circulate the claim.

B. The First Instance Decision by the Turin Court

8/28 On 16 March 2011 the court of Turin rejected the claim declaring the class action inadmissible for a number of reasons, thus leading the legal community to voice anew its concerns on the effectiveness of the new class action law.

8/29 *Altroconsumo's lack of standing to sue* – Primarily, the court stated that Altroconsumo did not have legal capacity to sue and, thus, its claim had to be declared inadmissible. In the court's view, the association was indeed only granted with the power to procedurally represent the three consumers before the courts. However, according to Italian procedure law (sec 77 of the Civil Procedure Code), such power can only be granted together with the substantial au-

10 Article 169 of the Treaty on the Functioning of the European Union (TFEU): '1. In order to promote the interests of consumers and to ensure a high level of consumer protection, the Union shall contribute to protecting the health, safety and economic interests of consumers, as well as to promoting their right to information, education and to organise themselves in order to safeguard their interests. 2. The Union shall contribute to the attainment of the objectives referred to in paragraph 1 through: (a) measures adopted pursuant to Article 114 in the context of the completion of the internal market; (b) measures which support, supplement and monitor the policy pursued by the Member States. 3. The European Parliament and the Council, acting in accordance with the ordinary legislative procedure and after consulting the Economic and Social Committee, shall adopt the measures referred to in paragraph 2(b). 4. Measures adopted pursuant to paragraph 3 shall not prevent any Member State from maintaining or introducing more stringent protective measures. Such measures must be compatible with the Treaties. The Commission shall be notified of them'.

11 Article 38 of the Charter: 'Union policies shall ensure a high level of consumer protection'.

12 Article 47 of the Charter: '1. Every citizen of the Union has the right to vote and to stand as a candidate at elections to the European Parliament in the Member State in which he or she resides, under the same conditions as nationals of that State. 2. Members of the European Parliament shall be elected by direct universal suffrage in a free and secret ballot.'

thority in relation to the rights under dispute, which were not conferred upon the association in the specific case.

Based on the above, the court stated that Altroconsumo had no standing to sue and, accordingly, considered the claim as if it had been brought by the three consumers only. 8/30

Also, the court found that Altroconsumo's claim was not admissible because the consumers were also parties to the proceedings themselves, and a representative cannot procedurally plead in the presence of the represented party in the same proceedings because an agent's procedural standing to sue postulates the absence of the principal in the proceedings. 8/31

Claimants' ability to adequately pursue the interests of the class – Having ruled on Altroconsumo's lack of standing to sue, the court addressed the issue of whether the case could nevertheless be pursued by the three consumers alone. As mentioned above, sec 140 *bis* provides that the class action can be deemed admissible (and then the merits stage follows), only if the lead plaintiff(s) appears to be able to adequately pursue the interests of the class. In this regard, the Turin court pointed out that the three consumers would not have been able to bear the costs arising from the class action proceedings. The court particularly focused its attention on the massive (and necessary) costs for advertising the class action claim in order to allow other class members to exercise their opt-in rights. 8/32

In light of the above, the court declared the class action non-admissible and, as provided by para 8 of sec 140 *bis*, ordered the publication of the decision in a popular national newspaper at the plaintiffs' expense. 8/33

Constitutionality issue – Finally, the court rejected the constitutionality issue mentioned above, deeming it manifestly groundless. In the judges' view, the publication of the admissibility order is extremely important and indispensable as it allows other potential class members to join the class action and, thus, must be a condition of admissibility of the claim. Besides – the court concluded – sec 140 *bis* provides that the consumer may grant representation powers to associations which, due to their organisational and financial resources, can easily bear the class action-related costs and, therefore, adequately protect the interests of the class. 34

IV. Dynamics of the Case and Legal Issues Involved – The Appeal Proceedings

A. Grounds of the Appeal

8/35 Altroconsumo and the three consumers challenged the first instance decision before the Turin Court of Appeals on several grounds.

8/36 *Standing to sue* – The appellants argued that Altroconsumo had standing to sue in the class action context just like the three consumers:

- the Court should not have referred to (and applied) ordinary Italian civil procedure law, because sec 140 *bis* sets out a brand new form of representation before the courts which, accordingly, is autonomous and distinct. Indeed, sec 140 *bis* does not require the association representing consumers to be granted with any kind of substantial power;
- procedurally, the case law of the Supreme Court of Cassation allows a representative and a principal to be parties to the same legal proceedings.

8/37 *Claimants' ability to adequately pursue the interests of the class* – The appellants challenged the first instance decision insofar as it dismissed *a priori* the possibility that the three consumers could be able to adequately pursue the interests of the class at issue. In the plaintiffs' view, the first instance court had not even ascertained whether Altroconsumo and the three consumers had entered into any legally binding relationship under which the association would handle and administer the class action and bear the relevant costs. In any event, the plaintiffs filed a supplementary agreement with the Turin Court of Appeals, whereby the association expressly stated that it would bear the organisational and financial costs possibly arising from the class action proceedings.

B. The Decision of the Turin Court of Appeals

8/38 In a decision issued on 23 September 2011 the Turin Court of Appeals overturned the first instance judgment.

8/39 *Altroconsumo's standing to sue* – In the appellant judges' view, the first instance judgment did not adequately take into account the special nature of the new class action legal framework as set out by sec 140 *bis*, a provision establishing a brand new collective form of consumer protection with an independent regime. Accordingly, the special rule prescribing that consumers are entitled to grant associations a power of representation before the courts cannot be superseded by the general provision under sec 77 of the Italian Civil Procedure Code.[13] In conclusion, in the Appeals Court's view, class action law does not require the representative to be conferred with any kind of substantial power and, therefore, the agreement entered into by the three consumers and Altroconsumo duly granted the association the standing to sue in the proceedings at issue.

Claimants' ability to adequately pursue the interests of the class – In light of the foregoing reasoning, and considering that the three consumers and Altroconsumo had agreed that the association would bear the costs related to the class action suit, the Appeals Court held that the first instance decision was not justified insofar as it found that the claimants could not adequately pursue the interests of the class. **8/40**

Moreover, the Court of Appeals held that the simultaneous presence of Altroconsumo and the three consumers in the proceedings did not represent any kind of conflict or violation of the Italian civil procedure law because the association would not have taken part in the trial as a substantial party to the proceedings, given that its role was limited to providing technical support. **8/41**

Timing issues – Finally, the Court of Appeals examined the claim in light of the rule prescribing that the class action remedy only applies to illicit acts committed after 15 August 2009. Intesa SanPaolo's argument was that the class action had to be declared inadmissible since the illicit conduct had been carried out on 11 May 2009, that is when the clause imposing the new overdraft fee had been introduced by the bank. However, in the Court of Appeals' view, the bank performed an illicit act each and every time it enforced such a new contractual clause by charging the overdraft fees. Hence the Turin Court of Appeals overturned the first instance decision and declared the admissibility of the class action brought by the three account holders and Altroconsumo only with respect to any overdraft fees charged from 16 August 2009 onwards. **8/42**

The Court of Appeals found that the admissibility prerequisites established by sec 140 *bis* were met (namely because, in the specific case, the protection of individual, homogenous contractual rights of a group of consumers in homogenous circumstances vis-à-vis the same company was being sought). **8/43**

Following admission of the class action, by order of the Appeals Court, the case was transferred back to the first instance judges for the adoption of the measures set forth by sec 140 *bis* in order to publicly circulate the information on the class action claim and the opting-in criteria, and to proceed with the second phase of the proceedings aimed at assessing the claims on the merits. **8/44**

---

13 As explained above, under sec 77 of the Italian Civil Procedure Code, the power to procedurally represent consumers before the courts can only be granted together with the substantial authority in relation to the rights in dispute.

8/45 In the meantime, Intesa SanPaolo bank has challenged the appeal decision before the Supreme Court of Cassation, which has not yet addressed this case (this challenge does not suspend the progress of the proceedings on the merits).

C. Further Progress of the Class Action

8/46 Following a hearing held on 19 April 2012 before the first instance Court of Turin, the parties were ordered to file briefs to discuss the opting-in criteria. After a further hearing held on 24 May 2012, by an order issued on 15 June 2012 the Court defined the opting-in terms and the ways to publicly inform consumers of the class action.

8/47 The Court of Turin ruled that by 30 September 2012 the class action claim would have to be published for two days (a non-working day and a working day) in three national daily newspapers, and on their official websites for seven consecutive days. Holders of overdrawn accounts that had no previous agreement with the account provider could have joined the class action starting from 1 October 2012 until 21 January 2013. As to the opting-in crieria, consumers could either file a specific motion with the Court of Turin (following the model form provided by the Court) or send the motion to Altroconsumo who would in turn file it with the Court by 28 January 2013.

8/48 The Court ruling was issued in accordance with the recent reform amending sec 140 *bis* to facilitate consumers opting into the class action: class members can now opt in even through certified e-mail or by fax. Accordingly, the ruling specified that potential class members could also e-mail or fax their application forms to the Turin Court.[14]

8/49 After the initial hearings on 14 March and 12 April 2013, where the Court acknowledged the members of the class action, the next hearings (the first of which was held on 6 November 2013) will be devoted to the taking of evidence, which should not prove particularly complex in the specific case (as opposed to evidentiary issues arising in product liability class action cases), since the matter involves purely legal issues connected with the legality of contractual clauses.

8/50 As mentioned above, sec 140 *bis* requires that this stage of the proceedings be carried out as swiftly as possible and, thus, it is foreseeable that the merits phase will be free of unnecessary formalities.

---

14 If the class action instrument had been more successful, courts would probably have had to adopt organisational schemes to cope with large class action joiners. As this has not been the case so far, courts have employed existing resources to address the issue.

V. Conclusions

Contrary to other class action claims against banks that have been deemed inadmissible by courts, the case brought by Altroconsumo met all the admissibility prerequisites set forth by sec 140 *bis* of the Consumer Code. 8/51

Firstly, protection was sought for contractual rights of a group of consumers in homogenous circumstances vis-à-vis the same bank (as provided under sec 140 *bis*, para 2a). Secondly, the claim passed the 'homogeneity of rights' test, given that the individual rights asserted by the three bank customers were homogeneous (as provided under sec 140 *bis*, para 6). Thirdly, the claim referred to illicit acts allegedly committed after the fateful date of 15 August 2009. Finally, the plaintiffs were considered able to adequately pursue the interests of the class (the decisive element for the Court possibly was the agreement entered into by Altroconsumo and the three consumers, whereby the association agreed to bear all costs arising from the class action proceedings). 8/52

In light of the decision of the Turin Court of Appeals, a number of conclusions may be drawn on the elements that potential plaintiffs and defendants may take into account in a class action scenario. 8/53

On the plaintiffs' side, before choosing to engage in a class action claim, the actual potential of the class should be thoroughly assessed by means of a full survey on the number of possible joiners to the class action. This should enable prospective claimants to set up a plan as to the distribution of costs arising from an admissibility order defining the terms and conditions for publicly circulating information on the class action to allow others to opt-in. Obviously, a greater number of plaintiffs would allow each class member to bear costs which would otherwise be unaffordable, beyond adding persuasiveness to the overall claim. In this regard, it may be worth mentioning that a recent decision of the Court of Milan rejected a class action claim filed by one plaintiff only and where only one additional plaintiff opted-in. The Court ordered both plaintiffs to bear the litigation costs and the defendant was awarded € 17,000 in damages for vexatious action, to be redressed by the initial plaintiff only. 8/54

In light of the above, it is strongly advisable that the initial plaintiff be assisted by a consumer association which expressly agrees to bear all costs that may arise from the class action proceedings. The issue regarding costs should be part of an agreement between the plaintiffs and the consumer association and should possibly be then filed with the competent class action court. 8/55

On the defendants' side, companies should firstly attempt to understand how many class members could potentially join the class action by exercising their opt-in right. Estimates on the first class actions brought against banks, for 8/56 instance, predicted that almost 100% of the clients who were charged overdraft fees would have joined the claim. Once the number of potential class joiners is predicted, defendants will be in a better position to investigate whether there is any chance of entering into a settlement agreement with the plaintiffs and then assess whether amicably resolving the dispute represents the best option.

8/57 Due to its strict admissibility provisions, class action law in Italy has not achieved the expected success so far. In this context, the recent reform clearly aimed to foster the class action regime by softening the existing admissibility requisites. Nonetheless, these amendments are not likely to have a significant impact on the trends characterising class actions in Italy in the present scenario, although some authors share more optimistic views on the prospective increase of class action cases in the forthcoming years. On their side, Italian consumer associations appear to be progressively losing their interest in filing class action suits in Italy and are rather looking at the other side of the Atlantic, where the US-style class action regime seems to be less restrictive. In this context, however, the admitted class action against Intesa SanPaolo bank certainly represents a significant counter-trend and may open the way to similar claims in the near future.

Andreas W Tilp and Thomas A Roth

9 The German Capital Market Model Proceedings Act as Illustrated by the Example of the Frankfurt Deutsche Telekom Claims

I. Introduction

How can the German Capital Market Model Proceedings Act (*Kapitalanleger-Musterverfahrensgesetz,* KapMuG)[1] be described in a single sentence? The KapMuG is the only instrument of collective redress in the German legal system that permits multiple injured parties to bring compensation claims in respect of similar claims. But this already oversimplifies matters, as 'model proceedings' under the KapMuG themselves only involve decisions on questions of law or fact common to multiple disputes (the 'main proceedings'); no legal consequences are pronounced. The German legislature has been and remains averse to instruments of collective redress. It is repeatedly argued, by the 'wrongdoer industry'[2] in particular, that a situation 'like [that] in the US' would be undesirable. The KapMuG entered into force on 1 November 2005.[3] It represented the legislature's response to the mass litigation against Deutsche Telekom described in this article, which had proven unmanageable using the established instruments of German civil procedural law. As a result, the KapMuG has often also been referred to as the 'Lex Telekom'. The KapMuG was initially enacted for a limited period to expire on 31 October 2010. After efforts to revise the Act were slow to get started, however, the term of the Act was extended to 31 October 2012. The result of these reform projects, which included the solicitation of expert reports from practitioners who had worked with the KapMuG, was an amended Act which entered into force on 1 November 2012 and will expire on 9/1

1 References in the following to the 'KapMuG' with no additional information refer to the Act in force until 31 October 2012; a radically reformed KapMuG came into effect on 1 November 2012 ('new KapMuG').

2 Referring to this term see *AW Tilp/TA Roth,* 9 Thesen auf dem Wege zur kollektiven Rechtsdurchsetzung [Nine arguments towards collective legal redress], NJW-aktuell, Neue Juristische Wochenschrift (NJW) 10 (2009) XII.

3 See Bundesgesetzblatt (BGBl) I (2005) 2437.

1 November 2020 in accordance with sec 28 KapMuG.[4] TILP Rechtsanwaltsgesellschaft mbH also submitted various opinions during the revision process.[5]

9/2 As its title suggests, the scope of the KapMuG is restricted to matters relating to capital investment law. The key case for the KapMuG discussed in this article, the one involving Deutsche Telekom, arose out of share offerings by Deutsche Telekom AG in 1999 (second share offering – 'DT2') and 2000 (third share offering, or more accurately: share placement – 'DT3'). Deutsche Telekom AG is a former state-owned company which was privatised and floated on the stock market in the mid-1990s. The background to the Telekom case is the fact that, after being advertised prior to the share offerings as *Volksaktie* ('people's shares') – a reliable investment suitable for small-time investors – the company's share price crashed from its previous high and the shares lost over 90% of their value. The claimants argue that the capital market information provided was incomplete and inaccurate, and in particular that the prospectuses for the DT2 and DT3 share offerings were incorrect. The claimants in the proceedings described below are seeking compensation for their financial losses and the defendant requests that the claims be dismissed.

II. The Facts of the Case

A. Actors Involved in the Litigation

9/3 The claimants in the Deutsche Telekom AG case are approximately 17,000 small-time investors with claims totalling around € 100 million. The average claim value is just under € 5,900. There are no institutional investors among the claimants. The only institutional investor to bring a case was established overseas and withdrew its claim after being requested to pay a guarantee for court costs.[6]

9/4 Around 900 law firms represent the claimants.[7] TILP represents the 'model claimants' in both the DT2 and DT3 model proceedings plus almost 300 further claimants. Only a small number of these law firms have made any noteworthy

---

4 See BGBl I (2012) 2182.

5 See <http://www.tilp.de/files/BMJ_KapMuG_Stellungnahme_TILP.pdf>, <http://www.tilp.de/files/TILP_Stellungnahme_25-04-2012.pdf>; Andreas W Tilp appeared before the Bundestag Committee on Legal Affairs on 25 April 2012 as an expert on reform of the KapMuG.

6 *AW Tilp*, Das Kapitalanleger-Musterverfahrensgesetz: Stresstest für den Telekom-Prozess, in: Festschrift für Achim Krämer (2009) 331, 332 f.

7 Ibid, 332.

contribution to proceedings. Those that have include the firms *Rotter* from Munich, *Doerr & Partner* from Wiesbaden and *Philipp, Sudmann & Schendel* from Mannheim.

The model defendant is Deutsche Telekom AG itself, but other defendants are the Federal Republic of Germany and KfW (*Kreditanstalt für Wiederaufbau*, a state-owned development bank) in around 250 individual actions each, Deutsche Bank in around 70 individual actions and the global coordinators for the share offering Goldman Sachs and Dresdner Kleinwort.[8] The model defendant, Deutsche Telekom AG, is represented by the Frankfurt law firm *Schmitz & Partner*, and the Federal Republic of Germany and KfW are represented by *SALANS* from Frankfurt. 9/5

B. Actors not Involved in the Litigation

The action against Deutsche Telekom received a great deal of media attention, 9/6
particularly during the initial phase when the cases were pending at the Frankfurt Regional Court (*Landgericht*, LG) and when model proceedings were commenced at the Frankfurt Higher Regional Court (*Oberlandesgericht*, OLG).[9] This was due to the large number of plaintiffs, who had not least relied on the idea of Telekom shares as a 'people's share', as well as to the introduction of the KapMuG, but was also the result of the involvement of the federal government, which remains a major shareholder of Deutsche Telekom AG. The federal government also went to court in the US on several occasions to prevent documents from parallel proceedings in the US being handed over to the plaintiffs' bar.[10] By now, media interest has noticeably decreased.

In connection with the events that are now the subject of the model proceedings, public prosecutors in Bonn investigated against Deutsche Telekom AG executives on suspicion of balance sheet fraud and investment fraud in relation to the three share offerings. The result of this investigation was that conditions were imposed in exchange for proceedings being dropped (sec 153a of the German Code of Criminal Procedure, StPO). Regarding the 1996 prospectus, the Bonn public prosecution department found that the accused former Deutsche Telekom AG management board member [Joachim] Kröske had committed investment fraud and balance sheet fraud in the years 1995 to 1997.[11] These inves- 9/7

8 Ibid.
9 Ibid.
10 Ibid, 353 f, with further references.
11 Ibid, 342 f.

tigations were also used to explain why the federal German government intervened in the US litigation – 'endangerment of sovereign interests'(!).[12] A class action concerning the third Deutsche Telekom AG share offering was brought in the US but ended in 2005 with a settlement under US law. This involved a commitment by Deutsche Telekom to pay $ 120 million to US claimants.[13]

III. Proceedings

9/8 In view of the particularities of the Deutsche Telekom case, it appears appropriate to discuss the procedural issues *before* the substantive questions. The following focuses exclusively on the action involving the third share offering,[14] as the model proceedings in respect of the second share offering[15] are effectively suspended.[16]

A. Out-of-Court Proceedings

9/9 The first cases against Deutsche Telekom were brought in early 2001.[17] To prevent expiry of the statutory limitation period in respect of prospectus liability claims in accordance with sec 46 of the German Stock Exchange Act (BörsG), old version, an additional 17,000 or so further injured parties filed claims with the Hamburg Public Legal Information and Conciliation Office (ÖRA).[18]

---

12 Ibid, 342, 353f, with further references.

13 Stipulation and Agreement of Settlement of 28 January 2005, Civil Action No 00-CV-9475 (SHS), <http://securities.stanford.edu/1016/USD00/2005128_r04s_00CV9475.pdf>; see also German Federal Supreme Court judgment of 31 May 2011, II ZR 141/09.

14 Oberlandesgericht (Higher Regional Court, OLG) Frankfurt, 16 May 2012 – 23 Kap 1/06 (model proceedings).

15 OLG Frankfurt, 3 July 2013 – 23 Kap 2/06 (model proceedings).

16 Although the model claimant for DT2 was selected in 2007, an oral hearing did not take place until 27 February 2013. The decision was not in favour of the model claimant; however, also his appeal to the Federal Supreme Court will most likely not be decided upon before a decision on DT3.

17 See press release by the President of Frankfurt/Main Regional Court dated 8 June 2004, <http://www.lg-frankfurt.justiz.hessen.de> – 'Presse' – 'Pressemeldungen'.

18 See <http://www.hamburg.de/oera/>; under what circumstances the limitation period is suspended in accordance with sec 204(1) no 4 of the German Code of Civil Procedure (ZPO) by reason of such applications is disputed, see on the one hand *G Nobbe*, Verjährung von Forderungen im Bank- und Kapitalmarktrecht in der Praxis, Zeitschrift für Bankrecht und Bankwirtschaft (ZBB) 2009, 93, 108 (restrictively), and on the other *H-P Schwintowski*, Aktuelle

B. Judicial Proceedings Prior to Entry into Force of the KapMuG

The Telekom case is unusual in KapMuG terms in that the majority of actions were filed with the competent Regional Court in Frankfurt before the KapMuG entered into force. It was only this flood of claims that led to the enactment of the KapMuG.[19] 9/10

Two oral hearings had already been held before the Frankfurt Regional Court (in 2004 and 2005) before the KapMuG entered into force.[20] In preparation for these hearings, the Court had selected ten 'pilot cases', which presented a variety of complex legal and factual issues.[21] Shortly before the KapMuG entered into force, the party who would later become the model claimant submitted an application for model proceedings (*Musterfeststellungsantrag*) in accordance with sec 1 KapMuG. In view of this, the Regional Court issued advice on how, in its view, such applications for model proceedings should be worded.[22] 9/11

C. KapMuG Proceedings

In accordance with the KapMuG, proceedings begin when at least ten corresponding applications for model proceedings have been submitted from among the main proceedings before the Regional Court. On the basis of these applications, the Regional Court issues an order to refer the case, which de facto defines the programme of work for the Higher Regional Court in the subsequent model proceedings. The scope of the order to refer can be extended subsequently by applications under sec 13 KapMuG. However, jurisdiction for such extensions lies with the Regional Court that issued the original order to refer rather than the Higher Regional Court. Several such extensions were made during the DT3 proceedings. 9/12

Thus model proceedings are triggered by the ten corresponding applications for model proceedings from among the main proceedings before the Regional Court, which lead to an order to refer (secs 1–4 KapMuG). The main pro- 9/13

Verjährungsfragen aus dem Bank- und Kapitalmarktrecht, Zeitschrift für Bank- und Kapitalmarktrecht (BKR) 2009, 89, 97.

19 *Tilp* (fn 6) 331, 333.

20 Ibid.

21 See Landgericht (Regional Court, LG) Frankfurt/Main, Order of 3.9.2004 re Winkler, case No 3-07 O 53/11; these proceedings were the pilot case for TILP.

22 *Tilp* (fn 6) 347.

ceedings are then suspended and the 'model parties' are determined (secs 7 and 8 KapMuG). Actual model proceedings then begin before the Higher Regional Court and the questions of fact and law raised in the order to refer are decided on (sec 9ff KapMuG). Once final, the decision reached in the model proceedings is binding for the main proceedings (sec 16 KapMuG). When the decision in the model proceedings is final, the main proceedings continue in the Regional Court. There, except as regards the binding decision in the model proceedings, the usual instances of appeal under the German Code of Civil Procedure (*Zivilprozessordnung*, ZPO) are available.[23] And it is this that makes KapMuG proceedings so cumbersome, among other things.

9/14 In general, it can be presumed that KapMuG proceedings – including the Telekom case – will proceed to the German Supreme Court for final decision, on the one hand because decisions of this kind are usually of great importance for the parties involved and on the other due to the option of appeal to the Supreme Court by reason of fundamental significance provided for in sec 15(1) KapMuG.

9/15 In the original order to refer of 11 July 2006 in relation to DT3, which comprised 193 pages, the Frankfurt Regional Court referred 33 individual questions, or 'issues', for decision by the Higher Regional Court. All sought to achieve a single objective: that of determining whether Deutsche Telekom's DT3 prospectus was incorrect.

9/16 The Regional Court has since issued further nine extension orders in accordance with sec 13 KapMuG and several amendment orders varying the order to refer.[24] The Higher Regional Court also deleted parts of the order to refer with the agreement of both parties.[25] An extension application by the model claimant seeking to include a second objective of determining whether Deutsche Telekom had violated ad hoc disclosure duties in connection with the acquisition of the US company VoiceStream Wireless Corporation (see below no 9/26) was rejected (Regional Court decision of 23 November 2009). After his appeal against this decision was rejected by the Higher Regional Court, the model claimant brought a constitutional complaint, arguing that his right to a fair hearing had been violated. However, the complaint was not accepted for adjudication by the Constitutional Court (decision of the Constitutional Court, 14 September 2010).

9/17 In its order of 25 July 2006, the Higher Regional Court determined the model claimant in respect of the third share offering.[26] Subsequent proceedings to sus-

---

23 Ibid, 349.

24 The decisions of Frankfurt Regional and Higher Regional Courts cited below are available from the register of claims at the website <www.bundesanzeiger.de>.

25 *Tilp* (fn 6) 335.

26 Ibid, 351.

pend all complaints in the main proceedings were beset with complications: under sec 7(1) sent 3 KapMuG, parties to suspension proceedings must be heard and Deutsche Telekom objected to suspension in around 73% of main proceedings.[27] For a claim to qualify for suspension, the result of the model proceedings must be of relevance to the decision in the main proceedings. There was uncertainty as to whether strict criteria should be applied when assessing qualification for suspension or whether only a cursory review was required.[28] The Regional Court resolved these problems by prioritising pragmatism over dogmatism.[29]

In accordance with sec 8 KapMuG, the other parties to the main proceedings besides the model claimant and model defendant have the status of interested third parties. Due to concerns regarding the possible infringement of the right of third parties to a fair hearing, the Higher Regional Court issued an order on 25 September 2007 also permitting these parties access to the content of pleadings on both sides. To this end, all pleadings submitted by all parties were placed on a password-protected internet site. Only legal representatives were permitted to use the password and disclosure of the password was prohibited.[30] This action was taken as a result of the huge number of parties involved (approx 17,000). 9/18

Oral proceedings in the Higher Regional Court began on 7 April 2008 and the court began hearing evidence on the third day of proceedings, 14 April 2008. On 1 August 2008, the Higher Regional Court requested the model defendant to surrender depositions taken in the course of the US class action suit.[31] 9/19

On 28 and 29 April 2009 and 1 May 2009, four American witnesses were examined regarding the acquisition of VoiceStream by Deutsche Telekom AG at the German Consulates General in San Francisco and New York in the presence of the three adjudicating Higher Regional Court judges and the legal representatives of the model parties. 9/20

On 15 December 2010, the 16th day of court proceedings, the chair of the division of the Higher Regional Court hearing the case was replaced for age reasons. On 18 January 2012 and 26 April 2012 the Higher Regional Court issued orders incorporating further issues into the model proceedings by way of interpretation of the order to refer. 9/21

---

27 *M Wösthoff*, Das Kapitalanleger-Musterverfahrensgesetz zwischen Theorie und Praxis, p 9, Vortragsskript zum 4. Tag des Bank- und Kapitalmarktrechtes, Potsdam, 22 November 2007.

28 *B-W Schmitz* in: M Habersack/PO Mülbert/M Schlitt (eds), Handbuch der Kapitalmarktinformation (2008) sec 32 no 177 ff.

29 *Wösthoff* (fn 27) 13.

30 *Tilp* (fn 6) 355.

31 Ibid, 356 ff.

9/22 On 16 May 2012 the Higher Regional Court delivered its model decision.[32] It held that Deutsche Telekom had committed no material breaches of duty under capital market law. On the same day, after eleven years of litigation, a group of claimants, represented by TILP, lodged an appeal on a point of law from this model decision with the Federal Supreme Court. The model claimant has now also filed an appeal. The appellants are represented by Supreme Court lawyer Volkert Vorwerk.[33] A decision by the Federal Supreme Court is not expected until the second half of 2014 at the earliest.

IV. Legal Issues

A. Competent Courts

9/23 The main proceedings are pending before the Regional Court in Frankfurt am Main, which has general jurisdiction in regard to the main defendant Deutsche Telekom AG under sec 17(1) ZPO. A single division of the Regional Court, the 7th commercial division, chaired by Judge Wösthoff, had jurisdiction. As such, the model proceedings were brought before Frankfurt Higher Regional Court, which had jurisdiction in accordance with sec 4(1) sent 1 KapMuG. A final decision on the appeal will be handed down by the Federal Supreme Court in accordance with sec 15 KapMuG.

9/24 As mentioned previously, a class action was brought in the US in connection with the third share offering, which ended with a settlement in favour of US investors in 2005.[34] However, this action had no connection with the German KapMuG proceedings.

---

32 <https://www.bundesanzeiger.de/ebanzwww/wexsservlet?session.sessionid=40066b69c767cedb1c0b63c05f7bac0e&page.navid=detailsearchlisttodetailsearchdetail&fts_search_list.selected=aa8e640c62ab7c42&fts_search_list.destHistoryId=11030>.

33 Co-editor of the first commentary on the KapMuG: *V Vorwerk/C Wolf,* Kapitalanleger-Musterverfahrensgesetz: KapMuG, Kommentar (2007).

34 *Tilp* (fn 6) 343.

B. The Central Questions of Law

1. The original material questions

As mentioned previously, the order to refer of 11 July 2006 submitted 33 issues to the Higher Regional Court for decision. The main issues included for example the question of whether the defendant's prospectus constituted a prospectus within the meaning of sec 44 BörsG, whether certain items of information given in this prospectus were incorrect or incomplete, and many others.[35] 9/25

The central points – and almost the only ones to receive attention in the media in particular[36] – concern the failure to provide information regarding the acquisition of the US telephone company VoiceStream Wireless Corporation by Deutsche Telekom AG and the incorrect real estate valuation information given in the issue prospectus.[37] The common denominator ('objective') here is the question of whether the model defendant's prospectus was incorrect or incomplete and whether the claimants have any claims arising from and/or in connection with such incompleteness or incorrectness.[38] 9/26

These substantive questions chiefly concern claims against the defendant for prospectus liability, especially specific statutory prospectus liability under the BörsG (old version), and in tort. 9/27

2. Questions of procedural law

The following terms are of crucial importance for KapMuG actions: matter in dispute (*Streitgegenstand*), body of circumstances (*Lebenssachverhalt*), objective (*Feststellungsziel*) and issues (*Streitpunkte*). 9/28

The term 'matter in dispute' is not given a statutory definition in the KapMuG but is used in sec 16(1) sent 2 KapMuG in connection with the binding force of the model decision. Model decisions '[have] binding force insofar as the matter in dispute in the model proceedings has been decided.' As such, in accordance with sec 16(1) sent 3 KapMuG, the model decision is effective 'for and against all third parties to the model proceedings, irrespective of whether those third parties expressly raised all issues themselves.' The term 'body of circumstances' is likewise not given a statutory definition in the KapMuG but is used in 9/29

35 LG Frankfurt/Main, Order ref: 3/7 OH 1/06, pp 6–140.
36 *Tilp* (fn 6) 334 f.
37 LG Frankfurt/Main, Order to refer of 11. July 2006, ref: 3/7 OH 1/06, points 6 and 11.
38 Extension of the order to refer per Order of 18. June 2008.

sec 2(1) sent 5. Here 'corresponding applications for model proceedings' are defined as 'the objective which concerns the same underlying body of circumstances'.

9/30 In contrast, the Act does give a statutory definition for the term 'objective' in sec 1(1) sent 1 KapMuG. Here 'objective' is defined as the desire for 'establishment of whether or not conditions on which claims may be founded or excluded are met, or clarification of legal issues'. Finally, a statutory definition of the term 'issue' is given in sec 1(2) sent 2 KapMuG. Here 'issues' are defined as 'information regarding all factual and legal circumstances on which the objective is based'.

9/31 The four terms specified above are of central importance throughout a KapMuG action, namely as regards its commencement,[39] execution[40] and conclusion.[41]

9/32 The abovementioned questions and concepts have also proved to be significant in relation to the limitation of actions. In its model decision, the Frankfurt Higher Regional Court hearing the model proceedings, expressed the – in the authors' opinion incorrect – opinion that the statute of limitations for each error in the prospectus should be considered separately, with the result that errors in the prospectus being revealed after 27 May 2003 could be incorporated into the model proceedings by way of applications for extension, but any claims in connection with such errors had expired. However, it was held, no doubt correctly, that lodging the original claims with the Regional Court had suspended the limitation period for claims in respect of all prospectus errors.

3. Other substantive questions of law

9/33 Using the option of subsequent extension of the order to refer, further substantive questions were incorporated into the model proceedings as additional issues during the period between April 2007 and November 2011. To mention only the most important:

- Liability for non-disclosure in the prospectus of a contingent liability on Deutsche Telekom resulting from potential claims by disadvantaged share-

39 Regarding the corresponding nature of the applications for model proceedings see sec 2(1) sent 5 KapMuG.

40 Due to the wording of the order to refer, which in accordance with sec 4(2) KapMuG must specify the objective and the issues.

41 As regards the binding force of the decision, which takes effect only insofar as the matter in dispute in the model proceedings has been decided, see sec 16(1) sent 1 KapMuG.

holders on the basis of the deliberate investment fraud in relation to the Initial Public Offering in 1996 and the deliberate balance sheet fraud in the years 1995 to 1997 established by the Bonn public prosecution department.[42]

- Liability of Deutsche Telekom for prospectus errors in relation to the issues surrounding Sprint.[43]
- Liability for defects in the three supplementary prospectuses.[44]
- Extension order regarding determination of the target audience for the issue prospectus.[45]
- Liability for prospectus errors in relation to the issues surrounding the global acquisition agreement.[46]

V. Summary

The course of proceedings in the Telekom case shows that the KapMuG is afflicted by structural slowness and procedural complexity. Suspension proceedings and the large number of interested third parties, all of whom have the right to participate in proceedings,[47] have also proved to be potential 'stumbling blocks'.[48] The Telekom proceedings were rendered manageable chiefly because the District Court approached the suspension proceedings 'pragmatically rather than dogmatically'[49] and because the overwhelming majority of interested third parties played no active part in the case. However, given that sec 16(2) KapMuG excludes any objection by third parties to the model decision in their own main proceedings, it is clear that such inaction on the part of the third parties is not provided for in the Act. This shows that the dogmatic nature of the KapMuG is an obstacle to manageability of the Telekom case.[50] 9/34

42 LG Frankfurt/Main, decision of 23. November 2009, 3/7 OH 1/06.

43 LG Frankfurt/Main, decisions of 1. December 2009, 8.6.2011 and 11.8.2011, all 3/7 OH 1/06.

44 LG Frankfurt/Main, decision of 10. February 2010, 3/7 OH 1/06.

45 LG Frankfurt/Main, decision of 8. June 2011, 3/7 OH 1/06.

46 LG Frankfurt/Main, decision of 29. November 2011, 3/7 OH 1/06.

47 See in this regard *Tilp* (fn 6) 359 f, who argues that the active involvement of all interested parties would have effectively paralysed proceedings in the Telekom case.

48 See *Wösthoff* (fn 27) 9.

49 Ibid, 13.

50 *Tilp* (fn 6) 360; Wösthoff too bemoans the practical difficulties involved in 'genuine mass proceedings', see idem, Das Kapitalanleger-Musterverfahrensgesetz KapMuG in der Praxis, Bamberger Verbraucherrechtstage 2009, 96.

9/35 As regards the KapMuG itself, even in its revised form, the authors remain pessimistic:[51] The Act does not provide a workable instrument of effective collective redress – and whether it was the genuine intention of the German legislature to provide such is, in the opinion of the authors, also to be doubted.

51 See the opinions by *Tilp* (fn 6).

Jenny Boldon

10 The Madoff Ponzi Scheme*

I. Background

As most readers will be aware from the widespread media coverage this scandal has attracted around the globe, Bernard Madoff was a legendary Wall Street trader and US hedge fund manager, as well as a former chairman of the US NASDAQ stock market and adviser to the US financial regulator, the Securities and Exchange Commission (SEC). However, for many years, he perpetrated a fraud of an unprecedented magnitude on investors through a massive Ponzi scheme, ie a pyramid selling scheme where money is taken from new investors to pay off existing investors. 10/1

Madoff's New York company, Bernard L Madoff Investment Securities LLC (BLMIS), consisted of three divisions, one of which was the investment advisory business – the other two were his better known market-making business and the proprietary trading division. He purported to run the investment advisory business as a legitimate business, with an impressive client list that included wealthy individuals, banks and hedge funds. Madoff employed his mythical '*split-strike conversion strategy*' but, whilst impressive sounding, no one appeared to truly understand how it produced such good returns. 10/2

In reality, it appears that the investment advisory business made no material investments. Instead, clients' money was paid into a single bank account. When Madoff appeared to pay his clients consistent annual returns of 10–12% (or more) on their investments, he was actually paying them with later investors' money: the scheme being financed by a constant flow of funds. It was only when the global financial crisis took hold in the second half of 2008, and the requests for redemption of funds exceeded incoming investment monies, that Madoff was undone. 10/3

The recession caused anxious investors to seek to withdraw US$ 7 billion in redemptions from the fund, when there was far less than that in it, leading to its collapse – and leaving customers approximately US$ 17.5 billion out of pocket. 10/4

On 11 December 2008, Madoff (then aged 70) was arrested by US federal agents and charged with securities fraud – having allegedly confessed the previous day to his two sons, Mark and Andrew, who reported him to the FBI. Madoff is reported to have confessed that '*it's all just one big lie*' and he was '*fin-* 10/5

* This report is based on the facts up to November 2013.

ished' and estimated that he had channelled in excess of US$ 50 billion through his fraudulent scheme.

10/6 Madoff pleaded guilty to an 11-count criminal complaint on 12 March 2009 and was later sentenced to 150 years in prison. He was also charged with securities fraud by the SEC, which it soon transpired had never properly inspected Madoff's hedge fund, despite numerous tip-offs including persistent allegations by Wall Street rivals. Madoff pleaded guilty to offences including 'securities', investment adviser-, mail- and 'wire' fraud, international money laundering, making false statements, perjury, false filings with the SEC and theft from an employee benefit plan.

10/7 Those losing monies in the fraud included a number of charities and non-profit organisations (which Madoff targeted as they were less likely to demand the immediate return of investment monies), pension funds and pensioners, individuals – including a number of celebrities – and institutional investors.

II. The Aftermath

10/8 At the time of writing, it is almost five years since the discovery of Madoff's fraud and the fallout continues. It has manifested itself in a litany of lawsuits across the world, targets of which have included a host of individuals and entities other than Madoff and his companies, such as:

- individual investors who benefitted financially from the BLMIS fund;
- some of the hedge and feeder funds which invested in Madoff's scheme;
- investment managers who recommended such investments, as well as trustees/fiduciaries who approved them; and
- Banks/custodians of funds

10/9 Very soon after the fraud was uncovered in December 2008, a trustee in bankruptcy, Irving H Picard ('the Trustee'), was appointed under the US Securities Investor Protection Act 1970 (SIPA) to liquidate BLMIS and the Madoff estate in the US. The Court-appointed Trustee is tasked with locating and securing assets for distribution to investors who were victims of the fraud. Under wide-ranging US bankruptcy/SIPA rules, the Trustee has the power to seize assets and records, demand documents and summon witnesses in the quest for the recovery of assets. These assets form part of the 'Customer Fund', which will be distributed to defrauded investors and, thereafter, to general creditors of BLMIS.

10/10 The Trustee has initiated litigation in a number of jurisdictions – over 1,000 legal actions in more than 30 jurisdictions, according to some press reports – but perhaps unsurprisingly the concentration of litigation is in the US.

III. The US

A. Trustee Recoveries/Clawback Claims

Under US bankruptcy laws, there is a legal principle of '*fraudulent conveyance or preference*', which means that investors who withdrew their monies before the fraud was revealed can be compelled to return their profits. Accordingly, those who made money from their Madoff investments – who have been termed '*net winners*' – can be pursued to disgorge past returns. 10/11

The Trustee can sue investors for fictitious profits in the six years prior to the discovery of the fraud. This is, however, subject to the investor's good faith defence, that is that they were not aware of the fraud or of facts which should have put them on notice of a potential problem that they should have investigated, in which case profits can only be traced back for a two-year period. Rulings in Madoff litigation have required the Trustee to prove that the investors had *wilfully blinded* themselves to the Ponzi scheme. 10/12

223 investors who had a direct personal relationship with Madoff and his family have been targeted by the Trustee, such as Madoff's relatives, employees and friends and feeder fund managers, who fed[1] billions of dollars of investors' monies to Madoff in return for substantial commissions. Significant sums have been recovered. Many of these '*avoidance*' or clawback actions have been brought by the Trustee in the Manhattan Federal Bankruptcy Court, which has sought to assert jurisdiction over a large number of foreign entities based in jurisdictions such as Europe, Bermuda, the Cayman Islands, the British Virgin Islands, Gibraltar and so on. A number of settlements have also been reached without the need for litigation. 10/13

The Trustee was required to bring these clawback claims within two years of the initial bankruptcy filing in December 2008 and, therefore, there was a flurry of claims brought in late 2010. According to press reports, by the end of 2010 almost 60 lawsuits had been filed by the Trustee, seeking in excess of US$ 40 billion from banks, hedge funds and investors he claimed had made millions with Madoff. Notably, the Trustee brought claims in the Manhattan Bankruptcy Court against a number of entities including banks administering feeder funds and providing services to Madoff including UBS, JP Morgan, UniCredit Bank Austria, Sonja Kohn HSBC and others. The claims included allegations that the banks/custodians 'looked the other way' and effectively aided and abetted Madoff by giving his scheme an 'aura of legitimacy'. 10/14

---

1 Without knowledge of Madoff's fraud in a large number if not the majority of cases.

10/15 Between July and November 2011, there were a number of rulings by US District Judges which concluded that the Trustee had no standing to bring claims against JP Morgan and others. The US Courts held that, under US federal law, only the victims themselves, not the Trustee, could sue third parties such as banks for damages. Further the *in pari delicto* principle prevents lawsuits between 'wrongdoers' so the Trustee cannot accuse banks of fraud where he is the Trustee of a fraudulent enterprise.

10/16 An appeal by the Trustee to the Second US Circuit Court of Appeals upheld the dismissal on the same basis in June 2013. In early October 2013 the Trustee filed a petition to the US Supreme Court requesting it hear an appeal of the case. The Trustee argues that he ought to be able to pursue third party claims – worth approximately US$ 30 billion – on behalf of investors and the current ruling undermines the intent of SIPA.

10/17 As of 15 November 2013, the Trustee had recovered or entered agreements to recover approximately US$ 9.508 billion, ie just over half of the estimated US$ 17.5 billion lost. This includes settlements reached with Santander's Swiss-based fund Optimal, Tremont Group Holdings Inc, Union Bancaire Privée, Fairfield Funds, Greenwich Funds, Carl Shapiro and the Picower Estate and others. Details of the recoveries and recovery actions can be found at www.madofftrustee.com.

10/18 According to figures published by the Trustee, he has, as of 15 November 2012, distributed approximately US$ 4.883 billion to Madoff investors' claims which have been made in the liquidation. Some monies cannot as yet be distributed due to Court appeals and reserves required to be held. For example, victims of the fraud are now appealing a ruling that they are not entitled to interest or inflation adjustments on their claims.[2] Ongoing litigation is leading to frustration for many of the fraud victims in the US.

10/19 Settlements between third parties and either the Trustee or US States have been approved by either the US Bankruptcy Court or the Southern District of New York but some challenges have been made. These challenges have been made by investors who have wished to bring direct claims, or sometimes by the Trustee in the case of settlements made by US State Attorneys and third parties.[3]

2 BLMIS, US Bankruptcy Court, Southern District of NY No 80-1789.

3 For example, *Picard v Schniederman* (State of NY), 13-01785 US Circuit Court of Appeals.

B. Restitutionary Claims against Investors by Feeder Funds

A number of feeder funds – for example, Fairfield Sentry/Greenwich (which are in liquidation) – have separately, by their liquidators, pursued restitutionary claims against investors who received significant redemption payments before Madoff's fraud was exposed. These claims are put on the basis of '*unjust enrichment*', that means that it is unfair that particular investors should have received returns on their funds when other investors have lost their principal invested. 10/20

Much of this litigation is, and claims filed by the Trustee are, going on in the British Virgin Islands. To date, the BVI Courts have rejected the liquidators' claims, at first instance and on appeal, but an appeal to the Privy Council in England is expected. 10/21

C. Investor Claims

A number of US class action claims were immediately instigated in the New York State Supreme Court and in other State and Federal Courts following Madoff's arrest. More recently, following the rejection of the right of the Trustee to bring claims against various banks, class action claims have been instigated against a number of banks, including JP Morgan. 10/22

D. Regulatory Aspects

A number of investors and funds who lost money have been vocal in blaming US regulators for '*systemic failures*' for the Madoff debacle. One Wall Street rival, in particular, had written repeatedly to the SEC stating that Madoff could not legitimately make the profits he was claiming. The SEC investigated this claim in 2005 and 2007 but, according to press reports, appears to have done little other than ask Madoff to justify his position. Following a full investigation, a number of SEC staff were disciplined but none lost their jobs. Some commentators consider that, despite all regulatory efforts, if a clever fraudster is determined to carry out fraudulent activity, there is little a regulator can do to prevent that. In this instance, it appears that Madoff lied to the SEC and falsified documents to conceal his fraud. The problem with disclosure-based regulation – such as in the US and the UK – is that it relies on truthful information being provided. 10/23

A civil action was brought in the US against the SEC for negligently failing to detect the fraud, but failed. In April 2013 the US Court of Appeals for the Sec- 10/24 ond Circuit, NY, upheld the dismissal of the lawsuits against the SEC since the SEC is protected by a law that shields federal agencies from liability.[4]

E. Criminal Prosecutions

10/25 Madoff claimed he acted alone in the fraud but Madoff's brother Peter pleaded guilty to conspiracy in 2012 and is currently serving 10 years in prison for falsifying documents and lying to regulators. He may face further charges. Other associates of Madoff have pleaded guilty to various misdemeanours.

10/26 Five former employees of Madoff are currently[5] standing trial in federal court in Manhattan. Madoff's former accountant has also been charged and prosecutors are rushing to bring charges before an 11 December 2013 statutory cut-off.

IV. The European Landscape

10/27 A number of European banks have announced potential client losses in the order of many millions and, in some cases, billions of dollars arising from the Madoff affair. Law firms across Europe worked together to form an international group of lawyers, the 'Global Alliance'[6], with the aim of securing settlements against these banks by maximising their bargaining position. The investors argued that the banks failed to carry out due diligence on the investments and also misrepresented the products as low risk.

10/28 Some investor claims have been filed in the US as the jurisdiction of first choice as a result of favourable factors such as the class action procedure, contingency fees, the extensive discovery procedure and so on. Claims have also been filed, however, in jurisdictions such as Luxembourg, Ireland and Switzerland. These investors' claims have been numerous and have been launched against various banks for allegedly helping to channel money into Madoff's fraudulent scheme. A number of actions against European funds, notably Luxembourg-based LuxAlpha American Selection and Lux Invest (of which UBS was a custodian) and Thema (of which HSBC was a custodian) have been brought. There are also actions against former directors and officers, investment

4 *Molchatsky v US*, 2nd US Circuit Court of Appeals, No 11-2510.

5 The trial began in early October 2013.

6 The 'Global Alliance' or 'Madoff Lawyers' Alliance' was formed by the Spanish law firm Cremades & Calvo-Sotelo.

managers and auditors. Investors allege that these entities/individuals are liable to compensate them for losses allegedly caused by their failure to detect Madoff's fraud, despite the existence of red flags that should have alerted them. It is alleged that feeder funds were blinded by the commissions paid to them for channelling investment monies to Madoff and that funds and custodians of funds were negligent in failing to carry out due diligence and breaching duties of care.

It is not clear what success the Global Alliance has had. Conflicts of interest have created difficulties in sharing information and deals reached are confidential. It appears that a number of European financial institutions have taken commercial decisions to reimburse customers for losses without the need for litigation. **10/29**

In addition to settlements and direct claims for damages and compensation in Europe, there have also been some interesting rulings on providing assistance to the US Trustee in gathering information and assets, both under principles of international comity and global insolvency practice and on jurisdiction and cross-border enforcement of judgments. **10/30**

A. England and Wales

The attempts of the Trustee to recover funds have led to a number of pieces of litigation in England: **10/31**

1. Requests for information

In early 2009 litigation[7] began concerning Madoff's British operation, Madoff Securities International Ltd (MSIL), which, initially, Madoff denied was involved in the fraud but subsequently was found to have been used by Madoff to launder funds.[8] Following a request by the Trustee and an application for directions by the joint provisional liquidators under the Insolvency Act 1986, the English High Court ordered that information in the possession of MSIL's joint provisional liquidators should be transferred to the trustee in bankruptcy of its **10/32**

---

7 *In the Matter of Bernard L Madoff Investment Securities LLC sub nom In the Matter of Madoff Securities International Ltd* [2009] England & Wales High Court (EWHC) 442 Chancery Division (Ch).

8 Note: In the UK, the Serious Fraud Office investigated MSIL but ultimately decided not to bring criminal charges. See below for discussion of MSIL's knowledge of Madoff's fraud.

parent company (BLMIS), ie to the Trustee. The Court was satisfied that it was in the public interest that an alleged fraud of such scale and complexity be investigated and, accordingly, held that transfers of the information specified were '*necessary for reasons of substantial public interest*', in accordance with the exception contained in the Data Protection Act 1998.

10/33 In May 2010 the Trustee applied to the High Court[9] under the Cross-Border Insolvency Regulations 2006. The Trustee sought an order that an English company produce to him various documents relating to the assets, affairs and so on of BLMIS, which he claimed were essential for the purposes of discharging his statutory duties. That company had established two investment companies which invested most of their monies in BLMIS, as well as provided extensive consultancy services to them but contested the scope of the Trustee's request. The High Court exercised its discretion under the 2006 Regulations and ordered the English company to disclose to the Trustee documents relating to a 16-year period. The judge decided that it was appropriate to do so as these documents were necessary for him to discharge his duty to investigate what claims BLMIS and its investors might have and against whom.

2. Jurisdiction

10/34 In further litigation[10] concerning MSIL, in November 2011, the London Commercial Court was asked to decide issues under art 6(1) of the Brussels Regulation 44/2001.

10/35 A claim was brought by MSIL (through its liquidators) as the first claimant, the second claimant being the Trustee. The first five defendants were the English directors of MSIL, whereas the sixth, seventh and eighth defendants (Madoff's brother and sons) were also MSIL directors but were not domiciled in the UK. The ninth defendant was Sonja Kohn (of Bank Medici), who was born in Austria but lived and conducted her affairs internationally through a series of corporate vehicles, two of which were the eleventh and thirteenth defendants.

10/36 MSIL pursued the directors for alleged breach of contract and fiduciary duty and the Kohn defendants for alleged knowing receipt and constructive trust. The Trustee was pursing the Kohn defendants on the basis that, as a matter of New York law, they received monies from BLMIS as constructive trustees and,

9 *In the Matter of Bernard L Madoff Investment Securities LLC, between Picard v Fim Advisers LLP and others* [2010] EWHC 1299 (Ch).

10 *Madoff Securities International Ltd and another v Raven and others* [2011] EWHC 3102 Commercial Court (Comm).

therefore, were liable to make restitution. The English court decided that art 6(1) only applied if the same claimants were bringing claims against both a defendant domiciled in the UK and a non-UK domiciled defendant. However, it did *not* grant jurisdiction in instances where one claimant was pursuing a UK defendant, whilst another claimant was pursuing a non-UK domiciled defendant.

3. Enforcement

In October 2012, the UK Supreme Court gave judgment in a conjoined appeal[11] in which it had to decide whether an order of a foreign court in avoidance proceedings in insolvency would be recognised and enforced in England. The Trustee applied to intervene in this case because of his Madoff interests. It was argued that a 'universalist' approach should be taken to cross-border insolvencies to avoid inconsistencies as between creditors. **10/37**

The Supreme Court decided that the insolvency proceedings could not be directly enforced in England, as that would be an expansion of common law and statutory powers which is appropriate for the legislature not the judiciary. There should not be more liberal rules for insolvency proceedings than other judgments. This means that the 'universal bankruptcy' principle has not been extended, as some thought it might be, and liquidators are left needing to bring proceedings in different jurisdictions. **10/38**

4. MSIL Liquidator Action against MSIL Directors and Others

The decision in the claim brought by MSIL and the Trustee against the directors of MSIL, Madoff's sons, Sonja Kohn and others referred to above[12] was given on 18 October 2013.[13] As mentioned above, the directors were pursued by MSIL liquidators for breach of directors' duties in failing to prevent 'improper payments' passing between Madoff's London and US operations and it was argued that Mrs Kohn (of Bank Medici/Uni Credit Bank Austria) had provided 'valueless research' as a pretext for payments. **10/39**

---

11 *Rubin v Eurofinance SA* and *New Cap Reinsurance Corp (In Liquidation) v AE Grant* [2012] United Kingdom Supreme Court (UKSC) 46.

12 See no 10/35 above.

13 *Madoff Securities International Ltd (In Liquidation) v Raven & Ors* [2013] EWHC 3147.

10/40 Mr Justice Popplewell found that none of the defendants[14] were guilty of any wrongdoing nor did they have any knowledge of the fraud. There were no breaches of directors' fiduciary duties, no dishonest assistance or knowing receipt and no unjust enrichment; all claims failed. In the final paragraph of the decision,[15] the judge was extremely critical of the Trustee's conduct referring to 'this unfounded claim… [which] has been pursued aggressively and relentlessly', commenting 'Mrs Kohn has suffered poisonous press releases by the SIPA Trustee' and that the defendants' 'honesty and integrity has been vindicated'.

B. Spain

10/41 Following the discovery of the Madoff fraud, the Spanish Anti-Corruption Public Prosecution began investigating Fairfield Greenwich, which had operated in Spain as the principal feeder fund. In July 2010, the public prosecutor concluded that there was no evidence of embezzlement or money laundering or wrongdoing by Fairfield and, therefore, closed the investigation. This dissuaded lawyers and investors in Spain from filing actions against Fairfield in Spain, since they would not be supported by the public prosecutor's evidence.

10/42 As mentioned above, and as throughout Europe, many private investors have reached confidential settlements. The main Spanish banks suffering losses, Santander and BBVA, have not commenced any legal actions, even though their exposure is thought to be around US$ 6 billion.

C. Ireland

10/43 Press reports have predicted that the Madoff litigation is likely to become the biggest in Ireland's history. Two Irish funds, Thema International and Alternative Advantage, brought claims against HSBC Institutional Trusts Services, a custodian of the funds, claiming losses of more than US$ 1 billion and US$ 100 million respectively, after it allegedly used BLMIS as a sub-custodian in the US.

14 As above Madoff's brother Peter pleaded guilty to conspiracy in 2012 and is currently serving 10 years in prison. Whilst originally a defendant, the MSIL liquidators settled with him earlier this year. Peter Madoff provided evidence in the trial but repeatedly invoked his right against self-incrimination per the 5th Amendment of the US Constitution.

15 At para 672.

Further, a number of investors in turn have brought claims against Thema and HSBC (as custodian) and 27 others. This investor litigation has given rise to a number of interesting interlocutory judgments of the Commercial Court in Dublin on case management procedures in dealing with related proceedings, on champerty[16] and issues of *forum non conveniens*. **10/44**

In November 2012 the press reported on a settlement reached between HSBC and BVI registered Kalix Funds Limited. Kalix had sought US$ 35.6 million from HSBC arguing that HSBC should have safeguarded the money it placed in Thema. The settlement was reached on the first day of a six-week trial and settlement terms are confidential. The settlement with Kalix was predicted to be the first of many but that remains to be seen. HSBC went on to settle its claim with Thema in early 2013 – again on a confidential basis and without 'admission of liability on the part of any party.' **10/45**

Thema was a European-regulated fund per Undertakings for Collective Investment in Transferable Securities (UCITS). Custodians are responsible for managing the profits and payments. The legal issues being considered in the Irish cases include whether a custodian has an obligation to account to a fund or its investors arising from the UCITS directive/regulations and whether, aside from those regulations, the relationship between HSBC and Thema investors is that of a trustee and beneficiary in equity giving rise to a fiduciary relationship and in turn a duty to account. **10/46**

Some commentators consider that these settlements are likely to encourage others to pursue claims against banks which acted as custodians. They say that whilst the terms of the settlements are not known, it appears that a custodian bank has compensated the final investors, so whilst there has been no formal admission that custodians owe investors fiduciary duties or a duty of care or that they accept breaches of such duty, nonetheless it appears compensation has been paid. Naturally for HSBC there may be a host of commercial reasons why settlement was appropriate. Whether there will be ramifications for other custodian banks and litigation in other jurisdictions remains to be seen. **10/47**

---

16 In a hearing in *Thema v HSBC* in 2011, the Irish Court confirmed that maintenance and champerty still exist in Irish law; it is therefore unlawful for a party without a legitimate interest to fund the litigation of another or to fund litigation in return for a share of the proceeds. It is permissible for third parties to fund litigation in which they have a legitimate interest but such third party funders would however be exposed to potential cost orders.

D. Luxembourg

10/48 In a 2010 test case, a Luxembourg court held that victims who had invested via the US$ 1.4 billion Luxembourg-based LuxAlpha Fund established by UBS could not directly sue UBS or the auditor of the fund, Ernst & Young. The court found that the investors had not demonstrated damage separate from that suffered by LuxAlpha, nor that they had suffered individual damage caused by the alleged behaviour of UBS and Ernst & Young. Accordingly, they must file claims through the fund's liquidators. Over 100 sets of proceedings had been commenced against UBS, which was custodian for the LuxAlpha fund. UBS maintained that it set up its LuxAlpha fund (another UCITS fund) at the request of wealthy clients who wanted to invest in Madoff products and that it had no responsibility for the performance of the investments.

10/49 The EU, in July 2013, unveiled new proposals for banks to safeguard investment funds' (such as UCITS) assets to prevent fraud similar to Madoff's. The directive is still in its draft stages.

E. Switzerland

10/50 According to press reports, Switzerland has the dubious honour of being considered the 'most swindled nation in Europe' as a result of the Madoff fraud.

10/51 As discussed above, the Trustee's attempts to recover from UBS directly have been thwarted to date. However, press articles at the end of 2011 reported that the Trustee had filed lawsuits against Credit Suisse and Bank Julius Baer in the US Bankruptcy Court in New York and, in mid-2012, it was reported that a further three lawsuits had been issued against private banks EFG Bank SA, Lombard Odier & Co and Banque Cantonal Vaudoise.

10/52 According to press reports, Switzerland's banking privacy laws have made it more difficult for claims to be brought. In addition some investors do not want to reveal their losses in legal proceedings as they held their money in secret accounts.

F. Austria

10/53 In late 2010 the Trustee sued the Austrian bank Bank Medici for US$ 19.6 million in the US according to press reports, alleging that Sonja Kohn, its former president, masterminded the funnelling of billions of dollars to BLMIS from soon after she met Madoff in 1985. Litigation is also on foot in Austria and the Vienna public prosecutor is investigating Bank Medici (which has lost its Austrian banking license) and Sonja Kohn. Bank Medici has in turn brought various actions as a result of losses to its Herald funds.

There have been various Hague Convention requests made for deposition evidence from Austrian citizens involved in Madoff investments in addition to various orders made for the freezing of assets. 10/54

V. Insurance Issues

The myriad allegations levelled against various directors, officers and the like have given rise to a range of insurance issues in respect of claims made on financial institutions, errors and omissions, directors' and officers', fidelity and other insurance policies. Many issues arise in relation to what might be considered perhaps more standard coverage issues, such as the payment of defence costs, allocation issues and the payment of mitigation costs. For example, there have been discussions as to whether restitutionary/clawback claims are claims for '*damages*' which are covered under liability policies at all. There have also been debates with insureds as to their knowledge of 'circumstances' and whether such was pre-policy inception. 10/55

RICO (Racketeer Influenced and Corrupt Organizations Act 1961) exclusions and exclusions for SEC liabilities and/or money laundering have all been subject to scrutiny. Some insurers are running arguments that there can be no cover provided, for example, to custodians or investment managers where Madoff's conduct (who, following his guilty plea, it could be said was a money launderer and violator of SEC regulation and RICO *par excellence*) is at the heart of the fraud. Questions arise as to whose conduct the policy exclusion is directed to and whether there is a sufficiently strong causal link between such conduct and the loss to satisfy the exclusion. 10/56

Few Madoff-related coverage disputes have proceeded to trial – and these have been in the US and largely involved individual issues on a homeowner's policy or a professional liability policy. Most coverage disputes will remain confidential as between policyholders and insurers. 10/57

VI. The Market for Madoff Claims

In the last couple of years, it has emerged that there is a market for the claims that investors or funds might have for losses incurred investing with Madoff. For 10/58 example, there have been press reports of Deutsche Bank being sued by two hedge funds (Kingate Global Fund and Kingate Euro Fund) to enforce an alleged deal by which Kingate claim it was agreed that they would receive US$ 1 billion for US$ 1.6 billion of claims they have against the Madoff estate.

10/59 Speculators hope that claims can be bought up at an undervalue and then made good for substantially more value. Accordingly, both those buying and selling Madoff claims continue to monitor carefully the Trustee's progress on recoveries.

VII. Conclusion

10/60 Whilst the cynics argue that the Trustee, who along with his lawyers have incurred in excess of US$ 800 million in fees and disbursements (paid out of a separate state fund, not out of investor monies), is deliberately drawing matters out, others consider that he is doing a good job and has recovered more than has ever been recovered in any other Ponzi scheme. It can be no surprise that a grand fraud of this type, involving many billions of dollars in assets around the globe, is taking time to unravel and triggering substantial litigation.

10/61 What is clear is that the Madoff litigation is far from over and that there will be a number of issues still to play out across the European and US courts.

Harald Koch

11 Mass Damage in Europe: Aggregation of Claims, Effective Enforcement and Adequate Representation

I. Introduction

A. Relevance and Notion of Mass Damage

The topic of 'mass damage' in Europe has become the focus of discussion due to the increasing number of cases, incidents, and occurrences which have been reported[1] and which we describe as 'mass damage' – somewhat imprecise for several reasons: one is the bafflement and perplexity with which lawyers tend to react in the face of unforeseen and harmful events, disasters, catastrophes not being prevented and, hence, difficult to cope with spontaneously. The legal system, unlike other social systems, is very much dependent on precisely defined prerequisites for regulatory intervention. **11/1**

B. European Initiatives

Another reason to pay more attention to the subject of mass damage is the obvious incapability of our traditional private law systems to adequately react to such mass phenomena. Substantive tort law, as well as procedural principles, are firmly based on individual rights being protected or challenged, so that mass torts and mass damages are looked at from an individual angle, that is they are split up and at best may be gathered and then brought and enforced collectively by a representative. **11/2**

This perception of a lacuna is shared by the European Commission which has repeatedly pointed to the deficits of European law in varying constitutions, and which finally, in June 2013 drafted a set of Communications and Recom- **11/3**

1 See the *Case Studies* in this volume. For earlier collections of mass damage incidents see *H Koch/A Willingmann* (eds), Großschäden – Complex Damages: Rechtliche und alternative Regulierungsstrategien im In- und Ausland (1998); *iid* (eds), Modernes Schadensmanagement bei Großschäden (2002).

mendations for 'Common Principles for Collective Redress Mechanisms in the Member Sates Concerning Violations of Rights Granted under Union Law'.[2]

11/4 Apart from the confusing mix of European legal sources which was obviously due to different ideas within the Commission on the degree of their binding force, a number of crucial positions were agreed upon and these can be summarised as follows:

11/5 The Commission strongly recommends collective claims for compensatory relief in mass harm situations in the Member States (Recommendation recital 12), They suggest the designation of non-profit entities to bring representative actions (recital 18), the claimant party operating under the opt-in principle (Recommendation recital nos 21–24), and they agree on the key role that should be given to courts in managing collective redress actions effectively, thus ensuring fundamental safeguards against misuse (Recommendation recital 21).

11/6 As a number of Member States have already introduced procedures to bring collective claims for compensation, the Recommendations propose a set of principles common across the Union (Recommendation no 13) and want to strengthen collective redress mechanisms, supplementing public enforcement by private institutions. As mentioned already, the Commission's Recommendations are not binding, so that the Member States are now (only?) under political pressure to meet the Commission's and the Parliament's expectations.[3]

C. Double Meaning of 'Damage' and Claims Mentality

11/7 'Mass damage' is often the disastrous result_of an accident or another violation of the law we are confronted with, and so the second reason for the inaccuracy of the mass damage notion becomes apparent. It is not only a description of the economic disadvantages to many people, but also includes a remedial aspect in the sense of the victim's right to claim damages from a third party. Here we are touching on a problem which has been intensively discussed by lawyers and social scientists alike, and that is the widely diverse claim mentality in different legal cultures. What in some countries is accepted as bad luck or an Act of God, in other countries immediately can lead to a desire to find a liable party ('sue

2 Communication from the EU-Commission 'Towards a European Horizontal Framework for Collective Redress', 11.6.13, COM (2013) 401, and Commission Recommendation on common principles for injunctive and compensatory collective redress mechanisms in the Member States concerning violations of rights granted under Union law, 11.6.13, C (2013) 3539/3.

3 In 2012 the European Parliament adopted a Resolution 'Towards a Coherent European Approach to Collective Redress', 2011/2089 (INI), see also Recommendation no 4.

the bastard!') – Francis McGovern in last year's MunichRe Liability Forum convincingly showed the tendency in the US where a shift to individual responsibility and a new type of opportunistic plaintiffs' bar seems to have produced an extremely articulate claims consciousness and, hence, a high mass litigation rate even after natural disasters.[4] According to the European Co-Speaker in that Forum (Alexander Mack),[5] however, there is no such tendency in the rest of the world (which does not mean that there is no coverage by first party insurance like property insurance, being exposed to claims!).

What does all this mean for our mass damage topic? Here I can only try to 11/8
raise some questions and sketch some model answers in order to draw up something like a system of different procedural means to deal with mass damages being arranged in a certain order of priority.

II. Focus: Damage as a Result of Mass Torts

The focus is on the damaging results of the respective original cause – which 11/9
may be mass torts, man made disasters, but also natural catastrophes, which also increasingly lead to damages claims, because of failures to warn, to take necessary safety measures, to prevent foreseeable harmful consequences of a natural disaster, etc. Therefore, this damage concept already shows that it is difficult – if not impossible – to draw a sharp line between mass torts and natural disasters affecting a large number of people. We cannot exclude natural catastrophes from our analysis of mass damage, and the insurance industry is in a position to say a thing or two about the inclusion of 'hybrid disasters' in our considerations.[6]

III. Effective Enforcement of Mass Damage Claims

How are mass damages – in the sense of claims – effectively realised, enforced, 11/10
not only asserted with great publicity, but also recognised and turned into real damages awards? It does not help the victims if legal research shows that they have a case unless their claims are successful. This presupposes that enforce-

---

4 *F McGovern*, Litigation after 'Natural Disasters', in: MunichRe (ed), 15th International Liability Forum: Is there a potential shift from first-party insurance claims to liability insurance as a consequence of natural catastrophes? (Munich 2012) 13.

5 *A Mack*, The Perspective of the Primary Insurer, in: MunichRe (fn 4) 37.

6 *McGovern* (fn 4) 15, 17.

ment is desirable at all, and then (if affirmed) we have to discuss what effective enforcement means.

A. Functions of Mass Damage Enforcement

11/11 The true function of liability (in tort) and, hence its enforcement, is still highly controversial in different legal systems. Although it is not specific to mass torts, the question of objectives of liability (reduced to the two overriding principles of compensation and deterrence)[7] in mass tort situations by its simple volume is put in an intensified and multiplied way so that it becomes increasingly relevant, and, due to the sheer volume, it is of major social and economic importance.

11/12 If we follow the prevailing view in many civil law countries – that compensation is the primary function of liability – then, for procedural enforcement, it is necessary to carefully examine all the claims, all of which may not be identical. This could be a very difficult and cumbersome task. From the perspective of an economic approach to liability, however, it is deterrence and prevention of future losses that is clearly favoured as the core function of liability. I cannot go deeper into the debate of legal versus economic principles at this point.[8] It should be noted, though, that in those mass tort situations where every single claim by itself is of a substantial amount already and not only of a minimal or petty character, this individual volume of course requires compensation, whereas in *de minimis* cases this may be different as somebody who 'suffered' a 75 cent damage individually (having paid an excessive price, for instance) does not feel the need to take action. In this case collective legal action does not serve compensation purposes but makes sense only as a sanction for illegal behaviour which might prevent the offender from future harmful activities.

11/13 What is striking with this reaction to the two different scenarios is the change of perspective of those who decide to take legal action: Considering compensation aspects, it is solely the victim whose damage is under scrutiny, whereas the sanctioning and preventive purpose of enforcing liability focuses primarily on the wrongdoer whose behaviour is to be influenced.

---

7 See the discussion of these principles by *H Koziol*, Grundfragen des Schadensersatzrechts (2010) para 1/7, and by *KS Abraham*, The Liability Century: Insurance and Tort Law from the Progressive Era to 9/11 (2008).

8 Cf *G Wagner*, Prävention und Verhaltenssteuerung durch Privatrecht, Archiv für die civilistische Praxis 206 (2006) 352, 451 ff; also *H Kötz/G Wagner*, Deliktsrecht (12th edn 2013) no 59 ff.

Also, from the ex-post perspective of compensation, the damage is looked at after the harm has occurred, while deterrence and prevention take the ex-ante position and are aiming at future behaviour. Considering mass damage from the victim's perspective, this first of all (due to psychosocial reasons) triggers the need to help – which means: to make good, to redress an injury, to compensate. But as regards the wrongdoer, the primary reaction will be to impose a sanction, a penalty which, on the civil side of adequate remedies, may be a lump sum or flat rate summary payment, not precisely calculated according to damage and claims adjustment principles (*Differenzhypothese*, 'but for test'). 11/14

In summary, even if the awarding of mass damages primarily aims to compensate many victims, it has a strong deterrent and preventive effect as well, simply because of the much stronger effect of a damages amount multiplied many times. 11/15

B. Effectiveness and Efficiency

What then is 'effective' enforcement? It may be taken as the most efficient way to realise the legislative programme. This is in particular the European law mandate of efficiency: 11/16

Article 120 Treaty on the Functioning of the European Union (TFEU) expressly 'favors an efficient allocation of resources' and hence, has to be considered seriously in any given case. In the procedural context, the efficiency mandate confronts the judicial system and its actors with two related demands: One is for the plaintiff to receive the highest possible damages award (in relation to his minimal input of expenses). And the other demand is the public treasury's inevitable austerity and saving policy that prevents the (political) economy (= the judicial budget) from incurring unnecessary costs. For procedural enforcement of mass damages claims, this means that the accumulation of many similar claims into one set obviously is potentially more favourable in terms of the cost/benefit ratio. And it also saves the judiciary's budget from being charged with the surplus/remaining costs of numerous individual law suits, at least in systems where small claims do not completely cover the full costs.[9] 11/17

---

9 For an economic appreciation of the American way of accumulation cf *G Calabresi/ KS Schwartz*, The Cost of Class Actions: Allocation and Collective Redress in the US Experience, European Journal of Law and Economics 32 (2011) 169.

IV. Suitable Ways to Handle Mass Damages Claims Procedurally

11/18 What is the best way to handle mass damages claims procedurally? What are the appropriate devices we might use for mass disputes?

A. Out-of-Court Negotiations, ADR, Arbitration

11/19 Before we go to court, are there any out-of-court instruments we might consider to negotiate collective agreements, or to refer mass damages claims to arbitration?

11/20 In the (international) debate, there is a widespread longing for ADR without really getting to the problem and evaluating the pros and cons more precisely (in particular the cons!). The same is true for the very popular praise of an easy-to-use, flexible, unbureaucratic (= non-judicial) 'solution' to a mass damage situation. As Chris Hodges covers these questions more thoroughly in this volume,[10] it suffices for me to name but a few of the drawbacks of over-hasty out-of-court arrangements. There are in particular two pro-ADR arguments to be reconsidered, presented in the 'time-and-money-saving' formula, and in the appreciation of its greater flexibility as opposed to the judiciary.

11/21 As to the allegedly lower costs of ADR, this does not apply in every situation. Arbitration, for instance, is not generally cheaper for the parties involved, especially when complex disputes with many parties have to be resolved.[11] Also, arbitration institutions and arbitrators usually charge the parties quite considerable fees. The time-saving argument, indeed, is very much a point in favour of arbitration and ADR in general.

11/22 The really critical issue with ADR in mass damage disputes seems to be the relaxation of precise procedural and substantive legal requirements which are associated with ADR. Proposals for an early settlement tend to cover up the differences amongst the numerous claims (their size, their qualification) and thus 'level-off' these many differences and rather establish a flat-rate estimate. This is due to ADR's rejection of rigid procedural requirements and its much more flexible approach to legal consequences and remedies, which makes it much easier to handle many, possibly heterogeneous claims in one collective scheme.

10 *C Hodges*, Delivering Redress through Alternative Dispute Resolution and Regulation, 14/1 ff, in this volume.

11 As to the costs of arbitration see *GB Born*, International Commercial Arbitration (2009) 84 ff.

This gain in flexibility (and adaptability) of collective action is, however, very often coupled with a dubious loss of due process guarantee which is to be granted in state court proceedings: If there is not equal access to enforcement tools, possibly at reasonable costs, if individual notice, if a fair hearing, or the right to adequate representation cannot be provided in the same way for everyone this seems highly questionable and not in accordance with the rule of law.[12] This skepticism does not only sound pathetic but is reflected in the reluctance shown towards all kinds of class arbitration cases.[13] In order to recognise collective arbitration awards (as enforceable), it is either necessary that all the claimants and the respondent have submitted to arbitration or instead state court approval is indispensable, as provided for in the Dutch Collective Mass Claims Settlement Act (WCAM)[14] which is not an easy task due to the lack of clear legal criteria to be fulfilled. 11/23

B. Individual Pursuit of Claims, Test Litigation, and its Relevance for other Claims

Advising every single claimant in mass damage situations to take individual action is obviously not a solution on inefficiency grounds and due to the socially ruthless attitude regarding access to justice. But test litigation seems to be a way out of this dilemma, in particular if you can provide the test decision with binding force for all other similar cases.[15] This is what the German Capital Investment Model Proceedings Act (CIMPA or *Kapitalanleger-Musterverfahrensgesetz*, KapMuG) tries to achieve. We have been familiarised with the merits and the problems of this Act by Mr Tilp and Mr Roth already.[16] 11/24

Let me just point to two insufficiencies with respect to our general goal of finding adequate ways to deal with mass damages: One is the belated court intervention in the course of proceedings. Treating one case as a test case is only 11/25

12 *Hodges* (fn 10).

13 *SI Strong*, Class, Mass and Collective Arbitration in National and International Law (2013).

14 Wet collectieve Afwikkeling Massaschade, cf *W van Boom*, Collective Settlement of Mass Claims in the Netherlands, in: M Casper/A Janssen/P Pohlmann/R Schulze, Auf dem Wege zu einer europäischen Sammelklage? (2009) 171.

15 Cf already *H Koch*, Class and Public Interest Actions in German Law, Civil Justice Quarterly (CJQ) 1986, 66, at 75.

16 *A Tilp/T Roth*, The German Capital Market Model Proceedings Act as Illustrated by the Example of the Frankfurt Deutsche Telekom Claims, 9/1 ff, in this volume. – As to deficiencies of the KapMuG, see *H Micklitz*, Collective Private Enforcement of Consumer Law: The Key Questions, in: W van Boom/M Loos, Collective Enforcement of Consumer Law (2007) 11, at 16.

ordered after numerous cases have been brought already and are now pending in the same court, so that this procedure is simply intended to decongest, to relieve the court from duly processing every single case individually. This type of test litigation cannot really be an example for a model case being brought before many others, encouraging non-parties to join in, or otherwise exercise their right of action so far not considered.

11/26 The other pitfall is the extremely limited applicability regarding the subject matter: it is restricted to a very narrowly-defined detail of securities fraud cases, so that experiences with this Act – and there are few enough! – cannot be generalised. This does not mean that test litigation is never capable of meeting the requirements for the efficient enforcement of mass damages claims. As long as there is no statutory *res judicata* (binding) effect of the test case with respect to the absentees, it might be a very suitable informal procedural tool to advance one single exemplary case and then later trust in the precedential value or persuasive authority the model case will deploy for the similar cases which will follow.

C. Aggregation of Claims

11/27 Among the different procedural techniques to aggregate numerous claims and pursue them together in one proceeding, I would like to focus on three basic forms used in most European countries: joinder, assignment, and other forms of representation.

1. Joinder

11/28 The traditional procedural way to deal with a multitude of claims is the use of joinder devices. It is either the parties that join in or it is the court that chooses to consolidate a group of (pending) cases. This kind of joinder in most countries simply requires the existence of common questions of law or fact so that a joint procedure may be appropriate. The effects, however, are not very far-reaching (at least not in Germany):[17] There is not necessarily one uniform decision, and one party is not bound by the other parties' procedural conduct, but instead there is extensive legal autonomy of the single cases, so that joinder is more or less a matter of procedural convenience left to the parties' and court's discretion. Furthermore, joinder require, that the court is competent to hear each and every claim so

17 See *H Koch*, Class and Public Interest Actions in German Law, Civil Justice Quarterly (CJQ) 1986, 66, at 76.

that aggregation across venues or even jurisdictions is not possible. Hence, joinder may have some practical advantages such as saving a multiplicity of trials/ hearings, repetition of evidence in the same questions and the like.

2. Assignment

Assignment is another way of aggregating many similar claims without special procedural treatment: All the claimants simply transfer their claims by contract to one new creditor, the assignee, who can then bring his case in court, now suing in his own right. This is the technique used by a Belgian company named Cartel Damage Claims (CDC) which purchases claims from numerous victims of the defendants' antitrust violations and then asserts these claims by legal action in court.[18] The 'customers' (assignors) first receive a token consideration and share in the (advance on) costs of proceedings. In case of success, they receive the greater part of the amount sued for (up to 85%). A similar technique of collective law enforcement is the pooling of claims by claimants who set up an ad hoc (civil law) association with each contributing a sum of money in order to cover the costs of litigation and then assign their claims to the association.[19] **11/29**

All these forms of assignment and pooling require an agreement between the assignors and the leading plaintiff, it is true, which sometimes might be cumbersome to achieve; in some countries it is even necessary to observe certain form requirements. But if successful, it avoids many of the obstacles that most procedural systems put in a collective litigant's way: There are no representation problems (as the assignee acts on his own behalf) and no more joinder or consolidation actions are necessary – which in some countries cannot even be initiated by counsel as this might be unethical or an unlawful solicitation of business.[20] In this constellation, however, we have to pay attention to circumvention rules in some countries where assignment might be regarded as an unlawful evasion of such ethical standards. **11/30**

---

18 See approval of this assignment by the German courts: BGH in Betriebsberater (BB) 2009, 905; before already OLG (Oberlandesgericht, Higher Regional Court) Düsseldorf, Wirtschaft und Wettbewerb (WuW) 2008, 845 and LG (Landesgericht, Regional Court) Düsseldorf, BB 2007, 847.

19 See *B Hess*, Verbesserung des Rechtsschutzes durch kollektive Rechtsbehelfe?, in: H-P Mansel et al, Zugang zum Recht: Europäische und US-amerikanische Wege der privaten Rechtsdurchsetzung (2007) 61, at 70 ff.

20 This was the state of law in Germany until 2008 when a new 'Legal Services Act' (*Rechtsdienstleistungsgesetz*) came into force, allowing for more freedom of objective and functional information on lawyers' services (advertising) and, hence, their assumption of representation of numerous (assigned) claims as well.

3. Court controlled representation

11/31 Should we accept the simple assertion of numerous minor or petty claims being brought in court by a self-appointed representative of all people similarly situated? As the US class action model demonstrates, this self-appointment principle for lawyers is an extremely attractive procedural tool since the American cost and fee rules encourage the filing of a class action and are *the* incentive to bring suit. Where such incentives do not exist (as in Europe), self-appointment is much less attractive, of course. But there is another principle of representation that may enable a right of action on behalf of many others: quasi-public associations (like consumer or environmental protection associations) are licensed in the public interest – which means they exercise public duties (of effective law enforcement) – and they have a right of action by operation of law instead of those who would otherwise not have access to the legal system. In this model it is the court that reviews and confirms the representation on behalf of those persons affected by the association's activity: The court also re-examines the number of claims, their size and their merits, and thus ensures that this authority is legitimate and not only motivated by fee promises.

D. Adequate Representation

11/32 This brings me to the true and original representation question: Who is the most suitable representative of the many? Who has a right of action, who is in a position to bring suit, to answer to the adversary's and the court's questions, to negotiate a settlement? What about the authority of the representative to go forward on behalf of many claimants?

1. Conflict of interests

11/33 To start with, the principal-agent theory may give some answers which will be presented here, as it is this theory – also termed as 'agency dilemma' – that concerns the difficulties in motivating the representative (agent) to act in the best interest of the claimants (principal) rather than in his own interest.[21] First,

21 For a general introduction see *KM Eisenhardt,* Agency Theory. An Assessment and Review, Academy of Management Review 14 (1989) 57. More specific on civil procedure cf *JS Parker,* Comparative Civil Procedure and Transnational 'Harmonization' – A Law and Economics Per-

we have to make sure that these interests do not conflict, which means that the self-interest of the agent (to get a sufficient fee) coincides with what the principal strives for (the highest possible compensation amount). The American class action model solves the dilemma by distributing an award among the class members only after having set aside reasonable attorneys' fees (court approved!) from the awarded sum.

Whether this is a practicable solution for European collective procedures in particular depends on the nature of the respective remedies that are at stake: If the claimants ask that excessive profits be skimmed-off, then the costs for successfully disgorging these profits have to be debited to this account at the outset. 11/34

In Germany, for example, the problem with this solution is that the illegal profits can be claimed by consumer and trade associations, indeed, but not for their own benefit but only in favour of the treasury.[22] So there is no real incentive for private law enforcement by associations. 11/35

If the remedy is a simple action for (collected) damages then total compensation for the victims does not allow for a deduction of the agents' costs and fees from the award. Under the European loser-pays rule, too, the defendant has to pay damages plus costs and fees. Therefore, under cost allocation principles, a representative is ultimately paid by the defendant in any case.[23] 11/36

2. Representative's authority

As far as the right of action is concerned, this procedural question is answered differently in the European countries: Under German law, you cannot simply delegate the right of action to someone else without fully assigning the substantive right in question as well – unless the representative has a 'genuine legal interest' in the matter himself.[24] (This is different when it comes to the *lawyer*'s right of audience in court, however, which is taken for granted). Trustees, lead plaintiffs, and associations acting as representatives have to be authorised to do so.[25] 11/37

---

spective, in: R Bork et al, Ökonomische Analyse des Verfahrensrechts (2008) 387; *J Backhaus/B Cassone/GB Ramello*, The Law and Economics of Class Actions in Europe (2012).

22 This is the rule in § 10 UWG (Unlauterer-Wettberwerbs-Gesetz, Unfair Competition Act) and in § 34a GWB (Gesetz gegen Wettbewerbsbeschränkungen, Antitrust Act).

23 *R Stürner*, Rechtsdurchsetzung durch Gewährung von Klageanreizen?, in: Mansel et al (fn 19) 113, at 128 ff.

24 *L Rosenberg/Kl-H Schwab/P Gottwald*, Zivilprozessrecht (17th edn 2010) § 46 no 34.

25 *P Murray/R Stürner*, German Civil Justice (2004) 156, at 161 ff.

11/38 This seems to be a German speciality, and in other countries it is not an obstacle that the 'real party in interest' is represented by someone else. So the least burdensome and elaborate construction would be to create a trust, establishing a fiduciary relationship between claimants and their representative to enable the trustee to pursue the collected claims entrusted to him or her in the best interest of the beneficiaries – which would then shift the problems of distribution of the proceeds among the members of the claimant group to the trustee and the beneficiaries themselves.

E. Notice to all Parties Potentially Affected

11/39 It is a fundamental component of due process that everyone potentially affected by the proceeding has 'the right to be heard'.

1. Notice of representation

11/40 In mass damage cases we sometimes come up against the limits of this right of audience as there are always some people who are innocent (in the sense that they are not even aware of a suit pending on their behalf). The problem is very well known from the US class action's notice requirement: For a damages class action 'the court must direct to class members the best notice practicable under the circumstances, including individual notice to all members who can be identified through reasonable effort' (Rule 23 (c)(2)(B) Federal Rules of Civil Procedure).

11/41 This problem, however, will rarely arise in cases of mass damage of a considerable size, as everybody will have actively joined in from the beginning already. Hence, there is no need for a special notice. Only in cases of widespread minor damage affecting numerous people not even known to the promoters of the case, they might feel induced to publicly announce their initiative in order to solicit the additional joinder of claimants or mandates to pursue the aggregate amount.

11/42 Here we have the significant difference to the American class action: In mass damage cases most European systems of collective litigation will operate only under an opt-in rule; so far absent members of the affected group having suffered losses must have the option to join the other claimants or to exclude themselves and to proceed individually.[26]

---

26 *Murray/Stürner* (fn 25) ch 6 (E) 3; *Micklitz* (fn 16) at 20; *H Koch*, Europäischer kollektiver Rechtsschutz vs. amerikanische 'class action': Die gebändigte Sammelklage in Europa, WuW

2. Notice of settlement and appropriation of award

Once the exact size of the group of claimants and their identity has been ascertained (by way of original joinder or opting-in upon due notice), then the notice question may become relevant again in further stages of the proceeding: If the lead plaintiff and the defendant have agreed on a settlement and a way to distribute the awards among the claimants, all the absentees have to be notified of the settlement in order to be able to approve it – or to request exclusion. Again, this notice requirement serves to meet the fundamental due process mandate effective in all the countries dealt with. And that is why it should not be underestimated. 11/43

F. Financing Mass Litigation

Last but not least it is the matter-of-fact question of financing that is crucial for the selection of the most appropriate instrument to proceed in mass damage cases: 'It's all about money' and we all know that in the US it is the cost and fee issue that is the salient point of paramount importance in mass litigation cases over there.[27] 11/44

I shall limit myself to Europe, however, and here in most countries the starting point for the attribution of legal costs is the loser-pays principle (as opposed to the so-called American rule of costs). This of course considerably curbs the willingness of a claimant to take legal action not only for himself but also on behalf of many others similarly situated. 11/45

In weighing up the desirability of effective procedural enforcement of mass claims against the social costs incurred by the judicial system, we have to assess both the value of enforcement and the costs of the judiciary proceedings which are not borne by the parties. This is what legislators have to observe when adopting rules for right of action and standing to sue. And it is the court's task, too, to handle these rules in a responsible way when certifying a representative action on behalf of many others in a given case. 11/46

Of course there are certain procedural and constitutional guidelines to be met by legislators just as by courts – such as equal opportunities for the parties, access to justice, and procedural efficiency. And this ultimately means that we 11/47

2013, 1059. The execption is the Dutch WCAM (see fn 14) which operates under the opt-out principle.

27 See *HL Buxbaum*, Incentives to Promote Private Enforcement of Law: A View from the United States, in: Mansel et al (fn 19) 91, at 93ff.

have to determine whether these services can be granted free of charge: Is it in the public interest that as many claimants as possible can realise their claims? Or are the parties to be charged for their respective activities?

11/48 In the mass tort situations we are discussing here, that is damages of a considerable individual size already, there is a specific public interest only in providing for fundamental procedural guarantees like equal and efficient justice, but not for effective enforcement for as many individual claims as possible. This is different in mass cases concerning many small claims only: There it is access to justice, law enforcement, and public control of illegal behaviour that is at stake – with the corresponding costs.

V. Coping with Mass Damages outside the Law: Delegalisation?

11/49 Finally let me again point to the tendency of mass claims debtors to attempt to satisfy these claims without strictly and meticulously observing every legal standard. I mentioned this widespread practice already in the context of ADR (no 19ff above), and I would like to stress the delegalising effect of these practices which, in a way (at least for lawyers), highlights their own shortcomings, not to mention their risk of unemployment connected with it.

11/50 But delegalising also demonstrates that coming to terms with mass damages is not only a legal matter and definitely not only a procedural task. From a number of disastrous events with mass injuries and casualties we know that victims also need something other than pure financial compensation. Rather, the significance of complex and mass proceedings is also due to the public perception, appreciation and recognition of the victims' harm as being taken seriously. Part of this appreciation by enterprises being held liable is to prepare for simple ways to communicate with victims, to provide for counselling and advisory services, for emergency aid and immediate assistance in case of need, also for informal complaint bodies like ombudsmen or grievance proceedings and even to be in the position and willing to apologise, to ask for forgiveness in a non-binding, informal way, that is without prejudice for legal proceedings.[28]

28 'Wir brauchen eine Entschuldigung!' (we need an apology), Press release by victims' representatives 15 years after a railway catastrophe with 102 casualties in Eschede, Germany, Süddeutsche Zeitung 3.6.2013, p 8. As to the non-legal reappraisal of mass torts (contentment and social peace) see *H Koch*, Lessons from Mass Litigation in and for Europe: Effective Policies to

The big airlines, railway companies, and other enterprises running high-risk activities have prepared themselves beforehand for catastrophic events with emergency plans and staff training in order to be able to respond to more than just the financial challenges of mass damage. In this way, 'risk management' becomes another, more extensive concept, including the precautionary measures necessary to supplement legal processing and pure compensation.

Deal with Mass Disputes, Social Peace and Regulatory Goals, in: MunichRe (ed), Mass Litigation Conference. The Globalisation of Private Law Enforcement (2008) 54, at 67.

Bernhard A Koch

12 Multiple Tortfeasors in Mass Tort Cases

I. Introduction

In an ideal world, people would co-exist without interfering with each other's interests, in particular without inflicting harm on each other. The runner-up would be a world where such damage – being unavoidable – is occasionally done, but where the very person that caused such impairment subsequently makes sure that the damage is made good again, thereby either restoring the status quo ante or at least providing for a satisfactory equivalent thereto. 12/1

Needless to say, neither of these two worlds really exists. While the first option is objectively impossible to realise, if only for the mere co-existence of people per se, the second-best equally seems to be out of reach. Major obstacles along the way include uncertainties about the identity of the actual wrongdoer (if there is any) as well as problems of enforcing the latter's responsibility (if only due to her lack of funds and means), even if the damage could indeed be attributed to her. This unsatisfactory outcome is worsened, at least in the eyes of the victim, if the law prevents or at least curtails her claim for policy reasons, be it in light of a balancing of the competing interests or due to some other equitable reason. 12/2

This dilemma is already troublesome in a simple one-on-one setting, but gets more problematic the more individuals are involved on either side of the harmful event. The sheer magnitude of the overall losses, specifically in a mass torts scenario, sometimes seems to completely blur or even conceal the traditional mechanisms of tort law. Secondary or even tertiary defendants appear on the scene if the primary addressee of a claim for compensation is out of reach. 12/3

For the purposes of this paper, we shall mostly limit ourselves to a multitude of tortfeasors on the one hand versus one victim on the other and thereby disregard both the mirror image thereof (not triggering questions regarding multiple tortfeasors anyhow) as well as a combination of the two, that is, more than one individual on both sides, which may be a rather frequent scenario (if not the most likely in the context of mass torts). However, in deciding whether and how to shift a mass loss onto more than one potential tortfeasor, it does not make a tremendous difference whether it results from an addition of many individual losses or whether it was suffered by one single victim instead. Still, at the latest when it comes to procedural aspects, in particular regarding the cost of pursuing a claim and the availability of mass claim procedures, there will be 12/4 obvious differences that will be addressed under the respective heading below (no 12/53 ff) and in a separate paper contained in this volume.[1]

12/5 In order to facilitate the presentation, the term 'defendant(s)' will be used in the following for all addressees of claims for recovery, since they will not necessarily be tortfeasors in the classic sense. However, while the term presupposes court actions against them, in practice there may very well be out-of-court settlements, of course.

II. Range of Possible Outcomes

12/6 Before addressing various arguments leading to one or the other solution, let us first look at these possible outcomes in comparison. We will thereby disregard variations resulting from pre-existing contractual relations between the victim on the one hand and one or more defendants on the other and focus on non-contractual liability alone. Alternative compensation regimes will at least be mentioned at the end of this list in order to complete the picture; a more detailed analysis is provided elsewhere in this volume.[2]

A. No Liability of Any Defendant

12/7 'Casum sentit dominus.' This starting point of tort law in many jurisdictions – though often forgotten – means that a victim has to absorb her own losses unless there is good (ie legally acknowledged) reason to shift it at least in part onto someone else.[3]

12/8 An important factor turning the switch is the applicable standard of proving causation. It suffices in some jurisdictions (such as in the common law part of the world) to prove that the likelihood of a certain conduct or activity to indeed have caused the harm at stake merely exceeds the probability that it has not, in particular in light of some competing other potential cause. Other jurisdictions insist on a higher degree of probability to persuade the fact-finder. Traditionally, civil law countries even required that the judge be convinced with almost

1 See *H Koch*, Mass Damage in Europe: Aggregation of Claims, Effective Enforcement and Adequate Representation, 11/1 ff.

2 See *C Hodges*, Delivering Redress through Alternative Dispute Resolution and Regulation, 14/1 ff.

3 Cf *H Koziol*, Basic Questions of Tort Law from a Germanic Perspective (2012) no 1/1.

certainty, however, that high threshold has been lowered over time in many jurisdictions, though sometimes only with respect to certain risky activities.[4]

The choice between the one and the other approach significantly impacts the outcome of cases brought in either jurisdiction if it applies an all-or-nothing approach: If there is a 51% chance that at least one of the defendants caused the harm, the victim will recover up to her entire damage; if the overall probability that the cause lay anywhere within the sphere of the defendants remains below the 50% margin, the victim will not be able to shift at least part of her loss. In jurisdictions raising the bar higher, the victim will leave the courthouse empty-handed even if there was a proven 74% chance that at least one of the defendants caused her injuries (if 75% should be the applicable standard of proof), a scenario where she would have been indemnified entirely in the first group of countries. **12/9**

The higher the standard of proving causation, the more likely this option A will apply unless the jurisdiction concerned recognises paths towards partial compensation linked to a mere probability of causation (see no 18 ff below). **12/10**

Even if the hurdle of proving causation is passed, all other requirements of liability must be given, and no (full) defence must apply. However, the defendants may not have been at fault when causing the loss, there may be no basis for holding them liable without fault, the victims may have filed suit too late, thereby missing the deadline of prescription – to name just some of the obstacles along the way towards compensation irrespective of the proof of causation. **12/11**

Needless to say, the loss may still be indirectly spread via a first-party insurance system which may cover at least part of the victim's loss. This is certainly true for European jurisdictions offering more or less far-reaching social insurance cover for personal injuries, for example. To the extent social or private (first-party) insurers cover the victim's loss directly, they will invariably be eligible to pursue potential claims against possible tortfeasors subrogated to them by the beneficiary, that is the victim. While that leads to a change of the identity of the claimant, the claim as such remains the same, and if the victim herself has no claim against any of the defendants, neither will the insurer taking over the claimant's role from the victim. **12/12**

For pragmatic reasons, one also needs to keep in mind the possibility that despite partial or even full liability of one or more defendants, the economic outcome for the victim may be equivalent to no liability at all if neither of these **12/13**

---

4 See *I Gilead/M Green/BA Koch*, Causal Uncertainty and Proportional Liability: Analytical and Comparative Report, in: *I Gilead/M Green/BA Koch* (eds), Proportional Liability: Analytical and Comparative Perspectives (2013) 47 ff; in the following: *Gilead et al*, Proportional Liability for more details.

defendants is sufficiently solvent. In case of multiple victims, this may well mean that some of them may face the risk of insolvency if others win the race to the court and manage to collect compensation from the defendant(s) as long as the latters are still able to pay.[5]

B. Full Liability of one Defendant

12/14 If causation is the prime variable in assessing the liability of all defendants, depending upon the applicable standard of proof as just mentioned, we may end up with one defendant as the payor of the entire loss despite others who were suspected of at least having contributed thereto, with no possibility for the defendant to pass on at least part of her obligation onto the latter. This may be the outcome if neither the victim nor the defendant concerned (in whose interest the argument primarily lies) manage to prove the contribution of others with a likelihood exceeding the threshold of the applicable standard of proof. So if there is a 75% or higher probability that X caused the entire loss, but the likelihood that the remaining suspects Y and Z contributed thereto at all (irrespective of their respective shares) is significantly lower, a jurisdiction applying that percentage as the threshold will traditionally let Y and Z off the hook and shift the entire loss onto X.

12/15 X may also be the exclusive payor (though not of the full loss) if the share of causation attributed to her is, for example, 75% (proven by a 75+ % likelihood), with the remaining 25% caused by some unknown third party, even if that might have been Y and/or Z (but a 50% likelihood applied to either one of them would not even suffice if the jurisdiction applied a preponderance of the evidence standard). The victim will consequently have to bear the remaining 25% of her loss herself.

12/16 Even if more than one cause of the harm is proven, there may be insufficient grounds to attribute at least a segment of the loss to each of these causes, in particular if none but one of the potential tortfeasors was at fault and no other basis of liability applies, which again leaves just one defendant to turn to for the victims.

12/17 From a legal policy (but also economic) perspective, identifying one single payor among many other (at least at first sight possible) addressees of claims may not appear to be a desirable outcome – after all, in a mass tort scenario in particular, the one defendant singled out as liable may not have sufficient funds

5 Thereby disregarding potential limits set by insolvency laws, of course, as well as procedural alternative solutions.

to cover all losses and go bankrupt, leaving at least some victims undercompensated. While the desire to indemnify victims in itself cannot (and should not) outweigh the lack of justifications to shift the loss onto others, it may contribute to tipping the scales in favour of the innocent victims if the sole defendant fulfilled the requirements to be held liable and none of the others for which this would be equally true can be brought before a court of law and/or are insolvent. However, the weight of the reasons establishing liability play a role, as do the ordinary risks of life which the victims themselves have to bear.[6]

C. Proportional Liability of Some or All Defendants

1. Proportional liability in general

While the term 'proportional liability' may be interpreted broadly so as to include all cases where the loss does not remain with one single party involved, for example by way of contribution or via contributory negligence,[7] a narrower definition was used by a recent comparative project conducted by members of the European Group on Tort Law:[8] 12/18

> 'Proportional liability is tort liability imposed on D for harm suffered by P, for part of it, or for harm that P may suffer, according to the causal probability that D's tortious conduct may have caused the harm or caused part of it or may cause harm in the future.'[9]

In addition (and beyond the scope of said project), apportionment of harm according to causal probabilities may be adjusted according to the applicable bases of liability (such as comparative fault) or other aspects. Nevertheless, an evaluation of the interplay of various potential causes is the necessary starting point and will be considered further at no 12/35ff below. 12/19

In contrast to solidary liability (no 12/26ff below), the victim has to sue all potential tortfeasors in order to recover her full loss (or at least the portion thereof that may be attributable to causes outside her own sphere). If one of the latter is insolvent, that risk consequently falls onto the victim. While this may 12/20

---

6 Cf *J Spier* in: Principles of European Tort Law. Text and Commentary (2005) art 3:201 no 19f (p 62f).

7 As such, it would include what is covered under D (no 23ff) and E (no 26ff) in the following.

8 *Gilead et al*, Proportional Liability (fn 4).

9 *I Gilead/M Green/BA Koch*, Causal Uncertainty and Proportional Liability: Analytical and Comparative Report, in: Gilead et al, Proportional Liability (fn 4) 2, no 4.

seem unfair at first sight, the alternative may also be, if someone is held solidarily liable for the whole loss (equally without a chance to pass at least parts of it onto another suspect) even if there is a significant chance that she had not contributed to causing that loss at all. This is why the European Group on Tort Law in their Principles of European Tort Law (PETL) opted in favour of proportional liability in cases of alternative causation (arts 3:103 and 3:106 PETL).

2. Loss of a chance

12/21 A similar outcome may be achieved by applying the doctrine of the loss of a chance as developed in France and recognised in other jurisdictions such as the Netherlands or Spain, at least if one of the potential causes lies in the victim's own sphere (such as a predisposition).[10] The doctrine may be interpreted both from a damage as well as from a causation point of view. Under the former (which seems to be the prevalent one[11]), the victim's loss is redefined and distinguished from the actual harm suffered: If it remains unclear whether the defendant(s) caused it, but if her (their) contribution at least lowered the victim's chance of avoiding said harm, the latter can recover a portion thereof corresponding to the ratio of probabilities. If successful, she will recover the entirety of said portion (ie the full 'secondary' harm as redefined by the doctrine) while having to bear the remainder herself (the difference between what she was awarded and the actual – 'primary' – harm which was the starting point of the action).

12/22 Awarding compensation for the mere loss of a chance has been labelled 'proportional liability in disguise',[12] and truly so, as it conceals the award of partial compensation behind the fiction of indemnifying a standalone harm which per se does not exist, but is the mere product of calculation on the basis of a 'true' loss.[13] Nevertheless, in light of its recognition in some jurisdictions, it may there be applied as one possible solution also in the mass torts scenario, particularly in cases of causal uncertainty involving risks within the victim's own sphere. However, it will not serve as a peculiar solution to the problem of multi-

10 See eg *BA Koch* in: B Winiger/H Koziol/BA Koch/R Zimmermann (eds), Digest of European Tort Law II: Essential Cases on Damage (2011) 26/30 (p 1120 ff).

11 *BA Koch* (fn 10) 26/30 no 1 (at fn 133).

12 See the quotation from a ruling of the Israeli Supreme Court in *B Shnoor/I Gilead*, Causal Uncertainty and Proportional Liability in Israel, in: Gilead et al, Proportional Liability (fn 4) 192, no 36 (at fn 40).

13 Cf *H Koziol* in B Winiger/H Koziol/BA Koch/R Zimmermann (eds), Digest of European Tort Law I: Essential Cases on Natural Causation (2007) 10/29 no 4.

ple tortfeasors as such, even though it may add further complexity to traditional approaches.[14]

D. Several Liability of Some or all Defendants

Under certain conditions it may be possible that more than one defendant has to indemnify the victim for a portion of the latter's harm, but not calculated on the basis of probabilities, but rather linked to an actual part of the damage itself. This is first of all true if the causal impact of the defendant's conduct can be attributed to one specific aspect of the victim's injuries: If, for example, the single one bullet in the victim's upper right arm can clearly be traced to only one defendant's weapon, even though further shots hit the victim in other parts of her body, which clearly were not fired from that defendant's gun, the latter only (or at least) may have to indemnify the victim for the injuries sustained to her upper right arm and the consequences thereof.[15] Such partial compensation may also be due if the quantum of harm that the defendant's conduct caused or her exact share in the overall outcome can be identified.[16] **12/23**

Several liability is only an option if the victim's harm is divisible – either in reality or economically, which may be the case if a second defendant at least contributed to aggravating a harm already caused by the first defendant.[17] **12/24**

---

14 Cf *O Moréteau*, Causal Uncertainty and Proportional Liability in France, in: Gilead et al, Proportional Liability (fn 4) 144, no 7, giving the example of a case 'where two tortfeasors are held liable *in solidum*, yet one for the whole damage and the other one only to the extent that there has been loss of a chance'.

15 If shooting the victim was a concerted action, however, the actual consequences of one participant's conduct may not be assessed in an isolated manner, but she may still be solidarily liable (now:) for her participation in the overall attack, no matter how precisely the impact of her shots could be reconstructed by ballistics. Cf *WVH Rogers*, Comparative Report on Multiple Tortfeasors, in: WVH Rogers (ed), Unification of Tort Law: Multiple Tortfeasors (2004) 271, no 14.

16 Cf the Austrian rule of art 1302 Allgemeines Bürgerliches Gesetzbuch (Austrian Civil Code, ABGB): 'In such a case, if the damage was caused negligently and the contributions to it can be determined, each participant is liable only for the part of the damage caused through his negligence. ...' Translation by *BC Steininger*, Austria, in: K Oliphant/BC Steininger (eds), European Tort Law, Basic Texts (2011) 1, 3.

17 See also no 12/47 below (including fn 34, where the economic impact upon the victim's assets is distinguished from the damages award indemnifying such loss, which as a matter of course is 'divisible'). Cf *K Oliphant*, Causal Uncertainty and Proportional Liability in England and Wales, in: Gilead et al, Proportional Liability (fn 4) 134, no 29: 'In English law, the starting point is to ask whether the claimant's injury is divisible or indivisible. If the latter, joint and several liability will be imposed. If the former, each party will be liable for the proportion of the

12/25 Several liability in particular may often be one partial outcome combined with another, if at least with respect to one specific portion of the victim's harm one of the defendants can be identified as the exclusive cause, with the remainder, for example, spread amongst other suspects (including or excluding said defendant) according to the likelihood of their respective contribution or – if unclear – in equal shares.

E. Joint and Several (Solidary) Liability of Some or All Defendants

1. Solidary liability[18]

12/26 At present, perhaps the most common outcome in cases involving multiple tortfeasors seems to be solidary liability,[19] which is summarised by Horton Rogers as follows:

> 'Persons whose acts cause a single, indivisible harm are generally each called upon to answer to the victim for the whole of that harm, whether or not they have acted in pursuit of some common design; and as between themselves they may call for the damage as a whole to be apportioned according to their relative responsibility.'[20]

12/27 This is also true for those jurisdictions (and again these are in the majority) which hold merely suspected tortfeasors liable for the harm they potentially caused. If there is more than one such suspect, the same rule applies, and again

overall harm that may be attributed to his or her tortious act.' Oliphant gives the example of *Holtby v Brigham & Cowan (Hull) Ltd* [2000] Industrial Cases Reports (ICR) 1086, where asbestosis was treated as a divisible injury, linked to the period of exposure at each employer.

18 In this paper, the term 'solidary liability' will be used instead of 'joint and several liability' even though a common law terminology may prefer the latter. This is in line with a decision of the European Group on Tort Law to use the former term as explained by *WVH Rogers* in: Principles of European Tort Law. Text and Commentary (2005) Title V no 2 (p 138): The term 'solidary' is used 'to describe the situation where each of a number of tortfeasors is individually liable for the whole of the damage suffered by the victim. It is difficult to find a suitable form of words here. It is essentially the same as the common law expression "joint and several liability" but we consider that to be very unclear. We consider "solidary" to be preferable even though it is used as a term of art in some systems and not in a wholly consistent manner.' See also *Rogers* (fn 15) no 3 ff.

19 For the US position, see *M Green*, Multiple Tortfeasors under US Law, in: WVH Rogers (ed), Unification of Tort Law: Multiple Tortfeasors (2004) 261, no 16.

20 *Rogers* (fn 18) no 8.

they are all liable for the full damage vis-à-vis the victim but can try to spread payments made to the latter onto all remaining suspected tortfeasors, again 'according to their relative responsibility' (though in this case influenced by the probabilities of causation).

As stated by art 9:101 para 1 PETL, which tried to build upon the common core identified in a comparative survey:[21] 12/28

> 'Liability is solidary where the whole or a distinct part of the damage suffered by the victim is attributable to two or more persons. Liability is solidary where:
> a) a person knowingly participates in or instigates or encourages wrongdoing by others which causes damage to the victim; or
> b) one person's independent behaviour or activity causes damage to the victim and the same damage is also attributable to another person;
> c) a person is responsible for damage caused by an auxiliary in circumstances where the auxiliary is also liable.'

Needless to say, the victim can only recover her loss once. 12/29

2. Contribution (recourse)

Only if the victim can claim her full loss from one of several (actual or potential) tortfeasors will the question arise if and how that defendant can recover the shares attributable to the respective others. The full picture of solidary liability therefore only shows after a second step (or series) of claims for contribution,[22] which have to be taken into account also when assessing the overall administrative costs of that solution. 12/30

---

21 *Rogers* (fn 18) nos 7, 10. See also *id* (fn 15) no 23: '[O]n balance solidary liability is so deeply embedded in the European systems we have surveyed that its abolition would amount to a legal revolution of a profoundly "anti-claimant" nature.' Cf also art VI-6:105 Draft Common Frame of Reference (DCFR): 'Where several persons are liable for the same legally relevant damage, they are liable solidarily.'

22 The latter term was chosen by the European Group on Tort Law as preferable to 'recourse' for two reasons: 'First, "recourse" is used in other contexts where the parties are not multiple tortfeasors. For example, one may speak of a subrogated loss insurer having "recourse" against the tortfeasor who has caused damage to the property insured. Secondly, "recourse" perhaps implies that the person seeking it has made a payment which he seeks to recover. However, in practice the apportionment of liability will often take place as a side issue attached to the main suit brought by the victim.' *Rogers* (fn 18) no 4.

12/31 On this second level of litigation, the liability of each remaining tortfeasor will typically be several,[23] so only the victim is protected by solidary liability, whereas with respect to the internal distribution of the risk that was provisionally passed onto the one defendant singled out by the victim's action, none of the remaining tortfeasors will commonly have to absorb any portion of the overall loss that is ultimately attributable to another (even if that person should be unable to pay). However, some jurisdictions would divide the contribution claims only among those ultimately solvent, therefore also effectively reassigning a portion whose payment is not enforceable vis-à-vis one of the tortfeasors to the remaining others.[24]

12/32 From a legal policy perspective, one needs to keep in mind upfront that the bigger the gap between the amount for which someone was held solidarily liable on the one hand and the amount she can recover from the other tortfeasors by way of recourse on the other, the less attractive a system of solidary liability appears to be (although it certainly remains the eternally ideal solution through the eyes of the victim, of course). After all, if the one defendant singled out by the victim as solidarily liable for the latter's whole loss ends up bearing only a comparatively small portion of that damage after spreading what she had to prefinance onto many other tortfeasors (or onto few with bigger shares than hers), it appears questionable why the victim should be allowed to address her as the effective insurer of the others in the first place. This analysis is influenced, though, by factors such as *ex ante* knowledge of the shares attributable to all potential defendants, the degree of fault attributable to the payor and the weight of other arguments triggering her liability. Furthermore, the burden of prefinancing may be split between the claimant and the defendant if the former has to bear part of her loss herself due to uncertainty of causation, in which case both sides may have to take additional steps to distribute their respective share onto third parties.

12/33 In certain specific scenarios of solidary liability, recourse may effectively only work in one way, but not in the opposite direction. Take the example of a terrorist attack: Assuming that the terrorists themselves are not sued, be it because they never got caught or because they have insufficient funds justifying litigation efforts, possible secondary or tertiary defendants include financers of

---

23 *Rogers* (fn 15) no 43. Cf art 9:102 para 4 PETL.

24 This is also the solution preferred by art 9:102 para 4 PETL: 'The obligation to make contribution is several, that is to say, the person subject to it is liable only for his apportioned share of responsibility for the damage under this Article; but where it is not possible to enforce a judgment for contribution against one person liable his share is to be reallocated among the other persons liable in proportion to their responsibility.'

terrorism, but also companies or authorities in charge of security which allegedly was not provided adequately.[25] These latter defendants could at least theoretically pass on what has become their loss to the terrorists, though subject to the same practical restraints. In the unlikely case that the terrorists had indemnified the victims themselves, however, they would not have a corresponding claim in recourse against these other potential payors.

F. Alternative Compensation Schemes

Apart from tort law, a jurisdiction may offer alternative compensation schemes, 12/34
be it via a pre-existing fund scheme or one established ad hoc in the aftermath of a mass tort event, for example, via some insurance model. The victims may effectively recover at least in part via such regimes, however, in light of the typical uniqueness of such approaches and the deviations from tort law models, they shall be disregarded in the following. To the extent tort claims are subrogated to such funds, the same rules for recourse actions apply as if the victims had pursued such claims themselves, so that essentially the same factors apply when answering the question to what extent (and against whom) such recourse claims will be successful, even though the interest of the victim in obtaining fast and easy compensation will already have been taken care of.

III. Key Factors

A. Causation

1. Categories of causal scenarios

Depending upon the combination of possible or proven causes that indeed have 12/35
or may have led to the harm at stake, one may be more or less inclined to let the victim shift her loss altogether, or to shift it onto only one of several potential defendants and let the latter subsequently further divide the loss among the remaining others.

The first and most fundamental differentiation is between cases where the 12/36
victim had no influence whatsoever on the chain of events leading to her harm

25 See eg *BA Koch*, Comparative Analysis of Liability for Acts of Terrorism, in: BA Koch (ed), Terrorism, Tort Law and Insurance (2004) 282, no 7 ff.

on the one hand,[26] and, on the other hand, scenarios where at least one possible reason for the victim's loss may be found in her own sphere, either by her own improper and/or inadequate conduct. The latter may be subdivided into cases where the victim's contribution as such is certain or just possible, and these in turn may be grouped into instances where the victim's (actual or potential) share is known and others where it remains uncertain.

12/37 Moving on to differentiations on the tortfeasors' side, one could identify the following groups of cases, all subdivided into those where the respective share is certain and others where it remains uncertain:

- ll defendants contributed to the victim's loss.
- At least one, but up to all defendants contributed (or might have contributed) to the victim's loss (all may have set a cause, one certainly did, no-one was necessarily innocent).
- Less than all defendants contributed (or might have contributed) to the victim's loss (ie at least one was innocent, but also at least another one set a cause).
- If at all, only one of the defendants contributed (or might have contributed) to the victim's loss (all minus one defendant are innocent).
- Either none, but (possibly) even all defendants contributed (or might have contributed) to the victim's loss (so even all addressees of the victim's claim may have nothing to do with the latter's loss).

12/38 This leads to the following matrix of 50 different combinations with only the above criteria (needless to say, there may be more[27]):

	contribution by victim	certain		possible		none
2+ defendants	share	known	unknown	known	unknown	
all certain	known	1A	1B	1C	1D	1E
	unknown	2A	2B	2C	2D	2E
1 – all	known	3A	3B	3C	3D	3E
	unknown	4A	4B	4C	4D	4E

26 This is already a legal assessment, though – if the victim had not been at the scene of the accident, no harm would have been done to her.

27 There may be at least one further level of complexity disregarded in the main text, namely whether the damage has already occurred or is just feared in the future. See categories C in *Gilead et al*, Proportional Liability (fn 4).

	contribution by victim	certain		possible		none
2+ defendants	share	known	unknown	known	unknown	
less than all	known	5A	5B	5C	5D	5E
	unknown	6A	6B	6C	6D	6E
1	known	7A	7B	7C	7D	7E
	unknown	8A	8B	8C	8D	8E
0 – all	known	9A	9B	9C	9D	9E
	unknown	10A	10B	10C	10D	10E

Depending upon the combination, sympathies may move from one side to the 12/39
other side of the claim. If it is certain, for example, that the victim had not contributed at all to her own harm, and all defendants certainly had (1E and 2E), calls for merely proportional liability of the latter may be rather scarce. On the other hand, if at least one defendant must have been innocent (even though her identity may remain unclear), one could argue at least in cases where one possible cause lay within the victim's own sphere that the risk of identifying the true cause should not be shifted entirely onto all (possibly innocent) defendants.

2. Proportional liability as one potential outcome

In the above-mentioned project on proportional liability,[28] several of these com- 12/40
binations were tested against the range of possible outcomes listed before. A comparative assessment of each alternative identified several key factual effects of the choice of either solution that need to be considered before proceeding to make the final decision:[29]

- How would the chosen outcome influence the conduct of potential defendants vis-à-vis its alternatives?
- Would the number of tort suits increase or decrease under any given scenario?
- How much would litigating each alternative cost?
- How uncertain are the respective scenarios?
- To what extent can informational difficulties be resolved?

28 *Gilead et al*, Proportional Liability (fn 4).
29 *Gilead/Green/Koch* (fn 9) no 146 ff.

- How are the probabilities of each potential cause distributed in light of the applicable standard of proof?
- How much – if at all – was either party at fault?

12/41 After ascertaining each of these effects with respect to the various potential outcomes in any given causal scenario, an evaluation of this assessment must be done with an eye to justice considerations on the one hand (balancing freedom of action and freedom from harm) and to efficiency on the other, that is whether the chosen solution 'increases overall welfare of society by promoting efficient deterrence, efficient loss-spreading and reduction of administrative costs'.[30]

12/42 Even though the project focused on causal proportional liability (CPL), this outcome was of course not perceived as the single one optimal solution in all scenarios. Instead, the project rather aimed at streamlining a more open-minded discussion by categorising scenarios and by providing commonly acceptable terminology for openly discussing the various choices including proportional (and not limited to solidary) liability.

12/43 The authors conclude, therefore, that 'there is no "right" or "general" prescription of CPL that would suit the needs of all jurisdictions. Each jurisdiction should find its own course. A major factor in this regard is the standard of proof.'[31]

3. Legal causation

12/44 Apart from factual causation as marked by the *condicio sine qua non* principle or deviations therefrom, legal causation may add a further layer of complexity onto the analysis and thereby influence the weight of each causal contribution to the harm with regard to the outcome of the case: Bearing in mind that policy arguments ultimately decide where to draw the line between *condiciones sine quibus non* that lead to liability and others which are deemed too remote, one may consider using the degree of proximity attributed to each cause's link to the harm as yet another element in weighing the factors supporting the ultimate outcome. There is a felt difference, for example, between actually triggering environmental harm by discharging toxic waste into a river in disregard of certain regulations on the one hand and the neglect of the regulatory authority to monitor compliance with its rules on the other. Both conduct may lead to liability, but between the two, the actual wrongdoer seems to be closer to the inflic-

---

30 *Gilead/Green/Koch* (fn 9) no 154 ff.
31 *Gilead/Green/Koch* (fn 9) no 178.

tion of harm than the supervisory authority at first sight. This is not necessarily so – the regulatory and/or supervisory system may have flaws in itself, if the polluter, for example, erroneously relied on false assessments by the monitoring body.[32]

B. Type of Harm

The type of harm may play a role in the ultimate decision on where to place the risk. To begin with, as expressed by art 2:102 para 1 PETL, '[t]he scope of protection of an interest depends on its nature; the higher its value, the precision of its definition and its obviousness, the more extensive is its protection'. The range of potential tortfeasors may be drawn wider in cases of personal injury or even fatal accidents as compared to incidents leading to pure economic loss,[33] but that need not necessarily be so – think of minor one-time allergic reactions without lasting effects on the one hand and major financial losses leading a large group of victims into bankruptcy on the other. **12/45**

Furthermore, one needs to distinguish between primary and secondary victims – losses incurred by the direct victim may appear to call for more urgent compensation than the indirect harm suffered by relatives or other persons closely associated to the immediate victim. However, at the same time one needs to bear in mind that mass torts cases in the past have at least contributed to shifts in tort law regimes from compensating merely direct victims towards acknowledging indemnifying at least certain secondary losses. The best example is the Kaprun ski train fire in Austria which is perceived to have been an important trigger for recognising the indemnification of damages for bereavement in that jurisdiction. **12/46**

Another important distinction regarding the type of harm concerns the divisibility of the damage:[34] If it is a single damage and therefore cannot be divided into several distinct parts,[35] a multitude of tortfeasors can only be solidar- **12/47**

32 Needless to say, the assessment may also be different where the two conspired or otherwise have to be treated as if there had been a concerted action.

33 *Rogers* (fn 15) no 6.

34 On this issue, see generally *K Oliphant/M Steininger*, Aggregation and Divisibility of Damage in Tort Law and Insurance: Comparative Summary, in: K Oliphant (ed), Aggregation and Divisibility of Damage (2009) 473 ff (in particular no 36 ff).

35 This obviously refers to the actual impact on the victim's assets and/or interests as well as the immediate effects thereupon, not on the harm as expressed by the damages awarded for it, since monetary amounts necessarily are divisible. On the question of divisibility of harm and when one speaks of 'the same' damage, see *Rogers* (fn 18) no 12 ff.

ily liable for the whole loss (or proportionally to the likelihood each member of said group contributed to the overall harm), so at least option II.D is ruled out by the nature of the harm.[36] However, this conclusion may not necessarily only be drawn on the basis of objective scientific assessment, but also be the outcome of sheer resignation – Gilead therefore concludes:

> 'that courts that seek to divide past losses among past actors in ways that would increase aggregate well-being through the effect of division on deterrence, loss-spreading and administrative costs, can often rely on no more than rough estimations or common sense. Given the complexities, uncertainties and the informational difficulties, neither economic analysis nor actual rules of division provide sufficiently effective guidance in this labyrinth.'[37]

C. Link(s) between the Parties

12/48 An important factor contributing to holding multiple defendants liable is the relationship among these. If all of them acted entirely independently from one another, they may possibly be sued individually, but some jurisdictions at least historically would refuse to hold them solidarily liable as they would otherwise in cases of (actual or presumed) concerted action or in cases of procurement, incitement or encouragement.[38] Where causation is uncertain, the relationship between the potential wrongdoers may therefore be decisive for the question of whether the victim will be compensated at all – as could be seen at least in the history of the hunters' cases in several countries: Apart from joint hunting sprees (or at least a presumption thereof) no liability could be established if only one shot hit the victim and there was more than one potential shooter, since the likelihood that it was either one of them necessarily failed to exceed even a 50% threshold of the standard of proof (and even more so if that standard was higher). In the meantime, the distinction between 'joint' and merely 'concurrent' wrongdoers seems to have faded away in most jurisdictions with

36 See also *Rogers* (fn 15) no 5 on the 'logical fallacy' of the idea of partial causation 'since there is only one harm and each who played a part in bringing it about must be regarded as having caused all of it'.

37 *I Gilead*, Introduction to Economic Analysis of Loss Division, in: Oliphant (fn 34) 449 ff, no 59.

38 Cf the separate rule for 'collaboration' in art VI-4:102 DCFR: 'A person who participates with, instigates or materially assists another in causing legally relevant damage is to be regarded as causing that damage.'

respect to the outcome of such cases, with a majority response of solidary liability attached to either relationship.[39]

A separate aspect thereof obviously has an impact upon who ultimately bears the loss among several potential defendants – recourse claims can be predetermined via indemnification clauses, for example, so an *ex ante* relationship such as a contract between multiple tortfeasors may be an essential factor at least in attributing the loss *inter se*[40] (or – if the victim was included or at least concerned – also vis-à-vis the latter). Comparably, a contractual or other preexisting relationship between the victim and one of the (or less than all) defendants[41] may limit or even exclude liability vis-à-vis the victim, who may still recover from the remaining others.[42] 12/49

D. Bases of Liability

While the reasons for holding someone liable are only relevant for the victim of multiple tortfeasors inasmuch as they must be given at least against one of them, they may bear some importance on the question of recourse if that one defendant is singled out as a (solidarily liable) payor and subsequently seeks recourse from some or all of the others. In a regime of proportional or several liability, the bases of liability have to be established vis-à-vis each individual defendant and lead to success against one or more but not all of them, if only because too much time has lapsed since the victim brought suit against the first defendant. 12/50

Whereas the difference between strict and fault liability no longer seems to have so much of an impact on the question of recourse,[43] it nevertheless still 12/51

---

39 *Rogers* (fn 15) no 9 f.

40 *Rogers* (fn 15) nos 37, 50; *id* (fn 18) art 9:102 no 6 and art 9:102 para 1 PETL: 'A person subject to solidary liability may recover a contribution from any other person liable to the victim in respect of the same damage. *This right is without prejudice to any contract between them determining the allocation of the loss ...*' (emphasis added).

41 Ex post arrangements between both sides of the claim, in particular a settlement reached between the victim and some (but not all) defendants shall be disregarded in this context. On the effect of settlements on contribution claims, see *Rogers* (fn 15) no 36.

42 On that problem, see *Rogers* (fn 15) no 18.

43 The PETL propose a flexible approach; cf art 9:102 para 2 PETL: '... [T]he amount of the contribution shall be what is considered just in the light of the relative responsibility for the damage of the persons liable, having regard to their respective degree of fault and to any other matters which are relevant to establish or reduce their liability. If it is not possible to determine the relative responsibility of the persons liable they are to be treated as equally responsible'. See also *Rogers* (fn 18) art 9:102 no 7.

plays a role in at least several jurisdictions,[44] though not necessarily in the extreme form that someone held strictly liable can subsequently recover all she has paid to the victim from other tortfeasors who had been at fault. It may be decisive, though, whether the victim can recover at all if someone within the latter's sphere had acted with fault and the only basis of a claim against a third person is strict liability, as evidenced, for example, by art 8 para 2 of the Products Liability Directive.

12/52 Even amongst multiple faulty tortfeasors, their respective degree of fault may have an impact upon recourse claims *inter se* in a solidary liability regime, either with respect to their availability altogether[45] or at least with respect to the extent someone held solidarily liable may recover from the others.

E. Procedural Aspects

12/53 Needless to say, effective access to justice is an important theme influencing the distribution of risks, particularly in a mass torts environment. The more potential defendants there are, the higher the costs of pursuing claims individually against each of them would obviously be, and the less attractive a system of proportional or several liability appears, at least from the perspective of restoring the victims' interests.

12/54 The cost aspect is further influenced by the question of who ultimately bears the expenses of litigation and therefore carries the costs and risks of successful litigation. An important side aspect thereof is the legitimacy of contingency fee arrangements, which traditionally were not looked at favourably at least by continental European legal systems, but now seem to be on the rise, if only through the backdoor of insurance schemes effectively replicating such cost-bearing schemes.

12/55 Apart from the monetary aspect, procedural systems may offer more or less attractive ways to join claimants and/or defendants, so the availability of mass claim settlement procedures not surprisingly is an important factor shaping also the recoverability of claims against a multitude of potential defendants.[46]

---

44 *Rogers* (fn 15) no 39.

45 On the US approach that intentional wrongdoers cannot claim contribution from other concurrent tortfeasors, see *Green* (fn 19) no 10.

46 *H Koch* (fn 1) 11/10 ff.

Further procedural aspects include problems of diversity of jurisdiction over all defendants and the availability of ways to actually enforce possible awards, particularly in a (partial or full) cross-border setting.[47] 12/56

While at first sight such procedural factors should play no role in reaching the decision whether or not substantive law shall allow a claim against one or all of multiple tortfeasors, it is evident that tort law always sneaks a glance at the possibilities of realising the claims it plans to foresee, which may tip the scales into one or the other direction if the aggregate weight of other factors would keep them balanced. 12/57

F. Further Factors

More pragmatic arguments may also play a role in assessing the preferable outcome of a specific case involving a multitude of potential defendants in a mass torts scenario. This includes, inter alia, the availability of a public fund system or other non-tort law solution that at least might buffer the immediate needs of the victim. Also, there is at least the suspicion that deep pocket arguments also play a role in attributing a loss to one (or more) of several parties involved, if only such pocket is supposed to be filled by (first-party or liability) insurance cover. This is undeniably true with respect to the choice of the victim's first addressee of a claim against several defendants who all would be solidarily liable – naturally, the insolvent ones among them will not be the obvious first pick. 12/58

Legal barriers may add further complexity to distributing mass torts risks if some of the potential defendants are granted absolution from liability via specific rules channelling liability, for example in labour law: Several jurisdictions hold employees immune from personal liability to the extent losses incurred by customers of their employer can be absorbed by the latter. While tort law proper would often provide a clear path towards holding these individuals liable, reasons taken from an entirely different balancing of interests (here the employment market and/or social security law) interfere with the genuine tort law analysis and derail such claims from the traditional track. 12/59

47 Cf *A Stadler*, Mass Damages in Europe – Allocation of Jurisdiction – Cross-Border Multistricit Litigation, 13/1ff in this volume.

IV. Policy Arguments in the Mass Torts Scenario

12/60 Allocating losses in a mass torts setting requires playing with the above factors (and more) even though these were at least originally developed for a much less complex scenario. While the goals pursued in a simple one victim–one tortfeasor case are still valid (compensating losses that originated at least in part from external sources without justification, justice and fairness in general, efficiency, deterrence of undesirable conduct, etc), expanding the range of potential defendants against whom the victim may turn may already shift the focus, but specific arguments arise (or traditional arguments are applied specifically) in a mass torts scenario due to the unique features of this (qualitatively and/or quantitatively) massive clash of interests.

12/61 One obvious question is whether the mass aspect per se should justify a unique solution. At first sight, huge losses seem to call for more generous approaches towards indemnifying victims, with an eye to multiple tortfeasors particularly by expanding the range of potential payors to secondary or even tertiary tortfeasors.[48] However, that seems to be a rather illegitimate argument in a more general perspective: Why, for example, should liability be extended to public authorities for failures of supervising a fireworks factory that exploded if even more deaths could have been avoided year-round on the streets by more intensive and elaborate control of traffic? Needless to say, if such blame is based upon a specifically dangerous omission on the side of the authorities in the fireworks case, whereas the traffic accident scenario is more generally a matter of insufficient means, the decision may indeed speak in favour of holding the state liable,[49] but a mere reflex shift towards the state à la 'casum sentit res publica'[50] cannot (and should not) suffice.

---

48 The further away from the immediate wrongdoing, the less suitable the term 'tortfeasor' appears – while these tertiary parties may be held liable, they did not necessarily 'commit' a wrong in the classic sense.

49 Cf also the role of the SEC in the Madoff Ponzi Scheme (*J Boldon*, The Madoff Ponzi Scheme, 10/1, 10/6 and 10/23f in this volume).

50 As expressed earlier in *BA Koch*, Comparative Overview, European Tort Law (ETL) 2005, 602, no 17. See also ibid, at no 14: 'On a more general level, public response to recent large-scale losses, whether caused by natural catastrophes or by man-made disasters, has confirmed once again that citizens apparently see their states as providers of unlimited insurance against any risk of life imaginable. It is also a figment of the public's imagination that the state is the guardian of the deepest pocket of them all, though nobody seems to realise who fills these pockets, even if they should be full.'

Also, the mere fact that there is more than one suspected tortfeasor does not in itself justify a more favourable outcome for the victim[51] – after all, why should the victim be compensated more readily (or even more extensively[52]) only because the same harm was perhaps not caused by just one, but by two or more wrongdoers?[53] If the victim was entirely innocent, though, and the uncertainty of the other parties' involvement in causing harm only relates to causation (or even just to the degree thereof), but not to the culpability of their conduct, that answer may very well be given in favour of the victim. 12/62

The latter also finds support from a deterrence point of view,[54] since it is desirable for a legal system to signal that improper conduct will be sanctioned. However, the less clear the inappropriateness is (at least ex ante), the weaker that argument gets. If a secondary or tertiary tortfeasor, for example the financer of an ultimately harmful undertaking, is only held liable if such activity materialises in massive losses, but not if it causes only minor harm to a single victim, one and the same conduct of the financer will be met by two entirely different reactions of the legal system. The weaker the case against the financer is (in particular the less predictable for the latter the harmful nature of the enterprise was), the less convincing the deterrent argument is (but also vice versa).[55] 12/63

One must also generally not lose sight of the simple fact that holding someone other than the victim liable for the latter's loss does not make it disappear 12/64

---

51 Cf *Koziol* (fn 3) no 2/80 on victims of catastrophes for which a special fund is available (but not for victims of other risks within their own sphere).

52 In mass tort cases, it seems rather common that victims receive considerably more compensation than what they would collect in a single tort case against a single tortfeasor, even if the latter acted more culpably than those contributing to the mass tort settlement. From a deterrence point of view, this is certainly undesirable, and from the perspective of equality, one wonders what justifies that the same harm deserves higher compensation just because more people were involved in the case. Cf the settlements in the Eschede case (*OE Krasney*, Ombudsman for the Victims of the Rail Accident at Eschede on 3 June 1998, 5/1 ff). Needless to say, higher compensation may be justified if the harm had been more significant, for example if the mass aspect per se increased the trauma or otherwise added to the immaterial harm in an objectively calculable way.

53 Needless to say, if the additional tortfeasors also caused additional harm, that of course deserves (only to that extent: more) compensation subject to the general conditions of tort law.

54 But see *Gilead/Green/Koch* (fn 9) no 15 fn 29 and no 45 fn 44: 'The extent to which tort law actually deters socially sub-optimal conduct is a matter of considerable controversy.' A recent empirical study questions the deterrent effect particularly with respect to private (non-commercial) conduct: *WJ Cardi/RD Penfield/AH Yoon*, Does Tort Law Deter Individuals? A Behavioural Science Study, 9 Journal of Empirical Legal Studies 567 (2012).

55 It remains to be seen how the role of the various banks involved in the Madoff Ponzi scheme will be assessed by the courts; cf *Boldon* (fn 49).

but simply passes it onto another, 'hence the damage is merely shifted and someone else suffers a loss by having to cover it'.[56] This is not less correct if the loss is ultimately shifted onto more than one alleged wrongdoer – it even becomes the more untrue the more defendants there are, since tort law should not turn into an ex post insurance scheme trying to spread losses onto a risk pool as large as possible. Needless to say, there may be good reason to alleviate the victim at least in part of the harm she incurred, be it by spreading it onto more than one other party, but the sole fact that there are more such others is no justification in itself in the absence of further convincing arguments – despite the fact that the share of these others gets smaller the more contribute, which in itself may be perceived as at least a minor point in favour of involving them.

12/65 On a more pragmatic note, however, one needs to bear in mind that the higher the aggregate losses, the more likely at least one of the defendants will run out of funds to cover her share (and even more so to pre-finance compensation of all victims under a system of solidary liability). However, bankruptcy can occur also on a much smaller scale, and here again one must conclude that if victims of single tortfeasors are not protected beyond the applicable rules of bankruptcy law against the latter's insolvency, why should they be better off just because there may be other parties involved? As long as the reasons for holding the latter liable in a simple setting would not suffice, they should not be disregarded in a mass tort case either.

12/66 In a mass tort case in particular, the goal of administrative efficiency is challenged more substantially since the cost of determining who should ultimately bear the aggregate losses may be disproportionately higher than in less complex scenarios. The mere cost of identifying the facts tend to be much more significant – just think of a mass collision versus a traffic accident involving merely two cars.[57] However, a complex mass tort scenario with a multitude of victims on the one side and a multitude of (potential) tortfeasors on the other with uncertainties as to who harmed whom may ultimately only be resolved by using the sword-stroke of an innovative solution like market-share liability to resolve such Gordian knot instead of disentangling every potential strand of causation, which may be significantly more expensive if feasible at all. Similarly, if it is a single harmful incident with the same kind of losses incurred by all victims, pooling their claims into one case may obviously already be more cost-efficient as compared to individual actions by all claimants sepa-

56 *Koziol* (fn 3) no 1/2.

57 However, the more complex such cases in particular get, the more likely an alternative settlement will be attempted; cf eg the German insurers' special system of handling mass collisions explained at <http://www.gdv.de/2012/05/inferno-auf-der-autobahn/>.

rately.[58] Procedural costs are substantially higher, though, in jurisdictions which do not offer these or other special solutions for aggregating claims, even if they should provide for a 'loser-pays' rule at the end. This is even more true when proportional liability applies, as underlined by Rogers:

> '[U]nder a system of proportionate liability the victim will be under pressure to bring suit even against defendants against whom he has a weak case, for fear that those against whom he has a strong case will seek to use that liability to reduce their "shares"; furthermore, it may often be the case that a defendant is in a better position to identify other persons liable than is the victim. However, where one or more tortfeasors is absent or not worth powder and shot, the significance of solidary liability is critical, for even with a system for recourse *inter se*, it is the remaining members of the group of tortfeasors who bear the risk that one of their number cannot be made to pay "his share".'[59]

V. Conclusion

Mass torts are – luckily – rare and singular events. One may wonder, therefore, 12/67 to what extent solutions foreseen for the run-of-the-mill bipartisan tort cases are suitable under such extraordinary circumstances, or if they can at least provide guidance. Bearing in mind that even in such simple cases problems of causal uncertainties coupled with complications of legal attribution may cause headaches, a one-size-fits-all solutions seems to be out of reach in mass tort cases involving multiple tortfeasors.

This may be at least one of the reasons why such extraordinary cases in the 12/68 past have often been resolved by inventing ad hoc solutions, at least in jurisdictions whose procedural laws do not provide for special tools such as class or representative actions that allow such a multitude (and/or magnitude) of claims to be handled adequately.

From a substantive tort law perspective, it seems advisable at least in such 12/69 complex scenarios to rely on what the Austrian scholar Walter Wilburg has called a 'flexible system':[60] Instead of applying a strict checklist of pre-defined factors, where liability is only confirmed if all such factors are given, irrespec-

58 Cf the German Capital Market Case (*AW Tilp/TA Roth*, The German Capital Market Model Proceedings Act as Illustrated by the Example of the Frankfurt Deutsche Telekom Claims, 9/1ff), which has even triggered ad hoc procedural legislation by the state in order to cope with the multitude of claims filed.

59 *Rogers* (fn 15) no 4.

60 See eg *BA Koch*, Wilburg's Flexible System in a Nutshell, ETL 2001, 545, with further references.

tive of their weight in the individual case, the latter is taken care of specifically in a more flexible approach, where weaknesses with respect to one element are counter-balanced by another element that shows particularly strongly in a given case. This would allow all the key factors listed above under no 12/35 ff (and more) to be considered individually and with an eye to the specific circumstances of the case, thereby bearing in mind the various policy arguments on which this list of factors and their interplay is based.

12/70 While this may lead to deviations from the classic tort law analysis, this may still be justified on the basis of the individual circumstances. More generally, one is tempted to look at the way rules are made in the conflicts of laws arena, where the overall goal is pre-defined (identifying the jurisdiction that is most closely connected to the case at hand), and the actual rules identifying the connecting factors are meant to implement these goals for the run-of-the-mill cases, whereas escape clauses allow a jurisdiction other than the one that is manifestly more closely connected in light of all the circumstances of the actual case at hand to be chosen. Insofar, in tort law we should strive for an escape clause for mass tort cases, which would not only allow us to apply the tort law tests more flexibly in such cases, but at the same time would avoid that these exceptional analyses backfire on the standard cases which typically do not deserve such special treatment.

12/71 Either way, resolving problems of multiple tortfeasors in a mass torts scenario can ultimately be boiled down to a very basic question of tort law in general: Which side of the claim should be favoured – the victims' or the defendants' side (even before proceeding to address the individual members of each group)? Jurisdictions building strongly onto the principle of *casum sentit dominus*[61] will tend to solutions preferring the latter group, whereas legal systems with a more pragmatic victim-friendly approach will not surprisingly tip the scales towards the former group in case of doubt. This alone indicates more generally (as has been said before with respect to proportional liability specifically[62]) that there is no one-size-fits-all solution for each and every legal system alike, which would not be a very predictable regime anyhow in light of the fact that complex cases such as the ones under survey here tend to require a case-by-case analysis rather than a standard procedure.

61 Above no 12/7.
62 Above no 12/43.

Astrid Stadler

13 Mass Damages in Europe – Allocation of Jurisdiction – Cross-Border Multidistrict Litigation

I. Cross-Border Mass Torts and the Need for Forum Shopping

Mass torts or mass damages occur frequently all over Europe. They are a consequence of mass accidents,[1] production,[2] mass consumption, and standardised contract terms in the financial,[3] telecommunications and energy sector. They may also arise from dubious financial instruments[4] as well as false or misleading capital market information causing considerable loss to investors.[5] Coping with mass disputes prompts considerable procedural problems, particularly as a great number are cross-border cases and the claimants or tort victims are often domiciled in different countries. 13/1

With respect to international jurisdiction over mass torts, a minimum harmonisation of the instruments of collective redress in the EU is a key issue for claimants. Until recently one could have taken as a starting point that the efforts at the European level towards 'a coherent approach to collective redress'[6] had ended in a deadlock. Since 11 June 2013 the situation has changed to some extent. The Commission finally published its long awaited policy on collective redress, but the proposed horizontal framework is far from establishing a uniform procedural instrument for mass torts. The Commission's policy includes a Communication to the European Parliament and the Council 'Towards a Euro- 13/2

---

1 Case Study by *C Perrella*, The 'Costa Concordia' Case, 4/1 ff.

2 Case Study by *MR Ferrari*, Silicone Breast Implants: Mass Tort and Massive Damage in Europe, 3/1 ff.

3 Case Study by *F Rolla*, Bank Charges, 8/1 ff.

4 Case Study by *J Bolden*, The Madoff Ponzi Scheme, 10/1 ff.

5 Case Study by *A Tilp*/*T Roth*, The German Capital Market Model Proceedings Act as Illustrated by the Example of the Frankfurt Deutsche Telekom Claims, 9/1 ff.

6 Consultation paper of the EU Commission, SEC (2011) 173; the results of the public consultation are summarised and evaluated in the study of *B Hess*/*T Pfeiffer*, Evaluation of contributions to the public consultation and hearing: Towards a Coherent European Approach to Collective Redress, <http://ec.europa.eu/competition/consultations/2011_collective_redress/study_heidelberg_summary_en.pdf>.

pean Horizontal Framework for Collective Redress'[7] and a proposal for Recommendations 'on common principles for injunctive and compensatory collective redress mechanisms in the Member States concerning violations of rights granted under Union Law'[8] (the 'Recommendation'). For the sector of competition law, the Commission proposes a directive 'on certain rules governing actions for damages under national law for infringements of the competition law provisions of the Member States and of the European Union'[9] and published an impact assessment,[10] and some ideas on the calculation of damages in competition cases.[11] Neither of the Commission's papers suggests an obligation of the Member States to implement particular instruments of collective redress. With respect to the broad field of 'rights granted under Union Law', which includes consumer law, product liability, environmental law and protection of investors, all that the Member States will get is a general recommendation to put in place collective redress mechanisms at national level for both injunctive and compensatory relief. There is also a bundle of non-binding common principles and safeguards against misuse. They cover key issues such as the recommendation to implement only opt-in mechanisms, recommendations on financing and on the representation of interested parties, and a ban on punitive damages. Even the more specific draft for a directive in competition law does not direct Member States to implement particular procedural instruments. Thus the Commission yields to the strong political resistance against any binding instrument of collective redress and accepts the different pace of reform in the Member States.

13/3 At this stage, instead of harmonisation there is increasing competition among some Member States to attract the 'big cases' to their courts (and law firms) by implementing new procedural instruments or expanding the existing 'tool box'. The Netherlands had an impressive international success with its Collective Settlement Act 2005 (WCAM) and some improvements of the WCAM proceedings came into force in 2013.[12] There is even a debate on whether representative organisations should be granted legal standing to file class action lawsuits in mass disputes – an approach which was almost uniformly rejected in 2005 in order to prevent a US-style 'litigation culture'. In the UK, there are

---

7 COM (2013) 401/2.

8 COM (2013) 396/EU.

9 COM (2013)404 final.

10 Commission Staff Working Document, Impact Assessment Report: Damages actions for breach of the EU antitrust rules, SWD (2013) 203 final.

11 COM (2013) 3440.

12 <http://www.parlementairemonitor.nl/9353000/1/j9vvij5epmj1ey0/vivie6xp2swk>.

also various ideas for opt-out class actions in competition law[13] or similar instruments with respect to consumer law.[14] In January 2013, the UK Department for Business Innovation and Skills (BIS) announced its intention to implement a settlement proceeding before the Competition Appeal Tribunal which will be similar to the Dutch WCAM.[15] Even without these rather new proposals, we can already observe a very heterogeneous landscape of collective redress in Europe,[16] albeit with some Member States remaining more or less passive in this respect. This applies in particular to Germany.[17] The Commission's non-binding recommendations of June 2013, for example not to introduce opt-out proceedings or not to allow contingency arrangements, will probably not prevent the UK and the Netherlands from proceeding with their initiatives; France also intended to establish an opt-out instrument for the effective enforcement of consumer claims but decided for an opt-in mechanism in a last minute change. Even the German provisions on test case proceedings under the *Kapitalanleger-Musterverfahrensgesetz* (KapMuG) as described in the Case Study by Tilp and Roth are not in line with the Commissions Recommendations which require that

---

13 Department for Business Innovation & Skills, Private actions in competition law: a consultation on options for reform, <http://bis.gov.uk/assets/biscore/consumer-issues/docs/p/12-742-private-actions-in-competition-law-consultation.pdf>.

14 BIS, November 2012: Civil enforcement remedies: Consultation on extending the range of remedies available to public enforcers of consumer law, <http://www.bis.gov.uk/assets/biscore/consumer-issues/docs/c/12-1193-civil-enforcement-remedies-consultation-on-extending>.

15 BIS, January 2013, Private Actions in Competition Law: A consultation on options for reform – government response, available at the BIS website <http://www.biicl.org/files/6310_10_12_2012_urn_13_501_front_and_back_covers_22-jan-13_private_actions_in_competition_law__a_consultation_on_options_for_reform__government_~_response_pdf.pdf>. The paper suggests inter alia to implement opt-out class actions with special safeguards and a settlement proceeding like the WCAM.

16 *R Stürner*, The Role of Judges and Lawyers in Collective Actions, Equality among Parties, Conflict of Interest, in: I International Conference and XXIII Iberoamerican Procedural Law Convention, Procesos colectivos – Class Actions (Buenos Aires 2012) 67 ff.

17 In November 2012 a moderate reform of the Kapitalanleger-Musterverfahrensgesetz (KapMuG) came into force, for details *A Stadler*, Developments in Collective Redress: What's New in the 'New German KapMuG'? European Business Law Review (EBLR) 2013, 733. In June 2013 the Green Party submitted to the Parliament a proposal for the implementation of opt-in group actions (following in part the draft published by *HW Micklitz/A Stadler*, Das Verbandsklagerecht in der modernen Informations- und Dienstleistungsgesellschaft, (edited by the Bundesministerium für Verbraucherschutz, Ernährung und Landwirtschaft, 2005), available at: <http:/www.jura.uni-konstanz.de/stadler/forschung/publikationen/hinweis-verbandsklagerecht/>.

claimant parties should be free to leave the collective proceedings at any time before the final judgment.[18] Thus, competition will continue.

13/4 Given such a diversity of instruments of collective redress and national idiosyncrasy, extensive *forum shopping* is pivotal for claimants or representative organisations filing lawsuits or entering into settlement negotiations on behalf of the victims of mass torts. Selecting the 'right' Member State in which to proceed with mass claims is important not only with respect to the conflict of laws regime[19] and hence the applicable substantive law. But it is even more important to find a Member State or a jurisdiction outside the European Union where appropriate instruments of collective redress are available in the first place. Without devices which allow a bundling of similar claims in one litigation beyond the traditional joinder of claims (*Streitgenossenschaft*), there is often no effective handling of 'the mass' – at least in cases with a very large number of claims. Since even the new proposals of the European Commission do not address the question of international jurisdiction, Regulation 44/2001 (the Brussels I Regulation) applies to collective redress litigation in Europe. Nevertheless it will be necessary to take into consideration how the situation can be improved and to discuss what regulations would be desirable if the Commission – as announced – will consider further action in four years from now.

13/5 In the first part of this chapter, I will analyse the existing regulatory framework in the EU with respect to contentious litigation and mass settlements. In the second part, it will be necessary to discuss the future of jurisdictional rules and address two different scenarios:

13/6 (1) Without a binding European instrument on collective redress in the near future, we cannot take it for granted that all Member States will implement instruments for the effective enforcement of mass claims in their national procedures – on the contrary. In this case, only *forum shopping* can provide access to courts where such instruments are available and we will have to accept that as a start.

13/7 In the absence of a particular procedural framework for collective redress in Europe, it is very likely that a single mass tort (for example, the horse meat scandal which misled thousands of consumers of convenience food, or any price-fixing cartel with effects all over Europe) will produce parallel or subsequent proceedings in different Member States, initiated by various plaintiffs (depending on national rules on legal standing of group or class representa-

18 In the KapMuG proceedings claimants cannot escape the binding force of the test case decision by opting-out as interested parties of the test case proceedings and not even by withdrawing their claim against the defendant.

19 Due to the Rome I and II Regulations this aspect carries less weight today.

tives) and on behalf of different groups of consumers or tort victims. The existing provisions of the Brussels I Regulation (arts 27, 28) will not be able to prevent repetitive proceedings or reduce the risk of conflicting results. Therefore, in the absence of uniform European instruments of collective redress, we should at least consider a new approach to handling these situations. We might need (i) new rules on the cooperation of courts and the coordination of mass litigation, and/or (ii) a European register for class or group actions pending in the courts of the Member States.[20] One could even consider (iii) flexible rules for the consolidation of multiple cross-border mass disputes following the example of the US Multi District Litigation Panel,[21] but probably not in the near future.

(2) In a second scenario, *forum shopping* may become less important one **13/8**
day. Provided that there is a uniform or harmonised instrument of collective redress at least for cross-border cases in all Member States, the plaintiffs' incentive for selecting a particular forum will be reduced depending on the degree of harmonisation. Given the existing differences in national rules on procedural costs, remuneration of lawyers and on the access to evidence, it could, however, still make a difference where mass claims are filed. A complete harmonisation of these procedural aspects – even restricted to mass litigation – is not very likely, but a certain degree of harmonisation might be achieved if the Member States follow the Commission's Recommendation with respect to the ban on contingency fees and the application of the loser pays rule. However, it is more likely that Member States will insist on continuing to apply their traditional rules of civil procedure to the new instruments of collective redress. European law could also grant Member States the right to choose between various instruments of collective redress in order to preserve national idiosyncrasies such as the German representative actions by consumer and trade associations (*Verbandsklage*) or settlement proceedings like the Dutch WCAM.

---

20 In Canada, the Canadian Bar Association has established such a register. The Commission's recommendations include only the idea of registers at the national level (COM [2013] 3539/3 paras 35–37).

21 United States Code (USC) § 1407. For the important role of the Multidistrict Litigation Panel cf for example the silicone breast implants cases, illustrated in the Case Study by *Ferrari* (fn 2) 3/30.

II. The Regulatory Framework of International Jurisdiction

A. European Union – Regulation 44/2001 (the Brussels I Regulation)

13/9 Within the European Union, the Brussels I Regulation in its present and future form (to be applied from January 2015) provides a rather clear regulatory framework for the international jurisdiction of the courts of the Member States. The system, which was originally established by the Brussels Convention of 1968, is well accepted and is based on the principle of mutual trust. Corresponding to the – more or less – clear catalogue of rules in its second Chapter (art 2ff), the Brussels I Regulation provides that any examination of the jurisdiction of the court of origin in the state of recognition or enforcement is permitted only in exceptional cases (art 35). Solely where the rules on jurisdiction provide a special safeguard for consumers, employees[22] and policy holders or beneficiaries of an insurance contract may courts review whether the court of origin did in fact have jurisdiction. Hence, where no cross-border recognition or enforcement is necessary, the Regulation relies on a correct application of the rules in each Member State.

13/10 The jurisdictional system of the Brussels I Regulation is based on the principle of *actor sequitur forum rei* (art 2 [1]): persons domiciled in a Member State shall, whatever their nationality, be sued in the courts of that Member State. In addition, the Regulation offers several 'special jurisdictions' which are often based on the rationale that the matter in controversy is closely linked to the territory of a particular Member State. For cases with a very close connection to the territory of one Member State, the catalogue in art 22 of the Regulation establishes exclusive jurisdiction. Jurisdictional rules for insurance and consumer contracts and for individual contracts of employment are also mandatory and plaintiffs have no choice where to sue the defendant if he or she is the 'weaker party'.

13/11 The Brussels I Regulation does not provide any special rules for mass claims or class actions.[23] Thus, in cross-border mass damage cases, an individ-

---

22 The new Brussels I Regulation coming into force in 2015 will extend the scope of protection provided by art 35 to employees.

23 Some Member States have already implemented class or group action proceedings; for example, Bulgaria, Denmark, Finland, Italy, Poland, and Portugal. Christopher Hodges has pointed out, rightly, that the terminology has changed in recent years from 'collective action'

ual claimant, a representative organisation or whoever has legal standing to bring such a lawsuit must carefully examine the scope of the collective redress and international jurisdiction. The requirement that courts must have jurisdiction applies to all claims which are subject to a court decision or a binding decision on a settlement of the case, irrespective of whether the collective mechanism is based on an opt-out or opt-in system.

B. Mass Litigation on a Global Scale and the forum non conveniens Doctrine

If we take a look at international cases and jurisdictions outside the European 13/12
Union, it is of course well known that the USA not only offers class actions at the level of Federal and State courts,[24] but is also quite generous in assuming international jurisdiction as long as the case or the defendant has 'minimum contacts' with US territory (except for securities cases and cases under the Alien Tort Statute as explained below). Together with the typical 'plaintiff-friendly' features of US procedural law (for example, pretrial discovery, American rule of costs) and substantive tort law (like punitive or treble damages), there has been a global tendency for many years to litigate mass claims in US courts whenever possible. The *Costa Corcordia* case[25] recently provided an excellent example for this strategy of plaintiffs. Although the *Costa Concordia* capsized in Italy and was both operated by an Italian company (Costa Crociere, Spa) and was flying the Italian flag, crew members and some passengers initiated class action proceedings in the US.[26] Presently, the outcome of the US litigation is not clear. US courts may dismiss the actions on *forum non conveniens* grounds or enforce the forum selection clauses in favour of Italian jurisdiction which are part of the

to 'collective redress'. The latter includes not only contentious litigation but also instruments for achieving mass settlements or declaring them binding on 'interested parties', see *C Hodges*, The European Approach to Justice and Redress (2011) Supreme Court Law Review 301, 313. For a more detailed discussion on the jurisdiction for cross-border antitrust damage claims *W Wurmnest*, Internationale Zuständigkeit und anwendbares Recht bei grenzüberschreitenden Kartelldelikten, Europäische Zeitschrift für Wirtschaftsrecht (EuZW) 2012, 933.

24 Due to the 'diversity' regulation in 28 USC § 1332, class actions including foreign class members will often be filed in Federal courts. The Class Action Fairness Act 2005 was explicitly designed to expand federal jurisdiction for class actions, see 28 USC § 1332 (d), 1453, 1711–1715.

25 Case study by *Perrella* (fn 1) 4/1 ff.

26 *Lobaton v Carnival Corp*, no 12-cv-598, US District Court, Northern District of Illinois; *Scimone et al v Carnival Cruise Lines et al*, no 12-3496, Florida Circuit Court.

passenger ticket contracts. Even if the US actions are successful, enforcement in Italy remains doubtful. Particularly with respect to punitive damage awards, in 2012 the Italian *Corte di Cassazione* confirmed that they are contrary to public policy and hence not enforceable in Italy.[27]

13/13 The broad concept of international jurisdiction is restricted by the common law doctrine of *forum non conveniens* which allows US courts to refuse to take jurisdiction over cases where there is a more appropriate forum outside the US.[28] The doctrine also applies – with modifications – in Canada,[29] Australia[30] and – with restrictions owing to the Brussels I Regulation – in the UK. US courts will balance the plaintiff's choice of forum against the inconvenience for the defendant and also for the court (including public interest) to have the litigation in the selected forum. Thus, *forum non conveniens* is the gatekeeper against a flood of claims filed by foreigners in the US. This chapter will not go into details of the doctrine and its application by US courts. We must, however, accept that conceding such a broad discretion to courts in terms of jurisdiction brings about great uncertainty for the parties. Therefore and with respect to the clear cut jurisdictional system in the EU, the European Court of Justice (ECJ) in its *Owusu* decision has made clear that, within the scope of application of the Brussels I Regulation, courts in the UK are not allowed to apply the doctrine.[31] There is, however, still some dispute about the scope of the *Owusu* decision. English courts try to preserve at least part of the *forum non conveniens* doctrine and it is often invoked by defendants indirectly. Two types of cases become relevant in this context and are described in the case studies of this book. For example, some English courts have decided that, even within the scope of application of the Brussels I Regulation, situations may occur when English courts are seized based on art 2 (defendant's domicile in the UK), but non-EU courts claim exclu-

---

27 *Soc Ruffinati v Oyola-Rosado*, Cassazione, 8 February 2012, no 1781/2012, Foro italiano 2012, I, 1449. The German Federal High Court (Bundesgerichtshof, BGH) decided so already in the 1990s: Neue Juristische Wochenschrift (NJW) 1992, 3102.

28 The most instructive example of the factors which courts take into consideration when applying the *forum non conveniens* doctrine is the famous Bhopal case: *In re Union Carbide Corporation's Gas Plant at Bhopal*, United States Court of Appeals, 809 Federal Reporter, Second Series (F 2d) 195 (2d Cir 1987).

29 For example, *Amchem Products Inc v British Columbia Worker's Compensation Board* [1993] 1 Supreme Court Reports (SCR) 897.

30 According to Australian case law, the doctrine applies only if the selected forum in Australia is 'clearly inappropriate', *Regie National des Usines Renault SA v Zhang* (2002) 210 Commonwealth Law Reports (CLR) 491 (High Court of Australia).

31 ECJ C-281/02, *Owusu v Jackson and Others* [2005] European Court Reports (ECR) I-1383; <http://www.bailii.org/eu/cases/EUECJ/2005/C28102.html>.

sive jurisdiction over the dispute based on regulations similar to art 22 of the Brussels I Regulation.[32] The situation is neither covered by art 22 nor by art 25 of the Brussels I Regulation which both explicitly refer only to the exclusive jurisdiction of another Member State. Absent an ECJ decision on the question whether art 22 should have at least a 'reflexive application' (whatever that may be), there is some tendency to accept such a reflexive effect of art 22 even though this comes close to *forum non conveniens* considerations.[33] Another gateway to *forum non conveniens* considerations is illustrated by the South African silicosis cases where plaintiffs frankly admit their tactical reasons for filing a lawsuit on behalf of approximately 1,500 South African miners in the London High Court despite the fact that the litigation relates to wrongs allegedly committed in South Africa and all the victims are South African miners.[34] Jurisdiction of the English court is based on art 2 Brussels I Regulation and on the argument that the defendant, Anglo American South Africa (AASA), although a South African based company, has its 'central administration' and its 'principle place of business' (art 60 of the Regulation) in London because AASA is a wholly-owned subsidiary of Anglo American Plc with headquarters in London. The case raises very interesting issues with respect to art 2, 60 of the Brussels I Regulation (details will be discussed under no 13/16 ff below). The question whether the High Court will give these articles a rather broad or a more strict interpretation will indirectly depend on whether the judges consider courts in South Africa a more appropriate forum. Plaintiffs also rely on a former South African case litigated in the UK which involved 3,000 South African plaintiffs suffering from asbestos related personal injuries. In the *Cape v Lubbe*[35] decision, the House of Lords overruled the decision of the Court of Appeals and accepted the defendants' argument that a refusal to accept jurisdiction would amount to a denial of justice because South African laws would not provide legal aid or any other chance of funding proceedings for a group action of the numerous

---

32 *Ferrexpo AG v Gilson Investment Ltd* [2012] England & Wales High Court (EWHC) 721 (Comm); in *Catalyst Investment Group v Lewinsohn* [2009] EWHC 1964 (Ch) Barling J conceded that the application of *lis pendens* (art 27 of the Brussels I Regulation) in these cases 'would introduce the wide *forum non conveniens* discretion by the back door, contrary to the ruling of the EJC in Owusu'.

33 For example *A Borrás/R Hausmann* in: T Simons/R Hausmann, Internationales Zivilprozessrecht, Brüssel I Verordnung, unalex Kommentar (2012) art 22 paras 9–11.

34 Case Study by *P Tansley*, South African Silicosis Litigation in London, 7/10 ff.

35 *Lubbe and others v Cape plc* [2000] United Kingdom House of Lords (UKHL) 41 (20 July 2000), 4 All England Law Reports (ALL ER) 268.

claimants. However, this case was based on the *forum non conveniens* doctrine and was decided before the ECJ 2005 *Owusu* decision.[36]

13/14 It is very likely that a certain tendency to litigate mass disputes before courts in Europe will increase. Despite the broad jurisdictional concept in the US, class actions are not available for European tort victims in all cases. In its 2010 landmark decision, *Morrison v First National Australian Bank*, the US Supreme Court restricted the access to US courts and hence to US class actions at least for so-called 'f-cubed'[37] securities cases.[38] As long as the US legislature does not revise the Supreme Court's rulings,[39] European shareholders who lost monies due to false capital market information or other violations of securities laws will be unable to pursue their claims through litigation in US courts but will have to pursue them in other (European) jurisdictions. As securities cases in the past have shown, the Dutch WCAM might be very attractive for shareholders to settle their disputes.

13/15 Another decision of the US Supreme Court which is in line with the *Morrison* decision was issued on 17 April 2013 and will probably strongly influence plaintiffs' tactics as to where to litigate some types of mass torts. In *Kiobel v Royal Dutch Petroleum Co*[40] the US Supreme Court restricted the scope of application of the US Alien Tort Statute (ATS)[41] and held that 'the presumption against extraterritoriality applies to claims under the Alien Tort Statute, and nothing in the statute rebuts that presumption'. Therefore claims filed under the ATS now require that the claims touch and concern activities occurring 'in the territory of the US'. In the same case, the Court of Appeals[42] had already ruled that corporations like the defendant Royal Dutch Petroleum Co cannot be held liable for violations of customary international law. The South African silicosis litigation case study has pointed out that English courts have already expanded their ju-

36 For similar cases cf Case Study by *H Marangos*, International Environmental Mass Litigation in the UK, 6/1 ff.

37 'F-cubed' securities fraud class actions are cases which are almost exclusively related to foreign territory: foreign shareholders bought shares of a non-US company outside US stock exchanges.

38 *Morrison v First National Bank of Australia*, US Supreme Court, 129 Supreme Court Reporter (S Ct) 2762 (June 2010).

39 *M Lehmann*, Eine neue Ära der extraterritorialen Anwendung US-amerikanischen Rechts, Recht der Internationalen Wirtschaft (RIW) 2010, 841–850.

40 *Kiobel v Royal Dutch Petroleum*, 569 United States Supreme Court Reports (US) (2013).

41 The Alien Tort Statute (28 USC § 1350) provides that '[t]he district courts shall have original jurisdiction of any civil action by an alien for a tort only, committed in violation of the law of nations or a treaty of the United States.'

42 *Kiobel v Royal Dutch Petroleum*, 621 F 3d 111 (2d Cir 2010).

risdiction towards a forum for victims who have suffered harm anywhere in the world as the result of actions of multinationals domiciled in England. The *Kiobel* decision may stimulate the trend in England to accept extra-territorial jurisdiction.

C. International Jurisdiction for Contentious Mass Litigation in the EU

1. Defendant's domicile

Court decisions and settlements (see no 13/28ff below) in group or class action proceedings regularly have a *res judicata* effect for all members of the group or class. Therefore courts must have jurisdiction over all the claims of the group, although the group members formally do not become fully-fledged parties to the litigation. Under the present regime of the Brussels I Regulation, this does not create problems with respect to jurisdiction if the claims are filed in the Member State where the defendant is domiciled (art 2 [1] Brussels I Regulation). Article 2 allows all kinds of civil proceedings to be initiated, but the downside of this rule is that the defendant benefits from its 'home' jurisdiction while group representatives and group members may suffer from higher costs and risks.[43] 13/16

If more than one defendant is potentially liable for the mass damage, art 6 no 1 of the Brussels I Regulation provides an ancillary jurisdiction for 'closely connected' claims. Defendants domiciled in any Member State may be sued in the courts of the place where one of them is domiciled. The requirement of a close connection between the claims filed against several defendants is not very clearly defined by the case law of the ECJ. However, if all claims are based on the same set of facts or on a joint action of the defendants, art 6 no 1 will apply. Even if – according to the applicable choice of law rule – different substantive tort or contract laws apply to the claims against several defendants, the court will have jurisdiction if the legal bases of the claims are basically the same.[44] 13/17

---

43 *E Lein*, Cross-Border Collective Redress and Jurisdiction under Brussels I: A Mismatch, in: D Fairgrieve/E Lein (eds), Extraterrioriality and Collective Redress (2012) ch 8, 133.

44 ECJ C-145/10, *Eva-Maria Painer v Standard VerlagsGmbH* = EuZW 2012, 182, 185, para 80, and Opinion of Attorney General Trstenjak, para 92. In a former decision, ECJ C-539/03, *Roche Nederland BV v Frederick Primus and Milton Goldenberg* [2006] ECR I-6535, para 26 = EuZW 2006, 573, the ECJ had applied stricter standards and had refused to apply art 6 no 1 of the Regulation to a case where different national patent law was applicable to the claims against the defendants.

Article 6 no 1 is an exception to the Regulation's rationale that international jurisdiction should not be solely based on the fact that various claims are closely connected. The exception applies only to the defendants' side and cannot be invoked to establish jurisdiction if various plaintiffs file claims in a cross-border mass litigation.

13/18 At first sight, art 2 Brussels I seems to be a rather rigid jurisdictional rule. Despite the 'home field advantage' it provides for the defendant, it turned out that in case of mass torts which took place outside Europe, plaintiffs sometimes prefer to rely on an art 2 based jurisdiction in order to obtain access to courts in Europe. The South African silicosis case mentioned earlier[45] illustrates the potential advantages for plaintiffs and the problems it raises under the Brussels I Regulation. In this litigation it is undisputed that the alleged wrongs were committed in South Africa. The plaintiffs are thousands of African miners who have contracted silicosis as a result of their work in South African gold mines. They allege that the mine operators at least negligently ignored the dangers of dust in gold mines, that they did not provide adequate safety equipment and permitted levels of dust in the mines which they knew to be dangerous.[46] For various reasons explained in the Case Study, the claimants picked as a defendant not those persons or companies operating the mines at the relevant times, and which were all domiciled in South Africa. Instead AASA became a defendant, a company which is via several holdings a wholly-owned subsidiary of Anglo American Plc domiciled in the UK. AASA developed mines in South Africa by obtaining outside investment and listed them in South Africa only retaining a minority shareholding. However, AASA provided services to the mines under management contracts. The claims are based on the assumption that AASA did at least have a de facto control over the mines which gave rise to a duty of care between them and the injured mine workers. The claimants thus try to benefit from English case law which allows individuals in countries with emerging economies to hold multinationals with a substantial presence in England liable for the activities of their subsidiaries abroad.[47] With respect to substantive law, it is a question of whether the parent company has responsibility towards its subsidiaries' employees. In *Chandler v Cape* the English Court of Appeals re-

---

45 Case Study by *Tansley* (fn 34) 7/1ff.

46 Ibid, 7/18.

47 For example *Chandler v Cape* [2012] England & Wales Court of Appeal 525: The victim had suffered injury due to the exposure to asbestos while working for a South African wholly-owned subsidiary of the English defendant. The subsidiary no longer existed at the time of the litigation and had no policy of insurance covering damage claims for asbestosis. The Court of Appeal imposed on the parent company responsibility for the health and safety of the workers employed by its subsidiary.

jected the suggestion that liability of the parent company in such cases is based on the 'piercing-the-corporate-veil' doctrine. It accepted that the parent company and its subsidiaries are separate legal entities. Nevertheless exercising control over subsidiaries may give rise to a special relationship and a duty of care to employees of subsidiaries. For the purpose of this chapter it is only important to realise that expanding the principles of liability with respect to groups of companies and imposing responsibility on parent companies has a considerable influence on the question of jurisdiction. The more potential liable parties with domiciles in different countries can be taken into consideration, the better the chances for plaintiffs to find an appropriate forum. On the other side *forum shopping* becomes even more attractive.

In terms of jurisdiction, the South African silicosis litigation offers another 13/19
interesting aspect which is also of importance for the London High Court. There is no doubt that the Brussels I Regulation applies in cases like this simply due to the plaintiff's allegation that the defendant is domiciled in the UK. The ECJ has held that application of the Brussels I Regulation does not require that the case before the court of a Member State has certain connecting factors to another Member State. Although the jurisdictional rules of the Brussels I Regulation require an 'international element', it suffices that the defendant is domiciled in a Member State whereas his nationality or the domicile and/or nationality of the plaintiff are irrelevant.[48] The core issue in the South African silicosis litigation in terms of art 2 is whether AASA is really domiciled in the UK. In contrast to the former Brussels I Convention, art 60 of the Brussels I Regulation has adopted a rather broad concept of domicile of companies and other legal persons. They are domiciled where they have a) their statutory seat, b) their central administration or 3) their principal place of business.[49] With respect to art 60 Brussels I Regulation, there is no ECJ case law dealing with the domicile of a company which is part of a corporate group. As a basic principle the domicile of each company (although member of a corporate group) has to be examined individually as it is a separate legal entity. The plaintiffs in the South African silicosis litigation allege that AASA, although not having a statutory seat in the UK, nevertheless has its central administration and/or principle place of business in the UK because the parent company Anglo American Plc has its headquarters in London. Indeed the English judge found that there was a good arguable cause that AASA has its central administra-

48 ECJ *Owusu* [2005] ECR I-1383; ECJ C-412/98, *Group Josi v Universal General Insurance Company* (UGIC) [2000] ECR I-5925.

49 Article 60 (2) provides a special definition of 'statutory seat' for the UK and Ireland where it means the registered office or, where there is no such office anywhere, the place of incorporation or formation.

tion in London, but there is no final decision.[49a] The final decision will depend on the interpretation of 'central administration' and/or 'principle place of business'. Is it sufficient that important decisions for the business activities of AASA are taken in the London headquarter of the parent Anglo American Plc? The plaintiffs' arguments in this respect are similar to those which have been discussed in recent years in the context of a company's 'centre of main interests' (CoMI) under art 3 of the European Insolvency Regulation (EIR). In a number of insolvency cases which involved debtor companies belonging to a multinational corporate group, UK and Italian courts had taken the position that a 'mind-of-management' theory should apply in order to define the debtor company's CoMI. This approach refers mainly to the internal structure of the corporate group and the way decisions are taken. It therefore often allows allocating a subsidiary's CoMI in the Member States where the parent company has its headquarters.[50] Other courts and authors preferred a 'business-activity' approach and pointed out that the subsidiaries' own activities and administrative structures are important. The whole debate was strongly influenced by the particular aspects of insolvency and the question whether a place of jurisdiction for a whole corporate group might result in better chances of reorganisation of the debtor. Therefore the arguments invoked are at least to some extent specific to the EIR and the interpretation of art 60 Brussels I will require different aspects to be taken into consideration.

13/20 However, despite the advantages a 'mind-of-management' approach could have in case of the insolvency of companies which are part of a corporate group, in its *Eurofood* decision[51] the ECJ clearly favoured the 'business-activity' approach and emphasised that jurisdiction over a (debtor) company has to be decided individually for each legal entity. With respect to the presumption in art 3 EIR that the debtor's CoMI coincides with his registered office, any rebuttal must be based on factors that are objective and discernible by third parties, particularly the debtor's main creditors.[52] The ECJ rightly points out that, with respect to interna-

---

49a On 24 July 2013, the High Court ruled that it had no jurisdiction over the claims filed against AASA. Claimants were, however, allowed to appeal the decision to the UK Court of Appeal, [2013] EWHC 2131 (GB).

50 *Daisytek-ISA* nos 861–876/03 (EWHC, 16 May 2003); *BRAC Rent-A-Car* no 0042/2003 (EWHC, 7 February 2003); *Eurofood v Parmalat* no 53/04 (Tribunale Civile Parma, 19 February 2004) Zeitschrift für Wirtschaftsrecht (ZIP) 2004, 1220; for further references see *N Probst*, Die internationale Zuständigkeit zur Eröffnung von Insolvenzverfahren im europäischen Insolvenzrecht (2008) 88 ff.

51 ECJ C-341/04, *Eurofood IFSC Ltd* [2006] ECR I-3813.

52 For a more detailed discussion see *A Stadler*, International Jurisdiction under the Regulation 1346/2000/EC on Insolvency Proceedings, in: R Stürner/M Kawano (eds), Cross Border Insolvency, Intellectual Property Litigation, Arbitration and Ordre Public (2011) 13.

tional jurisdiction of courts, legal certainty and predictability for potential litigants are important criteria. Thus it seems likely that the ECJ might give art 60 of the Brussels I Regulation a similar interpretation.[53] In the South African silicosis litigation, it remains to be seen whether the Court of Appeal will nevertheless apply a kind of 'mind-of-management' approach to art 60 Brussels I. It is probably inevitable in this case to refer the case to the ECJ for a preliminary ruling. Obviously the plaintiffs are not very confident that the English court will confirm its jurisdiction based on the argument that the UK parent company had a strong de facto influence on AASA's administration and activities, because shortly before a two-day hearing on that issue scheduled for May 2013, in March 2013 claimants launched another class action application against AASA in South Africa.

2. Tort cases

If none of the Member States where the defendant or one out of several allegedly 13/21
liable parties is domiciled provides any instruments of collective redress, plaintiffs may seek to take recourse to courts in other jurisdictions where appropriate devices are available. Depending on whether the mass damage is a tort or contract case, art 5 no 1 or no 3 of the Regulation may be invoked. In tort cases, all tort victims, regardless of their nationality or domicile, may sue the defendant(s) in the courts of the Member State in which the 'harmful event occurred' (art 5 no 3). This can be the Member State where the tortious act took place (which will often coincide with the defendant's place of business or domicile) or the Member State in which the victims suffered injury or harm (irrespective of the place where the financial loss caused by the injury occurred). The chance of a joint action of all tort victims against the liable party will therefore depend on the nature of the tort. In many international settings, like product liability cases or securities cases ('single cause mass torts'), the tort victims will suffer harm in different places which leaves only the place where the tortious act was committed as a possible forum for all claims. In other situations, such as a plane or train crash, or similar accidents (so-called 'single event mass torts'), all victims are injured at the same place and at the same time. Thus, the place of the accident is another forum which plaintiffs may select and in the *Costa Concordia* case for example all claims could be pursued in Italy.

53 The Commission's proposal for a reform of the EIR published in 2012 (COM [2012] 742 final, 12 December 2012) also confirms the ECJ decision in *Eurofood* and rejects the idea of corporate group insolvency. Instead it emphasises that the debtor company's CoMI must be determined individually and based on objective criteria discernible for third parties.

3. Contract cases

13/22 The chance for bundling various claims is a good deal worse in contract cases.[54] Mass damages may appear as contract cases because of the use of standardised contract terms in various sectors of law and very often customers, consumers or policy holders in several Members States may be affected by illegal contract practices. Although art 5 no 1 of the Brussels I Regulation establishes a special jurisdiction in the Member State of performance of the contractual obligation(s), for most cases it seems rather unlikely that the place of performance of the individual contracts will be the same for all parties.[55] Furthermore, with respect to consumer contracts, arts 15–17 of the Regulation provide special safeguards for consumers and exclude the application of art 5 no 1.[56] However, they apply only to claims filed by consumers (or against consumers). According to ECJ case law, these provisions are not applicable if consumers have assigned their claims arising from a consumer contract to a representative association or any other representative which is not a consumer.[57] One might thus assume that collective redress instruments which give legal standing to non-profit organisations, consumer ombudspersons, consumer agencies or other legal entities will not be restricted by arts 15–17 of the Brussels I Regulation and may use art 5 no 1 when suing on behalf of consumers or after an assignment of consumer claims, albeit that bears little practical importance owing to the requirement of a common place of performance. Even if all contracts contain a choice of forum clause, for example for the court of residence of the defendant, in consumer contracts such clauses violate art 17 of the Brussels I Regulation and are thus invalid.

---

54 It is noteworthy, however, that in some cases claims can be based on both, tort and contract. The 'Costa Concordia' case (Case Study by *Perrella* (fn 1) 4/1 ff) is a good example.

55 Nevertheless in some cases the place of performance of different contracts might be the same despite the fact that the claimants come from different countries – take for example an event like a football match or a concert with internationally sold tickets.

56 According to art 16 (1) of the Regulation, consumers may bring proceedings against the other party to the consumer contract either in the courts of the Member State in which that party is domiciled or in the courts of the Member State in which the consumer is domiciled. For actions against consumers art 16 (2) provides only the forum of the consumer's domicile.

57 ECJ C-167/00, *Verein für Konsumenteninformation v Henkel* [2002] ECR I-8111, para 3; *A Stadler* in: HJ Musielak, Kommentar zur Zivilprozessordnung (2012) art 15 Brussels I Regulation, para 1.

4. Choice-of-forum agreements

Finally, another option to establish jurisdiction of the courts of a particular Member State which offers instruments of collective redress are forum selection agreements. Due to the mass phenomenon, such clauses or agreements (art 23 Brussels I Regulation) will normally not exist between the liable party and all the victims in tort cases *prior* to the lawsuit. In contract cases, forum selection clauses may exist in some situations, but – as mentioned before – are invalid if they violate arts 15–17 of the Brussels I Regulation. Consumer claims may, for the purpose of pursuing them together with identical or similar claims in a single litigation, be assigned to representative associations or be sold and transferred to third parties who are not consumers. Then the question arises whether the assignees may rely on forum selection clauses included in the consumer contracts. It is, however, not very likely that courts will come to the conclusion that an invalid contract clause becomes revitalised only due to the assignment of the consumer's rights under the contract. 13/23

One might, however, take into consideration that once a mass damage claim has been filed in the court of a Member State which has no jurisdiction under the Brussels I Regulation, the parties may enter into a 'choice-of-forum' agreement. According to art 17 no 1 of the Brussels I Regulation, such an agreement entered into after the dispute has arisen may even depart from the special protection granted to consumers by arts 15, 16 of the Regulation. The group plaintiff who has legal standing to bring a group or class action may negotiate such an agreement with the allegedly liable party thus representing the whole group of tort victims. Even if the liable party is willing to enter into such a forum selection agreement, I have serious doubts whether such a contract will be valid with respect to art 23 of the Regulation. It is an agreement which is not clearly for the benefit of the absent plaintiffs only – some claimants might wish to sue the liable party individually before the courts of another Member State depending on the amount of damage they have suffered.[58] In February 2013, the ECJ decided in the *Refcomp* case[59] that a jurisdiction clause agreed in the contract concluded between two parties cannot be relied on against a third party '*unless it is established that that third party has actually consented to that clause*' under the conditions laid down in art 23. In that particular case the third party was a sub-buyer of goods and the forum selection clause had been agreed upon 13/24

58 For minimal damages it is very unlikely that claimants will prefer individual litigation over class or group actions.

59 ECJ C-543/10, *Refcomp SpA v Axa Corporate Solutions Assurance SA*; see also *Wurmnest*, EuZW 2012, 933, 935.

between the manufacturer of the goods and the first buyer. The ECJ found no reason to assume that the sub-buyer had entered into the original agreement. In the situation of mass damage claims, the absent group or class members represented by the lead plaintiff during the litigation will normally not explicitly consent to such an agreement.

13/25 Unfortunately the ECJ does not specify the requirements for the consent of the third party, but refers only to art 23 of the Brussels I Regulation. In this context an explicit consent is not necessary, implicit consensus suffices[60] but there must be a strong indication that the third party accepts the jurisdiction of the court seized or accepts the choice-of-forum agreement. If the collective mechanism is based on an opt-in system, one might assume that any opting in of the 'absent plaintiffs' gives the lead plaintiff the representative power to handle the whole proceedings including a choice-of-forum agreement with the defendant. With an opt-out system (which is rejected now in the Commission's Recommendations) one may doubt whether the ECJ would take the absence of an opt-out as a fictitious consent of the 'absent parties' to litigate the cases in the courts of a Member State which has no jurisdiction unless the forum selection clause can be relied upon. Considering that the court will never know exactly why an absent party did not opt-out – he or she may indeed wish to participate in and benefit from the proceedings, but he or she may also have not received any information about the pending litigation – implicit consent is difficult to establish. Interpretation of the 'absent parties' intentions will probably depend on the efforts of the court seized with the case regarding notification of the 'absent parties' and thus the probability that not opting-out is based on an informed consent. National courts might still take different positions if there was no individual notification of the group members, but only a public announcement without a guarantee that all group members received the information and had a fair chance of opting-out. Therefore, the representative power of the group or lead plaintiff will often depend on a case-by-case decision and on the general attitude of the Member States towards the opt-out mechanism. The Commission's Recommendation not to implement opt-out proceedings can probably not be interpreted in a way that existing opt-out mechanisms will always constitute a violation of public policy. Invoking public policy considerations is always a matter of *ultima ratio* and the Commission's Recommendation are a political statement rather than a legal or constitutional one. Furthermore Recommendation no 21 is open to exceptions if the opt-out is duly justified 'by reasons of sound administration of justice'.

---

60 *U Magnus/P Mankowski*, Brussels I Regulation, Commentary (2nd edn 2012) art 23 para 78 with further references.

In any case the ECJ reference to art 23 of the Brussels Regulation makes clear that any agreement with third parties requires that the consent of the 'interested/third parties' fulfills the formal requirements of this article. Subsection 1 requires either an agreement in writing, or in a form which accords with practices which the parties have established between themselves, or finally according to lit (c) a form which accords with the usage of international trade or commerce. The first two options will be of minor importance in mass tort cases. Only if the 'interested parties'' opt-in is declared in written or electronic form (art 23 [2]) will this constitute his or her consent to the choice-of-forum agreement in the form described in lit a of art 23 (1). In all other cases – particularly in proceedings with an opt-out mechanism – it goes without saying that the passivity on behalf of the 'interested parties' does not fulfill any requirements of 'writing' and one cannot assume – at least not today – that there is any custom in international trade or commerce which allows the passivity to be interpreted as such a consent. 13/26

In conclusion, presently the jurisdictional rules applicable in the EU do not offer a good chance of bundling the claims of all consumers or tort victims in a case of mass torts apart from some clear 'single event' tort cases. In the majority of cases, a lawsuit can be brought only in the Member State in which the defendant (or one of the defendants) is domiciled or – in tort cases – where the tortious act has been committed. If those Member States do not offer any instruments of collective redress, the effective handling of 'the mass' will often fail. 13/27

D. Mass Settlements and the Brussels I Regulation

1. Settlements negotiated in the course of contentious court proceedings

Today there is a global tendency for mass claims, once court proceedings have been initiated, to be settled by the litigating parties.[61] There are several reasons for this. Settlement is often a means to avoid the cost of litigation, but it also avoids lengthy proceedings with an often unpredictable outcome, and – if there is a risk of the liable party becoming insolvent owing to the total amount of damages claimed – a settlement can be a trade-off for the claimants who face the risk of being left behind as unsecured creditors once they have won the case. If a settlement is achieved after a lawsuit has been filed, then the general rules on international jurisdiction apply to the proceedings. Only with respect to 13/28

61 For national reports see *C Hodges/A Stadler*, Resolving Mass Disputes – ADR and Mass Settlements (2013).

recognition and enforcement may the situation be different depending on the outcome of the lawsuit. Most jurisdictions consider settlements to be a contract between private parties (and an instrument to terminate a lawsuit) without a *res judicata* effect. Therefore, both Chapter 4 of the Brussels I Regulation ('Authentic instruments and settlements') and the European Enforcement Order Regulation[62] on uncontested claims (which includes settlements) apply with respect to the *enforcement* of the settlement but not to the *recognition* of any preclusive effects. As regards mass settlements, the situation is, however, often different. Due to the principle of representation being the basic concept of collective redress, settlements in mass litigation are negotiated by the lead plaintiff who has legal standing to bring the lawsuit. Typically the absent group or class members are not involved in the negotiations and may not even have a chance of accepting the settlement or of opting-out of its binding effect. As a safeguard to the rights of the absent group members, and in order to cope with principal-agent conflicts which might arise between the lead plaintiff and the lead counsel on the one side and the group members on the other, many group action regulations require court approval of the proposed settlement.[63] Given that the court has the right to examine the settlement terms and to refuse the approval if certain requirements are not met, the approved settlement is not a 'settlement' within the meaning of the Brussels I Regulation but it is deemed to be a court decision.[64] Therefore the decision bears a negative preclusive effect, like a judgment, which may be invoked against any subsequent individual lawsuit

62 Article 24 (3) and art 5 European Enforcement Order Regulation (EEO).

63 Rule 23(e)(1)(C) FRCP. Many (European) regulations have adopted this principle, for example art 7:907 Dutch Civil Code; sec 26 Swedish Group Litigation Act 2003; § 254h Administration of Justice Act Denmark; sec 35-11 Norway Dispute Act; art 19 (2) Polish Group Litigation Act 2009; art 300 (3) – as a general rule – Portuguese Code of Civil Procedure; in the UK there is no particular rule requiring court approval of settlements in GLO proceedings or representative actions. Article 19 of the Israeli Class Action Law 2006 also requires court approval of settlements. In Germany, the 2012 reform of the KapMuG permits a settlement of the whole dispute during the intermediate test case proceedings and also requires court approval of the settlement, §§ 17–19 KapMuG.

64 The question is often raised for WCAM settlements. Many scholars classify the approved settlement as a court decision: *H van Lith*, The Dutch Collective Settlements Act and Private International Law (2011) 108–111; *T Arons/W van Boom*, Beyond Tulips and Cheese: Exporting Mass Securities Claim Settlements from the Netherlands, EBLR 2010, 857, 880f; *A Stadler*, Grenzüberschreitender kollektiver Rechtsschutz in Europa, Juristenzeitung (JZ) 2009, 121, 126; *A Halfmeier*, Recognition of a WCAM Settlement in Germany, Nederland Internationaal Privaatrecht (NIP) 2012, 176, 178–180; arguably also *B Hess*, A Coherent Approach to European Collective Redress, in: Fairgrieve/Lein (fn 43) ch 6, 114.

filed by a group member who is bound by the settlement. As a consequence, a court approving such a settlement must have jurisdiction to do so.

2. Settlements without contentious litigation

Another type of mass settlement may be entered into before or without any contentious court proceedings. The Dutch Collective Settlement Act 2005 (WCAM) is based on the idea that a representative organisation enters into negotiations with the liable party in a mass damage case on behalf of the victims ('interested parties'). Once a settlement has been achieved, the parties to the settlement contract may file a joint application to the Amsterdam Court of Appeals for a court approval of the settlement and a decision declaring the settlement binding on all 'interested parties'. The proceedings before the Amsterdam Court of Appeals begin on the initiative of one or several representative organisations and the party who allegedly caused the mass damage. It is important to note that the liable party, who will normally be the defendant in any contentious court proceedings, thus becomes an 'applicant'. This reversal of roles becomes important in terms of jurisdiction (see below). The Amsterdam Court will notify the 'interested parties' either by personal notification if their names and addresses are known or by public notification in newspapers, on websites, etc if they are not identified. If the 'interested parties' do not opt-out of the proceedings within a certain period fixed by the court, the approved settlement will be binding on them. 13/29

With respect to the international jurisdiction of the Amsterdam Court of Appeals, WCAM cases have caused quite a headache to the court and to legal scholars. In recent years, the WCAM has attracted global attention and has been used to settle some of the 'big' international securities cases. In the aftermath of the *Morrison* decision of the US Supreme Court, the WCAM will probably be of increasing importance for the compensation of shareholders domiciled outside the USA. Some of the international settlements approved by the Amsterdam Court of Appeals[65] had only minimal contact with the Netherlands. In *Converium*, a securities case, only approximately 3% of the investors on whose behalf the settlement had been negotiated were domiciled in the Netherlands. The parties liable for the damages in this case were Swiss companies and only the 13/30

65 Court of Appeal Amsterdam, 1 June 2006, Landelijk Jurisprudentie Nummer LJN: AX6440 (*DES*); 25 January 2007, LJN: AZ7033 (*Dexia*); 29 April 2009, LJN: BI2717 (*Vie d'Or*); 29 May 2009, LJN: BI5744 (*Shell*); 15 July 2009, LJN: BJ2691 (*Vedior*); 17 January 2012, LJN: BV1026 (*Converium*).

representative organisations acting on behalf of the shareholders to be compensated were foundations under Dutch law. In the *Royal Shell* case the approximately 500,000 'interested parties' were residing in more than 100 countries (except the USA), the liable parties were companies registered in the UK and the Netherlands.

13/31 The Amsterdam Court of Appeals established international jurisdiction over non-resident 'interested parties' domiciled outside the EU on the domestic provision of art 3 of the Dutch Code of Civil Procedure. With respect to those 'interested parties' residing in the European Union, Norway, Iceland and Switzerland, it decided that the Brussels I Regulation and the Lugano Conventions respectively apply. Both sets of rules assume that there is a 'party to be sued' in the first place, so the first question to be answered was 'who is the party to be sued?': the liable party or the tort victims as 'interested parties'? Another open issue was whether the cause of action in these proceedings would be the settlement to be approved by the court or rather the original claims of the tort victims. Considering the objective of the WCAM proceedings – to grant a binding effect of the settlement on parties who were not involved in the negotiations – it seems clear that the 'interested parties' are arguably to be considered as 'defendants' in the sense of the Brussels I Regulation (and the Lugano Convention). They become involved in the litigation without their prior consent, they bear the risk of a court decision which might have a negative effect (they can pursue any claims against the party liable for the mass damage only as fixed in the settlement), and therefore, they must enjoy the safeguards provided by the jurisdictional regime of European procedural law.

13/32 As a consequence, it is only with respect to those 'interested parties' residing in the Netherlands that art 2 of the Brussels I Regulation provides international jurisdiction for the Dutch court. For non-EU residents, according to art 4 of the Regulation, the Dutch Code of Civil Procedure applied (giving jurisdiction to the courts where the applicants are domiciled in petition proceedings like the WCAM proceedings). For non-Dutch EU residents, however, the Brussels I jurisdictional rules applied and the Amsterdam court offered different explanations to establish its jurisdiction in the *Royal Shell* and in the *Converium* cases. In *Shell*, the court relied on art 6 no 1 of the Regulation. Any person or 'interested party' domiciled in a Member State 'may be sued where he or she is one of a number of defendants in the Member State where any one of them is domiciled, provided that the claims are so closely connected that it is expedient to hear and determine them together to avoid the risk of irreconcilable judgments'. The decision drew criticism from many legal scholars and apparently prompted the Amsterdam court to reconsider the matter in the *Converium* case in a separate partial judgment published in November 2011, in which jurisdiction was based on art 5 no 1 of the Regulation arguing that the settlement is a contract which is – according to the settlement terms – to be performed in the Netherlands.

Neither of the two explanations offered by the court is satisfying. Even if one agrees to consider the 'interested parties' as 'defendants' in the sense of art 6 no 1, one may doubt whether this provision should apply. At first sight the claims are 'closely connected'. Due to the reversal of the roles of the parties in the WCAM proceedings, the court did not look at the original claims for compensation arising from the mass tort or accident, but only at the settlement. This was indeed negotiated in order to meet all claims in a single stroke and it is the explicit objective of the joint application that the settlement is declared binding on all potential claimants irrespective of their nationality or place of residence. According to the provisions of the Dutch Code of Civil Procedure, the Amsterdam Court of Appeals has only two options: to dismiss the application or to approve the settlement and to declare it binding upon all the 'interested parties'. Thus the connection of all claims is simply a consequence of the particular features of the WCAM proceedings. 13/33

Obviously the idea that the 'interested parties' are deemed to be 'defendants' eventually does not offer adequate protection – at least with respect to art 6 no 1 of the Brussels I Regulation and in cases where the clear majority of them live outside the Netherlands. On the contrary, it will come as rather a surprise to non-Dutch residents that the whole settlement is subject to the Amsterdam court's jurisdiction if only a single claimant is domiciled in the Netherlands. One might argue that this is inherent to art 6 no 1, but when this provision is used for establishing jurisdiction for mass claims, a disparity between a small number of 'defendants' domiciled in the forum state and a vast majority of them domiciled elsewhere becomes apparent which does not exist in other cases. Moving the focus on to the original claims, however, will restrict the scope of application of the WCAM proceedings considerably. The Amsterdam court would have jurisdiction for approving settlements only if the liable party (or one of them) was domiciled in the Netherlands, such as in the *Royal Shell* case or if the tortious act was committed there (which might be assumed for torts relating to stock traded in Amsterdam). 13/34

Perhaps this was the situation the Amsterdam judges had in their minds in the *Converium* case, in which the liable parties were registered in Switzerland and only a few 'interested parties' resided in the Netherlands. Finally the court took recourse to art 5 no 1 of the Regulation. Compared with the arguments advanced in favour of art 6 no 1 this is, however, an even weaker basis for its jurisdiction. Although art 5 no 1 does not require that a valid contract exists between the litigating parties, the ECJ defined 'contractual obligations' as obligations arising from activities the parties (at least allegedly) entered into voluntarily. 13/35

The WCAM settlement cases are different. The representative organisation initiates negotiations on behalf of the tort victims without any power of attorney and it is only the court's approval of the settlement which brings about the binding effect. None of the tort victims enters into anything like a pre-contractual relationship with the liable party with respect to the settlement negotiations. Despite the fact that there is in a technical sense a contract at least between the applicants it has no effect whatsoever for the 'interested parties' unless there is a court decision approving the contract and giving it a binding effect. The argument that the contract is a contract 'for the benefit of third parties' does not carry much weight because a settlement almost always curtails the original claims arising from the mass tort. Although settlements are often contracts concluded under uncertainty in terms of liability and causation, it is an essential feature that both sides make compromises compared to the positions they have taken or would take during litigation. The argument that an agreement is a binding contract for 'the benefit' of persons who did not participate in the contract negotiations only seems acceptable if there is clearly no disadvantage for those persons involved. Making decisions over the head of those persons requires that the contract is exclusively favourable for them. Therefore in terms of substantive law, one might argue that to abstain from further litigation or litigation at all means the claimants giving up the chance of receiving full compensation. Furthermore particularly with respect to any choice-of-court clauses, the settlement contract is not only for the benefit of the 'interested parties' because any exclusive jurisdiction of Dutch courts prevents the tort victims from bringing individual claims elsewhere. Therefore, in order to establish jurisdiction over the 'interested parties', art 5 no 1 can only be invoked based on a circular argument: The court has jurisdiction because there is a contract – and there is a contract (with respect to the 'interested parties') solely because the court assumed jurisdiction and approved the settlement at the end of the proceedings.

13/36 Given that neither art 5 no 1 nor art 6 no 1 of the Regulation offers a solid basis for jurisdiction, one might again consider art 23 and the choice-of-forum clauses which are regularly part of the settlement agreement. According to these settlement terms, any 'interested party' who claims compensation under the settlement thereby accepts that the Amsterdam Court of Appeals has jurisdiction. Such a retroactive consent may be a safe haven for those victims who are satisfied with the settlement and do not wish to sue the liable party for more money. Those 'interested parties' who neither opted-out nor accepted the settlement later cannot be bound by forum selection clauses which are part of the settlement. Even so, the ECJ has held that a person who was not a party to a contract which included a forum selection clause may profit from such a clause if he or she sues one of the contracting parties, and the 2013 decision of the ECJ implies that third parties must actually consent to that clause.[66]

As a consequence one should consider looking at the original claims of the 'interested parties'. They are also subject to the proceedings before the Amsterdam court albeit indirectly. By approving the proposed settlement, the original claims of the tort victims change – with respect to their legal basis and most likely as regards the amount of damages. Furthermore, the original claims arising from the infringement of the liable party should be taken as a benchmark when deciding whether the settlement is fair and adequate. From this perspective, the reversal of party roles implemented by the WCAM can be ignored and the liable party can be considered to be a 'defendant'. This means, however, that, under the present regime of the Brussels I Regulation, Dutch courts can assume jurisdiction in few cases – the *Converium* case would not have been settled in Amsterdam then. **13/37**

Thus, as long as it is only the Netherlands (and maybe in the future the UK) that offers mass settlement proceedings a strict interpretation of the Brussels I Regulation would prevent global settlements which are sometimes the only way for liable parties 'to buy peace'. For the time being the parties to a WCAM settlement must be aware that there is no guarantee of a Europe- or worldwide recognition of its preclusive effect. Some Member States may refuse recognition based on a general aversion to opt-out systems, others will probably at least scrutinise whether there was adequate notice to the 'interested parties' and will not recognise the binding effect of the settlement with respect to those who were not aware or could not be aware of the Amsterdam proceedings.[67] This is, however, a scenario only for situations where one or more of the 'interested parties' are not satisfied with the terms of the settlement contract and may try to obtain a higher damages award by ignoring the settlement and filing an individual lawsuit outside the Netherlands. Then the court seized will have to take into consideration whether the court approved settlement has a preclusive effect. **13/38**

III. The Future of Jurisdictional Rules over Mass Claims in Europe

When addressing the future of jurisdiction in mass tort cases we must take into consideration different options. These are the following: (1) there may be no **13/39**

66 See ECJ C-543/10, *Refcomp*.

67 *D Fairgrieve* in: Fairgrieve/Lein (fn 43) ch 10; *Halfmeier*, NIP 2012, 176, 180.

specific regulation at the European level at all (which is the present situation described already and which is not satisfactory); (2) European legislation might address only the problem of international jurisdiction of collective redress (including a better co-ordination of parallel proceedings) without harmonising instruments of collective redress; (3) EU regulations on new and harmonised instruments of collective redress might include new rules on (even exclusive) international jurisdiction.

A. No Harmonisation of the Instruments of Collective Redress in the EU

13/40 As the EU Commission failed to pave the way for a uniform European collective redress instrument with its June 2013 policy, the competition for mass disputes among some Member States will continue. *Forum shopping* for plaintiffs will continue to be important unless there is a change to the jurisdictional rules of the Brussels I Regulation. As explained above, the present regime allows for a bundling of claims mainly in the Member State where the defendant is domiciled or – in tort cases – where the tortious act was committed. New rules providing an additional option for plaintiffs in collective redress proceedings to bring a lawsuit also in the Member State where a majority of the 'interested parties' are domiciled would increase the chance of finding a forum that provides the necessary procedural instruments. It has to be admitted, however, that in some cases like the fraudulent activities of Bernard Madoff[68] it might be quite difficult to decide where the majority of victims reside.[69] Also extending art 6 (1) to cover collective redress cases is another good option.[70]

13/41 In any case, we must be aware that, with an increasing number of different collective redress instruments in the Member States, we will face more and more situations where proceedings arising from the same event will be pending in several Member States at the same time or subsequently.[71] Depending on the rules on legal standing, litigation might be initiated by different plaintiffs and the absent class or group members may be the same, completely different or 'overlapping'. Articles 27 and 28 of the Brussels I Regulation (arts 29, 30 of the

68 Case Study by *Boldon* (fn 4) 10/27 ff.

69 *T Arons*, Cross-Border Enforcement of Listed Companies' Duties to Inform (2012) 325.

70 *A Stadler* in: M Casper et al, Auf dem Weg zu einer europäischen Sammelklage (2009) 160; *E Lein* in: Fairgrieve/Lein (fn 43) ch 8, 35.

71 *R Money-Kyrle/C Hodges*, European Collective Action: Towards Coherence?, (2012-4) Maastricht Journal of European and Comparative Law (MJ) 477, 485.

new version applicable from 2015) dealing with parallel proceedings are not sufficient to handle these situations. Very often the core of the different proceedings might be identical in the sense of the ECJ case law developed in the *Tatry* and *Gubisch* cases.[72] However, the plaintiffs involved may not be exactly the same in different proceedings. The *lis pendens* provision in art 27 (29 Brussels I new), however, requires 'proceedings involving the same cause of action and between the same parties' in order to give the court first seized the right (and obligation) to stay its proceedings. Thus the question appears whether we must have particular rules for a better co-ordination or even a consolidation or merger of these proceedings in the interest of the parties and for the sake of procedural economy. The following example may illustrate the situation:

Example: Companies A (from the UK), B (from Japan) and C (from Germany), all producers of artificial vitamins, have entered into a price fixing agreement for their products for the whole European market. The agreement was allegedly entered into during a meeting of company officials in Warsaw. Once cartel authorities have started an investigation and have confirmed the violation of competition rules, the following civil proceedings are initiated: **13/42**

- A follow-on class action for the recovery of damages in the UK (based on an opt-out mechanism for UK residents and an opt-in system for other class members)[73] against all three companies.[74]
- Disgorgement proceedings initiated by a German consumer association against companies C and A in Germany for handing out the profit illegally gained by the cartel agreement in Germany.[75]
- An opt-in group action for the recovery of damages on behalf of end-consumers domiciled in Germany, Austria and Poland is filed in Poland based on art 5 no 3 of the Brussels I Regulation in Poland.[76]

---

72 ECJ 144/86, *Gubisch Maschinenfabrik v Giulio Palumbo* [1987] ECR 4861; C-406/92, *Tatry v Maciej Rataj* [1994] ECR I-5439.

73 This might become reality once the reform of UK competition law announced by the BIS in January 2013 enters into force.

74 Jurisdiction over the Japanese company may be based on domestic rules.

75 A draft for a revision of the German Antitrust Act came into force in June 2013. It expands legal standing for skimming-off or disgorgement proceedings to consumer organisations. Based on art 6 (1) of the Brussels I Regulation, the plaintiffs may sue the German and the British, but not the Japanese company.

76 Cf *Wurmnest*, EuZW 2012, 933, 934: the place where companies enter into a price-fixing agreement may establish jurisdiction for claims arising from the cartel agreement. It is, however, disputed whether this applies for all the various places where the members of the cartel may meet over the time of a long-lasting cartel.

13/43 Article 27 of the Brussels I Regulation cannot be applied to these proceedings. Even if we assume that the price fixing agreement which becomes relevant in all proceedings establishes the 'same cause of action' and if we disregard – as the ECJ does – the different objectives of these proceedings (disgorgement/damages), the plaintiff's side and hence 'the parties' are not identical in these proceedings Article 28 (art 30 Brussels I new) allows a consolidation of 'related actions' pending at first instance under certain conditions (subsec 2), particularly if the local law in the Member State where courts were first seized with the proceedings permit consolidation. Notwithstanding the definition of 'related actions' in art 28 (3), national rules will often be reluctant to permit the consolidation of actions that are not clearly identical.[77] Moreover, consolidation can be based only on art 28 (2) if the court first seized has jurisdiction over both actions. Thus, in many cases art 28 (2) could not be used to consolidate proceedings. Another good example for a multitude of individual or collective proceedings arising from a single cause mass tort is the *Madoff* case. As explained in the Case Study[78] claims against various banks in Europe have been filed alleging that the defendants helped to channel money into Madoff's fraudulent scheme. Another couple of proceedings were instituted against funds in Luxembourg, Ireland and Switzerland based on an alleged liability of the defendants due to their failure to detect Madoff's fraud and warn investors.

13/44 Parallel litigation in international cases can be prevented only to some extent. Giving exclusive jurisdiction to the courts of one Member State, for example in the Member State where the liable party is domiciled, produces relief only for claims against the same defendant. Even then there might be a dispute where the liable party is domiciled in terms of art 60 of the Brussels I Regulation as illustrated in the South Africa silicosis case and various courts seized may adopt different interpretations as long as there is no settled ECJ case law. With respect to collective settlement proceedings, T Arons recommends the adoption of a provision that the courts in the Member State where the liable party has his or her statutory seat have exclusive jurisdiction.[79] This would also provide legal certainty and predictability for contentious proceedings.[80]

77 If the national rules of the court first seized with mass tort proceedings do not provide the remedy of disgorgement but only actions for damages, it will not be very likely that proceedings can be consolidated.

78 Case Study by *Boldon* (fn 4) 10/27 ff.

79 *Arons* (fn 69) 325.

80 The German legislature has adopted such a provision for securities cases. Section 32a of the German Civil Procedure Code was enacted together with the KapMuG and establishes exclusive jurisdiction for the KapMuG cases for the courts where the defendant has its (statutory) seat (sec 17 German Code of Civil Procedure). The provision must of course stand back in interna-

However, as rules providing exclusive jurisdiction for civil actions are not acceptable as long as similar instruments of collective redress are not available in all Member States, and would considerably restrict the plaintiffs' options of finding a forum which is able to handle a mass case efficiently, there is a need for at least a better co-operation of courts in these situations. In the US, the Judicial Panel on Multidistrict Litigation (MDL) has broad discretion, with authority to temporarily transfer cases filed in different Federal courts to a single district 'for coordinated or consolidated pretrial proceedings'.[81] However, the Multidistrict Litigation (MDL) Panel will always take into consideration whether a transfer would cause unnecessary additional costs and whether there is a sufficient degree of 'commonality' among the parties of the different actions.[82] If no defendant or category of defendants is a party to all actions, consolidation is likely to be denied. Furthermore the plaintiffs must also constitute a homogenous group.[83] Therefore an order for a transfer of actions under USC § 1407 will be issued only if it serves the convenience of the parties or promotes an efficient conduct of litigation (USC § 1407 [a]).[84] The American Law Institute's project on 'Principles of the Law of Aggregate Litigation' adopted in 2010 emphasises that 'aggregate treatment of litigation is a matter of judicial discretion that flows from the general authority of courts to exercise early and effective supervision of litigation'[85] and suggests a number of principles which cannot be discussed here. In any case, for the purpose of this chapter it suffices to point out that ba- 13/45

tional cases against the provisions of the Brussels I Regulation. However with respect to securities cases in the US, sec 32a German Civil Procedure Code provides an argument to deny recognition of US decisions (sec 328 no 1 German Civil Procedure Code).

81 Furthermore Rule 42 Federal Rules of Civil Procedure allows multiple cases which have been filed in one judicial district to be consolidated for a single trial if the actions involve common questions of law or fact.

82 For example *In re Asbestos and Asbestos Insulation Material Products Liability Litigation*, Judicial Panel on Multidistrict Litigation, 431 Federal Supplement (F Supp) 906 (1977); *L Mullenix*, Mass Tort Litigation, Cases and Materials (2nd edn 2008) ch 2 paras 22.33, 22.341.

83 Thus the MDL procedure is an often used consolidation mechanism in airplane disaster cases. Recently it also became a preferred instrument to cope with pharmaceutical product liability cases, cf *Mullenix* (fn 82), 'Notes and Questions' with further references to case law.

84 *In re Asbestos School Products Liability Litigation*, Judicial Panel on Multidistrict Litigation, 606 F Supp 713 (1985); *In re AH Robins Co 'Dalkon Shield' IUD Products Liability Litigation*, Judicial Panel on Multidistrict Litigation, 610 F Supp 1099 (1985). In 1991, however, the MDL Panel finally granted a motion to transfer actions to a single district in the asbestos products liability litigation, *In re Asbestos Products Liability Litigation*, Judicial Panel on Multidistrict Litigation, 771 F Supp 415 (1991).

85 *American Law Institute*, Principles of Law of Aggregate Litigation, § 2.02 Comment a.

sic parameters and general rules for handling mass torts in Europe are different from the US.

13/46 It must be taken for granted that any consolidation or merger of proceedings – as an exception to existing rules of jurisdiction – needs a well-balanced legal basis and should not be accepted if it involves fundamental disadvantages for the parties. In the US, civil procedural rules at least for Federal Courts are identical (Federal Rules of Civil Procedure). Therefore it seems reasonable that the parties must accept a different forum (for consolidated pretrial discovery proceedings, for example) in order to have faster and more efficient proceedings irrespective of venue and jurisdiction. In Europe, the situation is different.[86] Although there has been some convergence of continental and common law procedural rules[87] some of the basic pillars such as the (active or passive) role of judges, the allocation of cost and risk, the obligation of parties and third-parties to produce evidence, etc still differ to a considerable extent and might influence the outcome of the litigation. Therefore pending claims in mass damage cases cannot simply be transferred from one Member State to another in order to try all claims in a single proceeding. Particularly an irrevocable transfer of actions from one jurisdiction to another for a single trial and a final decision is – if at all – a dream for the future. Under the present Brussels I regime, plaintiffs will carefully weigh where to bring an action against the defendant if there are several options. The possible outcome of litigation also has a strong influence on the decision of third-party funders who become increasingly important in mass proceedings. They will carefully assess procedural risks in advance by taking into consideration the procedural and substantive law parameters in a given forum. The prospect that the litigation could be transferred either temporarily or finally to a completely different jurisdiction brings considerable legal uncertainty and would make it even more difficult to predict the plaintiff's chances of winning the case. This will probably reduce access to third party funding and ATE insurance if the risk becomes incalculable. Therefore the US instruments of multidistrict consolidation cannot be adopted by the European Union at the present stage.

13/47 However, even without the prospect of consolidating proceedings, a better co-operation of courts trying similar proceedings might help to cope with mass

---

86 This is not taken into account in the paper of *JN Stefanelli*, Parallel Litigation and Cross-Border Collective Actions under the Brussels I Framework: Lessons from Abroad, in: Fairgrave/Lein (fn 43) 143 ff.

87 In particular, the reform of civil procedural rules in England and Wales has brought these countries closer to the continental European tradition of civil procedure, *Hodges/Stadler* (fn 61) Introduction.

damage cases. First of all an EU register, in electronic form, for collective redress proceedings[88] would assist litigating parties (particularly plaintiffs) to receive information about parallel proceedings. It might also be used as an instrument to distribute information and could, thus, increase the number of group or class members opting-in into certain proceedings. Different groups of plaintiffs or representative associations will be able to co-ordinate their efforts for collecting and presenting evidence, settlement negotiations, etc. Furthermore, courts may exchange information about pending litigation in the same cases and better assist each other in the taking of evidence and, selecting test cases, etc.[89] The EU Commission has also realised the necessity to make information on collective redress cases available to interested persons. In part VI of its Recommendations, the Commission suggests that Member States should establish national registries which should be available free of charge through electronic means and otherwise.[90] However, pure national registers will not contribute to a better co-ordination of cross-border cases. The Recommendation only suggests that, with the assistance of the Commission, Member States should endeavour to ensure coherence of information and interoperability of the national registers. We must probably go one step further. In its proposal for a reform of the European Insolvency Regulation[91] the Commission also envisages national registers, but also announces that it will provide a system of interconnection of the national registers which will be accessed via the European e-Justice portal.[92] The Commission will also ensure that minimum common criteria apply for searching the registers. The advantages of such a system for courts and creditors praised by the Commission also apply to mass tort claims and any other collective redress litigation. Given that the Commission favours opt-in group actions and that even in the UK the proposed group action in competition law as planned will not only be an opt-out instrument for claimants domiciled in the UK but an opt-in instrument for all claimants residing abroad,

88 *Arons* (fn 69) 326; the Canadian Bar has established a register for class actions in different provinces, see *Money-Kyrle/Hodges* (2012-4) MJ 477, 486.

89 The EU Commission has already proposed such a rule for the cooperation of courts in its recast of the Brussels I Regulation in 2011. The mutual obligation to cooperate then referred to provisional measures and injunctions. In this context any direct exchange of information among the courts might not be successful due to the time constraints and language problems (which are likely to occur in many situations). In collective redress proceedings these arguments against a co-operation clause do not carry weight since there is normally no need for decisions to be made within a short time frame of hours or days.

90 Recommendations paras 35–37.

91 COM (2012) 744 final.

92 COM (2012) 744 final, p 8.

an easily accessible European register would be a great help for interested parties.

B. Harmonisation of the Instruments of Collective Redress and New Rules on International Jurisdiction

13/48 It goes without saying that further considerations on jurisdictional issues depend very much on the degree of harmonisation and how a harmonised instrument at the European level will look. Once all Member States have to offer the same or at least similar instruments of collective redress, forum shopping becomes less important. Given the already existing harmonisation of the most important conflict of laws rules in the Rome I and II Regulations, one might consider a rather strict jurisdictional regime for mass claims. Exclusive jurisdiction would concentrate proceedings in one Member State. For this situation several options are being discussed. One solution could be to give exclusive jurisdiction to the courts of the Member State in which the defendant is domiciled (in accordance with the *actor sequitur forum rei* principle)[93] or – parallel to the European Regulation Insolvency Proceedings – where the tortfeasor's main interests are centred ('centre of main interest', COMI). Both solutions will raise questions of how to interpret 'domicile' or CoMI. The latter nevertheless has advantages as well: there is settled case law with respect to CoMI and, if the mass tort entails insolvency proceedings of the liable party, jurisdiction for them lies in the same Member State. As both options, however, fail to allow proceedings before EU courts if the liable party has his or her domicile or CoMI outside the EU subsidiary, jurisdiction should be provided within the EU and could take into consideration jurisdiction in the place where either the defendant allegedly committed the tortious act or the majority of (European) tort victims are domiciled[94] (despite the difficulty in some cases of deciding what and where the majority is[95]).

---

93 *Arons* (fn 69) 325: Member State where the alleged tortfeasors statutory seat is situated.

94 *A Stadler* in: J Steele/W van Boom, Mass Justice – Challenges of Representation and Distribution (2011) 82.

95 *Arons* (fn 69) 325.

IV. Summary and Questions to be Discussed in the Future

In summary, the European legislature should for the time being supplement the Brussels I Regulation by providing collective redress proceedings to take place in the Member State where a majority of the claimants of a mass damage is domiciled and should extend art 6 no 1 to cover mass torts claims. Furthermore a European register or interconnected national registers of the Member States with access via the European e-justice portal should be established as soon as possible to provide information about pending collective redress proceedings like the cause of action, the parties involved, the type of proceedings, etc. If harmonised European instruments of collective are implemented in the future, one might take into consideration the exclusive jurisdiction in a Member State having a close connection to the mass damage. This however requires a profound debate of the following questions: How far should a possible harmonisation of instruments of collective redress reach? Provided that the European legislature has legal competence to do so, should a new approach include regulations on the financing of mass litigation, rules on costs, lawyers' remuneration (contingency fees) and provisions on the taking of evidence particularly designed for collective redress? 13/49

Christopher Hodges*

14 Delivering Redress through Alternative Dispute Resolution and Regulation

I. Introduction

This chapter looks at the trend towards resolving disputes, and delivering redress, through pathways other than civil litigation through the courts. This approach has spread quickly in some Member States, and is gathering pace. Indeed, it seems that a major transformation is occurring in European legal systems, in which both courts and lawyers are being replaced, in mass consumer and injury contexts at least, by new approaches. These new approaches include Online Dispute Resolution (ODR), no-fault compensation, and regulatory mechanisms. We will start by describing the new mechanisms, then examine how they have come about and spread, and finish by imagining how things might develop further. 14/1

II. Describing the Mechanisms

This section will describe in general terms how the various options other than civil litigation work. It will not aim to be comprehensive since much detail exists, but it will illustrate some of the main techniques. Different ADR approaches have been developed for the differing contexts of personal injury and loss or damage arising from breach of contract. Those two contexts might traditionally be analysed by approaching the subject matter through the eyes of, respectively, tort law or contract law. Instead the 'alternative' approaches are more mechanistic, and approach the issues by taking the rights of the victims as a given starting point and trying to deliver appropriate solutions by means of the most user-friendly and efficient procedures. In some instances, the ADR solutions may be more flexible than the judicial remedies in response to a breach of a right of an injunction or an order to pay money. We look first at personal injury systems and then at breach of contract systems. 14/2

No-fault compensation schemes are familiar in some jurisdictions but not others. Experts are familiar with the New Zealand Accident Compensation 14/3

* Christopher Hodges receives research funding from Swiss Reinsurance Company Limited, European Justice Forum and the international law firm CMS.

Scheme, dating from 1972.[1] That accident scheme has survived cost issues and even thrived there, with different funds responding to workplace, road traffic or other injuries, effectively replacing tort litigation. The initial technical problem was to define what constituted an 'accident' but that term was largely dropped under the Accident Compensation Act 2001, and, for example, injuries resulting from medical treatment are compensated if they are a 'treatment injury'.[2]

14/4 Compensation schemes have long functioned in all Nordic states for the main types of personal injuries. The Nordic arrangements vary somewhat from country to country, but have strong similarities.[3] In Sweden, for example, insurance-based schemes cover personal injuries caused by medical treatment or by licenced medicinal products. The usual requirement for triggering a payment in relation to medical and drug injuries is that the injury was unavoidable, and the requirement for road traffic injuries is that for tort law.[4]

14/5 The Nordic schemes involve low transactional costs and short durations since they adopt investigative paper-based procedures, rather than adversarial procedures. Two important features of the Nordic arrangements are important. Firstly, the cost of damages for personal injuries that are paid out is relatively low because the schemes only cover part of the damages (ie not full compensation) because other social security schemes respond to a significant extent, and the 'no-fault' schemes merely 'top up' other entitlements.

14/6 Secondly, the fact that several schemes exist 'side by side' (eg for injuries caused by road traffic accidents, medical treatment or medicines) means that, where there is uncertainty over which scheme might respond, cases can be allocated to the right system and fund without delay, and one of the schemes is highly likely to respond. This wide coverage of different types of damage raises the collective profile of the general availability of the individual compensation schemes.

---

1 *K Oliphant*, Landmarks of No-Fault in the Common Law, in: WH van Boom/M Faure (eds), Shifts in Compensation between Private and Public Systems (2007).

2 Accident Compensation Act 2001, sec 32, which defines 'treatment injury' as caused by treatment and not a necessary part, or ordinary consequence, of the treatment, taking into account all the circumstances of the treatment, including (i) the person's underlying health condition at the time of treatment and (ii) the clinical knowledge at the time of the treatment. Failure to achieve a desired result does not of itself constitute a treatment injury. Injuries suffered in approved clinical trials are included.

3 *F Weber/C Hodges/N Creutzfeldt-Banda*, Sweden, in: C Hodges/I Benöhr/N Creutzfeldt-Banda, Consumer ADR in Europe (2012); *C Hodges*, Nordic Compensation Schemes for Drug Injuries, Journal of Consumer Policy (JCP) 29 (2006) 143–175.

4 *Weber/Hodges/Creutzfeldt-Banda* (fn 3) 234.

A similar approach towards wide coverage of medical injuries that might have been caused in different ways was established in France in 2005 under the ONIAM[5] scheme. Here, regional committees verify the injury and causation, and decide whether the injury was due to negligent medical treatment or resulted from a serious non-negligent adverse medical event. In the first situation, notification is sent to the insurer of the relevant practitioner, hospital or manufacturer, who is required to make a satisfactory settlement proposal within four months, failing which the patient may take the case to court and, if she wins, the insurer will have to pay a 15% punitive surcharge to the ONIAM. In the second situation, the ONIAM pays. 14/7

We turn now to systems for handling disputes arising from breaches of contract. Arbitration is well known and a widely used dispute resolution technique for disputes between commercial firms. It is not a controversial technique. Several well-established arbitration models and courts exist, and every major commercial centre has its own arrangements, whether large international fora such as those based in New York, Paris, London, Hamburg and Switzerland, or in local centres like *Handelskammern* and Chambers of Commerce. 14/8

Arbitration has attracted considerable interest in the United States in recent years since corporations have attempted to divert individual and mass claims away from lawyers and courts and into arbitration.[6] The commercial motivation for large defendants to avoid expensive discovery and class actions are obvious. Class arbitration has emerged as a possible technique.[7] The central issue, however, is whether a supplier can bind a customer, especially a consumer, in the contract of sale or supply to resolve any dispute that may arise from the contract, by means of arbitration. In Europe, that would be illegal in relation to a consumer contract as it would involve an unfair contract term, and breach of the consumer's fundamental rights.[8] It is not, of course, illegal to agree to resolve a dispute by arbitration after the dispute has arisen, but Europe prohibits binding the consumer before or at the time of entering into the substantive contract into agreeing to a form of dispute resolution other than through the courts. 14/9

---

5 Office National d'indemnisation des accidents médicaux, des affections iathrogènes et des infections nosocomiaux. See *R Cascão/R Hendrickx*, Shifts in the Compensation of Medical Adverse Events, in: WH van Boom/M Faure (eds), Shifts in Compensation between Private and Public Systems (2007).

6 See *AT&T Mobility v Concepcion*, 563 United States Supreme Court Reports (US) (2011).

7 *SI Strong*, Class, Mass and Collective Arbitration in National and International Law (2013).

8 Article 6 European Convention on Human Rights (ECHR). European Court of Justice (ECJ) C-168/05, *Mostaza Claro v Centro Móvil Milenium* [2006] European Court Reports (ECR) I-10421 and C-40/08 *Asturcom Telecomunicaciones SL v Cristina Rodríguez Nogueira* [2009] ECR I-9579.

However, in the United States the Federal Arbitration Act permits compulsory and binding arbitration.[9]

14/10 ADR comprises a set of techniques, notably mediation (or conciliation), early neutral evaluation, or mini-trial, which aim to settle a dispute without formal adjudication by a court.[10] In the EU, ADR is relatively well-known, although the extent of its use varies across different Member States. The seminal event in the spread of ADR was institutional inclusion of mediation into the civil procedure system of England and Wales in 1999,[11] following Lord Woolf's adoption of the idea from prior use in the United States.[12]

14/11 Mediation has spread quickly across Europe in the last decade, and was adopted by the EU in the 2008 Mediation Directive,[13] required to be implemented into the legal systems of every Member State by May 2011. This has not been uncontroversial. Those states that have enjoyed well-functioning, efficient and relatively low cost civil procedure systems, backed by predictable costs regimes and hence widespread insurance (such as Germany and Austria), were initially bemused by the need for the forcible inclusion of mediation into their civil procedure systems. Indeed, such forcible insertion might have adverse consequences for the efficient functioning of the civil procedure system, and might increase cost and duration rather than shorten them.[14]

14/12 A surprising number of multi-party cases are ultimately resolved through specific ADR schemes. Familiarity with an issue of liability that may be resolved through high-profile court proceedings may obscure the fact that what follows is a compensation scheme in which claimants' causation and scope of damages are assessed, before they receive money. English examples include miners' disease claims and investors in Equitable Life. Sometimes, courts may be bypassed: the ombudsman scheme appointed by the Deutsche Bahn to handle claims after the Eschede rail crash[15] and American examples after the

---

9 This separability principle was upheld in *Prima Paint Corp v Flood & Conklin Mfg Co* 388 US 395 (1967).

10 *Hodges/Benöhr/Creutzfeldt-Banda* (fn 3).

11 Civil Procedure Rules 1998, SI 1998/3132 as amended.

12 *Lord Woolf*, Access to Justice: Report to the Lord Chancellor on the Civil Justice System in England and Wales: Final Report (1996).

13 Directive 2008/52/EC of 21 May 2008 on certain aspects of mediation in civil and commercial matters, Official Journal (OJ) L 136, 24.5.2008, 3–8.

14 *KJ Hopt/F Steffek* (eds), Mediation: Principles and Regulation in Comparative Perspective (2013); *G De Palo/MB Trevor*, EU Mediation: Law and Practice (2012).

15 See *OE Krasney*, Ombudsman for the Victims of the Rail Accident at Eschede on 3 June 1998, 5/1 ff in this book.

2001 9/11 attacks and 2010 'Deepwater Horizon' Gulf claims are leading examples.[16]

Consumer ADR (CDR) has been another surprisingly sudden arrival on the EU landscape. CDR typically uses the ADR techniques of mediation followed by arbitration, but within the context of a dispute resolution structure that is entirely separate from the courts. The CDR architecture comprises ombudsmen and other ADR schemes that are attached to regulatory structures or to sectoral codes of business practice.[17] The European Commission claims that some 750 CDR schemes exist across the EU.[18] Whilst that figure may be too high, CDR is widely used in some Member States and is spreading quickly. Nordic states, the Netherlands and the United Kingdom have relied strongly on CDR systems for up to 40 years. Consumer arbitration arrangements are well-established in Spain and Portugal. CDR is set to expand considerably across the EU with the adoption in April 2013 of legislation that requires Member States to ensure full coverage of CDR options for (almost) all consumer-to-business (C2B) disputes by mid-2015.[19] 14/13

From the consumer perspective, CDR provides a swift, cheap and user-friendly means of resolving disputes with traders, which frequently involve little financial value and might not be worth spending time on, let alone further cost. Under many CDR systems, the CDR case-handler or ombudsman effectively assumes the role of an active intermediary, minimising the complainant's effort. This can be particularly useful where the dispute involves legal provisions that are unfamiliar to consumers or inherently complex, such as unfair competition and telecoms or financial services' regulation. EU consumer policy has moved away from private enforcement towards CDR and regulation.[20] 14/14

---

16 *S Issacharoff/DT Rave*, The BP Oil Spill Settlement and the Paradox of Public Litigation, New York University Law and Economics Working Papers, Paper 343 (June 2013), forthcoming in The Louisiana Law Review's 2013 symposium, Eastern District of Louisiana: The Nation's MDL Laboratory.

17 *Hodges/Benöhr/N Creutzfeldt-Banda* (fn 3).

18 Civic Consulting, Study on the use of Alternative Dispute Resolution in the European Union, 16 October 2009, <http://ec.europa.eu/consumers/redress_cons/adr_study.pdf>, 2 December 2009.

19 Directive 2013/11/EU of the European Parliament and of the Council of 21 May 2013 on alternative dispute resolution for consumer disputes and amending Regulation (EC) No 2006/2004 and Directive 2009/22/EC (Directive on consumer ADR), OJ L 165, 18.6.2013, 63–79; Regulation (EU) 524/2012 of the European Parliament and of the Council of 21 May 2013 on online dispute resolution for consumer disputes and amending Regulation (EC) No 2006/2004 and Directive 2009/22/EC (Regulation on consumer ODR), OJ L 165, 18.6.2013, 1–12.

20 See Guidelines for enforcement on consumer rights (Consumer Justice Enforcement Forum, 2013).

14/15 The existence of either strong CDR arrangements, or market reputational forces, or regulatory requirements, incentivises traders to operate effective customer care and service functions that are responsive to customers' complaints. In some sectors, such as telecoms,[21] energy,[22] consumer credit[23] and payment services,[24] traders are already required to belong to CDR schemes or even to have customer dispute resolution functions. It is striking that trade sectors in various countries that were initially highly suspicious of CDR have increasingly become strong supporters when they realise that it can repair customer relations and so retain customer loyalty as well as save money in dispute resolution. Although some Member States have efficient and low cost court procedures, which may be accessible through widespread legal expenses insurance, they are in the minority (and still do not offer coverage for all), whereas court cases last twice as long as the EU standard in one third of EU countries, and business perceptions of courts' independence is very low in some Member States.[25]

14/16 The involvement of regulatory authorities in delivering compensation to consumers or competitors is not yet widely known but is hugely powerful where it is used.[26] A range of possible powers can be deployed, which can have varying effectiveness. We can illustrate the effect through some examples. First, the Danish Consumer Ombudsman (who, perhaps unusually is the national consumer enforcement officer rather than a traditional ombudsman), possesses a range of enforcement powers in his toolbox, one of which is a power to bring a class action for damages on behalf of a defined class of consumers, and the sole power to request the court to declare that the proposed class action be on an opt-out basis.[27] Since this opt-out class action power was introduced in 2008, the Consumer Ombudsman has not yet found it necessary to make an applica-

---

21 Directives 2009/136/EC and 2009/140/EC – OJ L 337, 18.12.2009, 11–36 and ibid, 37–69.

22 Directives 2009/72/EC and 2009/73/EC – OJ L 211, 14.8.2009, 55–93 and ibid, 94–136.

23 Directive 2008/48/EC, OJ L 133, 22.5.2008, 66–92.

24 Directive 2007/64/EC, OJ L 319, 5.12.2007, 1–36.

25 The EU Justice Scoreboard (European Commission, 2013).

26 In 2013 the European Commission has proposed to accept commitments from a trader that include introduction of a new pricing system and paying some customers compensation: see *European Commission,* Antitrust: Commission market tests commitments proposed by Deutsche Bahn concerning pricing system for traction current in Germany (European Commission press release, 15 August 2013), IP/13/780.

27 Administration of Justice Act Pt 23, amended by Act No 181 of 28 February 2007. Class members or a relevant association may start an opt-in class action. See *C Hodges*, The Reform of Class and Representative Actions in European Legal Systems: A New Framework for Collective Redress in Europe (2008).

tion to the court based on it.[28] The reason is that traders and the Consumer Ombudsman have reached agreements on redress as part of the general settlement of all the public and private consequences of a matter. The key lies in having a toolbox that contains all necessary public enforcement powers together with the means for the public enforcement authority to resolve compensation or redress issues all at the same time. Negotiations can be strenuous, but are relatively speedy and avoid the costs of going to court.

Indeed, a second example comes from the existence of regulatory powers alone. Certain regulatory systems, such as in financial services, communications or utilities, rest on the ability of a regulator to withdraw licences from traders or to vary generic or individual conditions. The strength of such powers can result in a regulator being able to persuade undertakings to institute 'voluntary' repayment or restitutionary arrangements without any formal power to order this, or involve a court. **14/17**

A third example again combines public investigation and enforcement with a power to order a trader to make reparation, or to require all traders of a certain description to institute a consumer redress scheme, or to approve redress arrangements proposed by a trader, or some other technique. Various examples of such powers have been, or are being, introduced for many sectoral regulators in the United Kingdom, such as in financial services,[29] the environment[30] and utilities.[31] The published enforcement policies of many regulators have been amended in the period from 2010 to 2013 to include an objective of ensuring that victims receive redress, or that the environment or market is restored to its former equilibrium. **14/18**

In many jurisdictions, a civil party may 'piggyback' on a criminal case, and take advantage of the wider powers of the state in investigating the facts and of **14/19**

28 Presentation by the Consumer Ombudsman at the conference 'Building Effective Markets – The Role of an Integrated Legal System' at the Swiss Re Centre for Global Dialogue, Rüschlikon, Zürich, Switzerland on 29–30 January 2013; see note at <http://www.csls.ox.ac.uk/documents/EXECUTIVESUMMARY.pdf>.

29 The Financial Services and Markets Act 2000 as amended gives the Financial Conduct Authority power to make a consumer redress scheme under sec 404(1) or a single firm scheme under sec 404F(7).

30 The Environmental Civil Sanctions (England) Order 2010/1157 and the Environmental Civil Sanctions (Miscellaneous Amendments) (England) Order 2010/1159 give the Environment Agency and English Nature power to impose civil sanctions (specified in the Regulatory Enforcement and Sanctions Act 2008) that include restoration notices and compliance notices, and to accept undertakings that can include payment of compensation or other restoration.

31 Energy Act 2013.

the greater resources in funding the case.[32] If a relevant defendant is convicted, the court may award compensation, and even if there is no conviction, useful evidence may have emerged. The use of this technique in Belgium in a series of large cases has been described by Voet.[33] He shows that a key factor is that a Belgian criminal judge is required to deal with the civil party claims at the end of the criminal case, whereas criminal judges in the Netherlands and Germany have discretion not to do so – so the technique has unsurprisingly not been used so often in those countries. Since 2012 all criminal courts in the United Kingdom have been required to consider making a compensation order to any victims, without their being registered as civil parties to the proceedings. Procedures can be slow, but perhaps not as slow or duplicative as when criminal and civil tracks are pursued separately.[34] Belgium is reviewing its rules so as to improve the process.

14/20 The combined effect of all these dispute resolution pathways adds up to a range of options that are 'alternative' to courts. Few outside the Nordic states have realised until recently that essentially all C2B disputes are brought (and most solved) in the CDR systems, such as the Swedish *Allmänna reklamationsnämnden* (ARN) – and no such claims go to court (unless a trader refuses to comply with the non-binding decision of the CDR body, which is relatively rare in Sweden). (In some CDR schemes in other countries, and by definition in all arbitration-based CDR schemes, outcomes are binding on at least the trader, so subsequent enforcement proceedings in court are very rare.) In the United Kingdom, the Financial Ombudsman Service alone received 1,268,798 inquiries from consumers in 2011-12, which turned into 264,375 new formal disputes.[35] The scale of the demand can be compared with a total number of 1,553,983 non-family claims commenced in the English and Welsh courts in 2011: there were

---

32 See Directive 2004/80/EC of 29 April relating to compensation to crime victims, OJ L 261, 6.8.2004, 15–18, arts 1 and 2. See also Council Framework Decision of 15 March 2001 on the standing of victims in criminal proceedings (2001/220/JHA), and Proposal for a Directive establishing minimum standards on the rights, support and protection of victims of crime COM(2011) 275 final, 18 May 2011; and Proposal for a Directive on the freezing and confiscation of proceeds of crime in the European Union, COM(2012) 85, 12.3.2012, at <http://eur-lex.europa.eu/LexUriServ/LexUriServ.do?uri=COM:2012:0085:FIN:EN:PDF>. There should be little surprise that the piggy-back technique is used in Italy, where the civil procedure system has been notoriously clogged for years, and cases take too long.

33 *S Voet*, Public Enforcement & A(O)DR as Mechanisms for Resolving Mass Problems: A Belgian Perspective, in: C Hodges/A Stadler (eds), Resolving Mass Disputes: Alternative Dispute Resolution (ADR) and Settlement of Mass Claims (2013).

34 See *N Coggiola/M Graziadei*, The Italian 'Eternit Trial': Litigating Massive Asbestos Damage in a Criminal Court, 2/1 ff in this volume.

35 Annual Report 2011-12 (Financial Ombudsman Service, 2012).

275,920 defences and 52,660 trials and small claims hearings.[36] The usage figures of all CDR systems in the country are increasing and the court statistics have been falling for some years. These trends in the figures indicate not only that CDR is a major alternative to courts (and lawyers) but also that CDR is becoming the dispute resolution pathway of choice for C2B claims.

The 'regulatory redress' technique is relatively new, but has in some situa- 14/21
tions delivered large total sums, sometimes made up of multiple small amounts, to victims. Examples of negotiated voluntary reparation come from the Lithuanian Telecommunications Authority[37] and various UK agencies, such as in communications,[38] energy[39] and financial services.[40]

III. Origins of the Alternative Techniques

Where have these various new techniques come from? Arbitration is far from 14/22
new. Mediation as a technique is as old as humanity,[41] even if the introduction of mediation as a formal part of some Western civil procedure systems has only occurred within the past 15 years.

---

36 Judicial and Court Statistics 2011 (Ministry of Justice, 2012), available at <https://www.gov.uk/government/uploads/system/uploads/attachment_data/file/162459/judicial-court-stats-2011.pdf.pdf>.

37 Personal communication with the author.

38 In one case relating to the billing by a telephone company of customers for services that had been cancelled, the Office of Communications (Ofcom) required the company to repay customers and to pay compensation where it was appropriate. As a result, some 62,000 customers received a total of around £ 2.5 million in refunds and goodwill payments. Ofcom also imposed a fine of over £ 3 million in this case. Noted in: Consultation on a proposed new power for Ofgem to compel regulated energy businesses to provide redress to consumers (12D/060: DECC, April 2012), available at <http://www.decc.gov.uk/assets/decc/11/consultation/4975-consultation-on-a-proposed-new-power-for-ofgem-to-.pdf>.

39 See *Office of Gas and Electricity Markets (Ofgem)*, Ofgem secures £1.7 million for Consumers following E.ON Error (Ofgem press release, 27 November 2012) at <http://www.ofgem.gov.uk/Media/PressRel/Documents1/20121127_EON_Press_Release.pdf>.

40 In a case involving variable application of interest rate variations on Halifax tracker mortgages, the Financial Services Authority ruled that a bank should write to all customers, and reached agreement that the bank would automatically compensate some borrowers, after which £ 30 million was paid in compensation.

41 *S Roberts/M Palmer*, Dispute Processes. ADR and the Primary Forms of Decision-Making (2005).

14/23 Creutzfeldt-Banda's analysis found that CDR has multiple origins.[42] They include inspiration from the more ancient tradition of public sector ombudsmen; the requirements of business to maintain consumer loyalty and underpin the spread of consumer confidence, especially in cross-border and online trading; the spread of both consumer protection requirements and regulatory systems in the EU that tend to increase the potential for disputes, often relatively simple in nature, but also demand efficient means of resolving them; and, of course, dissatisfaction with the slowness, undue complexity and disproportionate cost[43] of civil procedure systems. Indeed, there does appear to be a developing European culture that seeks harmony and solidarity through communication, negotiation and settlement of problems, rather than more adversarial and argumentative means that rely on self-asserting individualism that creates distance and mistrust.[44]

14/24 There are examples of situations in which large companies actively seek customer feedback and support their reputations by going 'beyond compliance'. Major retailers who operate in competitive markets where critical publicity can have significant adverse effects on the business now have well-resourced customer care departments that operate with some zeal in seeking feedback and satisfying customers' expectations.[45] A significant number of companies publish statements of ethical business practice, and can act in accordance with them.[46] It would be unwise to estimate how widespread it is that virtuous or non-virtuous behaviour occurs, but the point is that it can occur in the right contexts. The 'corporate social responsibility' movement is a manifestation of this. It may be that the trigger in such circumstances for delivery of compensation is no longer the establishment of legal liability but the existence of the potential for damage to reputation, or even an ethical obligation.

14/25 The 'regulatory redress' technique also arose from multiple causes. The Danish example was noted above. In fact, the controversial class action mecha-

---

42 *N Creutzfeldt-Banda*, The Evolution and Origins of Consumer Dispute Resolution Systems in Europe, in: Hodges/Stadler (fn 33).

43 See data in *C Hodges/S Vogenauer/M Tulibacka* (eds), Costs and Funding of Civil Litigation (2010).

44 See *A Stadler/C Hodges*, Introduction, in Hodges/Stadler (fn 33).

45 *C Hodges*, Best Practice in Customer Care in the UK, in: Hodges/Benöhr/Creutzfeldt-Banda (fn 3).

46 An example of a multinational manufacturer voluntarily instituting a global recall, with a medical revision and damage compensation scheme, was given at the conference 'Building Effective Markets – The Role of an Integrated Legal System' at the Swiss Re Centre for Global Dialogue, Rüschlikon, Zürich, Switzerland on 29 and 30 January 2013: see note at <http://www.csls.ox.ac.uk/documents/EXECUTIVESUMMARY.pdf>, p 28.

nism was introduced into Sweden, Denmark, Finland and Norway in the same decade but with some important variations of detail between each state. One of the most controversial design features was whether to introduce an American opt-out procedure or a less aggressive opt-in procedure. The basic model in each of those states, and in Europe generally, is the opt-in model. But in Denmark, whilst the opt-in approach was adopted as a general rule, as noted above, the opt-out approach was also introduced but crucially, limited to being used by a single trusted public official (the Consumer Ombudsman). He was then able to exploit the new technique as a highly effective addition to his enforcement toolbox. In effect, the other states missed a trick in not giving their enforcement officials a power to facilitate redress.

The origins of the inclusion of redress functions, duties and powers into UK regulators can be traced through three critical developments. Firstly, the creation of such regulators was an essential component of privatised markets from the 1970s onwards; secondly, their functions were reviewed, driven by the 'Better Regulation' movement and as crystalised by Richard Macrory's review of enforcement penalties, which was inspired by the context of restoration of environmental damages;[47] and, thirdly, the need to prioritise redress and rectification of markets arose after the 2008 financial crisis. The redress/restorative power has now been included in the enforcement policies of almost all UK regulators, and mass redress is being either voluntarily arranged by traders 'in the shadow' of the enforcement powers or through formal enforcement action. 14/26

IV. Predicting the Future

The 'regulatory redress' technique has considerable potential to spread quickly across the EU, not least in view of the fact that the EU's primary activity is to regulate markets and in so doing is creating public authorities, whose enforcement powers and effectiveness will come under increasing scrutiny. The existence of the principles of subsidiarity and Member State procedural autonomy, expressed in the widely found EU legal rule that Member States must ensure that their domestic enforcement arrangements are 'effective, proportionate and persuasive'[48] has had the effect that the comparative spotlight has hitherto not 14/27

47 *R Macrory*, Regulatory Justice: Making Sanctions Effective (2006); reprinted in *R Macrory*, Regulation, Enforcement and Governance in Environmental Law (2010).

48 ECJ 68/88, *Commission v Greece* [1989] ECR 2965, paras 22–27; C-326/88, *Anklagemyndighedem v Hansen & Soen I/S* [1990] ECR I-2911; C-36/94, *Siesse v Director da Alfândega de Alcântara* [1995] ECR I-3573, paras 19–21; C-83/94, *Criminal Proceedings against Leifer* [1995] ECR I-3231,

been shined on the realities of enforcement. There have been few comparative studies of national investigation and enforcement powers, duties of regulators and their enforcement policies and practices, whether enforcement is the domain of specialist regulators or of general public prosecutors, and empirical reviews of effectiveness and outcomes. Such matters are only just beginning to rise to the surface,[49] but they will be studied closely in the coming five years, and the availability of empirical evidence will lead to strong moves towards sharing of best practices and standardisation. Amongst this general movement, the delivery of restitution, redress and equilibrium by public bodies is only likely to increase.

14/28 CDR systems will continue to spread, for reasons of competitive advantage – lower cost, faster duration, more user-friendly. In addition, CDR also possesses one major advantage over dispute resolution through lawyers and courts, namely enormous market regulatory potential. Systems can be designed so that data on every C2B complaint can be captured, aggregated, and fed back to traders, regulators and markets. The effect of such information about the problems that are perceived to occur, their causes and which traders they involve, is enormously powerful. It is capable of having significant effect on 'behaviour control' of market operators. The power of such a holistic feedback system suggests that it is likely to be far more effective than a traditional liability-based system, relying on the theory of a deterrent effect on affecting future behaviour, especially as diluted by insurance. Inquiry into *what* affects human behaviour, and *how* an *ex post* liability system might affect the behaviour of humans working in large and small organisations (in the private or public sectors) raises many question marks about the effectiveness of an *ex post* deterrence-based policy. Future developments are likely to concentrate on behavioural psychology (which differs from behavioural economics) and the integration of external and intra-organisational compliance systems within meta-regulatory constructs.[50]

---

paras 32–41; C-341/94, *Criminal Proceedings against Allain* [1996] ECR I-4631, para 24; C-29/95, *Pastoors v Belgium* [1997] ECR I-285, paras 24–26.

49 See concerns about enforcement in Communication from the Commission to the European Parliament, the Council and the European Economic and Social Committee On the application of the Unfair Commercial Practices Directive Achieving a high level of consumer protection – Building trust in the Internal Market (EC, March 2013), available at <http://eur-lex.europa.eu/LexUriServ/LexUriServ.do?uri=COM:2013:0138:FIN:EN:PDF>.

50 Originating papers were: *P Grabosky*, Using Non-Governmental Resources to Foster Regulatory Compliance (1995) 8(4) Governance: An International Journal of Policy and Administration 527–550; *J Black*, Critical Reflections on Regulation, Centre for Analysis of Risk and Regulation (CARR) Discussion Paper, DP 4 (2002); (2002) 27 Australian Journal of Legal Philosophy 1–35, reprinted in *F Haines* (ed), Crime and Regulation (2007).

CDR or compensation schemes are likely not only to 'fill in gaps' as the EU specifies, but also to spread beyond existing boundaries. The ombudsman system is, after all, well known as a means of complaining about mistakes in public sector administration. A single integrated ombudsman system could be envisaged for sectors in which providers straddle public and private sectors, such as healthcare. An example of this was recommended for healthcare in the UK in April 2013.[51] 14/29

ADR and CDR systems are not without challenges. The resolution of rights requires constitutional guarantees that the processes and decision-makers must satisfy certain essential requirements. Issues such as independence, impartiality, due process, fairness, absence of conflicts of interest, and so on, must be satisfactorily dealt with. A topical issue is that 'safeguards' are required for any European collective action.[52] The same is true of judges, courts, ombudsmen, mediators and regulators. 14/30

Competition is generally considered to be healthy for markets and consumers, and to incentivise innovation. The existence of different dispute resolution options gives rise to competition between them. This has already occurred, as online traders have swiftly adopted ODR arrangements and CDR systems have mopped up demand by consumers for effective dispute resolution pathways where they were not being served by slow and expensive lawyers and courts. In the United Kingdom, satisfaction of this consumer demand had been abrogated by suppliers and the state before it was quickly satisfied when CDR systems became available. 14/31

Do the new CDR and regulatory redress techniques signal the demise of lawyers and courts? The empirical evidence suggests that it is rational to predict at least a major reform in the structure of European dispute resolution and regulatory systems. Gaps are likely to remain in certain countries, or sectors, or types of dispute, whether by accident or otherwise. But the future will clearly be profoundly different. Our legal systems and their intermediaries will not be structured or operate in the way we have become accustomed to. Resolving cross-border disputes is a challenge now, and is likely to remain so. But cross-border technologies are likely to transform arrangements, such as through ODR plat- 14/32

51 Review of the Regulation of Cosmetic Interventions (DoH, April 2013), available at <https://www.gov.uk/government/publications/review-of-the-regulation-of-cosmetic-interventions>.

52 European Parliament Resolution of 2 February 2012, Towards a Coherent European Approach to Collective Redress, (2011/2089 (INI); *R Money-Kyrle/C Hodges*, Safeguards in Collective Actions (2012) 19.4 Maastricht Journal of International and Comparative Law 477–504.

forms,[53] and lodging claims and evidence online, which is already occurring with both CDR and courts.

14/33 If citizens who have disputes adopt the perception 'think ombudsman' rather than 'think lawyer or court', and the former delivers easy-accessible, fast, cheap and effective justice then ...

53 *J Hörnle*, Cross-border Internet Dispute Resolution (2009); *P Cortés*, Online Dispute Resolution for Consumers in the European Union (2011).

Moritz Brinkmann

15 Mass Tort Related Insolvency Proceedings: Choice of Jurisdiction, Treatment and Discharge of Tort Claims

I. Introduction

Mass tort situations frequently create claims that in number and amount exceed the funds of the tortfeasor. Hence, the examples for mass tort litigation forcing the defendant into bankruptcy are numerous. The US asbestos litigation[1] – where over 70 defendants went bankrupt –, Dow Corning,[2] Bernard Madoff[3] and Phoenix Kapitaldienste GmbH, are some of many cases which show that mass tort related bankruptcies not only challenge the law governing insolvency proceedings with respect to the efficient handling and administration of the proceedings but also raise normative questions as to the fair and equitable treatment of tort claimants. Moreover, the issue of the fair and equitable distribution of limited funds is at the core of many mass tort cases even when the tortfeasor has not filed for bankruptcy. In this sense, insolvency law may even inform the law applicable outside insolvency. 15/1

In this paper I shall deal with three problems which the commencement of insolvency proceedings may create: 15/2

- Which court is competent to hear tort claims after the debtor has filed a bankruptcy petition? (Choice of Jurisdiction, no 15/4 ff)
- Are mass tort victims ordinary insolvency creditors or do they enjoy any preferences over for example contract creditors? (Treatment of Tort Creditors in Insolvency Proceedings, no 15/30 ff)
- How are present and future tort claimants affected by a discharge? (The Effects of a Discharge on the Position of Tort Creditors, no 15/41 ff)

I will conclude with some remarks on lessons to be learned from the US asbestos bankruptcies. 15/3

1 For a brief history see *ST Brown*, Section 524(g) Without Compromise: Voting Rights and the Asbestos Bankruptcy Paradox, Columbian Business Law Review (Colum Bus L Rev) 841 (2008); *GM Vario*, Mass Torts Bankruptcies: The Who, the Why and the How, 78 American Bankruptcy Law Journal (Am Bankr LJ) 93, 109 (2004).

2 See *MR Ferrari*, Silicone Breast Implants: Mass Tort and Massive Damage in Europe, 3/43 ff in this volume.

3 *J Boldon*, European Aspects of the Madoff Ponzi Scheme 10/1 ff in this volume.

II. Choice of Jurisdiction

15/4 With respect to choice of jurisdiction, two issues have to be distinguished. One is the question which courts have jurisdiction to open insolvency proceedings (see no 15/5ff). The other question pertains to the effect the opening of insolvency proceedings might have on the competence of a court to hear the tort claims (see no 15/22). Depending on the applicable law, the insolvency court may have (exclusive) jurisdiction with respect to all insolvency claims. Such a *vis attractiva concursus* has the effect of aggregating all tort claims before the insolvency court.

A. Choice of Jurisdiction with respect to the Insolvency Proceedings

15/5 Choice of jurisdiction, particularly in insolvency law, is not just a matter of convenience but has direct consequences for the applicable substantive law as the general conflicts rule is the *lex fori concursus*. According to this rule, the applicable insolvency law will be the law of the state where the insolvency proceedings have been initiated. As the insolvency laws of the EU Member States differ fundamentally in terms of priorities, avoidance provisions and discharge proceedings, choice of jurisdiction is a crucial factor for the creditors as well as for the debtor. Consequently, forum shopping looms large over international insolvency cases.

15/6 Within the European Union (with the exception of Denmark) international jurisdiction is governed by art 3 European Insolvency Regulation (EIR).[4] According to this provision, the courts of the state 'within the territory of which the centre of a debtor's main interests is situated shall have jurisdiction to open insolvency proceedings. In the case of a company or legal person, the place of the registered office shall be presumed to be the centre of its main interests in the absence of proof to the contrary.' The concept of 'centre of main interests' is generally referred to by the acronym 'COMI'.

15/7 While locating a debtor's COMI in a specific case can be a very difficult and fact-sensitive question, the general approach as developed by the European Court of Justice (ECJ)[5] is rather straightforward: The presumption that the debtor

4 Council Regulation (EC) No 1346/2000 of 29 May on insolvency proceedings, Official Journal of the European Union (OJ) L 160, 30.6.2000, 1–18.

5 ECJ C-341/04, *Eurofood IFSC Ltd* [2006] European Court Reports (ECR) I-3813; C-396/09, *Interedil Srl, in liquidation v Fallimento Interedil Srl and Intesa Gestione Crediti SpA* [2011] ECR I-9915.

has its COMI in the state where it is incorporated may be rebutted, where, from the viewpoint of third parties, the place in which a company's central administration is located is not the same as that of its registered office.[6] In the ECJ's view, the ascertainability by third parties is the key criterion to determine the COMI:

'While the Regulation does not provide a definition of the term "centre of a debtor's main interests", guidance as to the scope of that term is, nevertheless, as the Court stated at paragraph 32 of Eurofood IFSC, to be found in recital 13 in the preamble to the Regulation, which states that 'the "centre of main interests" should correspond to the place where the debtor conducts the administration of his interests on a regular basis and [which] is therefore ascertainable by third parties.' (...) 15/8

'With reference to that recital, the Court also stated, at paragraph 33 of Eurofood IFSC, that the centre of a debtor's main interests must be identified by reference to criteria that are both objective and ascertainable by third parties, in order to ensure legal certainty and foreseeability concerning the determination of the court with jurisdiction to open the main insolvency proceedings. That requirement for objectivity and that possibility of ascertainment by third parties may be considered to be met where the material factors taken into account for the purpose of establishing the place in which the debtor company conducts the administration of its interests on a regular basis have been made public or, at the very least, made sufficiently accessible to enable third parties, that is to say in particular the company's creditors, to be aware of them.'[7] 15/9

According to the proposal for the amendment of the EIR, published by the Commission on 12 December 2012,[8] the ascertainability test shall be expressly adopted in a revised art 3 (1) EIR. For letterbox companies this test has the effect that their COMI is located not at the place where they are registered but at the place where they conduct their affairs. 15/10

The relevant date for the purpose of locating the centre of the debtor's main interests is in principle the date when the request to open proceedings was lodged. If the debtor relocates its COMI to another state after this point of time, such a subsequent change will be irrelevant.[9] Consequently, forum shopping strategies must be employed pre-emptively to be successful. Only COMI-shifts that occur prior to the filing date can have an effect on choice of jurisdiction. 15/11

---

6 ECJ C-396/09, *Interedil v Fallimento Interedil* [2011] ECR I-9915, para 51.

7 *Interedil* [2011] ECR I-9915, paras 47, 49.

8 COM 2012 (774) final.

9 ECJ C-1/04, *Susanne Staubitz-Schreiber* [2006] ECR I-701.

15/12 But even pre-filing COMI-shifting may not have the desired effect: If the seat of the company is relocated after it has ceased all its activities, the COMI may still be in the jurisdiction where the company (formerly) conducted its business. As the ECJ pointed out in the *Interedil* case:

15/13 '(T)he term "centre of main interests" meets the need to establish a connection with the place with which, from an objective viewpoint and in a manner that is ascertainable by third parties, the company has the closest links. It is therefore logical in such a situation [debtor has ceased its activities] to attach greater importance to the location of the last centre of main interests at the time when the debtor company was removed from the register of companies and ceased all activities.'[10]

15/14 The described interpretation of art 3 (1) EIR by the ECJ makes COMI-shifting difficult and expensive.[11] Particularly for companies other than service providers or holding companies, forum shopping by COMI-shifting is hardly a promising strategy.

15/15 If a company wishes to restructure itself under a law different from the one at its COMI, it should try to take recourse to non-insolvency mechanisms such as the English scheme of arrangement according to Parts 26 and 27 Companies Act 2006. As the scheme of arrangement is not listed in Annex A to the EIR, it is not an insolvency proceeding in the sense of the EIR. Thus, English courts may take jurisdiction to sanction a scheme even though the company has its COMI outside England (or Wales for that matter).[12]

15/16 Whether restructuring by way of a scheme of arrangement is a promising strategy for a company facing mass tort claims depends on two questions:

- Is the scheme of arrangement in principle a promising instrument in such situations?
- If so, will the effects of the scheme be recognised in other states where the tort claimants might subsequently sue the company?

15/17 In mass tort related restructurings, sec 899 (1) Companies Act 2006 might be an obstacle difficult to deal with.[13] According to this provision, a 75% majority in

---

10 *Interedil* [2011] ECR I-9915, para 58.

11 *H Eidenmüller/T Frobenius/W Prusko*, Regulierungswettbewerb im Unternehmensinsolvenzrecht: Ergebnisse einer empirischen Untersuchung, Neue Zeitschrift für das Recht der Insolvenz und Sanierung (NZI) 2010, 545.

12 High Court of Justice, 6 May 2011 – England & Wales High Court (EWHC) 1104 Chancery Division (Ch) *In the matter of Rodenstock GmbH* (2011) International Insolvency Law Review (IILR) 591.

13 I shall not discuss here the general issue of international jurisdiction with respect to the scheme of arrangements regarding non-English companies. See High Court of Justice, 6 May 2011 – EWHC 1104 (Ch) *In the matter of Rodenstock GmbH* (2011) IILR 591.

each class is required. If this burden is not met, the court will not sanction the scheme. As the tort creditors may be a very diverse and fragmented class – as opposed to financiers, for example, it may be very difficult to reach the required majority.

With respect to the issue of recognition, one has to appreciate that the scheme of arrangement is not listed in annex A of the EIR and does therefore not qualify as 'insolvency proceedings' in the sense of the EIR.[14] Automatic recognition according to art 25 EIR is not applicable with respect to schemes of arrangement.[15] As of now, no case law by the ECJ exists on whether the Brussels I Regulation (EC No 44/2001 of 22 December 2000 on jurisdiction and the recognition and enforcement of judgments in civil and commercial matters) is applicable with respect to the recognition of schemes of arrangement.[16] As a consequence, the applicable law is difficult to ascertain. **15/18**

For these reasons restructuring by way of a scheme of arrangement is a risky strategy, particularly in the situations where the success of the scheme depends on its recognition outside of England. **15/19**

B. Decisions as to the Allowance of Claims – The Concept of Vis Attractiva Concursus

The second aspect of choice of jurisdiction in the context of insolvency proceedings relates to the question where disputes as to the existence of insolvency claims will be adjudicated. In some jurisdictions, the opening of insolvency proceedings has the effect of bringing all proceedings that are connected to the **15/20**

14 ECJ C-461/11, *Ulf Kazimierz Radziejewski v Kronofogdemyndigheten i Stockholm*, OJ C 340, 19.11.2011, 10–10, para 24.

15 See *C Thole*, Sanierung mittels Scheme of Arrangement im Blickwinkel des Internationalen Privat- und Verfahrensrechts, Zeitschrift für Unternehmens- und Gesellschaftsrecht (ZGR) 2013, 109, 114.

16 On the applicability of the Brussels I Regulation, see *H Eidenmüller/T Frobenius*, Die internationale Reichweite eines englischen Scheme of Arrangement, WM – Zeitschrift für Wirtschafts- und Bankrecht (WM) 2011, 1210, 1214; *W Lüke/A Scherz*, Zu den Wirkungen eines Solvent Scheme of Arrangement in Deutschland, Zeitschrift für Wirtschaftsrecht (ZIP) 2012, 1101, 1104; *P Mankowski*, Anerkennung englischer Solvent Schemes of Arrangement in Deutschland, WM 2011, 1201 f; *K Schümann-Kleber*, Recognition of English Solvent Schemes of Arrangements Affecting Dissenting Creditors of German Companies (2011) IILR 447, 449; *Thole*, ZGR 2013, 109, 151; *L Westpfahl/M Knapp*, ZIP 2011, 2033, 2044.

insolvency proceedings under the jurisdiction of the bankruptcy court. Such an effect is called *vis attractiva concursus*.[17]

15/21 The strength of *vis attractiva concursus* varies from jurisdiction to jurisdiction. A strong *vis attractiva concursus* may concentrate all mass tort claims before one court. However, two questions have to be distinguished:

- When a claim is lodged within the insolvency proceedings and contested (by the trustee or another creditor), which courts are competent to determine the claim? (see no 15/22ff below)
- When a trial is already pending at the time the insolvency proceedings are opened, will the case be transferred to the bankruptcy court or will the trial court retain jurisdiction? (see no 15/27ff below)

1. The determination of a lodged and contested claim

15/22 In insolvency proceedings, usually only those creditors who have lodged their claims in time will benefit from distributions made in those proceedings. When a claim is lodged, the administrator (and – depending on the respective insolvency law – other creditors) can reject the claim or otherwise contest it. Under most laws the creditor can then turn to a court to have the claim determined.

15/23 With respect to questions of international jurisdiction for the determination of claims contested by the administrator, a specific form of the *vis attractiva concursus* applies: After insolvency proceedings have been opened in one Member State of the EU (with the exception of Denmark) the courts of that state have jurisdiction under art 3 EIR to determine the insolvency claims because such proceedings are regarded as proceedings ancillary to the insolvency proceedings.[18] As art 3 EIR provides for an exclusive jurisdiction,[19] this has the effect that any special jurisdiction, which is available to the tort claimants outside insolvency – for example under art 5 (3) Brussels I Regulation – is no longer applicable.

15/24 On a national level the strength of *vis attractiva concursus* varies from jurisdiction to jurisdiction. In systems that have a *vis attractiva concursus*, these determinations will be made by the bankruptcy court.[20] Hence, the bankruptcy

17 For a comparative perspective, see *C Willemer*, Vis attractiva concursus und die Europäische Insolvenzverordnung (2006).

18 See *B Laukemann* in: The External Evaluation of Regulation No 1346/2000 on Insolvency Proceedings, JUST/2011/JCIV/PR0049/A4 190.

19 See *Laukemann* (fn18) 206.

20 England: Insolvency Rules 1986 4.83, 6.105; Austria: § 111 Insolvenzordnung (IO); France: Decision by the 'juge-commissaire' according to art L 624-2 Code de Commerce; Italy: art 95 subpara 3 Legge Fallimentare.

court has jurisdiction to determine all lodged mass tort claims. Such a bundling of claims may help to coordinate the adjudication of mass tort cases. In this sense, the opening of insolvency proceedings may have effects that are somewhat similar to the bundling or grouping of claims outside of insolvency situations.[21] As the insolvency court has exclusive jurisdiction to determine the claims, the case can be handled more efficiently.

However, the coordinating effect the *vis attractiva* may have comes at a price. Not only do the tort creditors lose any advantages that might result from a special jurisdiction available to them outside insolvency. Moreover, bankruptcy courts may have a higher tendency to decide in favour of the trustee that is the estate. A bankruptcy court may not always be completely unbiased as it closely cooperates with the trustee during the bankruptcy proceedings with a view to maximising the estate. Hence, a bankruptcy court might feel more inclined to 'protect' the estate rather than to decide in favour of claims against it.[22] 15/25

It is for this reason that some jurisdictions have refrained from adopting the concept of *vis attractiva concursus*. In Switzerland, Germany and Greece, for example, it is not for the bankruptcy court to determine contested claims, but for the trial court at the place where the insolvency proceedings take place.[23] In other words, the cases are not centralised before one single court or judge but only locally in one district. The coordinating effects of such a rule are clearly less significant. However, the aforementioned problem of having a potentially biased bankruptcy court determining the insolvency claims is avoided. 15/26

2. The effect of the opening of insolvency proceedings on pending trials

Often tort claimants will already have initiated litigation against the tortfeasor when the insolvency proceedings commence. The consequences of the opening of insolvency proceedings on the pending trial depend not only on the applicable insolvency law but also on the *lex fori*. Under most laws the commencement of insolvency proceedings will lead to a stay of such trials. This stay is to give the trustee the opportunity to make himself acquainted with the case and to choose his procedural strategy. 15/27

21 *Vario*, 78 Am Bankr LJ 93, 109 (2004).

22 See *JK DiMugno*, Asbestos, Bankruptcy and Insurance: Fuller-Austin Insulation Company v Highlands Insurance Company, 27 No 3 California Tort Reporter 103.

23 Switzerland: § 250 Bundesgesetz über Schuldbetreibung und Konkurs (SchKG); Germany: § 180 IO. Turkey has adopted a similar approach, see Icra ve İflas Kanunu, art 235 subpara 1.

15/28 The more pressing question in our context is whether the opening of insolvency proceedings has any effects on the jurisdiction of the trial court. Under some laws the *vis attractiva concursus* is so strong that even pending cases may be transferred from the trial court to the bankruptcy court.[24] Under Spanish law, for example, a case that is pending in first instance can be moved to the bankruptcy court if the outcome of the case has substantial effects, for example, on the list of insolvency creditors.[25] Such a rule ensures that the debtor's affairs will be centralised in a single forum in order to prevent conflicting judgments from different courts and to harmonise all of the creditors' interests with one another.[26]

15/29 Again, for tort claimants such a strong *vis attractiva concursus* may have repercussions. Not only will they no longer be able to enjoy the advantages of any special jurisdiction that may be available to them outside insolvency. Moreover, they will have to litigate before a court which may be more inclined to protect the estate (with a view to reorganising the debtor) than to defend the tort victims' rights.

III. Treatment of Tort Creditors in Insolvency Proceedings

A. Tort Creditors are General Creditors! (?)

15/30 Under virtually all insolvency laws, tort creditors – with the notable exception of the Spanish *Ley Concursal*[27] – are treated as general creditors in the sense that the *pari passu* rule – the fundamental principle of insolvency law – applies to them. The *pari passu* rule has the effect that tort creditors are treated the same

---

24 Under US law, all bankruptcy related litigation will usually be assigned to the bankruptcy judge. The district court, however, has the right to retain jurisdiction, *Vario*, 78 Am Bankr LJ 93, 112 (2004).

25 Art 51 subpara 1 Spanish Ley Concursal. Under US law, original jurisdiction with respect to cases arising under the Bankruptcy Code is vested with the federal district courts. According to 28 United States Code (USC) § 157 subpara a, the district courts, however, 'may provide that any or all cases under title 11 (...) shall be referred to the bankruptcy judges for the district'.

26 See *Fidelity Mortgage Investors v Camelia Builders, Inc*, 550 Federal Reporter, Second Series (F 2d) 47, 55 (2d Cir 1976) with respect to the automatic stay and its effects under US Law.

27 Art 125 Ley Concursal. For more details, see *JM Garrido*, Some Reflections on the EU Bankruptcy Convention and its Implications for Secured and Preferential Creditors (1998) 7 International Insolvency Review 79, 93.

way as for example unsecured contract creditors notwithstanding the fact that tort creditors did not have the option to ask for a security right.

From a theoretical point of view, one might question this proposition underlying most insolvency laws. The difference between these groups of creditors is that tort creditors did not choose to become creditors as they never made a decision to finance the debtor's business. They are merely the victims of the debtor's pre-bankruptcy conduct and in this sense involuntary creditors. Some scholars argue that a rule which treats voluntary creditors and tort creditors alike creates inefficiencies[28] and implies a misconception[29] of the *pari passu* rule. 15/31

Notwithstanding this critique, only Spanish insolvency law grants tort claimants priority over general (unsecured) creditors. Other jurisdictions differentiate between tort creditors and other creditors only with respect to discharge provisions (see no 15/42f). US law, however, privileges tort creditors in yet another aspect: A tort victim has the same right to a jury trial in bankruptcy as would exist under non-bankruptcy law, whereas claims based on contract are determined by the bankruptcy judge without a jury.[30] 15/32

B. Treatment of Insurance Policy Proceeds in Insolvency Proceedings

One of the crucial questions for tort creditors in insolvency proceedings pertains to the treatment of insurance policies respectively proceeds thereof. As an (admittedly eclectic) comparative analysis shows, tort creditors will, under most laws, enjoy priority with respect to those proceeds. Hence, the proceeds are not distributed among all creditors following the *pari passu* rule but the proceeds will be reserved exclusively for the tort creditors. Such a priority seems well justified. If it did not exist, the general creditors would benefit from the tort victims' loss. If the insurance policy proceeds became part of the estate and were distributed among all creditors, the tort victims' loss would augment the estate and would in turn raise the expected distributions made to all creditors. Such a rule would not only ignore the debtor's pre-insolvency decision to buy insurance but, furthermore, unduly benefit the non-tort creditors. 15/33

---

28 See *DG Baird*, Elements of Bankruptcy (5th edn 2010) 92; *G Wagner* in: E Schilken/G Kreft/G Wagner/D Eckardt (eds), Festschrift für Walter Gerhardt (2004) 1043.

29 See *LA Bebchuk*/*JM Fried*, The Uneasy Case for the Priority of Secured Claims in Bankruptcy, 105 Yale LJ 857 (1996).

30 *Baird* (fn 28).

15/34 Priority for tort claimants with respect to insurance proceeds can be achieved by two fundamentally different concepts, either via substantive law (see no 15/35 ff) or via insolvency law (see no 15/37 ff).

1. The effects of a direct action approach in insolvency

15/35 Some jurisdictions have adopted the concept of direct action with respect to specific types of insurance policies. Under a direct action rule, the tort victim can sue the insurer directly without having to obtain a judgment against the tortfeasor first. Such an approach was provided for by the European Convention on Compulsory Insurance against Civil Liability in respect of Motor Vehicles.[31] German law has expanded the scope of this concept to the effect that direct action is permissible in all instances of compulsory insurance if the insured is insolvent.[32]

15/36 If the tort victims can sue the insurer directly, the proceeds of the insurance policy never become the property of the estate. Hence, the tort creditors' rights with respect to the proceeds remain unaffected by the insured's insolvency. In particular, the opening of insolvency proceedings will not trigger an automatic stay of cases pending between tort claimants and insurer. In *AH Robins*[33], however, the Bankruptcy Court used its equitable powers under the Bankruptcy Code to extend the automatic stay also to actions against co-defendants, that is the insurer.[34] Particularly when the insurance proceeds are likely to be insufficient to pay all tort claimants completely, such an extension of the automatic stay may permit a coordinated distribution of the insurance proceeds among all tort claimants.

2. Earmarking of insurance policy proceeds

15/37 When direct action is not permissible, insurance policies and proceeds thereof are in principle the property of the estate. Different mechanisms exist to guaran-

---

31 Strasbourg, 20 May 1959, see eg § 26 (Austrian) Kraftfahrzeug-Haftpflichtversicherungsgesetz (KHVG).

32 See § 115 subpara 1 subsec 2 (German) Versicherungsvertragsgesetz (VVG).

33 Beginning in 1971 AH Robins distributed the Dalkon Shield, a contraceptive device which caused a variety of injuries.

34 The order was affirmed in *AH Robins Co v Piccinin*, 788 F 2d 994 (4th Cir 1986).

tee that the tort claimants nonetheless enjoy priority with respect to those policies:

German and Austrian law treat the tort creditors as if they had a security right in the insurance policies.[35] Hence, they are deemed to be *absonderungsberechtigte Gläubiger* (secured creditors) to the effect that the policy proceeds will not be distributed among all creditors but used to satisfy primarily the tort claimants. The difference to the direct action approach is a matter of procedure: Under § 110 German VVG and § 157 Austrian VVG, the tort victims will have to lodge their claims within the insolvency proceedings (and – as the case may be – prove them), whereas, under the direct action approach, the victims do not become involved with the insolvency proceedings at all as they can sue the insurer directly. **15/38**

Under the US Bankruptcy Code, the courts distinguish between the insurance policy as such on the one hand and its proceeds on the other hand. The policy is part of the estate[36] because any rights the debtor has against the insurer, whether contractual or otherwise, become the property of the estate.[37] However, ownership of a policy 'does not inexorably lead to ownership of the proceeds.'[38] Whether the insurance policy proceeds are part of the estate depends on whether the debtor has a 'legally cognizable claim to the insurance proceeds (…). Under the typical liability policy, the debtor will not have a cognizable interest in the proceeds of the policy. Those proceeds will normally be payable only for the benefit of those harmed by the debtor under the terms of the insurance contract.'[39] **15/39**

This approach not only guarantees the tort creditors' priority with respect to policy proceeds notwithstanding the absence of a direct action rule but is also in line with the view that a discharge obtained by the debtor during the insolvency proceedings does not affect the tort victims' rights to the insurance policy proceeds[40] unless an injunction according to § 524 (g) (4) (a) (II) (III) US Bankruptcy Code has been issued.[41] **15/40**

---

35 § 110 German VVG, § 157 Austrian VVG.

36 *JM Silverstein*, Overlooking Tort Claimants' Best Interest: Non-Debtor Releases in Asbestos Bankruptcies, 78 University of Missouri at Kansas City Law Review (UMKC L Rev) 1, 46 (2009).

37 *Matter of Edgeworth*, 993 F 2d 51, 55 (5th Cir 1993).

38 *Louisiana World Exposition*, 832 F 2d at 1401 (5th Cir 1987).

39 *Matter of Edgeworth*, 993 F 2d 51, 56 (5th 1993). See also *In re Edoscopy Center of Southern Nevada LLC*, 451 Bankruptcy Reporter (BR) 527 at 547 (Bankr D Nev 2011).

40 *First Fidelity Bank v McAteer*, 985 F 2d 114 (3d Cir 1993); *Green v Welsh*, 956 F 2d 30, 35 (2d Cir1992); *In re Fernstrom Storage & Van Co*, 938 F 2d 731, 733-34 (7th Cir 1991); *In re Jet Florida Systems, Inc*, 883 F 2d 970, 976 (11th Cir 1989) (per curiam) (adopting the district court opinion).

41 On § 524(g) 4a US Bankruptcy Code, see no 15/51 ff.

IV. The Effects of a Discharge on the Position of Tort Creditors

15/41 Today, the notion that the debtor deserves a fresh start despite its bankruptcy is universally accepted. Following the example of Chapter 11 US Bankruptcy Code, many jurisdictions have adopted procedures that are aimed at the reorganisation rather than the liquidation of the debtor. With respect to reorganisation, it is important to understand that restructuring is not an end in itself. In many situations it may be more efficient to liquidate the debtor's business than to spend 'fresh' money on the futile attempt to reorganise it. However, in situations where reorganisation is economically sensible, it is also attractive for the creditors as they can expect to receive higher returns than in a liquidation scenario.

A. Discharge of Tort Claims in Principle

15/42 The arguments brought forward in favour of giving tort claimants priority over contractual creditors, which were discussed earlier (no 15/30ff), can also be applied to the question whether a discharge should affect tort claims. Moreover, it is not at all self evident that the debtor can enjoy a fresh start, continue to do business and keep whatever earnings thereby generated whereas the persons harmed by its former activity have to be satisfied with only partial compensation for their damage.

15/43 Hence, a strong case can be made that at least claims resulting from wilful and malicious injury should not be affected by a discharge. Rules exempting those claims from discharge in bankruptcy exist for example in Austria,[42] in Germany[43] with respect to discharges obtained by natural persons, and in the United States[44] in Chapter 7 proceedings – that is liquidation cases. Negligence claims, however, will be affected by a discharge notwithstanding the mentioned rules as these rules apply only to wilful injuries.

---

42 § 215 No 1 IO.

43 § 302 No 1 Insolvenzordnung (InsO).

44 11 USC § 523(a) 6. In *Kawaahua v Geiger*, 523 United States Supreme Court Reports (US) 57 (1998) the Supreme Court held that the debtor must maliciously intend to specifically injure the person or property in order for the liability not to be discharged.

B. Treatment of Tort Claims in Restructuring Plans – in Particular the Future Claimant Problem

One should bear in mind, however, that in mass tort related insolvency proceedings a reorganisation of the debtor will only succeed if the plan provides for a haircut of all claims including the tort claims relating to the debtor's pre-bankruptcy activities. If the debtor or any third party providing financing must fear that after confirmation of the plan new claimants turn up and demand compensation for their damage, the reorganisation is bound to fail due to the remaining uncertainty. The debtor needs what is often called 'global peace' in order to successfully reorganise its business. 15/44

A fundamental threat to this global peace is the future claimant problem which is perhaps the most intriguing issue in many mass tort cases. In situations such as asbestos cases, the injury takes a very long time to manifest itself due to its very long latency period. It may be many years after the confirmation of the plan that new claimants appear who only then have learned about their injuries and hence only now ask for compensation. Depending on the case and the kind of injuries, the amount of future claims can be extremely difficult to anticipate. 15/45

In reorganisation proceedings, potential future claims generate mainly two problems: One regards questions of due process and pertains to the adequate representation of the future claimants' interests in the voting procedures. The other issue is the question of how funds made available to the tort creditors by the plan are to be distributed. As the problem of future claimants is at the centre of the asbestos bankruptcies, US law provides many examples for strategies that have been developed to address the issue. For this reason, the following analysis will mainly concentrate on the experience in asbestos bankruptcies. European readers should bear in mind, however, that US bankruptcy courts are courts of equity. They enjoy a discretion and flexibility unknown to continental civil courts. 15/46

1. Representation of future creditors' interests in plan proceedings

If a court has evidence that there are victims who have not yet learned about their injuries and thus did not participate in the insolvency proceedings, the court will be very reluctant to confirm a plan that is binding also on such potential future claims as due process might be violated.[45] In order to address these 15/47

---

45 A similar problem arises outside bankruptcy with respect to the aggregation of claims and the negotiation of a settlement that is also binding on future claimants. See for example *Ste-*

concerns, the court in the bankruptcy of the asbestos producing company *Johns-Manville* appointed a legal guardian for the future claimants.[46] The court argued that future claimants were 'parties in interest' under 11 USC § 1109 and, therefore, were entitled to a representative. The other instrument for the protection of future claimants was the establishment of a trust which was funded with (among other sources) Manville's settlements with its insurers, stock of the reorganised Manville Corporation, and the right to receive up to 20% of Manville's yearly profits for as long as it would take to satisfy all health claims. The trust was designed to compensate all asbestos victims including any future claimants. To protect Manville's operating entities and its insurers from asbestos related claims, the court issued an injunction channelling all respective claims to the trust. The channelling injunction applied to all personal injury claimants, both present and future.[47]

15/48 The trust mechanism deployed in Manville was eventually used by Congress as a role model for 11 USC[48] § 524 (g) which was enacted in 1994. Under Sec 524 (g), an asbestos bankruptcy reorganisation plan can 'enjoin entities from taking legal action for the purpose of directly or indirectly collecting, recovering, or receiving payment or recovery with respect to any claim or demand that, under a plan of reorganisation, is to be paid in whole or in part by the trust established if – among other things – at least 75% of any class or classes of current asbestos claimants vote in favour of the plan'.[49] As in Manville, § 524 (g) furthermore provides for a legal representative 'for the purpose of protecting the rights of persons that might subsequently assert demands[50] of such kind'.[51] To-

---

phenson v Dow Chemical Corp, 27 F 3d 249 (2d Cir 2001) affirmed by the Supreme Court in 539 US 111 (2003): The question was whether a class action settlement was also binding on victims whose injuries had manifested themselves after a fund for the compensation of the victims had been established and subsequently depleted by payments made to other victims. The Second Circuit held that the settlement was not binding for the plaintiffs (who had 'future' claims), because they did not get proper notice and opportunity to be heard. Thus, their interests were not adequately protected.

46 See *In re Johns-Manville Corp*, 36 BR 743 (Bankr SDNY 1984).

47 *Vario*, 78 Am Bankr LJ 93, 102 (2004).

48 *Brown*, Colum Bus L Rev 841, 852 (2008).

49 See 11 USC § 524(g) 2 (B)(ii)(IV)(bb).

50 Subsec 5 says that 'the term "demand" means a demand for payment, present or future, that (A) was not a claim during the proceedings leading to the confirmation of a plan of reorganization; (B) arises out of the same or similar conduct or events that gave rise to the claims addressed by the injunction issued under para (1); and (C) pursuant to the plan, is to be paid by a trust described in para 2 subpara B subsec I'.

51 See 11 USC § 524(g) 4.

day, approximately 60 asbestos bankruptcy trust funds are said to have been established or are in the process of being established.[52]

2. Depletion of the established trust

Not only the Manville trust but also many other asbestos trusts were eventually depleted of funds as the funds were insufficient to pay the future claims as they were much more numerous and much higher in value than initially expected. In Manville, claimants received only pennies on the dollar and eventually the trust was restructured.[53] The settlement agreement essentially revised the processes for the payment of asbestos claims.[54] The objective of the established trust distribution process was 'to treat all claimants alike by paying all claimants an equal percentage of their claims' values over time.' In 2002, however, the process had to be revised again.[55] **15/49**

It has been argued that 'the design of Section 524 (g), the manner in which asbestos bankruptcies are administered, and the management structure and criteria of established trusts continue to work against the goal of ensuring equitable compensation for future victims.'[56] To address some of this criticism, a bill called the Furthering Asbestos Claim Transparency (FACT) Act of 2013[57] has been introduced in Congress. The bill is meant to enhance transparency with respect to the administration of trusts; its opponents, however, purport that 'the legislation is designed to make it more difficult for asbestos victims, including those with mesothelioma and other cancers, to receive compensation for their injuries through asbestos trusts and the court system'.[58] **15/50**

52 See the written statement of Professor *ST Brown*, Furthering Asbestos Claim Transparency (FACT) Act of 2013, 13 March 2013.

53 See *In re Joint Eastern and Southern Dist Asbestos Litigation*, 982 F.2d 721 (1992).

54 For details see *Vario*, 78 Am Bankr LJ 93, 104 (2004).

55 The TDP 2002 can be retrieved under <http://www.claimsres.com/documents/MT/2002%20TDPJanuary%202012%20Revision.pdf>.

56 *Brown* (fn 52) 11. For more critique see *Silverstein*, 78 UMKC L Rev 1 (2009).

57 House of Representatives (HR) 982.

58 See <http://cancervictimsrights.org/legislation/fact-act/> as of 26 June 2013.

V. Lessons to Be Learned From the Asbestos Bankruptcies

15/51 This is not the appropriate place to further elaborate on the details of the FACT bill or on the problem associated with § 524 (g) in its present form. What is clear is that the future claimant issue which looms large over asbestos cases and other mass tort related insolvencies has not been resolved yet.[59] However, the concept used in Manville, which also underlies § 524 (g) US Bankruptcy Code, seems in principle to be a sound approach to tackle the future claimant problem. The problems of current US asbestos bankruptcies appear to be more the result of the way the cases are managed and administered by courts and counsels than of defects of the law.

15/52 The idea to establish a trust for the compensation of future claimants, which is funded among other sources by a share of the future revenues the restructured firm generates, is sound in principle.[60] If reorganisation is efficient from an economic point of view, such a scheme is in any event much more preferable for future claimants than a liquidation of the debtor. In liquidation proceedings, all the debtor's assets will be distributed among the present creditors. Future claimants would be left with nothing. Hence, reorganisation and the establishment of a trust is – at least from the perspective of the future claimants – a sensible approach. The representation of the future claimants and the control of the management of the trust, however, must be addressed with great diligence. Judging from the US experience, it may be advisable to entrust an official body (eg a court) with the task of protecting the future claimants' rights rather than a private entity. A solution along these lines, though with no foundation in insolvency law, has been used in Germany in the Contergan tragedy[61] and again to deal with the HIV infections caused by the transfer of contaminated blood.[62]

---

59 See in particular the Report by the RAND Institute: *SJ Carroll et al/RAND Institute for Civil Justice*, Asbestos Litigation VII (2005) 112, available at <http://www.rand.org/pubs/monographs/MG162/>.

60 See *H Koch*, Haftung für Massenschäden – Recht, Abwicklungspraxis, rechtspolitischer Handlungsbedarf, JuristenZeitung (JZ) 1998, 801, 808.

61 Contergan was a barbiturate sold in the 1950s and 1960s in West Germany. It caused many different forms of birth defects. See Gesetz über die Errichtung der Stiftung 'Hilfswerk für behinderte Kinder', 17 December 1971, Bundesgesetzblatt (BGBl) I 2018.

62 Gesetz über die humanitäre Hilfe für durch Blutprodukte HIV-infizierte Personen, 24 July 1995, BGBl I 972. See for more details *E Deutsch*, Das Gesetz über die humanitäre Hilfe für durch Blutprodukte HIV-Infizierte, Neue Juristische Wochenschrift (NJW) 1996, 756.

Similarly, the Dutch WCAM settlement structure involves the incorporation of a 'legal entity' for the purpose of distributing the settlement sum.[63]

The contribution insolvency law has to offer to further enhance this design is the concept of a debt to equity swap which might be a useful tool to address the future claimant problem. A debt to equity swap has the effect of taking the debtor's stocks from the former share holders and putting them in the hands of its creditors, who in turn discharge the debtor from the debts. 15/53

One could envisage a mechanism that essentially requires four steps: 15/54

- In a first step all tort claims (present and future) are transferred to the trust.
- Secondly, as a compensation for the loss of their claims, the claimants acquire corresponding rights against the trust.
- In the third step the trust swaps the claims in exchange for shares in the debtor company. In the course of the last step, and as a consequence of step number 3, the former shareholders lose their equity in the debtor.

By making all tort claimants the beneficial owners of the debtor, such a design has three positive effects: 15/55

- The trust will be periodically refunded with revenues generated by the debtor, hence depletion problems are mitigated.
- Tort claimants receive dividends from the trust until their claims are satisfied to the extent agreed upon in the restructuring plan. The distribution process itself should be designed in a way that ensures equal treatment of present and future claimants to the greatest extent possible. To achieve this, one could rely on the concept of art 20 (2) EIR: A claimant who has in the past obtained a dividend on his claim shall share in future distributions only where all other claimants have obtained an equivalent dividend. Such a mechanism ensures that a claimant who learns rather late about its injuries enjoys priority with respect to the dividends until its claim is satisfied to an extent equal to satisfaction received earlier by the other claimants.
- Former shareholders will not benefit from the reorganisation (which is paid for by creditors, as their claims will only be satisfied in part or at least with considerable delay!)

Such an approach could be a promising strategy in scenarios where the debtor is insolvent, reorganisation is economically preferable to liquidation, and future 15/56

63 *F Weber/WH Van Boom*, Dutch Treat: The Dutch Collective Settlement of Mass Damage Act (WCAM 2005), (2011) Contratto e Impresa/Europa 69 fn 3.

claims are an issue. If this design should lead to the complete satisfaction of all tort claims, the trust may be used to fund charitable activities such as conducting research in the field or to support victims of other debtors.

Gerhard Wagner

16 Mass Tort Resolution: Competition Between Jurisdictions and Mechanisms

I. Introduction

Mass torts are a topic in themselves, but also part of a larger picture that includes instances of contractual liability. At the same time, fragments of the larger pool of problems and cases are grouped together and discussed under different labels. One such label that is of increasing importance in Europe is the one of collective redress.[1] It lumps together problems of competition law, namely the methods of calculating the tools for meting out damages, as well as aspects of consumer law, ie of providing compensation for consumers who have been wronged by violations of EU consumer law. In this context of collective redress, the main objective is enforcement of EU law rather than the development of pathways for dealing with scenarios of mass damage as such and for its own sake. The current project was designed to inform the European debate on collective redress without, however, neglecting the genuine aspects of the topic, ie the problems that are not linked to and aligned with the issue of law enforcement. 16/1

This project aspired to broaden the picture in other respects, too. Most approaches to the problems posed by mass torts remain confined to the field of civil litigation. Some systems of civil procedure, among them the systems of the US, offer special tools designed for the combined resolution of claims growing out of mass torts. The most prominent tool are, of course, the American class action, together with the rather generous and efficient rules on joinder of claims and consolidation of proceedings in one district. Much of the European debate on collective redress has taken place in the shadow of the American model. While some commentators suggested pushing ahead and adapting a European version of the American class actions, others warned against the perceived dangers of American-style litigation, of which the class action was held to be a major ingredient. In the course of this argument, issues such as the choice between an opt-out and an opt-in system gained in importance and dominated the de- 16/2

1 For a definition cf Commission Recommendation 2013/396/EU of 11 June 2013 on common principles for injunctive and compensatory collective redress mechanisms in the Member States concerning violations of rights granted under Union Law, Official Journal (OJ) L 201, 26.7.2013, 60–65.

bate. The downside was that alternatives to civil litigation as a means of dealing with mass torts remained outside of the limelight.

16/3 In contrast, the present project included other modes of settling mass torts, apart from civil litigation. One example, which can be counted among the alternatives to civil litigation, involves ad-hoc compensation schemes. While jurisdictions such as Germany lack general procedural mechanisms for aggregating numerous claims based on the same accident or other harmful event, Germany has a tradition of dealing with mass disasters on an ad hoc basis. The train crash near the city of Eschede, in which around 100 passengers lost their lives, provides an example that is represented by a case study in this volume. Ad hoc compensation schemes for victims of mass disasters make up only a small fraction of the spectrum of Alternative Dispute Resolution (ADR). Other options are mediation, conciliation and summary proceedings before non-judicial bodies that may be efficient in settling small claims at reasonable costs. It seems that the relationship between ADR and collective redress has remained unexplored. In particular, the potential of ADR to offer a low-cost disposition of claims case-by-case may offer an alternative to the aggregation of many claims into one large claim.

16/4 Another institution that has not yet been analysed for purposes of mass tort resolution is insolvency law. A considerable portion of mass tort scenarios raises questions of insolvency, simply because the damages are so vast that they may bankrupt the wrongdoer. In this respect, mass torts have always been linked to insolvency law. Particularly in the US, bankruptcy has been used by businesses as a response to an overwhelming flood of tort claims, as they have become familiar particularly in the field of product liability.[2] However, insolvency law must not be reduced to a mechanism for shaking off tort claims or for limiting the exposure to a large number of such claims. Insolvency law also has something to offer to tort law, namely mechanisms and tools for disposing of a large number of claims at low-cost. Insolvency proceedings are well-attuned to the tasks of resolving a large number of claims at low-cost and of distributing a limited pool of assets between many competing claimants. Furthermore, insolvency law includes tools that allow for the restitution of moneys that were paid out to particular claimants for the benefit of the full group of claimants.

16/5 Finally, the project also looked at the role that criminal procedure might have to play in the resolution of mass torts. From the perspective of many legal systems, it may be surprising to see the criminal justice system perform this function, but for others, the connection between crimes and tort, between civil

2 *Linda S Mullenix*, Mass Tort Litigation (2nd edn 2008) 478.

and criminal procedure was never severed. Most of the continental-European jurisdictions allow tort victims to join criminal proceedings against the wrongdoer and to claim damages in criminal court.[3] Particularly in the area of personal injury, mass tort scenarios are of high profile so that prosecutors and criminal courts get involved. In such cases, victims retain the option to take advantage of the criminal investigation and to add a mass of damages claims to the public charge.

II. The Spectrum of Mechanisms and Fora

A. Civil Procedure

1. The commission recommendation on collective redress

Naturally, civil procedure is the first area to look at in search for institutions 16/6 that allow for the efficient resolution of mass disputes. Not surprisingly, the European debate on collective redress has been focused on civil procedure. The Commission Recommendation on Collective Redress naturally focuses on measures within civil procedure, without even explaining why.[4] Recommendation recital 15 explicitly provides that 'collective redress mechanisms should preserve procedural safeguards and guarantees of parties to civil actions.' With this principle in mind, the Recommendation calls for the introduction of representative actions, ie civil actions brought by a representative entity on behalf of victims who claim to have been harmed in a mass harm situation.[5] In addition, Member States shall provide for group actions, ie the bundling together of claims growing out of a mass harm situation for disposition in a single proceeding.[6] Such group actions shall be based on the opt-in principle pursuant to

---

3 As to French law cf *R Vogler*, Criminal Procedure in France, in: R Vogler/B Huber, Criminal Procedure in Europe (2008) 241; as to Spanish law cf *FG Inchausti/ML Villamarín López*, Criminal Procedure in Spain, ibid, 609f. To be sure, criminal courts in England and Wales are authorised, and even required, to make compensation orders in favour of victims, in addition to sentencing the offender for the criminal wrong that he or she has committed. Cf *WVH Rogers*, Winfield & Jolovicz on Tort (18th edn 2010) para 4-2. More generally *C von Bar*, The Common European Law of Torts, vol 1 (1998) para 602.

4 Commission Recommendation (fn 1). The Recommendation does mention Alternative Dispute Resolution (ADR), but seems to envisage the amicable settlement of aggregate claims through means of 'collective ADR', not the ADR-treatment of individual claims; cf para 25ff.

5 Commission Recommendation (fn 1) para 3(d).

6 Ibid, para 21ff.

which victims are only allowed to participate in the proceedings and to benefit from an award of damages if they expressly joined the claimant party before judgment was rendered. Conversely, victims that do not join the claimant party are neither allowed to benefit from an award nor are they bound in case of an unfavorable outcome, ie where the claim has been rejected.

16/7 To be fair, the Recommendation does mention mechanisms outside of civil procedure, namely 'collective alternative dispute resolution and settlements'. As the adjective 'collective' suggests, collective ADR must be different from ordinary ADR, and the difference is that numerous claims are resolved in a single proceeding, rather than in many proceedings, case-by-case.

2. Lessons from the case studies

16/8 Several of the case studies dealt with mechanisms of collective redress developed and implemented within the civil justice system. The fact that the US-American class action, together with other distinctive features of American-style civil procedure, makes US jurisdictions particularly attractive for victims of disasters has been known for decades. Among the case studies, the one on the Costa Concordia case provides yet another illustration of the particular role that American courts play in the global supply of collective redress mechanisms: Even though the capsizing of the Costa Concordia bears almost no connection to the US, a class action on behalf of all the victims of the disaster was filed in the federal district court for the Northern District of Illinois.[7]

16/9 Within the European theatre, the law of civil procedure of England and Wales offers several forms of collective actions. Therefore, it is not surprising that this jurisdiction continues to attract cases from all over the world, even if the connection to England is at best slight. To begin with, English law allows for a joinder of claims, ie the consolidation of damages claims that were brought separately into one proceeding for joint disposition. As joinder of claims or equivalent institutions are familiar to practically every civil justice system, they cannot explain the attractiveness of English courts for collective actions. Rather, the other options that are available, ie the group litigation order and the representative action must have done the trick. While the representative action is based on the opt-out principle, the group litigation order follows the reverse opt-in model. The opt-out model dispenses with the requirement that every claimant must file a separate action or at least declare his or her consent with

7 *C Perrella*, The 'Costa Concordia' Case (contained in this volume) no 4/41, referring to *Lobaton v Carnival Corp.*

the collective action. Rather, a single claim filed by the lead claimant pulls the claims of other potential claimants, who are similarly situated before the court. In contrast, opt-in models require registration of each participating claimant, or at least failure to remove one's name from the court register.[8] The German Securities Litigation Test Case Act (Kapitalanleger-Musterverfahrensgesetz) is another example of group actions following the opt-in principle.

The case studies shed some light on the qualities and deficiencies of these 16/10 institutions, but also on other issues that bear on the practical impact of mechanisms of collective redress. As the report on the South African silicosis litigation makes clear, these cases, which, arguably, are most closely connected with South Africa, have been brought in London for a number of reasons.[9] Among these reasons, procedural efficiency, ie the availability of an opt-out representative action, is only one, and, it seems, not the most important.[10] The relative generosity of the English law of damages seems to have provided another strong motive for the claimants to file in London rather than in a South African court.[11] Funding is important as well, and even though litigation in England is rather expensive, the easy availability of funding mechanisms such as after-the-event-insurance (ATE insurance) and conditional fee agreements (CFAs) incentivize the use of the English forum.[12] A non-legal, but nonetheless important aspect for the claimants seems to have been the prospect of generating more negative publicity for the defendants if they trial is held in England than if proceedings take place in South Africa.

The analysis laid out in the case study on the silicosis cases is confirmed by 16/11 the report on international environmental litigation in the UK.[13] The report describes the background and contents of a damages suit against Shell Oil that sought recovery for the environmental harm caused by spills from Shell's oil facilities in the Niger delta in Nigeria. This claim did not proceed on the basis of a group litigation order or as a representative action. Rather, it was filed as a stand-alone claim by a public body, the Bodo Community, for the recovery of harm done to environmental resources in Nigeria, namely the mangrove population and the marine life of the Bodo Creek, the farmland along the coastal ar-

8 As to the English group litigation order cf *N Andrews*, English Civil Procedure (2003) para 41.31 f; *G Wagner*, Collective Redress – Categories of Loss and Legislative Options (2011) 127 Law Quarterly Review (LQR) 55, 77 f.

9 *P Tansley*, South African Silicosis Litigation in London (contained in this volume).

10 Ibid, no 7/22.

11 Ibid.

12 Ibid.

13 *H Marangos*, International Environmental Mass Litigation in the UK (contained in this volume).

eas of the Niger delta, and the water supply in the affected areas.[14] Again, the quantum issue seems to have been one major motive to bring suit in London rather than in Nigeria – the English rules for the computation of damages are perceived to be more generous than the ones operating in Nigerian law.[15] In addition, the English courts enjoy a strong reputation for procedural efficiency and fairness, something that cannot be said in equal measure of the Nigerian courts.[16] It is difficult to say whether particular institutions of English civil procedure such as the representative action also played a role in the claimant's choice of forum decision.

16/12 Vivid illustrations of the problems encountered by continental-European legal systems that introduced mechanisms of collective litigation are to be found in the reports on the Italian bank charges case and the German Telekom case. The Italian report highlights the obstacles that the Class Action Act no 99/2009 places before lead plaintiffs that, in this case, are primarily consumer associations.[17] Claims for collective redress are only permissible if they are able to survive an initial admissibility phase.[18] Furthermore, they were met with much resistance in the Italian courts, which refused to abandon traditional notions of civil procedure banning suits by parties who do not purport to be the owner of the entitlement that forms the subject matter of the law suit.[19] While the initial resistance of the lower court at Torino seems to have been broken in the appeals system, the number of cases brought under the Class Action Act remains strikingly low, the total remaining in the single digits.[20] One reason for this outcome is the narrow scope of application of the Act as it is limited to consumer law, products liability and unfair business practices; another lies in the procedural requirement of a 'homogeneity of right'.[21] The most important factor may be the issue of costs: under the Italian scheme, the claimant bears the full cost risk of litigation. The claimant must obtain funding for the fees of his own counsel, but also needs to compensate the respondent if the claim is rejected at the end of the admissibility phase.[22]

16/13 Following the account of the German Telekom case provided by *Tilp & Roth*, the German Securities Litigation Test Case Act (KapMuG) suffers from major

14 Ibid, nos 6/1, 6/7.
15 Ibid, no 6/19.
16 Ibid, no 6/19.
17 *F Rolla/F Chiaves*, Bank Charges (contained in this volume) no 8/4.
18 Ibid, no 8/5 ff.
19 Ibid, no 8/28 ff.
20 Ibid, no 8/9.
21 Ibid, no 8/11.
22 Ibid, no 8/10.

shortcomings, too. As the authors point out, it is 'the only instrument of collective redress in the German legal system that permits multiple injured parties to bring compensation claims in respect of similar claims'.[23] The KapMuG was passed in reaction to mass filings of around 17,000 claims of retail investors against Deutsche Telekom, alleging prospectus liability, and it remains limited to the area of securities litigation. Even though it was designed to promote the expedient and efficient resolution of mass claims, it has taken more than ten years for the competent court of appeals to issue its decision in the test case.[24] According to the authors, this long delay can best be explained by the reluctance of the German lawmakers and judges to strip the other claimants whose cases have not been singled out for model proceedings of their procedural rights.[25] In their view, the duty of the court to continuously accommodate the procedural rights of the remaining claimants placed a major 'stumbling block' in the path towards efficient dispute resolution.[26]

B. Alternative Dispute Resolution

Compared to the criminal justice system and insolvency law, ADR is only one 16/14
step away from civil procedure, but the step may be a large one. ADR encompasses a multitude of different mechanisms, ranging from arbitration, which is close to judicial dispute resolution in public court, to mediation, which, in some variants at least, deliberately avoids the resolution of disputes through the application of legal rules but rather seeks a reconciliation of the parties on the basis of their non-legal interests. The variations within the range of mechanisms regarding the status of the law and the faithfulness of its application to the facts of the individual cases are important for the functions of mass tort resolution.[27]

---

23 *AW Tilp/TA Roth*, The German Capital Market Model Proceedings Act (contained in this volume) no 9/1.

24 Ibid, nos 9/9, 9/22.

25 Ibid, nos 9/17 f, 9/34.

26 Ibid, no 9/34.

27 Cf no 16/32 ff below.

1. Ad hoc ADR

16/15 Among the case studies, the report on the train crash near the German village of Eschede in 1998 illustrates how ADR can be used to resolve disputes arising from a major accident that killed and wounded hundreds of people.[28] In an immediate response to the catastrophe, the potentially liable party and would-be respondent, Deutsche Bahn AG, appointed an ombudsman and conferred him with the task of communicating with and providing assistance to the victims and their descendants.[29] It was thought to be of particular importance to offer immediate psychological help and treatment to the victims and relatives. In an effort to enable the ombudsman to perform his tasks, Deutsche Bahn placed a sum of DM 5 million at his disposal. In addition to providing immediate advice and psychological help, the ombudsman was also involved in the processes for settling damages claims against Deutsche Bahn. Even though the ombudsman did not act as a mediator or decision maker, he did play an active role in the process of resolving individual disputes. He served as a discussant and advisor of Deutsche Bahn's in-house liability team that worked to settle the claims raised by the victims and the bereaved amicably.[30] For the success of the liability team it was crucial that Deutsche Bahn had made the decision to mete out damages for pain and suffering without regard to the contested issue of fault, and that they adopted a generous approach to quantifying damages. Still, the total sum of € 30 million as compensation for financial and non-pecuniary losses[31] appears to be rather modest if compared to the scale of the accident.

16/16 The ombudsman scheme set up by Deutsche Bahn in the aftermath of the Eschede disaster was of an ad hoc nature. Germany has no ADR-scheme as a fleet in being that can be brought to life when a major accident happens.[32] The effort by Deutsche Bahn was voluntary and ad-hoc, and it unfolded under the leadership and guidance of Deutsche Bahn as the potentially liable party. Deutsche Bahn seems to have been fully aware of the problems of this ap-

---

28 *OE Krasney*, Ombudsman for the Victims of the Rail Accident at Eschede (contained in this volume).

29 Ibid, no 5/4.

30 Ibid, no 5/19.

31 Ibid, no 5/23.

32 *U Magnus*, Germany, in: M Faure/T Hartlief, Financial Compensation for Victims of Catastrophes (2006) para 3; *G Wagner*, Catastrophic Damages – Liability and Insurance, in: J Basedow/U Kirschel/U Sieber (eds), German National Reports to the 18th International Congress of Comparative Law (2010) 39, 44 ff.

proach, ie to place a 'company man' in the quasi-neutral role of ombudsman.[33] In order to accommodate fears of one-sided practices, the board of Deutsche Bahn refrained from issuing any instructions to the ombudsman on how to deal with individual cases.[34]

2. The broader picture of ADR

Chris Hodges, in his contribution to the present volume, covers the topic of ADR more broadly, and primarily with a view to institutional ADR, meaning schemes that are not set up ad hoc, as an immediate response to a disaster, but that exist continuously and wait for cases to be brought into the system.[35] Such schemes did receive a major push by Directive 2013/11/EU on Alternative Dispute Resolution for Consumer Disputes.[36] The impact of this piece of European legislation on mass tort resolution will remain very limited as its scope is confined to claims brought by consumers against businesses that are based on sales contracts or service contracts between these two parties (art 2 (1) Directive). Compared to the scope of the present project, only the Italian dispute involving bank charges is within the purview of Directive 2013/11/EU.[37] 16/17

Regardless of the limited scope of the Directive, there is no doubt that ADR may also have a role to play in mass tort settings, such as personal injuries caused by defective products, by crashes of trains and airplanes, the sinking of boats and other disasters. In fact, there are precursors of ADR schemes designed to deal with mass tort cases. As Hodges points out, the Nordic countries, eg Denmark, Sweden and Norway have been operating ADR systems for medical as well as for other types of personal injuries.[38] France operates a similar system for dealing with medical injuries that were not caused by negligent behaviour of 16/18

33 *Krasney* (fn 28) no 5/3.

34 Ibid, no 5/7.

35 *C Hodges*, Delivering Redress through Alternative Dispute Resolution and Regulation (contained in this volume) 14/1 ff.

36 Directive 2013/11/EU of the European Parliament and of the Council of 21 May 2013 on alternative dispute resolution for consumer disputes and amending Regulation (EC) No 2006/2004 and Directive 2009/22/EC (Directive on consumer ADR), OJ L 165, 18.6.2013, 63–79; see also Commission Proposal, COM(2011) 793 final. For an overview cf *G Wagner*, Private Law Enforcement through ADR: Wonder Drug or Snake Oil? (2014) 51 Common Market Law Review (CML Rev) 165.

37 *Rolla/Chiaves* (fn 16).

38 *Hodges* (fn 35) no 14/4.

the medical practitioner.[39] The example of the Nordic countries and, to a lesser degree, France, clearly illustrates that mechanisms of ADR need not be confined to the area of contractual disputes but may also play a role in the resolution of tort claims. However, it is also apparent that the systems existing today are designed to deal with rank-and-file tort cases, not with masses of claims growing out of the same catastrophic event.

16/19 In essence, the ADR mechanisms already existing in the area of tort liability provide for an expedient and economical resolution of disputes on a case-by-case basis. In doing so, they are strikingly different, in fact opposed to, the mechanisms developed within civil procedure. The institutions that have been developed in order to enable civil courts to deal with mass claims all aim for aggregation, in lieu of, or as a precursor to, case-by-case dispute resolution. The approach of civil procedure is motivated by the idea that it would be a waste of resources to deal with every individual claim but that it is well worth the effort to litigate the large claim that can be created by consolidating the individual claims. ADR schemes share in the assumption that it would be wasteful to litigate each individual claim but the conclusion drawn from this is that, while the proceedings should remain on the individual level, the effort put into resolving them should be scaled down to a level below the one practised in the civil courts. It remains to be seen whether one or the other option is preferable.[40]

C. Criminal Procedure

1. Priority of criminal over civil procedure

16/20 For many observers, the idea of resolving mass claims within criminal trials may come as a surprise. Within legal systems that do not provide for a joinder of compensatory claims to the public at charge, this option is not available.[41] However, most legal systems allow such a combination, and in the jurisdictions following the French tradition, the victim may even be compelled to walk the criminal path due to the principle of *le criminel tient le civil en état*, pursuant to

39 *Hodges* (fn 35) no 14/7; for a broader picture cf *R Cascão/R Hendrickx*, Shifts in the Compensation of Medical Adverse Events, in: WH van Boom/MG Faure, Shifts in Compensation between Private and Public Systems (2007) para 52 ff.

40 Cf no 16/45 ff below.

41 As to compensation orders in English law cf no 3 above. However, compensation orders are ill-suited for cases involving complex issues of law and fact, as is generally true for mass torts; cf *Rogers* (fn 3) para 4-2.

which the civil trial cannot proceed until the criminal case has been concluded.[42] Furthermore, the judgment reached by the criminal court is binding for the civil judge who subsequently has to decide on the damages claim (*autorité de la chose jugée au criminel sur le civil*).[43]

2. The italian asbestos trial

This background explains why criminal procedures could be used in the Italian *Eternit* case not only for investigating the history of a substantial part of the European asbestos industry, but also for the purpose of aggregating thousands of damages claims brought by asbestos victims as so-called *parti civili*.[44] As the case study prepared by Coggiola and Graziadei explains, participation in the criminal investigation offered substantial advantages: Public prosecutors were able to look at the full picture instead of having to analyse a series of bilateral relationship between a particular victim and the manufacturer that had produced and marketed a potentially defective product.[45] They had even made the deliberate choice to disregard crimes such as manslaughter and battery that look at harm to individuals and rather to focus on other crimes that are based on wrongful conduct endangering the public.[46] Interestingly, this shift of the focus of the criminal investigation did not undermine the beneficial side-effects of the criminal judgment for the civil claims: Even though harm to individual victims or municipalities was not the subject matter of the criminal trial, the criminal courts still held in favour of victims complaining about personal injury, damage to property, and harm to the environment.[47] Another important advantage of criminal proceedings in mass tort cases concerns the issue of funding. In the Italian *Eternit* case, victims could avail themselves of public funding. While the pursuing of individual claims still required private funding, the criminal charge and work of the state prosecution fell on the public purse. On the other hand, they were in a position to help the criminal investigation by introducing facts and offering evidence. Finally, criminal trials receive much more media atten- 16/21

42 Art 4 (2) Code de procédure pénale (France); *G Viney*, Introduction à la responsabilité (3rd edn 2008) para 117; cf also *von Bar* (fn 3) para 602.

43 *Viney* (fn 42) para 120 ff.

44 *N Coggiola/M Graziadei*, The Italian 'Eternit Trial': Litigating Massive Asbestos Damage in a Criminal Court (contained in this volume) nos 2/2, 2/15, 2/25: at the beginning of the trial, there were 6,000 private parties.

45 Ibid, no 2/16.

46 Ibid, no 2/21.

47 Ibid, no 2/42 ff.

tion than civil proceedings, which puts the respondents under additional pressure.

16/22 As the case study further illustrates, the jurisdiction of the criminal courts in Italy is not confined to finding criminal liability of the individuals who serve as defendants. Rather, the criminal judges may also impute civil liability to the business enterprises, which were managed by the defendant individuals, on theories such as *respondeat superior*.[48] On this basis, the criminal trial led to an outcome that engaged the liability of the manufacturers of asbestos products in much the same way as private actions based on product liability could have done. Only the determination of quantum was left to the civil courts. Throughout the course of the proceedings, however, the civil claims remained contingent upon the finding of criminal liability on the part of the two defendant individuals. Thus, the death of one of the accused during the trial terminated not only the criminal charges brought against him but also led to the closure of the civil proceedings, not only against the deceased but also against the enterprises managed by him.[49]

16/23 The authors of the *Eternit* case study conclude by asking fundamental questions: 'What are the pros and cons of the 'mass claims procedure' through the criminal courts: is this an efficient and fair alternative to civil court adjudication? Are there drawbacks? Advantages? In addition, is it appropriate to shift industrial injuries into the sphere of the criminal law?'[50] These are indeed the issues raised by the Italian experience, and they cannot be answered easily.[51] What can be said for sure, however, is that criminal trials present another option for victims of mass torts to seek redress. In making the choice whether to sue in civil court or to join criminal proceedings, victims will weigh the advantages and disadvantages of either option – and choose the one more favourable to their interests. One factor that weighs heavily in favour of criminal procedure are the investigative powers of the public prosecutor that are lacking in civil proceedings. This is particularly important in continental-European jurisdictions that do not allow for far-reaching discovery within civil proceedings. Another crucial factor seems to be funding as resort to the criminal law shifts much of the cost of investigating the facts of the case to the public purse. Finally, arraignment in criminal court fixes the venue also for civil claimants and thus provides a natural forum for the aggregation of a multitude of civil claims.

---

48 Ibid, no 2/39.
49 Ibid, no 2/40.
50 Ibid, no 2/48.
51 See no 16/50 ff below.

D. Insolvency Proceedings

1. Bankruptcy as the debtor's response to a mass of tort claims

The intersection of insolvency law and mass torts presents a topic that has not attracted much scholarly attention. What is well-known is that a bankruptcy petition may be used strategically as a response to an avalanche of tort claims that is impossible to handle for the defendant business. Within the present volume, the case study on silicone breast implants provides a vivid account of one of the most spectacular scenarios. In this scenario, mass tort proceedings that originated in multi-district litigation (MDL) proceedings outside bankruptcy were essentially continued within bankruptcy after proceedings for reorganization of the debtor were initiated under ch 11 of the US Bankruptcy Code.[52] The motive for defendant Dow Corning, Inc., to file for bankruptcy protection under ch 11 was to force the burgeoning number of individual law suits that had been brought against it into a single proceeding for the purpose of expedient and comprehensive resolution.[53] Bankruptcy reorganisation offers an essential advantage that MDL litigation and settlement cannot provide, namely the immediate arrest of all proceedings brought by claimants individually by virtue of the automatic stay operating under 11 United States Code (USC) § 362. In essence, the defendant sought to achieve 'global peace' through reorganisation in bankruptcy after attempts to buy it through a proposed MDL settlement had not borne fruit.[54] Furthermore, within bankruptcy, plans for reorganisation may be imposed on recalcitrant creditors under the cramdown power of the bankruptcy court whereas MDL judges and procedures lack the authority to force claimants to consent to a settlement offer that they would rather reject. 16/24

2. Consolidation of claims via insolvency law

Plans for reorganisation offer, to some degree at least, settlements of mass torts outside of bankruptcy that are surprisingly similar to the mode in which contingent claims are being resolved inside bankruptcy. Within bankruptcy as outside 16/25

---

52 *MR Ferrari*, Silicone Breast Implants: Mass Tort and Massive Damage in Europe (contained in this volume) no 3/43 ff.

53 Ibid, no 3/44.

54 Ibid, nos 3/36 ff, 3/44. On defendants' interest to obtain 'global peace', ie full settlement of all claims that may potentially be brought against them *RA Nagareda*, Mass Torts in a World of Settlement (2007) 72 f, 95 ff.

of it, claims are not being resolved on an individual basis, after a thorough investigation of the facts underlying liability and after establishment of the amount of damages suffered in a given case. Rather, the parties negotiate, with the help of the court, a plan or grid that provides for a summary disposition of the claims involved. To this end, MDL-settlements and plans for reorganisation alike categorise claims into classes, define mechanisms that allow for the filing and evaluation of individual claims and set out criteria for compensatory relief that is meted out on a summary basis. Much like MDL-settlements, plans for reorganisation draw on tools familiar from alternative dispute resolution (ADR) in order to reap the familiar benefits, ie expedient and economical resolution of a mass of claims that would be very costly to litigate on a case-by-case basis. Even the option for claimants to opt out of the plan and to pursue their claims individually has been borrowed from mass tort litigation that is settled within MDL proceedings.[55] In summary, MDL settlements and plans for reorganisation seem to be substitutes for one another. This is hardly surprising in light of the rationale of bankruptcy law, namely to offer a collective debt resolution mechanism in lieu of individual enforcement of rights.[56]

16/26 But bankruptcy may have more to offer for the resolution of mass torts than providing an alternative – and maybe even more attractive – route towards global peace. The case study of the *Madoff* bankruptcy illustrates that bankruptcy law may work to broaden the class of claimants in order to then distribute a limited pool of assets equally between the enlarged group of victims.[57] The administration of *Madoff*'s estate has not been ordered for the purpose of reorganisation but with the aim of liquidation.[58] Again, the trustee in bankruptcy was confronted with a fairly large group of creditors, albeit not even close to the size of the group in product liability settings such as the one involving breast implants. Ultimately, the efforts of the trustee will result in a plan that provides for the distribution of the estate's assets among *Madoff*'s creditors. The interesting point to note is that the trustee in bankruptcy has the power to claw back payments from pre-bankruptcy creditors who were paid before the filing of the petition. Under the law of preferences, pre-petition creditors may be liable to refund payments made by the debtor even if they were made on perfectly legitimate claims,[59] while the law of fraudulent conveyances allows for the avoidance of payments made by the debtor with the intention to defraud his or her

55 *Ferrari* (fn 52) no 3/55.

56 *TH Jackson*, The Logic and Limits of Bankruptcy Law (1986) 151 ff.

57 *J Boldon*, The Madoff Ponzi Scheme (contained in this volume) 10/1 ff.

58 Ibid, no 10/9.

59 11 USC § 547; *Jackson* (fn 56) 122 ff.

creditors.[60] Bankruptcy law not only allows to avoid these payments and to augment the estate through refunds but also provides the jurisdictional advantage to litigate these claims in the bankruptcy court so as to avoid the need to pursue creditors in the forum of their respective residence.[61] As the case study reports, the trustee was able to collect more than USD 9 billion from pre-petition creditors, which compares to a total loss of USD 17 billion.[62] As the *Madoff* case proves, bankruptcy law offers remedies that ordinary mass tort litigation cannot provide; remedies that essentially help to recompose the class of potential claimants. In so far as the trustee in bankruptcy may avoid pre-petition transfers on the grounds of preference or fraudulent conveyance law, third parties that received value from the debtor before the filing of the bankruptcy petition are forced to refund such value and are to join the group of creditors. As such, they share proportionally in the proceeds generated from the liquidation of the estate and are thus placed on equal terms with pre-petition creditors. Bankruptcy law therefore helps to ensure that all victims of a *Ponzi* scheme are treated equally, regardless of whether they were lucky enough to be paid before the fraudulent nature of the scheme was discovered or whether they found themselves within the class of unhappy investors who stood to lose the principal of their investments after the truth came out.

The theoretical and normative underpinnings and problems involved in the **16/27** use of bankruptcy as a response to a mass of tort claims or as a substitute for mass tort proceedings are elaborated and discussed in *Brinkmann*'s contribution to the present project.[63] As *Brinkmann* points out, bankruptcy law leaves room for forum shopping as multiple fora may have jurisdiction over a particular debtor company.[64] Within the European theatre, the European Regulation on Insolvency Proceedings was designed with a view to restrict or even eliminate the room for strategic forum choice by vesting exclusive jurisdiction in the court at the debtor's centre of main interest (COMI).[65] The case law of the ECJ illustrates the manoeuvres of private parties who sought to avail themselves of per-

---

60 11 USC § 548; *Jackson* (fn 56) 146 ff.

61 *Boldon* (fn 57) no 10/13; as to the European law under the European Insolvency Regulation (EC) No 1346/2000 cf European Court of Justice (ECJ) C-339/07, *Seagon v Deko Marty* [2009] European Court Reports (ECR) I-767, para 21 ff.

62 *Boldon* (fn 57) no 10/17.

63 *M Brinkmann*, Mass Tort Related Insolvency Proceedings: Choice of Jurisdiction, Treatment and Discharge of Tort Claims (contained in this volume) 15/1 ff.

64 Ibid, no 15/5 ff.

65 Art 3 Council Regulation (EC) No 1346/2000 of 29 May 2000 on insolvency proceedings, OJ L 160, 30.6.2000, 1–18; *Brinkmann* (fn 63) no 15/6 ff.

ceived advantages of the insolvency regime of one jurisdiction over those of another.[66]

16/28 Once a bankruptcy petition has been filed in a competent court and insolvency proceedings have been opened, the court has exclusive jurisdiction to determine any claims brought against the estate under the principle of *vis attractive concursus* as embraced by art 4 Insolvency Regulation.[67] This results in a forced consolidation of all claims in the jurisdiction in which the insolvency proceedings are pending. If the liabilities of the debtor involve mass tort claims, those are consolidated for joint disposition by a single court, be it the bankruptcy court, be it the trial court sitting in the same district as the bankruptcy court before which the petition is pending.[68] In many jurisdictions the same jurisdictional regime applies even if the claims against the debtor were pending even before the insolvency proceedings were opened, so that law suits pending in other courts need to be transferred to the forum in which the bankruptcy proceedings are pending.[69] Together, the principles of exclusive jurisdiction of the bankruptcy court and of *vis attractiva concursus* lead to outcomes that are very similar to the consolidation of mass tort claims in one judicial district in that they ensure the joint hearing and disposition of all claims before a single judge within a single proceeding. In essence, these are the doctrinal pillars on which the observations made in the case studies involving silicone breast implants and *Madoff*'s *Ponzi* scheme rest.

3. Externalities imposed on tort creditors

16/29 However, insolvency law is no *panacea* for mass torts. Rather, the advantages of forced consolidation and joint disposition of claims come at a rather high price. One pronounced disadvantage is based on the fact that, almost universally, tort claimants are treated equally with voluntary creditors who failed to negotiate a security interest. The status of an unsecured creditor turns out to be fatal in cases where the proceeds generated by the estate are insufficient to cover more than the claims of the secured creditors.[70] As secured creditors enjoy priority over unsecured creditors, often the latter receive nothing or much less than they are owed. The harsh treatment of unsecured creditors may be justified for volun-

66 *Brinkmann* (fn 6e) no 15/11.
67 Ibid, no 15/22ff.
68 Ibid, no 15/26.
69 Ibid, no 15/28f.
70 Ibid, no 15/30ff.

tary creditors, ie those who decided to extend credit to the debtor in full awareness of the fact that they had not negotiated a security interest to ensure payment of the debt once it falls due. Assuming a well-functioning credit market, unsecured lenders will compensate for the absence of a security interest by charging a higher interest rate or by rejecting the application for a loan altogether. Involuntary creditors such as tort claimants have no such option. Therefore, it may be argued that they should enjoy priority over other unsecured creditors who assumed this position voluntarily, and perhaps even over secured creditors who were successful in imposing an externality on involuntary creditors. By negotiating a security interest for his or her own gain, the creditor automatically diminishes the prospects of recovery for all other creditors, including tort claimants. They, in turn, can do nothing to protect themselves against losses should the tortfeasor become insolvent. Regrettably, only Spanish insolvency law tries to protect tort claimants by according them priority over other unsecured creditors, if not over secured creditors.[71] In all other major jurisdictions, the only privilege that tort creditors enjoy relates to funds paid into the estate by liability insurers. In many jurisdictions, proceeds from liability insurance policies are earmarked for the benefit of tort claimants so that other creditors do not share in these assets.[72]

Another disadvantage served on tort creditors by the law of insolvency involves discharge.[73] Within insolvency proceedings leading to the liquidation of the debtor business, discharge of the liabilities that remain after distribution of the assets is unavoidable and thus nothing that discriminates unfairly against tort creditors. Where, however, insolvency proceedings aim for and result in the reorganisation of the debtor as a going concern, discharge becomes problematic. Reorganisation and the resulting discharge allow debtors to shake off tort liabilities, leaving victims without compensation. The option for distressed debtors to externalise costs to the detriment of tort victims is particularly pronounced in cases involving long-tail risks where a substantial part of the harm caused by the hazardous activities of the debtor have not matured because the injuries have not manifested yet. There is a high danger that the interests of those victims whose claims have not matured at the time of bankruptcy will be ploughed under so that the assets of the debtor are distributed among present creditors and nothing remains for future claimants. The US Bankruptcy Code tries to contain this danger by providing for a legal guardian charged to protect the interests of future claimants and for a trust fund that needs to be set up for 16/30

71 Ibid, no 15/32.

72 Ibid, no 15/33ff.

73 Ibid, no 15/42ff.

the benefit of future claimants. In practice, these instruments were proven to be insufficient to safeguard the equal treatment of such claimants.[74]

16/31 In summary, the case studies and *Brinkmann*'s analysis strongly support the thesis that mass torts cannot be analysed without a view towards insolvency law. On the one hand, proceedings for liquidation and, particularly, reorganisation, may be used strategically by the tortfeasor-debtor for the purpose of shaking off tort liabilities, thereby externalising risk to the detriment of tort victims. On the other hand, insolvency law offers well-oiled tools for consolidating a large number of claims into a single proceeding and for disposing of them expediently and efficiently. In this way, insolvency law may also function as a substitute for institutions such as class actions and multi-district litigation.

III. A Functional Approach towards Institutions Designed for Mass Torts

16/32 The preceding part has provided an overview of the many ways used by the legal system to deal with mass torts. A whole menu of choices is at the disposal of lawmakers, ranging from institutions within civil procedure, to ADR processes, criminal proceedings, and insolvency law. What to make of this oversupply of regulatory options? Do the contributions to the present project suggest that one option or institutional setting is preferable over another for the efficient resolution of mass tort claims? These are big questions that are difficult to answer. Before exploring some tentative thoughts it is crucial to briefly recollect the functions of mass tort resolution. The advantages and disadvantages of institutions cannot be evaluated in the abstract, but only with a view to certain goals. The classical goals of tort law are compensation and deterrence.[75] The degree to which those two ends are furthered must not be maximised but rather optimised. Any achievements in the form of better compensation and increased deterrence need to be balanced against the added administrative costs that are associated with such gains.

16/33 The compensation goal requires that tort victims receive payments designed to redress the harm that was suffered by the individuals. A perfect system would allocate a sum to each victim that is equal to the monetary equivalent of the harm suffered by that particular victim. This requires mechanisms and proce-

74 Ibid, no 15/49 f.

75 *H Koch*, Mass Damage in Europe: Aggregation of Claims, Effective Enforcement and Adequate Representation (contained in this volume) no 11/11.

dures designed to establish the exact extent of the harm suffered so that under-compensation of some victims – and overcompensation of others – is avoided.

The deterrence function of tort law calls for institutions that generate incentives for potential tortfeasors to adjust their behaviour so that accidents are avoided up front rather than made up for ex post. From an economic perspective, precautions against harm should be increased up to a point where the added cost of another increment in precautions is equal to its marginal returns in the form of reduced accident costs. In addition, the legal system should provide incentives to limit the amount of dangerous activities only to a threshold where the incremental gain generated from another unit of the activity is equal to the total costs associated with that unit, including the costs of accidents caused by the respective activity. **16/34**

In theory, the compensatory and the deterrence functions of tort law are well understood. However, at least initially, the theory disregards the real-world circumstances within which tort law operates. Compensation and deterrence not only require that the substantive law of torts has a certain shape and quality but presuppose that there are mechanisms to implement the rules of substantive law. In fact, many analyses of the functions of tort law implicitly assume that its rules are implemented perfectly and at zero cost. This mode of analysis is convenient and adequate in situations in which enforcement of the law may be taken for granted. In the area of mass torts, enforcement must not be taken for granted at all.[76] This area of tort law is all about implementation and enforcement. Therefore, most of the case studies and academic papers deal with issues of procedure and choice of law, ie with institutions designed to help enforce claims based on whatever rules the substantive law provides. **16/35**

The root of the problems associated with the enforcement of damages claims growing out of mass scenarios is administrative costs.[77] In a world where judicial resources were not scarce and where litigation were costless, mass torts would not create major problems. Courts would process claims and resolve disputes one by one, and the only concern might be that of conflicting verdicts with regard to the same set of facts. In reality, however, judicial resources are scarce and litigation is expensive. Therefore, case-by-case adjudication of individual claims would be unattractive for the private parties involved and it would be wasteful for society at large. If a single event gives rise to thousands of claims, the judicial system will be clogged which not only delays the resolution of the mass tort claims but also the processing of all other claims that are wait- **16/36**

---

76 Ibid, no 11/10.

77 Cf also *BA Koch*, Multiple Tortfeasors in Mass Tort Cases (contained in this volume) no 12/66.

ing in line. The German *Telekom* case provides a vivid example: the court in Frankfurt would have been clogged for years if it had been required to deal with each and every one of the 17,000 claims filed in response to Telekom's alleged misstatements in its prospectus.[78] As this case illustrates, it is a matter of necessity to devise mechanisms that allow for a more efficient resolution of mass tort cases than ordinary one-on-one litigation does. Thus, the common rationale of the various procedural mechanisms that were canvassed above is to economise on administrative costs.

16/37 In principle, savings in administrative costs can be achieved in two different ways. One strategy would be to consolidate the resolution of the many individual claims into a single procedure that allows for a joint disposition, at least of the common issues, within one procedure or other mechanism. The alternative strategy points into the opposite direction of leaving the claims separate as they are, but offering a less ambitious, cheaper and quicker mechanism of dispute resolution with regard to each individual claim. In the next section of this paper, the several mechanisms that are in use in one jurisdiction or another and that have been analysed in the contributions to this project will be evaluated with regard to the question as to whether and to what extent they help to achieve the desired savings in administrative costs without sacrificing the substantive goals of tort law, ie compensation and deterrence.

IV. Evaluation

16/38 The review of the case studies and academic contributions has identified four different options for addressing the fundamental problem of mass torts, namely reforms of civil procedure, increased supply of alternative dispute resolution (ADR) services, the resolution of civil claims within criminal proceedings and regimes of insolvency law.

A. Civil Procedure: Aggregate Litigation

16/39 If mass claims resolution is to be achieved within the framework of civil procedure, aggregation is the preferred strategy. On an international level, the Anglo-American class action serves as a benchmark as it provides for an almost comprehensive consolidation of claims into a single proceeding, administered by a

---

78 *Tilp/Roth* (fn 23) nos 9/3, 9/9.

single claimant, the lead plaintiff. Within Europe, the American-style class action is not an attractive model. In its Recommendation on collective redress, the Commission was careful to embrace group actions based on the opt-in principle, as opposed to American-style class actions following the opt-out principle meaning victims must take affirmative action if they want to avoid becoming party to the class.[79]

The choice between the opt-in and opt-out principles raises complex and highly controversial issues that cannot and need not be discussed in the present context.[80] For purposes of the present analysis it suffices to point out that opt-in group actions remain comparatively close to one-on-one litigation of individual claims. While several claims may be combined into one proceeding, the claims remain separate, and potential claimants are neither forced nor even 'nudged' to join the common procedure. If this mechanism worked perfectly, the compensation and deterrence goals of tort law would be served well. Victims would join their claims to the collective proceedings, and courts would render accurate decisions on liability and quantum in order to mete out fully compensatory awards that generate the right incentives to take care and adjust activity levels. Aggregation of claims will even make things easier for substantive law as it spares the parties and the courts the task of establishing causation on a case by case basis. As *Bernhard A Koch* has indicated in his report, aggregate resolution of claims may make it easier to resolve problems of causation that seem impossible to overcome in the bilateral scenario.[81] **16/40**

However, the problem with mass torts is efficient enforcement, and in this regard, it must be asked whether group actions organised under the opt-in principle go far enough. The account of the German securities litigation test case procedure given by *Tilp* & *Roth* casts doubt on the performance of such institutions in effectively dealing with mass claims.[82] While the German test case procedure for securities cases is different from a group action in pure form, it includes the essential character of group actions, namely that victims need to opt-in, through filing a complaint, if they intend to participate in the proceedings and have their claim adjudicated by the court. In the view of *Tilp* & *Roth* the German Act places too much emphasis on vindicating procedural rights of individual parties and thus fails to deliver an efficient mechanism for dealing with **16/41**

---

79 Commission Recommendation (fn 1) para 21ff.

80 Cf, eg *Wagner* (2011) 127 LQR 55, 70ff.

81 *BA Koch* (fn 77) no 12/66.

82 Cf nos 9/9, 9/22 (fn 23) above.

mass tort scenarios. Given that it took more than a decade of litigation to resolve only a single case, this sceptical account seems plausible enough.[83]

16/42 The disappointing German experience with a variant of the group action is in sharp contrast to the attraction that the English courts exert on overseas claimants who shop for a favourable forensic environment for the enforcement of mass tort claims. The gravitation of claimants toward England is not based on procedural rules only, but includes factors such as the easy availability of litigation funding as well as access to a well-oiled and reputable judicial system. On the other hand there can be no doubt that the existence of the representative action – which is a variant of the opt-out class action – but also of other procedural forms of aggregation is an important factor in attracting mass tort cases.[84] For obvious reasons, claimants shop for a court that offers expedient and efficient mechanisms for dealing with mass claims. Where claimants have a choice between jurisdictions, those systems that fail to make such an offer lose out.

16/43 It is important to identify the normative implications of the 'voting with one's feet' that occurs at the inter-jurisdictional level. In the area of mass torts, as opposed to consumer collective redress that involves small claims for the compensation of scattered losses,[85] the important choice is not between the opt-out and the opt-in principle. Tort victims who have suffered massive personal injuries or substantial financial losses will be ready to join a group of claimants in order to enforce their rights to redress. Thus, the problem created by mass torts for judicial systems is not a dearth of claims but a flood of claims. As a consequence, for the success of a given judicial system, it is crucial to develop procedural tools that allow for a cost-effective management and expedient resolution of a multitude of claims in one proceeding. In this respect, English law seems to perform reasonably well while the German securities litigation test case procedure is doing poorly. The reasons for this failure are manifold: the framers of the German Act were far too timid in cutting back on the procedural guarantees of the many parties whose claims were not singled out as the test case. They failed to provide incentives for the lawyer representing an individual client to join the test case procedure and also for the lawyer representing the test case claimant to vigorously pursue the claim on behalf of the group of

83 Cf nos 9/9, 9/22 above.

84 Cf no 7/22 (fn 9) above.

85 The Italian bank charges case (fn 17 above) is an example of a case in which the harm to the individual is small, while the aggregate harm to society is large. In this area, representative actions brought by consumer associations are a valid alternative to opt-out class actions. Cf also *H Koch* (fn 75) no 12/31; *Wagner* (2011) 127 LQR 55, 62f, 74ff.

claimants as a whole.[86] Thus, financial incentives of the lawyers who are expected to make use of the collective mechanism are as important as streamlined proceedings after the claims have been filed.[87]

In summary, civil litigation continues to offer the best mechanisms for enforcing damages claims, even where there is a large number of claims growing out of the same incident or related causes. The challenge must be to avoid congestion of the court systems and to reap the efficiency gains that collective proceedings for related claims have to offer. In doing so, lawmakers must be prepared to compromise – not sacrifice – established principles of civil procedure in the interest of efficient judicial administration of mass claims. 16/44

B. ADR: Piece Meal Dispute Resolution out of Court

The promise ADR holds for the resolution of mass claims is opposed to the one underlying respective institutions within civil procedure. Civil procedure may avoid the waste of resources associated with multiple litigation of the same issues by consolidating related cases into a single procedural framework. The alternative represented by ADR instead keeps the mass of claims separate and offers a simplified mechanism for their resolution. In his contribution to the present project, *Chris Hodges* is rather enthusiastic about the potential that ADR holds for mass torts and for collective redress at large. With regard to small claims of consumers against businesses, the European lawmakers have followed suit and passed the ADR Directive, which requires Member States to provide for a seamless web of ADR facilities and services.[88] In the field of collective redress, the promotion of ADR involves a paradigm shift away from high-powered litigation over a small number of aggregated claims and into low-key or even summary disposition of a large number of small claims. 16/45

In contrast, *Harald Koch* has struck a more sceptical tone regarding the potential of ADR to serve as an alternative to civil litigation for the purpose of resolving mass tort disputes.[89] One question is whether ADR will be able to live up to the promise of low costs. It is doubtful whether the piecemeal resolution of small claims will really be cheaper than the aggregate litigation of one large 16/46

---

86 Cf also *H Koch* (fn 75) no 11/25 ff; *G Wagner*, Neue Perspektiven im Schadensersatzrecht, in: Verhandlungen des 66. Deutschen Juristentags, vol I (2006) A 123 f; *A Halfmeier*, Zeitschrift für Wirtschaftsrecht (ZIP) 2011, 1900.

87 Cf *H Koch* (fn 75) no 11/44 ff citing the adage 'it's all about money'.

88 Cf no 16/17 at fn 36 above.

89 *H Koch* (fn 75) no 11/20 ff.

claim, even if the effort put into the ADR processes is much smaller than the cost of civil litigation. It seems plausible to expect that the costs for the publicly funded judicial system may be lower, because more cases settle out of court, but that the costs to the private parties will be much higher than they would be if enforcement were sought in aggregate litigation. In this way, ADR may relieve the public purse but imposes an overall cost on society.

16/47 If it is true that the costs of ADR will be higher than the share each claimant would have to bear in order to fund aggregate litigation, then it is questionable whether ADR will in fact be able to significantly improve the enforcement of damages claims in mass tort situations. Anecdotal evidence from the US suggests that this will not happen.[90] In the case of *AT&T Mobility LLC v Concepcion*, AT&T offered a voluntary scheme of ADR that was extremely favourable to potential claimants: Upon the filing of a complaint, the potential defendant was liable to make a settlement offer. If no offer was made or the customer did not accept the offer within 30 days of filing, the customer was free to invoke arbitration. The arbitral proceedings were to be funded by the defendant only and were to be held at the customer's place of residence, primarily upon documentary evidence. The minimum recovery for the claimant-customer was stipulated to be $7,500 plus the double amount of the attorney's fees, provided that the award exceeded the defendant's last written settlement offer.[91] This scheme was aptly described by an American judge as 'perhaps the most fair and consumer-friendly provisions this Court has ever seen'.[92] In spite of this characterisation, the number of complaints brought under the ADR scheme remained surprisingly low if compared to the defendant's large customer base.[93] This suggests that aggregation of claims yields better results than the out-of-court resolution of individual disputes on the basis of simplified procedures, even if these are costless to potential claimants.

16/48 The *AT&T* case involved small claims growing out of disputes over consumer rights and thus its lesson may not carry over to the field of mass torts where claims tend to be of substantial magnitude. Even so, it does show that it would be wrong to suppose that ADR procedures are inherently more attractive to potential claimants than those offered by courts of law. Furthermore, the question needs to be asked whether ADR provides adequate tools of dispute

---

90 For a more thorough discussion cf *Wagner* (2014) 51 CML Rev 165, 191 ff.

91 *AT&T Mobility LLC v Concepcion*, 131 Supreme Court Reporter (S Ct) 1740 (2011).

92 *Marakowski v AT&T Mobility*, LLC, 2009 WL 1765661 (CD Cal 2009).

93 *Coneff v AT&T Corp*, 620 Federal Supplement, Second Series (F Supp 2d) 1248, 1258 (D Wash 2009); cf also Brief of Contract Professors as *Amici Curiae* in Support of Respondents in *AT&T Mobility LLC v Concepcion*, p 19.

resolution in areas where stakes are high and where disputes tend to raise complex legal and factual issues, as is typically the case in mass tort scenarios. The procedures followed by courts of law have evolved over hundreds of years with a view to resolving contested issues of law and fact fairly and accurately, given a cost constraint. ADR has nothing to offer in these terms – accurate dispute resolution – that could compete with civil procedure. In fact, some forms of ADR, such as mediation, do not even aim for the accurate application of legal rules to established fact patterns but rather for the amicable resolution of personal or social conflicts – regardless of what the law has to say about them.[94]

The regulatory powers of ombudsmen and other ADR entities that are high- **16/49** lighted in *Hodges*' paper may be relevant in the area of consumer disputes but are much less so in the area of mass torts.[95] Disasters that affect large groups of people may raise regulatory issues, but, where they do, these are best resolved in the political process, and not by dispute managers whose primary task it is to process, assess and dispose of individual damages claims.

C. Dispute Resolution the Criminal Way

In the Italian *Eternit* case, private victims were able to piggyback on a criminal **16/50** investigation in order to vindicate their rights of redress.[96] This is a fascinating story that may repeat itself in any of the continental-European jurisdictions that allow for the adhesive action. The involvement of the public prosecutor and the criminal court help to overcome the funding problem, particularly where the case requires a thorough investigation of facts with the help of experts. Furthermore, criminal proceedings serve as a focal point for victims to join at low cost to themselves.

The potential of criminal procedure for the resolution of mass torts is most **16/51** pronounced in cases in which a large group of victims has contracted fatal diseases, suffered serious personal injuries or even death. In these settings, the public interest in punishment, but also in a thorough investigation of the facts that led to the disaster, is most pronounced. The establishment of the true facts of the case helps society to learn from the accident and to take measures to avoid similar events in the future. The funds needed for investigating the case

94 *KJ Hopt/F Steffek*, Mediation: Comparison of Laws, Regulatory Models, Fundamental Issues, in: idem (eds), Mediation: Principles and Regulation in Comparative Perspective (2013) 12.

95 *Hodges* (fn 35) no 14/13 ff, speaking about consumer ADR.

96 See no 16/21 above.

will be substantial, but such expense is warranted for the purpose of protecting the life and limb of citizens in the future.

16/52 While criminal procedure is an adequate tool to investigate the facts and to establish the true course of events, it must be doubted that it is equally well equipped to handle a large pool of damages claims brought by an equally large number of victims. For the purpose of criminal law, it will only be necessary to establish liability while quantum is of no concern to the criminal judge. The resolution of civil claims, however, requires a finding of liability and the assessment of the damages. It is difficult to see how this could efficiently be done within criminal proceedings. In particular, criminal procedure is subject to the same resource constraints as civil procedure. Thus, the cost-effective resolution of damages claims within criminal procedure would have to employ similar institutions as the ones designed for the civil context.[97] Of course, criminal courts could leave the damages issues in the open, and the parties could still use the outcome of the criminal trial as a blueprint for settlement negotiations between the wrongdoer and individual victims. This is being done anyway and fails to integrate the claims into the criminal trial.

16/53 Outside the field of major accidents that have been caused by the fault of particular individuals, criminal law offers no valid alternative. Many mass accidents are subject to regimes of strict liability and thus do not raise the question of fault at all. Therefore, the defendant may be liable even if the criminal investigation has not led to a conviction. Many mass tort scenarios do not involve personal injuries but damage to property or financial losses. In these areas, criminal liability may be absent, or the crime may not be backed up by civil damages claims, as is the case for violations of capital markets law and parts of competition law.

16/54 In summary, while criminal procedure may play a helpful role in the most salient cases, particularly those involving bodily harm or even death of many victims, it is unlikely to play a major role in the overall process of resolving mass tort disputes.

D. Insolvency Law: Dealing with Scarcity

16/55 Perhaps surprisingly, insolvency law has something to offer for the resolution of mass torts and is not confined to playing the role of a constraint. The trustee in bankruptcy has the power to augment the pool of assets with the help of claims

97 Cf no 16/22 above.

for the restitution of gains obtained from preferential transactions and fraudulent conveyances. In this way, the financial resources of the debtor-wrongdoer are increased and tort victims stand to recover more than they would absent the insolvency law system. Furthermore, insolvency law offers well-tested tools for the summary disposition of large numbers of claims brought against the estate and for distributing limited funds fairly across a large group of claimants. All the claims against the estate are consolidated in a single forum in the district in which the insolvency proceedings are pending. It also plans for reorganisation of corporate debtors, which look much like the compensation grids and schemes that are a characteristic of successful mass tort resolution.

In as much as insolvency law helps to compensate victims even if the 16/56
wrongdoer has fallen into financial distress, it serves the dual goals of tort law, ie compensation and deterrence. For obvious reasons, however, insolvency law cannot play the role of a valid substitute for mechanisms that are specifically designed for the resolution of mass torts. Insolvency law is limited to debtors who have fallen into financial distress and thus does not apply to wrongdoers who remain financially healthy even after claims for compensation have been successfully raised against them. The case study on silicone breast implants illustrates that there is leeway for a strategic choice of the insolvency regime by a corporate tortfeasor that is fully solvent but prefers to manage the avalanche of claims brought against it under the protection of bankruptcy's automatic stay.[98] This option is particularly powerful in combination with the debtor's ability to choose the bankruptcy forum most favourable to its interest in successful reorganisation.

V. Competition Between Modes and Fora of Dispute Resolution: Where Does the Race Lead?

A. The Range of Choices Available to Forum Shopping Claimants

Victims of mass torts face a choice between multiple fora that are competent to 16/57
hear their cases. The existence of intensive forum shopping for the friendliest

98 Cf no 16/24 above.

court by victims of mass torts or rather, attorneys of the plaintiffs' bar, is a well-documented phenomenon with regard to US-American jurisdictions.[99] Within the European theatre, the Brussels I system vests jurisdiction not in one court only but in a multitude of fora.[100] The claimant suing in tort or delict may choose between the court at the domicile of the defendant (art 2 Brussels I), and the courts situated at the place where the harmful act occurred and at the place where the injury was sustained (art 5 no 3 Brussels I). Recent cases, such as the claims brought by South African mineworkers in London, have highlighted the uncertainties surrounding the interpretation of art 60 Brussels I.[101] This provision defines the domicile of corporate defendants in a way that leaves ample room for interpretation. In particular, the concept of the 'principal place of business' used in art 60 (1) (c) Brussels I raises serious questions as to its meaning and scope in cases where the entity that has the closest connection to the harm is part of a larger group of companies.[102] Finally, the common law doctrine of *forum non conveniens* that helps to organise the division of labour between several courts that may exercise jurisdiction and thus works to limit the range of competent courts is not available under the European jurisdictional regime.[103]

16/58 In summary, the Brussels I Regulation and the analogous jurisdictional system of the Lugano Convention leave ample room for tort victims to choose between courts of different Member States. As the paper contributed by *Astrid Stadler* illustrates, the range of fora to choose from is even broader for mass torts, as the Brussels I Regulation lacks a special head of jurisdiction for mass claims.[104] While art 6 no 1 Brussels I addresses the case that a claim is directed against several defendants, a similar rule for the reverse scenario that one or more defendants are sued by several claimants is missing.[105] Thus, attorneys representing a group of victims who suffered harm caused by the same accident or defect or a number of related accidents or defects may invoke the jurisdiction

99 *G Wagner*, Dispute Resolution as a Product: Competition between Civil Justice Systems, in: H Eidenmüller (ed), Regulatory Competition in Contract Law and Dispute Resolution (2013) 347, 363 ff; one example from the case studies involves the 'Costa Concordia' case, *Perrella* (fn 7).

100 Council Regulation (EC) No 44/2001 of 22.12.2000 on jurisdiction and the recognition and enforcement of judgments in civil and commercial matters, OJ L 12, 16.1.2001, 1.

101 *Tansley* (fn 9) no 7/24 ff; *Marangos* (fn 13) no 6/28; *A Stadler*, Mass Damages in Europe – Allocation of Jurisdiction – Cross-Border Multidistrict Litigation (contained in this volume) no 13/18 f.

102 *Stadler* (fn 101) nos 13/13, 13/16 ff.

103 ECJ C-281/02, *Owusu v Jackson and Others* [2005] ECR I-1383; *Stadler* (fn 101) no 13/13.

104 *Stadler* (fn 101) nos 13/4 ff, 13/11.

105 Ibid, no 13/17.

of one court with regard to one group of victims and may file the claims of another group of victims with another court.

At this point, the lack of a uniform European mechanism of collective redress needs to be considered. Given that the European lawmakers have failed to provide for a collective redress tool that is uniform across the civil justice system of the Member States, each jurisdiction retains the authority to develop its own mechanism – or to refrain from doing so. Where institutions of collective redress exist in the national systems, the question arises whether their respective scope is restricted to 'local victims', ie to potential claimants who are domiciled in the particular Member State providing for the collective redress mechanism under consideration.[106] To the extent that the law of a Member State provides for a binding effect of mass proceedings (*lis pendens*) or judgments reached in mass proceedings (*res judicata*) or settlements entered within or before such proceedings even with regard to victims domiciled outside of the respective jurisdiction, the range of choices for claimants' attorneys becomes even broader. If Member State A and Member State B each provide for a collective redress mechanism that binds tort victims domiciled in the other jurisdiction, the attorney representing the class of victims may choose where to file the mass claim with regard to all the victims. The attorney faced with such a choice has a strong incentive, and even a contractual duty vis-à-vis his or her clients, to file the collective suit in the court that offers the best prospects of a favourable judgment. **16/59**

The concept of a 'favourable judgment' is a complex one, as it is not confined to the probability with which a court will resolve the liability issue in favour of the potential claimants but includes many more considerations. One important factor is quantum, ie whether the law of particular jurisdiction is comparatively generous or parsimonious in meting out damages.[107] Obviously, the availability of punitive damages contributes to the attractiveness of American jurisdictions, an effect that is mitigated by the inability to enforce such judgments in European jurisdictions.[108] Other issues that loom large in the practice of mass tort litigation are costs and funding.[109] Other things being equal, the lower the costs of litigation and the better the options for bringing in third-party funders, the more attractive a jurisdiction becomes for potential victims and their counsel. It must be expected that attorneys representing clients in large- **16/60**

106 Ibid, no 13/29, discussing the problem within the context of mass settlements under the Dutch WCAM.

107 *Tansley* (fn 9) no 7/22; *Marangos* (fn 13) no 6/19.

108 *Perrella* (fn 7) no 4/43 f.

109 Cf no 16/10 at fn 12 above; for a general treatment cf *Wagner* (fn 99) 359 ff.

scale litigation involving mass tort scenarios look at all of these factors and make conscious choices over where to file the mass claim. They will select the jurisdiction and the court that offers the best package of liability and quantum rules at least cost and with access to insurance against adverse cost orders and/or litigation financiers who are prepared to fund the litigation and to take on themselves a substantial part of the cost risk associated with it.

16/61 The premise that claimants and their lawyers will shop around for the jurisdiction and the court that best suits their interests finds support in the case studies mentioned earlier. Damages claims of South African mine workers were filed in London because its courts offer good prospects for a fair trial that ignores the local South African interest in a healthy mining industry, because the English law of damages is rather generous, because the English rule allows for a recovery of court and attorney's fees in case of success, and because access to funders is assured.[110] Perhaps surprisingly, the attractiveness of criminal procedure as a tool for compensating the victims of mass torts in jurisdictions such as Italy may be analysed and explained along the same lines. The involvement of the public prosecutors removes much of the financial risk as the costs of the investigation are borne by the public. At the same time criminal proceedings may offer better chances to establish liability as the prosecutor may use the police power to investigate the facts of the case while private parties are left to their own resources. ADR schemes may be attractive for potential claimants because they promise an expedient resolution of the dispute at low costs so that the overall balance for claimants may be positive. And finally, insolvency proceedings are particularly attractive for victims of financial fraud as they include the authority to claw back payments that were made to third parties by the tortfeasor-debtor before the opening of insolvency proceedings. In this way, the asset pool that is awaiting distribution to the victims may be enlarged.

16/62 The idea that claimants shop between courts and jurisdictions is hardly new, even though systematic treatments of the underlying assumptions and of its consequences remain rare.[111] The contributions to the present project suggest that the scope of options for potential claimants and their lawyers goes beyond the competent courts of the jurisdictions involved and includes ADR-schemes, insolvency proceedings, and criminal investigations. Each one of these additional options offers another set of choices, making the picture even more complex. For example, choosing the competent court for insolvency proceedings with regard to companies domiciled in Europe raises complex questions that

110 *Tansley* (fn 9) no 7/22; cf also *Marangos* (fn 13) nos 6/19, 6/37.

111 For such an effort cf *Wagner* (fn 99) 357 ff.

need to be answered within the framework of art 3 European Insolvency Regulation.[112]

B. The Supply Side: Responses by Lawmakers, Judges, and Respondents

Provided that potential claimants or rather the attorney representing the victims of a disaster will select the forum that best serves their interests in a favourable judgment for high damages at low costs, the perspective must now turn to the supply side, namely lawmakers and judges. Even respondents may contribute to the supply of dispute resolution services, by offering ADR procedures on a voluntary basis. In practice, this is done with a view to protecting the reputation of the respondent business and to economise on the substantial costs of mass litigation in court. Examples within the scope of this project include Deutsche Bahn's handling of the Eschede train crash and Costa Coceriere's claims management after the Costa Concordia capsizing.[113] 16/63

The most salient example of lawmakers deliberately and consciously entering the competitive arena for collective redress mechanisms is the Dutch WCAM.[114] The Dutch legislature resolved to offer a low-cost mechanism for the resolution of mass disputes that has turned out to be rather attractive for the parties involved. It promises the respondents 'global peace' in exchange for a sizable payment on the damages claims that are resolved in the mass settlement. The fact that the WCAM is applied to cases where the majority of victims is domiciled outside of the Netherlands, together with the difficulties in establishing the jurisdiction of the Dutch courts suggest that the main motive of the lawmakers was not to solve a social problem in the Netherlands but rather to export legal services by attracting primarily foreign cases into the Dutch civil justice system.[115] If this is true, the WCAM stands out as a bold move in interjurisdictional competition for big cases. 16/64

It seems that, within Europe, England and Wales is the jurisdiction that is most inclined to accept the challenge posed by the Dutch WCAM and to enter 16/65

112 Council Regulation No 1346/2000 (fn 65); as to the interpretation of art 3's 'CoMI' (centre of main interests) *Stadler* (fn 101) no 13/19.

113 *Krasney* (fn 28) no 5/19; *Perrella* (fn 7) no 4/35 ff.

114 *Stadler* (fn 101) no 13/29 ff; for more information on the WCAM cf *T Arons/W van Boom*, Beyond Tulips and Cheese: Exporting Mass Securities Claim Settlements from the Netherlands (2010) European Business Law Review (EBLR) 857.

115 The 'export value of the WCAM' is highlighted by *Arons/van Boom* (2010) EBLR 857, 875 f.

the competition for big, mass tort cases. One strategy to attract primarily foreign cases into English courts is to interpret the concepts of 'central administration' and 'principle place of business' used in art 60 Brussels I broadly and with a view to a group of companies as a whole, rather than to the local subsidiary company in the jurisdiction where the harm was sustained.[116] The downside of such a strategic interpretation of art 60 (1) (b) (c) Brussels I is that it hurts multinational business concerns with head offices in England. The better alternative may therefore be to devise a direct competitor of the Dutch Collective Settlement Act 2005 that would be able to target liable parties that are domiciled outside England.[117] It seems that English lawmakers are considering walking this path. If they did, it would intensify competition for the settlement of mass disputes.

16/66 While the Netherlands together with England and Wales seem to be the frontrunners in the competition of European jurisdictions for the resolution of mass disputes, other Member States have become active, too. The Italian class action acts that provided the basis for the bank charges case is an example in point, but also the German Securities Litigation Test Case Act. The case studies involving these legal instruments suggest that the local lawmakers in Italy and Germany were torn between the desire to offer a remedy and the fear of unleashing a flood of claims that would overburden the respective judicial system and put domestic industry under stress. These ambiguous attitudes reveal another aspect of inter-jurisdictional competition, namely its defensive use as a shield against mechanisms offered in foreign jurisdictions. Domestic lawmakers may develop and adopt mechanisms of collective redress with the motive to fend off competition from elsewhere by luring potential claimants away from the courts of other Member States and by using domestic jurisdictional rules to vest exclusive jurisdiction in the local courts.

C. Evaluation of the Competition for the Resolution of Mass Tort Cases

16/67 The final question to ask is whether the competition for the resolution of mass tort cases that is developing in the European Union is to be welcomed or should rather be restricted. The European Commission, consciously or unconsciously, subscribed to the optimistic view as it did close to nothing to restrict the compe-

116 *Stadler* (fn 101) nos 13/13, 13/19.

117 The WCAM may be used to enforce claims against non-Dutch companies; *Stadler* (fn 101) nos 13/30, 13/35, 13/37.

tition between Member States in this area. The Commission Recommendation on collective redress suggest that the Member States supply some mechanisms designed to deal with mass cases, such as representative actions brought by designated representative entities, opt-in group actions, and ADR-procedures.[118] However, the Recommendation outlines these mechanisms with a very broad brush only and thus leaves ample room for local variations. Most importantly, the Recommendation does not provide a jurisdictional rule, as this could only have been done through an amendment of the Brussels I Regulation. The recent reform of this Regulation that is to enter into force in 2014, declined to act in this regard as well. The reformed Regulation will not provide a mirror image of the current art 6 no 1, ie a special head of jurisdiction for several claims brought by more than one plaintiff against one or more defendants. Furthermore, the new Brussels I Regulation does nothing to narrow the broad and ambiguous definition of the domicile of companies in the current art 60. Finally, the reformed Brussels I Regulation fails to supply a special jurisdictional rule for collective redress, ie for representative actions and group actions based on the opt-in principle, let alone class actions following the opt-out principle.

It is submitted that the prospect should be welcomed rather than con- **16/68**
demned. The introduction of a European jurisdictional rule for collective redress would bring the competition between European jurisdictions in this area to a standstill. If the European lawmakers would vest exclusive jurisdiction for aggregate claims in the courts at the domicile of the respondent, as suggested by the *actor sequitur* principle of art 2 Brussels I, or in the courts of the jurisdiction in which the majority of the victims is domiciled, as suggested by place of injury principle underlying art 5 no 3 Brussels I,[119] the choice between courts and jurisdictions as it now exists would be eliminated. Leaving differences in the interpretation of the imagined jurisdictional rules aside, the class of victims and their counsel would have but one single choice, namely to file the suit in the court in which the European law vested jurisdiction. They would no longer have a choice between, eg the German courts and their securities test case procedure, the settlement procedure under the Dutch WCAM, and a representative action or group litigation in England. In eliminating the choice between mechanisms, a uniform jurisdictional rule would let the steam out of the competition for the best solution for the resolution of mass torts that has just developed. As long as the differences between the national legal systems are as pronounced as they still are today, it seems inadequate to quench competition and to force potential

118 Commission Recommendation (fn 1) paras 4 ff, 21 ff, 25 ff.

119 These are the most plausible connecting factors for the allocation of jurisdiction regarding aggregate claims, cf *Stadler* (fn 101) no 13/48.

claimants to file in a single court designated by jurisdictional factors, even if an efficient mechanism of collective litigation is unavailable in the competent jurisdiction. For these reasons, competition between the Member States for the resolution of mass tort cases should be allowed to continue into the foreseeable future. It is much too early to ring the bell on this process.

16/69 What remains is the fear that unrestrained competition for mass tort cases will lead jurisdictions to adopt rules that are ever more favourable to claimants – after all, it is the claimants who make the choice between courts and jurisdictions in exercising their discretion to file the claim here rather than there. While this apprehension is not without merit,[120] it seems unlikely that the competition between Member States for efficient mechanisms of collective redress will result in a race to the bottom in the sense that jurisdictions become exceedingly generous to the claimant side. After all, claims against multinational companies tend to harm local industry as well, and the European way of civil litigation holds little potential for blackmailing respondents into the settlement of suits that lack merit. Should this assumption have to be reversed in the future, as some Member States have become over-eager to offer redress mechanisms for groups of victims, it will still be early enough for the lawmakers to step in and to supply a uniform jurisdictional rule that would bring this development to a standstill. If more intervention were needed, harmonisation through the introduction of a European mechanism of collective redress would be an option. Until then, the process of search and development that is currently unfolding in the Member States should be allowed to continue.

120 *Wagner* (fn 99) 373 ff.

List of Contributors

Jenny Boldon
Kennedys, London, United Kingdom

Willem H van Boom
Leiden University, The Netherlands

Moritz Brinkmann
Bonn University, Germany

Filippo Andrea Chiaves
Hogan Lovells, Milan, Italy

Nadia Coggiola
Torino University, Italy

Melissa R Ferrari
Attorneys at Law & Civil Law Notary, P.A., Miami, USA

Michele Graziadei
Torino University, Italy

Christopher J S Hodges
Erasmus University Rotterdam, The Netherlands

Bernhard A Koch
Innsbruck University, Austria

Harald Koch
Humboldt University, Berlin, Germany

Otto Ernst Krasney
Gießen University, Germany

Hermes Marangos
DAC Beachcroft, London, United Kingdom

Claudia Perrella
LS LexJus Sinact, Milan-Bologna, Italy

Francesca Rolla
Hogan Lovells, Milan, Italy

Thomas A Roth
Federal Office of Bundeswehr Equipment, Information Technology and In-Service-Support, Koblenz, Germany

Astrid Stadler
Konstanz University, Germany and Erasmus University, Rotterdam, The Netherlands

Philip Tansley
RPC LLP, London, United Kingdom

Andreas W Tilp
TILP Rechtsanwaltsgesellschaft mbH, Kirchentellinsfurt, Germany

Gerhard Wagner
Humboldt University, Berlin, Germany

Index

The numbers refer to the number of the report and the marginal notes.

Publications

Principles of European Tort Law Series

Volume 1: *The Limits of Liability: Keeping the Floodgates Shut*
Edited by Jaap Spier
Kluwer Law International, The Hague. Hardcover
ISBN 90-411-0169-1. 1996, 162 pp

Volume 2: *The Limits of Expanding Liability. Eight Fundamental Cases in a Comparative Perspective*
Edited by Jaap Spier
Kluwer Law International, The Hague. Hardcover
ISBN 90-411-0581-6. 1998, 244 pp

Volume 3: *Unification of Tort Law: Wrongfulness*
Edited by Helmut Koziol
Kluwer Law International, The Hague. Hardcover
ISBN 90-411-1019-4. 1998, 144 pp

Volume 4: *Unification of Tort Law: Causation*
Edited by Jaap Spier
Kluwer Law International, The Hague. Hardcover
ISBN 90-411-1325-8. 2000, 161 pp

Volume 5: *Unification of Tort Law: Damages*
Edited by Ulrich Magnus
Kluwer Law International, The Hague. Hardcover
ISBN 90-411-1481-5. 2001, 225 pp

Volume 6: *Unification of Tort Law: Strict Liability*
Edited by Bernhard A Koch and Helmut Koziol
Kluwer Law International, The Hague. Hardcover
ISBN 90-411-1705-9. 2002, 444 pp

Volume 7: *Unification of Tort Law: Liability for Damage caused by Others*
Edited by Jaap Spier
Kluwer Law International, The Hague. Hardcover
ISBN 90-411-2185-4. 2003, 335 pp

Volume 8: *Unification of Tort Law: Contributory Negligence*
Edited by Ulrich Magnus and Miquel Martín-Casals
Kluwer Law International, The Hague. Hardcover
ISBN 90-411-2220-6. 2004, 300 pp

Volume 9: *Unification of Tort Law: Multiple Tortfeasors*
Edited by WV Horton Rogers
Kluwer Law International, The Hague. Hardcover
ISBN 90-411-2319-9. 2004, 313 pp

Volume 10: *Unification of Tort Law: Fault*
Edited by Pierre Widmer
Kluwer Law International, The Hague. Hardcover
ISBN 90-411-2098-X. 2005, 393 pp

Tort and Insurance Law Series

Volume 1: *Cases on Medical Malpractice in a Comparative Perspectiv*
Edited by Michael Faure and Helmut Koziol
Springer, Vienna/New York
Softcover. ISBN 3-211-83595-4
2001, 331 pp
Volume 2: *Damages for Non-Pecuniary Loss in a Comparative Perspective*
Edited by WV Horton Rogers
Springer, Vienna/New York
Softcover. ISBN 3-211-83602-0
2001, 318 pp
Volume 3: *The Impact of Social Security on Tort Law*
Edited by Ulrich Magnus
Springer, Vienna/New York
Softcover. ISBN 3-211-83795-7
2003, 312 pp
Volume 4: *Compensation for Personal Injury in a Comparative Perspective*
Edited by Bernhard A Koch and Helmut Koziol
Springer, Vienna/New York
Softcover. ISBN 3-211-83791-4
2003, 501 pp
Volume 5: *Deterrence, Insurability and Compensation in Environmental Liability*
Future Developments in the European Union
Edited by Michael Faure
Springer, Vienna/New York
Softcover. ISBN 3-211-83863-5
2003, 405 pp
Volume 6: *Der Ersatz frustrierter Aufwendungen. Vermögens- und Nichtvermögensschaden im österreichischen und deutschen Recht*
By Thomas Schobel
Springer, Vienna/New York
Softcover. ISBN 3-211-83877-5
2003, 342 pp
Volume 7: *Liability for and Insurability of Biomedical Research with Human Subjects in a Comparative Perspective*
Edited by Jos Dute, Michael G Faure and Helmut Koziol
Springer, Vienna/New York
Softcover. ISBN 3-211-20098-3
2004, 445 pp
Volume 8: *No-Fault Compensation in the Health Care Sector*
Edited by Jos Dute, Michael G Faure, Helmut Koziol
Springer, Vienna/New York
Softcover. ISBN 3-211-20799-6
2004, 492 pp

Volume 9: *Pure Economic Loss*
Edited by Willem H van Boom, Helmut Koziol and Christian A Witting
Springer, Vienna/New York
Softcover. ISBN 3-211-00514-5
2004, 214 pp

Volume 10: *Liber Amicorum Pierre Widmer*
Edited by Helmut Koziol and Jaap Spier
Springer, Vienna/New York
Softcover. ISBN 3-211-00522-6
2003, 376 pp

Volume 11: *Terrorism, Tort Law and Insurance. A Comparative Survey*
Edited by Bernhard A Koch
Springer, Vienna/New York
Softcover. ISBN 3-211-01867-0
2004, 313 pp

Volume 12: *Abschlussprüfer. Haftung und Versicherung*
Edited by Helmut Koziol and Walter Doralt
Springer, Vienna/New York
Softcover. ISBN 3-211-20800-3
2004, 180 pp

Volume 13: *Persönlichkeitsschutz gegenüber Massenmedien/The Protection of Personality Rights against Invasions by Mass Media*
Edited by Helmut Koziol and Alexander Warzilek
Springer, Vienna/New York
Softcover. ISBN 3-211-23835-2
2005, 713 pp

Volume 14: *Financial Compensation for Victims of Catastrophes*
Edited by Michael Faure and Ton Hartlief
Springer, Vienna/New York
Softcover. ISBN 3-211-24481-6
2006, 466 pp

Volume 15: *Entwurf eines neuen österreichischen Schadenersatzrechts*
Edited by Irmgard Griss, Georg Kathrein and Helmut Koziol
Springer, Vienna/New York
Softcover. ISBN 3-211-30827-X
2006, 146 pp

Volume 16: *Tort Law and Liability Insurance*
Edited by Gerhard Wagner
Springer, Vienna/New York
Softcover. ISBN 3-211-24482-4
2005, 361 pp

Volume 17: *Children in Tort Law. Part I: Children as Tortfeasors*
Edited by Miquel Martín-Casals
Springer, Vienna/New York
Softcover. ISBN 3-211-24480-8
2006, 476 pp

Volume 18: *Children in Tort Law. Part II: Children as Victims*
Edited by Miquel Martín-Casals
Springer, Vienna/New York
Softcover. ISBN 3-211-31130-0
2007, 320 pp
Volume 19: *Tort and Regulatory Law*
Edited by Willem H van Boom, Meinhard Lukas and Christa Kissling
Springer, Vienna/New York
Hardcover. ISBN 978-3-211-31133-2
2007, 477 pp
Volume 20: *Shifts in Compensating Work-Related Injuries and Diseases*
Edited by Saskia Klosse and Ton Hartlief
Springer, Vienna/New York
Hardcover. ISBN 978-3-211-71555-0
2007, 236 pp
Volume 21: *Shifts in Compensation for Environmental Damage*
Edited by Michael Faure and Albert Verheij
Springer, Vienna/New York
Hardcover. ISBN 978-3-211-71551-2
2007, 338 pp
Volume 22: *Shifts in Compensation between Private and Public Systems*
Edited by Willem H van Boom and Michael Faure
Springer, Vienna/New York
Hardcover. ISBN 978-3-211-71553-6
2007, 246 pp
Volume 23: *Tort Law of the European Community*
Edited by Helmut Koziol and Reiner Schulze
Springer, Vienna/New York
Hardcover. ISBN 978-3-211-77585-1
2008, 693 pp
Volume 24: *Economic Loss Caused by Genetically Modified Organisms*
Edited by Bernhard A Koch
Springer, Vienna/New York
Hardcover. ISBN 978-3-211-77987-3
2008, 747 pp
Volume 25: *Punitive Damages*
Edited by Helmut Koziol and Vanessa Wilcox
Springer, Vienna/New York
Hardcover. ISBN 978-3-211-92270-1
2009, 322 pp
Volume 26: *Aggregation and Divisibility of Damage*
Edited by Ken Oliphant
Springer, Vienna/New York
Hardcover. ISBN 978-3-211-92208-8
2009, 568 pp

Volume 27: *Damage Caused by Genetically Modified Organisms. Comparative Survey of Redress Options for Harm to Persons, Property or the Environment*
Edited by Bernhard A Koch
de Gruyter, Berlin/New York
Hardcover. ISBN 978-3-89949-811-0
eBook. ISBN 978-3-89949-812-7
2010, 954 pp

Volume 28: *Loss of Housekeeping Capacity*
Edited by Ernst Karner and Ken Oliphant
de Gruyter, Berlin/Boston
Hardcover. ISBN 978-3-89949-813-4
eBook. ISBN 978-3-89949-814-1
2012 (forthcoming)

Volume 29: *Medical Liability in Europe. A Comparison of Selected Jurisdictions*
Edited by Bernhard A Koch
de Gruyter, Berlin/Boston
Hardcover. ISBN 978-3-11-026010-6
eBook. ISBN 978-3-11-026016-8
2011

Volume 30: *Tort Law in the Jurisprudence of the European Court of Human Rights*
Edited by Attila Fenyves, Ernst Karner, Helmut Koziol and Elisabeth Steiner
de Gruyter, Berlin/Boston
Hardcover. ISBN 978-3-11-025966-7
eBook. ISBN 978-3-11-026000-7
2011

Volume 31: *Employers' Liability and Workers' Compensation*
Edited by Ken Oliphant, Gerhard Wagner
de Gruyter, Berlin/Boston
Hardcover. ISBN 978-3-11-026996-3
eBook. ISBN 978-3-11-027021-1
2012

Volume 32: *Medical Malpractice and Compensation in a Global Perspective*
Edited by Ken Oliphant and Richard W Wright
de Gruyter, Berlin/Boston
Hardcover. ISBN 978-3-11-026997-0
eBook. ISBN 978-3-11-027023-5
2013

Volume 33: *Proportional Liability: Analytical and Comparative Perspectives*
Edited by Isreal Gilead, Michael D Green and Bernhard A Koch
de Gruyter, Berlin/Boston
Hardcover. ISBN 978-3-11-028253-5
eBook. ISBN 978-3-11-028258-0
2013

European Tort Law Yearbook

European Tort Law 2001
Edited by Helmut Koziol and Barbara C Steininger
Springer, Vienna/New York
Softcover. ISBN 3-211-83824-4
2002, 571 pp

European Tort Law 2002
Edited by Helmut Koziol and Barbara C Steininger
Springer, Vienna/New York
Softcover. ISBN 3-211-00486-6
2003, 596 pp

European Tort Law 2003
Edited by Helmut Koziol and Barbara C Steininger
Springer, Vienna/New York
Softcover. ISBN 3-211-21033-4
2004, 493 pp

European Tort Law 2004
Edited by Helmut Koziol and Barbara C Steininger
Springer, Vienna/New York
Softcover. ISBN 3-211-24479-4
2005, 674 pp

European Tort Law 2005
Edited by Helmut Koziol and Barbara C Steininger
Springer, Vienna/New York
Softcover. ISBN 3-211-31135-1
2006, 711 pp

European Tort Law 2006
Edited by Helmut Koziol and Barbara C Steininger
Springer, Vienna/New York
Softcover. ISBN 978-3-211-70937-5
2008, 576 pp

European Tort Law 2007
Edited by Helmut Koziol and Barbara C Steininger
Springer, Vienna/New York
Hardcover. ISBN 978-3-211-77991-0
2008, 661 pp

European Tort Law 2008
Edited by Helmut Koziol and Barbara C Steininger
Springer, Vienna/New York
Hardcover. ISBN 978-3-211-92797-7
2009, 708 pp

European Tort Law 2009
Edited by Helmut Koziol and Barbara C Steininger
de Gruyter, Berlin/New York
Hardcover. ISBN 978-3-11-024606-3
eBook. ISBN 978-3-11-024607-0
2010, 735 pp

European Tort Law 2010
Edited by Helmut Koziol and Barbara C Steininger
de Gruyter, Berlin/Boston
Hardcover. ISBN 978-3-11-023941-6
eBook. ISBN 978-3-11-023942-3
2011, 702 pp

European Tort Law 2011
Edited by Ken Oliphant and Barbara C Steininger
de Gruyter, Berlin/Boston
Hardcover. ISSN 2190-7773
eBook. ISSN 2190-7781
2012, 789 pp

European Tort Law 2012
Edited by Ken Oliphant and Barbara C Steininger
de Gruyter, Berlin/Boston
Hardcover. ISSN 2190-7773
eBook. ISSN 2190-7781
2013, 816 pp

European Tort Law 2013
Edited by Ernst Karner and Barbara C Steininger
de Gruyter, Berlin/Boston
Hardcover. ISSN 2190-7773
eBook. ISSN 2190-7781
2014 (Forthcoming Oct 2014), approx. 700 pp

Principles of European Tort Law

Text and Commentary
Edited by the European Group on Tort Law
Springer, Vienna/New York
Softcover. ISBN 3-211-23084-X
2005, 282 pp

Digest of European Tort Law

Volume 1: *Essential Cases on Natural Causation*
Edited by Bénédict Winiger, Helmut Koziol, Bernhard A Koch and Reinhard Zimmermann
Springer, Vienna/New York
Hardcover. ISBN 978-3-211-36957-9
2007, 632 pp

Volume 2: *Essential Cases on Damage*
Edited by Bénédict Winiger, Helmut Koziol, Bernhard A Koch and Reinhard Zimmermann
de Gruyter, Berlin/Boston
Hardcover. ISBN 978-3-11-024848-7
eBook. ISBN 978-3-11-024849-4
2011, 1175

Others

European Tort Law. Basic Texts
Edited by Ken Oliphant and Barbara C Steininger
Jan Sramek Verlag, Vienna
Softcover. ISBN 978-3-902638-50-2
2011, 330 pp

Medienpolitik und Recht. Bd I Media, Governance, Wahrhaftigkeitspflicht und sachgerechte Haftung
Edited by Helmut Koziol, Josef Seethaler and Thomas Thiede
Jan Sramek Verlag, Vienna
Hardcover. ISBN 978-3-902638-36-6
2010, 214 pp

Medienpolitik und Recht. Bd II Presserat, WikiLeaks und Redaktionsgeheimnis
Edited by Helmut Koziol, Josef Seethaler and Thomas Thiede
Jan Sramek Verlag, Vienna
Hardcover. ISBN 978-3-902638-63-2
2013, approx. 200 pp

Journal of European Tort Law

The Journal of European Tort Law (JETL) is the first law review to be dedicated to this important and dynamic area of European private law. It aims to contribute to the analysis and development of tort law in Europe by the publication of scholarly articles, comments and reviews. Its focus is primarily comparative, but it will also publish analyses of the tort law of single legal systems where the subject matter is of sufficient interest to the Journal's general readership. Comparative analyses of non-European systems from the perspective of European tort law will also appear from time to time. The Journal embraces all scholarly perspectives, including economic analysis of law and socio-legal studies. Its subject matter is both substantive tort law, including its place in the general law of obligations, and the wider tort system, including its practical operation and its relationship with such institutions as private and social insurance.

The Journal is published three times a year. The General Editor is Professor Ken Oliphant, Director of ETL. Professor Helmut Koziol, Director of ECTIL, is Honorary Editor in Chief.

Further information, including subscription details and instructions for authors, is available on the JETL website: www.degruyter.com/jetl.

Queries may be addressed to information@jetl.eu. Articles, comments and reviews should be submitted for consideration to submissions@jetl.eu. The Journal applies a policy of double blind peer review.

Eurotort

EUROTORT is the first comprehensive database of European cases on tort law. This web-based research tool allows both researchers as well as practitioners to access the vast wealth of jurisprudence on tort law throughout Europe in a single language (English) and with a standardised index system.

With a single search string, the most important aspects of tort law can be researched either in any one of the jurisdictions covered, in a selection of countries or without geographical limitation. The interface allows various types of retrievals including simple pattern search (full text search) and more elaborate retrievals like the search in specific database fields such as time period or keyword.

At present, the collection contains over 1,800 decisions from 28 European countries, all categorised and indexed. The cases have been selected by experts from each respective jurisdiction, who have also drafted the English texts presenting the facts of the case and an abstract of the decision.

Access to the database is free (subject to prior registration) at www. eurotort.org.

European Tort Law Blog

A new feature recently added to the ECTIL/ETL homepages is the European tort law blog (www.europeantortlaw.net). This highlights important legislative changes and case-law developments in the European tort law field, as well as forthcoming events, new publications, useful web links and other items of topical interest. Suggestions of items for posting are always welcome.

Bei Fragen zur Produktsicherheit wenden Sie sich bitte an:
If you have any questions regarding product safety,
please contact:

Walter de Gruyter GmbH
Genthiner Straße 13
10785 Berlin
productsafety@degruyterbrill.com